Sustainability and Water Management
in the Maya World and Beyond

Sustainability and Water Management
in the Maya World and Beyond

EDITED BY

JEAN T. LARMON, LISA J. LUCERO, AND FRED VALDEZ JR.

UNIVERSITY PRESS OF COLORADO
Louisville

Published by University Press of Colorado
245 Century Circle, Suite 202
Louisville, Colorado 80027

 The University Press of Colorado is a proud member of
the Association of University Presses.

The University Press of Colorado is a cooperative publishing enterprise supported, in part,
by Adams State University, Colorado State University, Fort Lewis College, Metropolitan
State University of Denver, Regis University, University of Alaska Fairbanks, University of
Colorado, University of Denver, University of Northern Colorado, University of Wyoming,
Utah State University, and Western Colorado University.

∞ This paper meets the requirements of the ANSI/NISO Z39.48–1992 (Permanence of Paper)

ISBN: 978-1-64642-231-9 (hardcover)
ISBN: 978-1-64642-232-6 (ebook)
https://doi.org/10.5876/9781646422326

Library of Congress Cataloging-in-Publication Data

Names: Larmon, Jean T., 1988– editor. | Lucero, Lisa Joyce, 1962– editor. | Valdez, Fred, Jr.,
    1953– editor.
Title: Sustainability and water management in the Maya world and beyond / edited by Jean T.
    Larmon, Lisa J. Lucero, and Fred Valdez Jr.
Description: Louisville, CO : University Press of Colorado, [2022] | Includes bibliographical refer-
    ences and index.
Identifiers: LCCN 2021049363 (print) | LCCN 2021049364 (ebook) | ISBN 9781646422319 (hardcover)
    | ISBN 9781646422326 (ebook)
Subjects: LCSH: Mayas—Antiquities. | Water-supply—Central America—Management—History.
    | Water-supply—Climatic factors—Central America—History. | Water quality
    management—Central America—History. | Water—Symbolic aspects—Central America. |
    Climate change mitigation—Central America—History. | Sustainable development—Central
    America—History.
Classification: LCC F1434.2.W38 S87 2022 (print) | LCC F1434.2.W38 (ebook) | DDC
    972.81/016—dc23/eng/20211025
LC record available at https://lccn.loc.gov/2021049363
LC ebook record available at https://lccn.loc.gov/2021049364

Cover illustration: drone photograph of Pool 20 by Jean T. Larmon.

To Vernon Scarborough, who has inspired us all

Contents

Sustainability and Water Management
in the Maya World and Beyond

1

Introduction to a Path to Sustainability

The Past and Future Role of Water Management

Jean T. Larmon, Lisa J. Lucero, and Fred Valdez Jr.

This volume covers the intersection of sustainability and water management; because of their inevitable relationship with climate change, it, too, must be considered. Discussions of the changing climate must strike a tenuous balance—how lessons from past societal strategies for dealing with climate change inform our future, while still accentuating the uniqueness of our current condition. Humans have been confronting a changing climate sustainably for millennia and have adapted to these periods of flux in a variety of ways, but we have never confronted a changing climate under the pressures of our present globalized world. While this volume stresses how lessons from the past offer invaluable insight into current approaches of adaptation, we move forward with the recognition that our time *is* different. With this in mind, our collective goal is to make those inevitable discrepancies between past and present climate change less daunting, and to emphasize the sustainable negotiations between humans and their surroundings that have been mediated by the changing climate for millennia. This volume investigates climate change and sustainability through time, particularly as it was mediated with diverse methods of water management and

https://doi.org/10.5876/9781646422326.c001

through diverse ideological conceptions of water. We build off of and focus upon earlier investigations of the global diversity of water management systems and the successes and failures of their employment (e.g., Scarborough 2003), while applying a multitude of perspectives on sustainability.

By the year 2050, over half of the world's population will rely upon the resources of the tropical forest (Roberts et al. 2017). The changing climate and increased pressure from the movement of human populations into these ecosystems make them some of the most endangered. For this reason, we focus much of the volume on the ancient Maya, who lived and adapted within the neotropical system for millennia, particularly during the emergence of urbanization in the region. Through the Maya world and timeline, control of and access to water have played a pivotal role in social and political shifts and developments. The wealth of the archaeological record offers rich data for exploring past politics of climate change, while the epigraphic and ethnographic data show how integrated the ideological, political, and environmental worlds of the Maya were. In the ancient Maya world, water bodies, caves, and sinkholes (all openings in the earth) were portals to the underworld (Bassie-Sweet 1996). It was within these portals that ancestors and deities resided and through these portals that Maya communicated with ancestors and deities (Brown and Emery 2008, 300). Water was not only essential for subsistence, but for the spiritual sustenance of daily life. The Maya's relationship with water, then, offers valuable insights into sustainability in the tropical ecosystem.

Here, we explore the ways in which political control of water sources, the maintenance or degradation of sustainable systems, ideological relationships with water, and fluctuations between the extremes of water availability have impacted or been impacted by social change. To do so, however, without delving into the diachronic and synchronic pertinence of climate change, would do a disservice to its global nature. Throughout the volume, we have three chapters that unhinge *different* aspects of sustainability and water management—water management's sway on the unfolding and downfall of Angkor and its role in contemporary social policy development, as well as how past behaviors unfold in the present. In our critical approach to past water management and sustainability, these chapters allow us to move to the present and beyond so we can structure this volume around a hopeful and informed future.

The 2014 Intergovernmental Panel on Climate Change (IPCC 2014) rightfully continues to place humans as a prime mover in climate change, but it also promotes adaptation and moves away from the idea that we can "fix" the damage already done. Perhaps the most important recognition is that we exist in an ever-changing climatic context and, as has always been the case, to adapt is to persevere. The increasing intensity of the processes of globalization, by which time/space are seemingly compressed to make great distances feel less

(Jennings 2011) and people more intimately connect with those on the other side of the globe, changes our understanding of and approach to the climate. With the recognition that climate change is largely centered on the impacts of humans on their environments comes the understanding that without informed and intentional change climate change will intensify. What is sustainable at present may not be possible as climate change continues, requiring diverse and flexible adaptation strategies.

This necessary change has been accomplished by past peoples as evidenced in the archaeological record. Today, however, is set apart from the past by scale; we now have the ability to study climate change on a global scale, which is just as well because it is a global problem. While archaeological examples tend to focus on a single region or society, our current context is worldwide. We have climate information from Antarctic ice cores that informs our understanding of fluctuating temperatures (Kawamura et al. 2017) around the world, and we can access data that explore how people in Brazil (Bretan and Engle 2017) and Iran (Gohari, Mirchi, and Madani 2017) have adjusted to their shifting local climates. Such interconnectivity both is a representation of how humans have encouraged the current climate condition, and highlights our unique ability to identify, explore, and ultimately ease tensions between local and global. In this tension lies a goal of this volume: we will explore localized examples of relationships with water and water management, as well as how they contributed to sustainability in the Maya region and elsewhere.

The passing of centuries has afforded us the ability to explore how these archaeological examples, which in the past were perhaps only visible on a myopic scale, integrate into the more global archaeological context, ultimately better simulating today's highly integrated condition. Here, we reduce any scalar hindrance—both geographical and temporal—in order to problematize concepts of "past" and "present," "local" and "global." The integrative approach helps us to break through dichotomies that lessen the impact of climate change discourse and ultimately promote a singularly modern and "Western" perspective. Instead, this volume will culminate in a discussion of water and sustainability that considers all boundaries (scalar and temporal) permeable.

Vernon Scarborough eloquently outlines the essential role of water in discussions of sustainability:

> Water for life is a biological given; a construction that is both inalienable and immutable on our green-blue planet. From a cultural perspective, water is foundational for our societal institutions; the rules and norms that direct and influence its access and allocation, strongly affect all other raw and refined resources. Its scarcity or abundance to a region significantly dictates the kinds of social organizational adaptations we have made as a species. Our health and longevity depend

on its availability; how it is delivered, who accesses it, and its quality and quantity identify levels of well-being. (2016, 4)

The labor and time investment devoted to managing water systems, accessing water, and maintaining water quality in the past espouse a sustainability discourse with a continuous theme of water throughout. This volume centers water—in plentitude and in absence—in the discussion of sustainability.

Some definitions are necessary before moving forward. In this volume, three concepts are at the forefront of our discussion: climate change, sustainability, and water management. Starting with the broadest concept, climate change is defined simply as a noticeable change in regional or global climate patterns: "the magnitude of seasonal weather pattern changes that persistently interfered with the food and water supplies necessary to support growing populations and infrastructural systems" (Lucero, Fletcher, and Coningham 2015, 1139). It is most readily applied to changes occurring since the twentieth century but has been impacting humans for millennia (Fiske et al. 2015). Of late, sustainability, or "development that meets the needs of the present without compromising the ability of future generations to meet their own needs" (Brundtland, World Commission on Environment and Development 1992) has frequented discourse on climate change. For this volume, we employ a broad definition of sustainability to allow the contributing authors freedom to include diverse understandings of the concept. Christian Isendahl problematizes this definition in the volume's conclusion. Promoting a sustainable lifestyle, specifically one that avoids the depletion of endangered natural resources over the long term, has been a means of adapting the increasingly inevitable impacts of climate change. Fluctuations in precipitation levels are a frequently cited impact—too much or too little rain. Consequently, water management systems are often employed to sustain water supplies. Water management is the manipulation of constructed and natural water bodies and precipitation to either decrease damage or increase the benefits of the fluctuations.

Stemming from the work of Scarborough (e.g., 1998, 2003, 2009; Scarborough and Burnside 2010; Scarborough and Lucero 2010), the contributing authors both investigate singular cases of water management and sustainability efforts, as well as consider syntheses of larger data sets, ultimately allowing for a juxtaposition that highlights cultural, environmental, and diachronic diversity. This volume presents a timely political and environmental perspective that not only encourages archaeological and anthropological discussion, but also promotes readers outside of the discipline to think critically about the intended and unintended consequences of environmental policy. Understanding our cultural spheres as a rhizome (e.g., Deleuze and Guattari 1983) in which all threads are interwoven, we can better conceptualize the mutually molding tendencies of our multifaceted world.

ORGANIZATION OF VOLUME

This volume is divided into two parts. In the first, the authors discuss Maya perspectives on water and water management. In these chapters, the authors detail land and water use strategies, and the ideological and political importance of water. They also explore how the methods of land and water use, as well as water's ideological importance, are integrated. The second part contains three studies from geographically and temporally diverse contexts to make clear the pervasiveness, through time and space, of water's role in sustainability. Each author offers a unique theoretical, methodological, or conceptual perspective that both contrasts and bolsters each other. The volume ends with a synthesis and discussion chapter by Christian Isendahl. The complexity of the volume's perspectives mirrors the reality of academic and political understandings of sustainability and water management and is explicitly concerned with the direction of our, at times, inundated and desiccated planet.

In the first part, the contributors introduce the details of methods employed by the ancient Maya to sustainably live and flourish within their environments, including both land management and water management, two practices that are intimately related. In chapter 2, Nicholas Dunning and coauthors explore how inhabitants of the Elevated Interior Region (EIR) of the Maya lowlands first adapted methods of water collection and storage—methods that were maintained and adjusted from the Middle Preclassic period (ca. 800 BCE) and throughout their entire occupation. The authors follow the development of water management systems in the EIR, which varied interregionally, identifying which storage techniques allowed for more sustainable living in the naturally arid region, particularly as conditions became increasing dry. In chapter 3, David Lentz and colleagues shift gears to look more critically at the ways in which land management systems impacted lowland Maya agricultural intensification. In particular, they investigate how land use strategies allowed for urbanization in the EIR of the Maya lowlands. The increasing density of settlement populations during the Classic period (300–800 CE) required an increase in food production, and the Maya employed a variety of agricultural techniques to account for seasonal fluctuations in rainfall. Lentz and colleagues present data suggesting that these adaptations were ultimately unsustainable, encouraging major social transformations during the Terminal Classic period (800–900 CE).

The previous chapters outline Maya efforts of sustainability in regard to specific methods employed in the EIR, though these and other methods of land and water management were prevalent across the Maya region. Water also was vital for sustenance, agriculture, and spiritual needs of the Maya. In chapter 4, Wendy Ashmore presents a theoretical exploration and summary of the role that water and water imagery plays in Maya cosmology. Her chapter emphasizes a primary point of this volume—*water is life*. Although her primary focus is how this sentiment rings true for the Maya, she poignantly connects it to additional archaeological and present-day examples. In this, Ashmore calls attention to how water is inherently and unforgivingly political. Chapters 5, 6, and 7 focus on case studies exploring how methods of water and land management were integrated with the political and ideological world of the Maya.

In chapter 5, Joel D. Gunn introduces methods of water management that were less constructed than those employed in earlier chapters, such as using riverine networks for site planning and to dictate trade routes. He discusses the transition of water management techniques from those that utilized the natural landscape to those that were based on constructed watersheds and basins. Through an exploration of watery origins, tropical footprints, and "water cities," Gunn looks at the intersection of population intensification and sustainable social organization for cities in the Maya lowlands, the crux of which hinges on the manipulation of access to water. Just as Gunn discusses the exploitation of natural waterways, in chapter 6, David Freidel and colleagues revisit unconstructed water management in the form of water trails, exploited to link regions throughout the southern Maya lowlands and centralize three centers in the lowlands of Guatemala: El Tintal, El Achiotal, and El Perú-Waka'. Freidel and colleagues place water at the heart of the economic and political power of these three centers and explore how "water mountains" worked to integrate the political and ideological world of the ancient Maya, ultimately linking Maya relationships and management of water systems to integrated and thriving Maya communities. In the final chapter of this part, chapter 7, Arlen F. Chase and colleagues present a comparative case study of Tikal, Guatemala, and Caracol, Belize. In an exploration of the diversity of relationships shared between humans and their environment, they compare the ways in which Maya living at Tikal and at Caracol differently shaped their landscapes and access to water storage. Ultimately, they differentiate between centralized and decentralized control of water management systems and natural resources, an analysis akin to Sylvia Rodríguez's (chapter 10) discussion of acequias in New Mexico.

In chapter 8, Sander van der Leeuw ushers us into the next part of the volume. Following the work of Vernon Scarborough, van der Leeuw offers insight into how we might today make use of archaeological data from the Yucatán Peninsula. He considers the intersection of social organization and water management, examining how practices of water management (in concert with cognitive, technological, and societal developments) were integral to the emergence of complex societies. In viewing societies as "collective information-processing organizations," van der Leeuw highlights the unintended consequences of "solutions" and their impact within a vast spatial-temporal sphere. Such a perspective necessitates *informed* forward thinking in terms of sustainability. While his discussion focuses on the Maya, it can be easily applied to the final chapters, especially since he argues that to understand the complex dynamics of the present, we have to argue from the past.

Chapter 9 takes us to Southeast Asia, where Dan Penny and Roland Fletcher use sedimentation as a proxy for sustainability; they suggest that contrary to some previous hypotheses, Angkor's suburb agricultural practices were sufficient for maintaining soil content and productivity. Instead, they propose that the extensive erosion and sedimentation evidenced in soil profiles originated from within the large-scale channelized water system, irreversibly damaging the water management system, rather than from practices impacting topsoil. Their analysis of previous theoretical approaches to studying the human and environment negotiations at Angkor is critical; it addresses the consequence of the development of one of the world's largest preindustrial settlements and the impact of that development on the surrounding tropical forests. Their results show that it was the deluge of water impacting Angkor's extensive channelized systems that produced detrimental erosion. This case further highlights the necessity of identifying local solutions for local problems—as opposed to drought, it was too much water that halted the sustainability of this system.

In chapter 10, Sylvia Rodríguez explores the politics of water today through many of the concepts already discussed in the volume that apply to archaeological cases. Through a lens of acequias in Taos, Rodríguez explores the morals of sustainability governance and puts forth the question, "Can acequias survive"? Rodríguez exemplifies how these locally managed systems of water management link human and natural systems—as Deleuze and Guattari's (1983) rhizome did—in a way that encourages mutualism. Resilience of the natural system is resilience of the human system. Her chapter stands apart in that it centers upon an ethnographic example of community and water management, though she does draw from diverse temporal and geographic examples. Such a divergence from the remainder of the volume is necessary. The themes woven throughout the archaeological examples remain in this powerful ethnographic example. Her discussion allows the reader to imagine how archaeology as a discipline, and scientific inquiry as a collective, might start to approach research in a way that does justice to keeping hold of the daily while appreciating and paying credence to the long term. As in the Chase et al. chapter, Rodríguez explores the benefits, but also problems, with locally managed practices of sustainability.

In the concluding chapter, Christian Isendahl interrogates the idea of sustainability that we introduce here. In doing so, he offers a narrower definition of sustainability originally posed by Herman Daly (2006, 39): "The entropic physical flow from nature's sources through the economy and back to nature's sinks, is to be nondeclining." Isendahl suggests that most archaeological studies, including some of those in this volume, do not adhere to this definition of sustainability;

it is with this definition, however, that we might gain better insight into how the intended and unintended consequences, and, in some cases the tradeoffs, of human behavior leave "landscape legacies," or past impacts on the environment that are visible in today's landscapes. Isendahl argues that it is in understanding these landscape legacies and their causes—intended and not—that archaeologists might best contribute to conversations of sustainability. He points out, as many chapters in this volume exemplify, that archaeology is uniquely suited to undertake this study because of the discipline's long-term and case-study-based approach, ultimately leaving us with the final goal of contributing, even slightly, to a response to the question, "How do we get out of this mess?"

CONCLUDING REMARKS

As the global water crisis continues to worsen in the face of climate change and exponential population growth, an anthropological perspective of water management practices and sustainability offers a diachronic and synchronic understanding of how access to natural resources, specifically a dearth and/or plethora of water, has impacted people in the past and still does today. Because water management systems have been key components of sustainability, they have been well studied by anthropologists and archaeologists. This volume builds upon earlier investigations of the global diversity of water management systems and the successes *and* failures of their employment (e.g., Scarborough 2003), while applying a multitude of perspectives on sustainability. Here, contributors explore the ways in which political control of water sources, the maintenance or degradation of sustainable systems, and fluctuations between the extremes of water availability have impacted, or been impacted by, culture change. Rather than focusing efforts upon a single geographical or historical example, this volume pays credence to the complexity of human and environment interactions and the mediating role of culture.

In September 2015, the United Nations (UN) introduced a global initiative—the "2030 Agenda for Sustainable Development" (UN 2015). This program mobilizes the induction of global sustainable development, with its seventeen goals addressing poverty, inequality, and *climate change*. Seven of these goals address sustainability efforts and the other ten, in their political and inequality confronting nature, are intimately tied to such efforts. The present volume speaks directly to this agenda; at a time when global climate initiatives are many and inevitably tested, a view into the diverse and locally intricate approaches to sustainability is essential. This perspective will contribute to an understanding of how the UN 2030 Agenda can be mobilized *on the ground* at local, regional, and national levels.

REFERENCES

Bassie-Sweet, Karen. 1996. *At the Edge of the World: Caves and Late Classic Maya World View.* Norman: University of Oklahoma Press.

Bretan, E., and N. Engle. 2017. "Drought Preparedness Policies and Climate Change Adaptation and Resilience Measures in Brazil: An Institutional Change Assessment." In *Evaluating Climate Change Action for Sustainable Development*, edited by J. I. Uitto, 305–326. Cham, Switzerland: Springer International Publishing AG.

Brown, Linda A., and Kitty F. Emery. 2008. "Negotiations with the Animate Forest: Hunting Shrines in the Guatemalan Highlands." *Journal of Archaeological Method and Theory* 15 (October): 300–337.

Brundtland, World Commission on Environment and Development. 1992. "Report of the World Commission on Environment and Development: Our Common Future." Last modified March 20, 1987. http://www.un-documents.net/our-common-future.pdf.

Daly, Herman E. 2006. "Sustainable Development—Definitions, Principles, Policies." In *The Future of Sustainability*, edited by Marco Keiner, 39–53. Dordrecht, Netherlands: Springer.

Deleuze, Gilles, and Félix Guattari. 1983. *On the Line.* Translated by J. Johnston. New York: Semiotext(e).

Fiske, Shirley, Susan Crate, Carole Crumley, Kathleen Galvin, Heather Lazarus, George Luber, Lisa J. Lucero, et al. 2015. *Changing the Atmosphere: Anthropology and Climate Change.* Arlington, VA. American Anthropological Association Climate Change Task Force Report. https://s3.amazonaws.com/rdcms-aaa/files/production/public/FileDownloads/pdfs/cmtes/commissions/upload/GCCTF-Changing-the-Atmosphere.pdf.

Gohari, A., A. Mirchi, and K. Madani. 2017. "System Dynamics Evaluation of Climate Change Adaptation Strategies for Water Resources Management in Central Iran." *Water Resource Management* 31 (May): 1413–1434.

Intergovernmental Panel on Climate Change (IPCC). 2014. *AR5 Synthesis Report: Climate Change 2014.* IPCC. Geneva, Switzerland: Electronic Document. Accessed December 1, 2021. https://www.ipcc.ch/report/ar5/syr/.

Jennings, Justin. 2011. *Globalizations and the Ancient World.* New York: Cambridge University Press.

Kawamura, K., A. Abe-Ouchi, H. Motoyama, Y. Ageta, S. Aoki, N. Azuma, Y. Fujii, et al. 2017. "State Dependence of Climatic Instability over the Past 720,000 Years from Antarctic Ice Cores and Climate Modeling." *Science Advances* 3 (2): E1600446.

Lucero, Lisa J., Roland Fletcher, and Robin Coningham. 2015. "From 'Collapse' to Urban Diaspora: The Transformation of Low-Density, Dispersed Agrarian Urbanism." *Antiquity* 89 (347): 1139–1154.

Roberts, Patrick, Chris Hunt, Manuel Arroyo-Kalin, Damian Evans, and Nicole Boivin. 2017. "The Deep Human Prehistory of Global Tropical Forests and Its Relevance for Modern Conservation." *Nature Plants* 3 (17093): 1–9.

Scarborough, Vernon L. 1998. "Ecology and Ritual: Water Management and the Maya." *Latin American Antiquity* 8 (2): 135–159.

Scarborough, Vernon L. 2003. *The Flow of Power: Ancient Water Systems and Landscapes.* Santa Fe, NM: School of American Research Press.

Scarborough, Vernon L. 2009. "Beyond Sustainability: Managed Wetlands and Water Harvesting in Ancient Mesoamerica." In *The Socio-natural Connection: Integrating Archaeology and Environmental Studies,* edited by C. T. Fisher, J. B. Hill, and G. M. Feinman, 62–82. University of Arizona Press.

Scarborough, Vernon L. 2016. "A Framework for Facing the Past." In *Water and Power in Past Societies,* edited by Emily Holt, 297–315. Albany: SUNY Press.

Scarborough, Vernon L., and William Burnside. 2010. "Complexity and Sustainability: Perspectives from the Ancient Maya and the Modern Balinese." *American Antiquity* 75 (2): 327–363.

Scarborough, Vernon L., and Lisa Lucero. 2011. The Non-hierarchical Development of Complexity in the Semitropics: Water and Cooperation. *Water History* 2 (November): 185–205.

United Nations (UN). 2015. "The Sustainable Development Agenda." September. https://www.un.org/sustainabledevelopment/development-agenda/.

2

Harvesting *Ha*

*Ancient Water Collection and Storage in the Elevated
Interior Region of the Maya Lowlands*

Nicholas Dunning, Jeffrey Brewer, Christopher Carr,
Armando Anaya Hernández, Timothy Beach,
Jennifer Chmilar, Liwy Grazioso Sierra, Robert Griffin,
David Lentz, Sheryl Luzzadder-Beach, Kathryn Reese-Taylor,
William Saturno, Vernon Scarborough, Michael Smyth, Fred Valdez Jr.

*Among the wonders unfolded by the discovery of these ruined cities, what made the
strongest impression on our minds was the fact that their immense population existed
in a region so scantily supplied with water. —J. L. Stephens (1841)*

Today's human populations, including those occupying the Yucatán Peninsula,
face mounting water resource problems related to both quantity and quality.
Many of these problems are not new and were also faced by the region's ancient
Maya inhabitants. We contend that the methods of water harvesting developed
by the ancient Maya offer valuable insights, both positive and negative, for sustainable water management in a tropical karst landscape.

The important role of water in Maya thought and life has long been recognized, as have the great lengths gone to by the ancient Maya to secure an
adequate water supply (e.g., Adams 1991; Dunning 2003; Lucero 2002; Lundell
1937; Luzzadder-Beach et al. 2016; R. T. Matheny 1978; Morley 1938; Scarborough

https://doi.org/10.5876/9781646422326.c002

1998; Seefeld 2018; Stephens 1841; Winemiller 2003; Wyatt 2014).[1] Water management in the Maya lowlands emphasized "collection over diversion, source over allocation" (Scarborough and Gallopin 1991, 658). In elevated, interior parts of the Maya lowlands, elaborate rain collection and storage systems were devised at multiple scales and social levels because groundwater access and perennial surface streams were rare indeed.

The word *ha'* (or *ja'*) and its cognates designate "water" across the Mayan language family and also appear in Maya glyphic script of the Classic period (Kettunen and Helmke 2013). In Classic period texts *ha'al* refers specifically to rainfall and *nahb* references bodies of water, most commonly "pools" of water (*aguadas*/reservoirs). Water and water bodies, including those in caves, form fundamental components of Maya cosmology, reflective of the tropical karst environment of the Maya lowlands (Dunning 2003). Water-related landscape features became closely associated with the *ch'en* (sacred places of origin) referenced by Maya lineages and dynasties in Classic inscriptions (Tokovinine 2013). This fundamental link between Maya culture, society, place-based identity, and water reflects the critical nature and seasonal scarcity of this resource across much of the Maya lowlands. Almost all ancient Maya agriculture was rainfall dependent, and in many areas water for consumption and other needs had to be "harvested" and stored in the rainy season and meted out through the dry. This relationship was most pronounced in the Elevated Interior Region (EIR), where Maya water collection and storage technology evolved over many centuries. Unlike the northern karst plain of Yucatán where cenotes (sinkholes with perennial water) and caves offered easy access to groundwater, or the southern parts of the Maya lowlands where nonkarst rivers provided perennial water, the EIR posed greater water management challenges for its ancient inhabitants (Dunning, Beach, and Luzzadder-Beach 2012).

The EIR of the Maya lowlands is a rugged karst landscape of hills, escarpments, and valleys created by block faulting and variable limestone dissolution (figure 2.1). Drainage is complex, with some seasonally flowing rivers, but largely dominated by subsurface drainage and flow typical of karst geomorphology. Depth to permanent groundwater in the EIR is typically tens to hundreds of meters below surface, though a few accessible perched aquifers occur in places. About 90 percent of rain falls between late May and mid-December. Average annual rainfall totals vary from about 1,145 mm in the Puuc Hills (Yucatán and Campeche, Mexico) in the north to some 1,600 mm in the south around Tikal in northern Guatemala (Isendahl 2011; Rosenmeier et al. 2002). During the rainy season, the surface drainage systems come alive and course with runoff, only to

---

[1] Seefeld's 2018 book was published after this chapter was largely written. The book contains the most comprehensive synthesis to date.

FIGURE 2.1. *Map showing the situation of the Elevated Interior Region (EIR) with the Maya lowlands and sites discussed in the text.*

later dry into scattered, shrinking pools along river channels. The EIR contains numerous *bajos* (natural depressions) created by faulting and limestone dissolution and ranging in size from one or two to hundreds of square kilometers in size. Today, most bajos are characterized by seasonal swamp forest ecosystems. Limited paleoenvironmental data indicate that some of these depressions held perennial wetlands or shallow lakes at the outset of Maya occupation in the

Preclassic but gradually desiccated due to some combination of natural climate change and anthropogenic sedimentation (Dunning et al. 2002; Dunning, Beach, and Luzzadder-Beach 2006a).

The highly seasonal distribution of rainfall in the Maya lowlands and a lack of, or declining quantity of, natural perennial water sources in the EIR made collection and storage of rainwater essential for permanent settlement of the region (Dunning, Beach, and Luzzadder-Beach 2012). Additionally, the climate record of the Maya lowlands is punctuated by periods of more frequent and intense droughts that also posed challenges for water management (e.g., Lucero, Gunn, and Scarborough 2011; Luzzadder-Beach et al. 2016). Arguably, in the EIR, the need to collect and store sufficient water to survive the dry season became a significant urbanizing force (Dunning et al. 1999; Scarborough 1993). While natural sources could provide water for a small number of people at select locations, concentrating larger numbers of people in response to the availability of other resources (e.g., agricultural land) required either cooperative or coerced investment in water storage at multiple scales.

The Maya devised several types of features in which to collect and store water, including reservoirs, smaller-scale "tanks," *chultuns* (underground cisterns), and canals. The exact nature and origin of reservoirs and other water storage features, including actual dimensions, and construction and use history, are typically impossible to determine without excavation. Unfortunately, relatively few such features have been excavated across the EIR, thus constraining our ability to adequately understand the development history of these vital components of Maya civilization. Nonetheless, enough data have been amassed at this point to begin to discern a number of chronological and geographical patterns, which are the subject of this chapter. Overall, there is a demonstrable increase in the diversity and sophistication of water collection and storage between the Middle Preclassic and Terminal Classic periods (ca. 800 BCE–900 CE).

In this chapter we provide a synthesis of current knowledge on ancient Maya water collection and storage systems in the EIR. We take a developmental approach, first examining early (Preclassic) reservoirs, then later (Classic) systems, including the development of features to control inflow, outflow, and water quality.

NATURAL MODELS FOR WATER COLLECTION AND STORAGE

The Maya lowlands environment provided a number of natural features that might have served as models for the creation of water collection systems: *sartenejas*, natural *aguadas*, *bajos*, and deep pools within seasonal rivers. Especially in the northern lowlands, processes of limestone weathering and soil formation in the seasonally wet/dry climate combine to create a thick, case-hardened caprock layer anywhere from a few centimeters to two or more meters below the surface (Dunning 1992). Where this caprock is exposed at the surface, solution hollows often form, some of which hold pools of rainwater known locally as *sartenejas*. Sartenejas can hold volumes of water ranging from a few cubic to many tens of cubic meters of water, though few of these pools are sufficiently large to persist through the entirety of the dry season.

The term *aguada* (pond) is widely used across the Maya lowlands for self-contained bodies of water that typically hold water for much or all of the year, but, depending on year-to-year variation in precipitation, may desiccate for some period. Aguadas can form naturally, typically where a karst sinkhole has gradually become plugged with clay-rich sediment allowing water to accumulate (Dunning et al. 2015; Siemens 1978). Examples of natural aguadas can be found throughout the Maya lowlands. Many of today's aguadas were entirely or partly anthropogenic in origin, that is, are the product of ancient reservoir construction.

The word *bajo* ("low-lying area") is widely used in the Maya lowlands to designate natural depressions of varying size (as little as square kilometer, to many hundreds of square kilometers). We use the term "pocket *bajo*" to indicate smaller depressions, typically less than a few square kilometers is size. Bajos typically are floored with deposits of clay-rich sediments. Topographic lows within bajos often fill with water during parts of the rainy season—an aspect of the environment easily observable by early Maya settlers.

The rivers that originate in the EIR and flow toward the coast have highly seasonal discharge patterns. Although they are largely desiccated in the dry season, pools persist within deep solution pockets within the channel. Along the Río Holmul drainage in northern Guatemala, such pools were the loci of many Preclassic settlements (Fialko 2000, 2005).

Many early Maya settlements were established at natural water sources, including springs and water-bearing caves in addition to the four natural water collection features mentioned above. However, sartenejas, aguadas, bajos, and river channel pools would have provided natural models for early settlers to observe the manner in which rainwater and seasonal streams could be manipulated to enhance water availability.

WATER CAPTURE

There are a few examples of places where water emerging from natural springs was captured and stored locally or shunted off for use elsewhere, for example, at Chan and Itzan, sites outside of the EIR, where springs are much more common (Johnston 2004). Local, perched aquifers can result in springs in the EIR, though these are quite rare. One example was located at Tikal, in the so-called silting tank of the Temple Reservoir. Here a basin was constructed to capture spring water, perhaps a foundational part of the Preclassic colonization of Tikal (Scarborough and Grazioso Sierra 2015). Ironically, as Tikal grew and the recharge surfaces for the spring were covered by buildings and pavements, the usefulness of the spring would have waned.

For the EIR as a whole, water was only generally available in the dry season where it had collected during the preceding rainy season, either naturally (see above) or by human manipulation of the landscape, though it should be noted that hydrological conditions within bajos appear to have changed over time making water progressively less available during the course of Maya civilization (see above). During the rainy season, rainfall is often intense, most typically in the form of thunderstorms but also, with some frequency, tropical storms and hurricanes (e.g., Dunning and Houston 2011; Frappier et al. 2014; Medina-Elizade et al. 2016). These intense rainfalls have the capacity to generate considerable surface runoff even under forested conditions. In fact, ancient Maya water systems needed to be able to deal with excess runoff in addition to their primary function of collecting and capturing water. However, hurricanes and tropical storms also likely provided important "bumps" in precipitation that allowed reservoirs to fill completely.

As the ancient Maya cleared forest and urbanized the landscape, they changed its hydrologic characteristics. In the case of urban watersheds, these changes became progressively more intentional, with plastered structures and plazas canted specifically to shed water directly into storage features or into channels directing the water into reservoirs some distance away. This system of enhanced collection and capture was established as early as 800 BCE at Yaxnohcah (Dunning, Anaya Hernández, and Geovannini 2016; Dunning, Anaya Hernández et al. 2017) and became a fundamental part of urban design across the EIR. For example, at the Preclassic Puuc region site of Xcoch, water was collected from elevated paved buildings and plazas and shunted into plastered channels carrying it into the La Gondola Reservoir (Dunning, Weaver et al. 2014; Smyth et al. 2017). Apparently, that system was not always able to fill the reservoir adequately and later a large, elevated platform was constructed adjacent to the reservoir in order to generate additional runoff. Outside of site cores, runoff was collected off of many nonpaved surfaces in both urban and rural settings and funneled into reservoirs. At the household scale, small, paved surfaces within residential compounds were often used to collect water into local open-air tanks or chultuns.

RESERVOIRS

Reservoirs were both adapted from natural features or completely constructed across the EIR beginning at least as early as the Middle Preclassic (ca. 800 BCE). The origins of individual reservoirs are usually difficult to determine without excavation, and, because relatively few have been probed, their exact nature and chronology often remain obscure. Excavations at several sites have revealed that reservoirs were built by modifying hydrologic ponding points such as natural aguadas and parts of bajos, by sealing depressions created by quarrying, as well

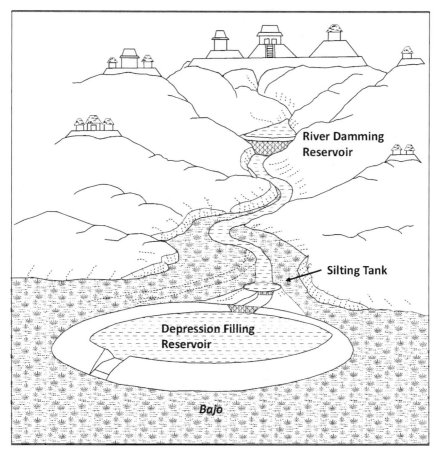

FIGURE 2.2. *Diagram showing stream-damming and depression-filling reservoirs.*

as created by impoundments created within stream channels. Examination of regional archaeological surveys in various parts of the EIR reveal the ubiquity of reservoirs embedded within the ancient settled landscape and their direct spatial association with sites of any size (e.g., Bullard 1960; Šprajc 2008). Examination of satellite imagery from areas within the EIR also quickly indicates that the Maya constructed thousands of reservoirs, only a fraction of which are visible after a thousand years of abandonment.

Vernon Scarborough (1993) proposed a model of Maya watershed manipulation in which he contrasted *concave* systems based on passive collection of runoff at the low point of local drainages with *convex* systems that involved water capture at higher points within a local watershed. He proposed that the concave systems were more characteristic of the Maya Preclassic, whereas convex systems were more typical of the Classic. While we do not refute the overall veracity of this model, we propose some refinements and changes in terminology, taking into account data that have become available over the past two decades. From a geomorphological standpoint, all stream channels are concave; that is, the floor of the channel drops in a general concave arc from upper watershed to lower, though the flow of this line is usually interrupted by grade changes for various reasons, most typically changes in bedrock hardness. We suggest that "depression filling reservoirs" be used to denote those features situated at a low point in a local drainage system (replacing Scarborough's "concave"), and "stream damming reservoir" be used to indicate those located higher in the drainage and created by damming an incised valley (replacing Scarborough's "convex") (figure 2.2). Reservoirs were also constructed further from the edges of bajos and with no visible intake breaks in their berms. This variant of depression-filling reservoirs was reliant entirely on rainfall for seasonal recharge, with their berms serving the dual purpose of increasing storage capacity and keeping out potentially sediment-laden water from the surrounding bajo. Natural aguadas and low, seasonally flooded areas within bajos provided early models for depression-filling reservoirs, and, in fact, many such places were developed as reservoirs.

Deep pools within descending streams may have provided a natural model for the potential of stream damming. Two useful characteristics of reservoirs that facilitate comparison are their relative location and capacity, both of which speak to their origins and control.

The location of reservoirs within ancient settlements has been presumed to offer information on their control. For example, centrally located urban reservoirs that are often intimately associated with monumental architecture have been used as evidence supporting the role of water management by ancient Maya political rulers (Ford 1996; Lucero 1999, 2002, 2006; Scarborough 1998; Scarborough and Gallopin 1991). In contrast, reservoirs and smaller-scale features in urban peripheries or associated with smaller settlements are suggestive of more decentralized water management (Weiss-Krejci and Sabbas 2002). This picture, however, is complicated by the presence of reservoirs of many sizes located in varied parts of urban centers, urban fringes, smaller settlements, and rural areas. We suggest that the terms "central," "community," and "household" be applied to water collection and storage features. Central reservoirs include spatial association with the monumental site core and elite control. Community reservoirs are characterized by association with locations outside of the site cores but are of a scale that required participation by many households for creation and maintenance. Household features (such as tanks and chultuns) are smaller features that are closely associated with an individual or small cluster of residential compounds. These terms are intentionally both spatial and social.

Another approach to comparing reservoirs is by their capacity; however, there are limitations to this approach. Available data are limited by the small quantity

TABLE 2.1. Estimated capacity of selected EIR reservoirs

Site Name	Reservoir Name	Estimated Capacity / m³
Calakmul	Aguada Grande	91,000
El Zotz	El Zotz Aguada	87,920
Yaxnohcah	Brisa Reservoir	84,000
Xcoch	Aguada La Gondola	79,200
Uxmal	Aguada ChenChan	75,000
Tikal	Palace Reservoir	74,630
Tikal	Corriental	57,559
Yaxnohcah	Fidelia	29,000
Xcoch	South Aguada 1	12,000
Uxul	Aguada Oriental	10,000
La Milpa	Aguada Lagunita Elusiva	7,800
La Milpa	Turtle Pond	785

of excavated features, which makes accurate measurement of volumetric capacity impossible because most reservoirs have experienced significant sedimentation, often both during their active use as well as postabandonment (table 2.1). Even surface area calculations can be difficult. While some reservoirs are rectangular, circular, or elliptical in shape, many others have very irregular outlines, and the original surface outline is often obscured by sedimentation and postabandonment vegetative succession. Additionally, even where capacity is known after excavation, it does not necessarily reflect the importance of a reservoir to a particular place. For example, even a small reservoir may have played a vital ("central") role in a relatively small site. Individual reservoir size may also not be especially important in places where there were multiple reservoirs or systems of reservoirs. Documented community and central reservoirs ranged in capacity from fewer than 1,000 to some 90,000 m³. Open-air, water-holding ponds smaller than 500 m³ are here considered as household "tanks"—essentially small-capacity reservoirs typically closely spatially associated with ancient residential groups. These capacity ranges are simply estimates, and the spatial settlement associations of reservoirs and tanks are critical to their interpretation; for example, tanks are typically closely associated with specific residential groups. These household-scale features will be discussed separately below.

Table 2.1 lists a sample of ancient Maya central and community reservoirs for which there is sufficient excavation data to assess origin, use history, and capacity. This list is meant to be illustrative and is not comprehensive. These data help illustrate the history of reservoir creation in the Maya lowlands, especially the EIR.

ARCHAEOLOGICAL EXAMPLES

Preclassic Period Reservoirs

The origin of ancient Maya reservoirs is typically impossible to ascertain without excavation. Given that relatively few reservoirs have been excavated at this time, our understanding of the origins of this form of water collection and

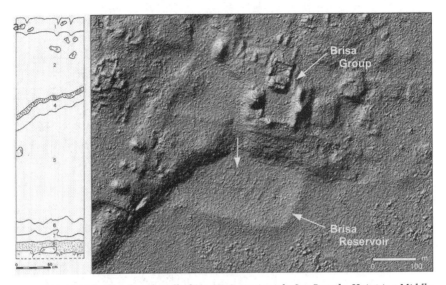

FIGURE 2.3. *(a) Profile of south wall of Op. SB3C-1 in Aguada San Bartolo. Unit 8 is a Middle Preclassic plaster floor; Units 4–7 are Middle and Late Preclassic sediments; 3 is a badly distorted Late Classic plaster floor; Units 1–2 are the modern soil formed on Late Classic and later sediment. (b) LiDAR-derived hill-shade image of a site center reservoir and associated ceremonial center (Brisa Reservoir, Yaxnohcah).*

storage in the Preclassic is very limited. Two of the oldest reservoirs known are at San Bartolo and Yaxnohcah, both with clear origins in the Middle Preclassic.

San Bartolo is a moderately sized site that is best known for its well-preserved Preclassic murals and inscriptions (Saturno, Stuart, and Beltran 2006). The site includes several groups of monumental architecture, one of which sits immediately adjacent to an aguada that gave the contemporary name to the site. Excavations in San Bartolo Aguada in 2005 revealed that it began as a limestone quarry (likely to provide material for the adjacent elevated plaza and pyramid), which was converted to a central reservoir by lining the floor with a thick coat of plaster (figure 2.3a; Dunning, Jones et al. 2006). Charcoal embedded in the plaster floor produced a radiocarbon date with a calibrated radiocarbon date of 780–410 BCE. Preclassic ceramics were recovered in abundance in the overlying reservoir sediments. San Bartolo was abandoned at the end of the Preclassic period (ca. 150 CE) but was reoccupied by the Late Classic, at which point the reservoir was partially dredged and a thin plaster floor was added atop remaining sediment.

Yaxnohcah is a sprawling site with numerous groups of monumental architecture featuring characteristic Preclassic triadic pyramid complexes (Reese-Taylor and Anaya Hernández 2013; Šprajc 2008). Although several reservoirs were known at the site, an airborne Light Detection and Ranging (LiDAR) survey in

2014 revealed more, including Brisa Reservoir, the largest at Yaxnohcah (Anaya Hernández, Peuramaki-Brown, and Reese-Taylor 2016; Reese-Taylor and Anaya Hernández 2017). Excavations in Brisa Reservoir have revealed that it originated around 800 BCE in the Middle Preclassic (Dunning, Anaya Hernández, and Carr 2017). The reservoir is enormous, with a surface area of over 28,000 m² and capacity of over 84,000 m³, but relatively primitive (figure 2.3b). It was created by walling off a section of the Bajo Tomatal adjacent to an angled quarried limestone scarp lying below the Brisa Group of monumental architecture that also appears to have originated in the Middle Preclassic. No floor was added to the reservoir, which relied on the slow permeability of the underlying bajo clay soil to retain water.

In both the case of San Bartolo and Yaxnohcah, the early reservoirs were at least partially filled by runoff directed from superadjacent monumental architecture, indicating that the relationship between central reservoirs and elite-directed activities in the site core existed early in Maya history. Due to lack of excavations, it is unclear how many other central reservoirs date to the Middle Preclassic. The sprawling Xpotoit Aguada at Yaxhom appears to have originated in the Middle Preclassic, though evidence to support this dating is preliminary (Ringle 2011).

Many additional reservoirs are known from the ensuing Late Preclassic period throughout the EIR. At Yaxnohcah, excavations have revealed that the Fidelia Aguada was created in the Late Preclassic period (Dunning, Anaya Hernández, and Geovannini 2016). A section of bajo floor adjacent to the Fidelia Group was walled off by a large berm creating an impoundment with a capacity of about 29,000 m³. Parts of the reservoir appear to have originated by rock quarrying. Where revealed by excavation, the floor of the reservoir was formed by bedrock, with lower pockets filled in with cobbles and clay. Excavation in Aguada La Gondola at Xcoch revealed a succession of three floors, the lowest of which was associated with Late Preclassic ceramics and a radiocarbon date of 89 BCE–1 CE (Dunning et al. 2014; Smyth et al. 2017). La Gondola was refloored twice, after a period of apparent abandonment in the Early Classic, and again in the Late Classic. At El Mirador, often considered the preeminent Late Preclassic Maya center, an elaborate system of reservoirs was constructed, including a number located within low points immediately adjacent to acropolis complexes, as well as several very large depression-filling, bajo margin components located at the end of drainages descending the tall escarpment on which the site core is situated (Matheny, Hansen, and Gurr 1980; Morales-Aguilar 2009). Excavation in the large Aguada Limon on the bajo margin revealed a plaster floor and two distinct episodes of sedimentation; construction was dated to the Late Preclassic by both ceramics and a radiocarbon sample (Dahlin, Foss, and Chambers 1980). Other Late Preclassic reservoirs are known from EIR sites including at Tikal, and the Xultun—San Bartolo area (Akpinar-Ferrand et al. 2012; Scarborough et al. 2012).

It is likely that a significant number of the hundreds of reservoirs in the EIR had Preclassic origins, but how many cannot be determined without excavation.

Classic Period Reservoirs

During the Classic period the number and diversity of reservoirs expanded, including the adoption of features designed to better control inflow and release of water, expand capacity, enhance access to water, and improve potability. We review several key attributes below.

Reservoir Seals

Reservoirs in the EIR exhibit a wide variety of strategies for retaining water by reducing loss via infiltration in their bottoms and sides. The default option was to simply rely on the natural impermeability of basal substrate. In a few instances, bedrock "floors" were exposed at the base of reservoirs during archaeological excavations. When not fractured, dense limestone and marl can have low permeability, but fractures would need to have been filled with clay or another dense material to provide a reasonable basal seal. Reservoirs located along bajo margins or other, localized depressions could have taken advantage of the low permeability of clay soils and sediments typically found in such locations, and examples of natural clay floors are not unusual. At Uxul, N. Seefeld (2013) found that the Aguada Occidental originated as a "natural *aguada*" in a small clay-bottomed depression on the margin of a larger bajo but was later modified to enhance water storage. One problem with reliance on clay seals, natural or anthropogenic, is the smectite-rich clays characteristic of the Maya lowlands have a propensity to shrink and crack when desiccated, potentially compromising water retention until fully rehydrated.

The ubiquity of clayey soils and sediments in the Maya lowlands can make it difficult to distinguish whether clay resulted from natural sedimentation or was intentionally introduced by the Maya. A case in point is the Aguada de Términos on the outskirts of Tikal (Dunning et al. 2015). This reservoir appears to have originated as a quarry targeting chert and limestone in the Late Preclassic but began to function as a reservoir after the accumulation of clayey sediment or its introduction. In either case, the depression was converted to a substantial reservoir that continues to effectively hold water today.

At some point in the Preclassic the ancient Maya discovered *tapial*, sometimes referred to as "rammed earth" (*pak'* in Yukatek Maya). In the Maya case, clay-rich soil was mixed with *sascab* or *sahcab* (natural limestone marl), which was pressure-packed into a hard, dense layer. This technique was used to create the floors of several reservoirs excavated at Xcoch, in the Puuc region, where it is still used today to line modern irrigation ditches (Dunning, Weaver et al. 2014). Examples of tapial seals can also be found in the southern parts of the EIR, including within at least one small tank investigated at Yaxnohcah (Brewer 2016).

In some instances, limestone slabs were used as part of the flooring of reservoirs, with plaster or clay tuck-pointed between or overlaid on the stones to complete the seal. Examples of such flooring in the EIR are documented for the Palace Reservoir at Tikal (Scarborough and Grazioso Sierra 2015); the large reservoir at El Zotz (Beach, Luzzadder-Beach, and Flood et al. 2015); the Aguada Oriental at Uxul (Seefeld 2013), Aguadas 4 and 6 at Calakmul (Domínguez Carrazco and Folan 1996; Geovannini-Acuña 2008), and Aguada Zacatal near Nakbe (Wahl et al. 2007).

Examples of plaster lining in reservoirs are relatively rare (e.g., Los Tambos at Xultun, Guatemala), probably reflecting the high cost of producing plaster and its need for other purposes, most notably on monumental architecture—though, as noted, such architectural complexes provided important runoff used to fill reservoirs and other water storage features.

Another rare treatment of reservoirs was the apparent application of a layer of ceramic fragments from broken vessels compressed into clay. Examples have been found at El Zotz (Beach, Luzzadder-Beach, and Flood et al. 2015) and Uxul. At Uxul, Seefeld (2013) noted that the ceramic layer on one floor of the Aguada Oriental was discontinuous, raising the question of whether this treatment was meant to enhance water retention or served another function. We speculate that such "tiling" may have been decorative.

Dams and Berms

Dams and berms are essentially variations of the same idea: walls constructed to restrict the movement of water. Dams can be distinguished as walls put in place across stream channels, whereas berms are walls constructed to impound water accumulated in depressions. Examples of dams can be found widely across the Maya lowlands wherever the Maya sought to manipulate the flow of moving water. In the EIR, dams were often used to create reservoirs within incised drainages. For example, the multiple dams constructed in the elevated site core of Tikal are of the stream-damming type (Grazioso Sierra and Scarborough 2013; Scarborough et al. 2012; Scarborough and Grazioso 2015). In many cases, the tops of dams doubled as causeways, facilitating passage across the valleys. The Palace Reservoir dam is the largest known thus far in Mesoamerica. When complete the dam was about 80 m long, 60 m wide at the base, and over 10 m in height, creating a reservoir with a capacity of about 74,630 m^3 of water. The dam was constructed with a fill of limestone rubble packed with clay soil obtained from bajos, and an armoring of limestone slabs. Buried deep within the dam is a much smaller Early Classic construction.

Examples of depression-filling reservoirs that employed berms are found ubiquitously across the EIR. Berms sometimes form partial enclosures, capturing runoff water at the base of a drainage. In other examples, berms encircle the entire reservoir except for restricted inlet and outlet points. Berms were constructed of a variety of materials, most typically expediently from readily available materials such as quarry rubble, bajo clay, and soil/sediment excavated while deepening the reservoir pool. Examples exist of more refined berm construction, most notably stone-lined inner walls sealed with clay, tapial, or plaster. While more elaborate berm construction is more often seen in urban reservoirs, it can sometimes also be found even in hinterland or rural areas, such as Aguada Tintal outside of San Bartolo (Dunning et al. 2008). Berms around larger reservoirs required large investments in labor. For example, at Xuch in the Puuc region C. Isendahl (2011) found that the massive berms ringing the huge central aguada represented the single-largest construction investment at the site.

Berms served two functions in reservoir construction and management. One was to limit the sourcing of water allowed to enter a reservoir and to exclude other water from entering. This is most clear in bajo-margin reservoirs that are flanked on one or more sides by low-lying, seasonally inundated terrain; inflow from surrounding areas needed to be prevented in the rainy season (e.g., Brisa Reservoir at Yaxnohcah; Dunning, Anaya Hernández, and Geovannini 2016; Dunning, Anaya Hernández 2017). Even in some reservoirs situated within stream channels, however, berms could function in a similar way. For example, the Corriental Reservoir at Tikal was created at the confluence of several seasonal streams where a natural wide spot was probably expanded and deepened by quarrying, and berms were used to control inflow and outflow of water, which could either be allowed into the reservoir or shunted around the outside of the berm (Scarborough et al. 2012).

Another function of berms was to enhance water storage capacity by allowing the water pool to elevate within the reservoir. At Xcoch's Aguada La Gondola, excavations revealed that the surrounding berm was increased in height and width three times over its history of use, taking into account the addition of new floors within the reservoir (Dunning, Weaver et al. 2014).

Dredging, Enhanced Capacity, and Access to Water

In order to maintain their water storage capacity, reservoirs were sometimes dredged of sediment to maintain pool depth, though the archaeological record offers few glimpses into how regularly this occurred. Excavations and sediment coring often produce evidence of severe disjunctions in the sediment record within reservoirs. A common finding is some depth of Preclassic age sediment in the lowest cultural level, separated abruptly from accumulations of Late or Terminal Classic and later sediments; sometimes these disjunctions are clearly visible in the sediment strata but not always. Good examples of such disrupted sediments can be seen in the Aguada de Términos at Tikal (Dunning et al. 2015),

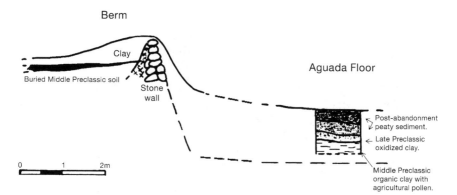

FIGURE 2.4. *Cross-sectional drawing of Aguada Tintal, northeast of San Bartolo, showing disjunction between Late Preclassic and Terminal Classic and later sediment within the reservoir.*

Aguada Fidelia at Yaxnohcah (Dunning, Anaya Hernández, and Geovannini 2016), and Aguada Tintal near San Bartolo (figure 2.4; Dunning, Wahl et al. 2014). Such dredging has proved to be a problem for studies attempting to use paleoenvironmental proxies, such as pollen, from reservoirs because sediment generated during much of the Classic period is often absent (Akpinar-Ferrand et al. 2012; Dunning et al. 2003).

How frequently dredging occurred during the Classic is difficult to ascertain. In the case of the Palace Reservoir at Tikal, a partial inward collapse of the reservoir dam in the Terminal Classic happened to preserve beautifully varved, visually distinguishable wet and dry season sediments representing 5.5 years of accumulation between a cleaning and dam collapse (Scarborough et al. 2012). This sample implies fairly frequent sediment removal even in the waning days of Tikal's political and economic power, though it is unwise to draw broad conclusions from one sample. Furthermore, this reservoir is located immediately adjacent to Tikal's royal palace and may well have been subject to more rigorous maintenance than was typical for Maya reservoirs in general. Coring in the berms of two reservoirs in the Puuc region indicates one, two, or more episodes of dredging with some of the excavated sediments heaped atop the berms (Dunning 1992, 23).

There are also many examples of reservoirs that were evidently not subject to dredging or to less thorough sediment extraction. As noted above, the central reservoir at San Bartolo was only partially dredged before a new floor was added when the site was reoccupied after a period of abandonment (see figure 2.3a; Dunning, Jones et al. 2006). Excavations in the huge reservoir at El Zotz revealed an original Early Classic floor buried by accumulated sediment, a Late

Classic floor, and a further accumulation of sediment (Beach, Luzzadder-Beach et al. 2015). Aguada La Gondola at Xcoch has three floors separated by thick zones of sediment accumulation (Dunning, Weaver et al. 2014). In this case, loss of pool depth due to sedimentation was partially offset by adding elevation to the surrounding berm. The decision to simply add a new floor atop accumulated sediment within reservoirs with no or only partial dredging may have been made for expediency, because dredging would have been a very labor-intensive undertaking and would have potentially kept a reservoir out of commission for a longer period. Partial rather than thorough dredging may have also been motivated by a desire to avoid potentially damaging underlying seals whose exact depth and composition may no longer have been in the collective memory of later site occupants.

In some instances, the Maya sought to prolong the dry season yield of water in reservoirs by excavating filtration wells in their floors. Known as *buk'té'ob* in Yukatek Maya (singular *buk'té*), these wells feature dry-laid stone walls surrounding openings of varying depth and width. In clay-bottomed reservoirs, or those with significant accumulated sediment into which the well was sunk, throughflow of water from surrounding saturated sediments could be accessed to obtain a final water yield from the drying reservoir. Buk'té'ob were first reported by John Lloyd Stephens (1841), who was told by a hacienda owner about his efforts to clean out and reuse these features. The practice of resurrecting ancient reservoirs, including their buk'té'ob, occurred elsewhere in the Puuc and Chenes regions during periods of economic expansion in the nineteenth century (for example, reopened buk'té'ob are still clearly visible in a reservoir at Ichpich; Dunning 1992, figure 2-11). J. Huchim Herrera and I. Sánchez (1990) excavated a buk'té in the floor of the ChenChan Reservoir at Uxmal that included a plaster floor at the base of the filtration wall. In the La Milpa Aguada, excavations exposed a buk'té visible as a stone ring on the reservoir floor after complete removal of grassy vegetation. This well proved to be the second of two, with the one visible at the surface having been excavated into an earlier, lower well after a period of apparent neglect and sedimentation (figure 2.5). How widespread such wells are within Maya reservoirs is difficult to assess since the majority are likely to be essentially invisible due to sedimentation and vegetation growth, though some aguadas contain small depressions in their floors that may indicate the presence of wells. Stephens (1841) was also told of, but did not observe, features resembling chultuns reportedly uncovered in the floor of an aguada.

Especially in wider and deeper reservoirs, the ancient Maya would have been faced with the problem of gaining access to water as levels dropped during the course of a dry season. Features observed in a number of reservoirs appear to have been put in place to facilitate access to water in the shrinking pool. In Aguada La Gondola at Xcoch, inclined stone-faced walkways were added at

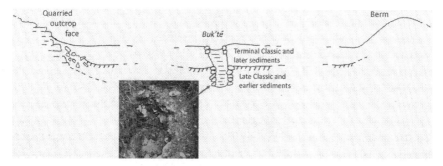

FIGURE 2.5. *Cross-sectional drawing of La Milpa Aguada, including* buk'té *in reservoir floor; inset photo showing earlier, lower part of the* buk'té *after excavation.*

different heights on each side of the reservoir's interior walls so that users could have followed the water down as it descended over time (Dunning, Weaver et al. 2014). Other reservoirs included stone piers that projected into the pool, such as Aguada de Carlos near Tikal (Dunning et al. 2015). In other instances, stone-based platforms or islands were built within reservoirs, perhaps to facilitate access to water, such as at Aguada Lagunita Elusiva, near La Milpa (Weiss-Krejci 2013).

Ingress Controls and Potability Features

If reservoir water was to be used for human consumption, measures needed to be taken to maintain potability. As noted above, the collection surfaces used to supply water to reservoirs varied greatly, ranging from plastered surfaces of varying sizes, that could presumably be kept relatively clean, to open slopes where residential and agricultural land use were likely intertwined. Another part of the collection and storage system in which cleanliness could be enhanced was via the control of water flow into the reservoir. Many reservoirs include restricted entry points that could potentially have been closed off to limit incoming flow; see, for example, the Perdido Reservoir at Tikal (Scarborough et al. 2012; Scarborough and Grazioso Sierra 2015). Such control would have served multiple purposes, including limiting inflow during times of excessive rainfall and potentially destructive volumes or velocities of runoff, as well as to exclude water that may have appeared dirtier than desired.

Water in channels leading into reservoirs was sometimes interrupted in its journey by the construction of silting or settling tanks such as at Kinal (Scarborough, Connelly, and Ross 1994), Oxpemul (Volta et al. 2013), and Aguada Los Loros near San Bartolo (Akpinar-Ferrand et al. 2012). Such features functioned to quickly slow water flow, allowing at least some particulate matter to precipitate before the water entered the main reservoir. At the Aguada Oriental at Uxul, channelized water was run through a thick, dry-laid stone "filter wall" before it could enter the reservoir (Seefeld 2013). The remains of this wall were not visible prior to excavation, and such features may be more commonplace than realized. Excavations in the Corriental Reservoir at Tikal produced findings suggestive of an even more sophisticated filtration system (Scarborough et al. 2012). Lenses of quartz sand were found stratified between typical clayey sediments within the reservoir. The nearest known source for such sand is some 39 km away in the Bajo de Azúcar; though sources from closer locations are possible, none are present in the reservoir watershed. This absence suggests that this "exotic" material was intentionally introduced and may well be the blown-out remains of former sand filtration boxes constructed in the reservoir's several intake points. The contributing watershed included residential areas interspersed with garden/orchard zones; thus, the ancient residents of Tikal may have sought a more thorough means of cleansing water entering the reservoir. A few less-clear sand lenses were also found in the sediments in the interconnected Temple and Palace Reservoirs suggesting that this filtration practice may have been more widespread at Tikal. The danger of contamination is evident in potentially toxic levels of cyanobacteria (from algal blooms) and mercury (from weathering of cultural surfaces pigmented with cinnabar) that were concentrated in the declining and eutrophying waters of the Temple and Palace reservoirs at Tikal during the droughts of the Terminal Classic period (Lentz et al. 2020).

Robert Rands (1953) noted the prevalence of water lilies in royal iconography from the Classic period, leading to suggestions that these plants may have played a role in maintaining water purity in reservoirs and as a mark of royal religious and political power (Ford 1996; Lucero 2006; Schele and Friedel 1990). Water lilies (*Nymphaea* spp.) are rarely found in ancient reservoirs that still hold water today, pollen recovered from sediments in some reservoirs contains lily pollen, supporting the idea that these plants were cultivated in reservoirs (Hansen et al. 2002). Lilies would have the beneficial properties of slowing evaporation from water surfaces, as well as biologically filtering some toxins that may have been present in reservoirs (Ford 1996; R. B. Gill 2000; Harrison 1993; Lucero 1999; Pohl et al. 1996).

Outflow Control

Many reservoirs include features that allowed for the release of water. Typically, these egresses are manifest today simply as gaps in the berms or dams used to create the reservoir. Examples include the Middle Preclassic Brisa Reservoir at Yaxnohcah and the Early Classic Perdido Reservoir at Tikal (Dunning, Anaya Hernández et al. 2017; Scarborough et al. 2012). Excavation revealed that these gaps are the badly blown-out remains of spillways. Presumably, features such as wooden gates may have existed in these spillways in the past, allowing for more regulated release of water. Perdido Reservoir, along with the nearby Pital Reservoir, was positioned to release captured water into a subadjacent pocket bajo, where there is isotopic evidence for intensive maize cultivation (Dunning et al. 2015).

The egress for Corriental Reservoir at Tikal was apparently more complex, at one point being transformed from a simple spillway to a "switching station" that could allow water to either enter or be released from the reservoir (Scarborough and Grazioso 2015). The Palace Reservoir and dam featured even more sophisticated outflow control; the dam included a series of stacked sluice channels that would have allowed water to be released at varying levels (Scarborough et al. 2012).

Religious and Ritual Aspects and Connections

Water played a central role in both Maya pragmatic and cosmological understandings of the world; thus, divine and elite political control of this substance became intertwined as Maya civilization evolved (e.g., Dunning 2003; Houston 2010; Lucero 2006; Scarborough 1998). This complex relationship is evident in the incorporation of water collection and storage features in the elite-sponsored monumental architecture within site cores from the Middle Preclassic onward, for example, the shedding of water from the Brisa Group into the Brisa Reservoir at Yaxnohcah (Dunning, Anaya Hernández et al. 2017). While the precise meaning and function of many Maya pyramid temples remain unclear, at least some of these buildings were apparently manifestations of the pan-Mesoamerican concept of a "water mountain" (Lucero 2006; see also Freidel et al., chapter 6 in this volume). Conceptually tied to mountain caves and springs, the architectural creation of such symbolically potent places was another symbol of the cosmologically endowed authority of rulers. The symbolic re-creation of water mountains as plastered pyramids and associated plazas and structures allowed these features to literally produce water as rain was shed, which could in turn be collected in reservoirs (Scarborough 1998).

In Maya cosmology, water-bearing caves are believed to be the home of the rain deity, Chaak (Brady 2010). Caves that penetrate to the permanent groundwater table are extremely rare in the EIR. One such cave is located at Xcoch, where a tortuous series of narrow passageways, drops, and wider chambers eventually reach a small pool of water. This pool was a focus of rain-related rituals from at least as early as 800 BCE and continuing into the modern era, including as a source of *zuhuy ha*, sacred water used in rain calling ceremonies to this day (Dunning, Weaver et al. 2014; Smyth and Ortegón Zapata 2008; Stephens 1841; Smyth et al. 2017; Weaver et al. 2015). On the surface, the Great Pyramid of Xcoch and an associated acropolis and plaza complex grew incrementally over many centuries, beginning in the Middle Preclassic, with numerous rebuilding episodes reinvigorating this sacred site—as well as literally creating a "water mountain," shedding rain that could be harvested. Over time a city grew around and above the cave, which remained at its ceremonial heart and the geomantic centering point for the community, its identity, its public architecture, and its water management infrastructure. Plastered channels funneled rainwater that was collected in several plazas into the city's largest reservoir, Aguada La Gondola. A *sacbe* (causeway) was constructed connecting an altar complex at the cave entrance to a temple group on the eastern lip of the reservoir. Rare "Chac Polychrome" and related Dos Arroyos water jars are found only deep within the cave and on the Preclassic and Early Classic floors of the reservoir. These specialized jars were likely used to bring zuhuy ha to the reservoir to symbolically initiate the refilling of the reservoir by the perceived combined actions of a shaman/ruler and the rain gods being called forth from the cave and sky.

The repetition of the urban pattern of pyramid, plazas, and reservoirs in the core areas of Maya cities and towns in the EIR is indicative of the pervasiveness of a belief system that included the close relationship between rulers and rain deities, which persisted from the Middle Preclassic through Terminal Classic periods. Many of these water catchment systems continued to evolve as central architectural complexes grew (e.g., a system documented at Nakum: Koszkul and Žralka 2013). Whether natural or created, water sources at the heart of Maya communities were intrinsically tied to place identity and the authority of dynastic rulership (Tokovinine 2013; Dunning and Weaver 2015).

Canals

The ancient Maya excavated canals for many reasons, including facilitating transportation (see Gunn, chapter 5 in this volume), draining perennially or seasonally inundated terrain to facilitate cultivation, aquaculture, and water storage. Canals clearly had the potential to store large volumes of water and cannot be ignored as at least a backup source for human consumption, as well as to facilitate agricultural production and aquaculture. Most documented canal systems are situated at considerable distances from urban population centers, but there are examples of systems that may have functioned as either vital or secondary urban water supply; they include Edzna, Dzibanche, and Baking Pot (Dunning and Beach 2010; Ebert and Hogarth 2016; Matheny et al. 1983). While the majority of the documented canal systems lie outside of the EIR in lower-lying areas with more abundant perennial water, examples of canal systems can be found in bajos within the EIR (e.g., the Bajo de Azúcar: Dunning, Griffin et al. 2017).

Community and Household Water Collection and Storage

The majority of the reservoirs discussed previously, though not all, are examples of central reservoirs intimately associated with core monumental architecture. Central reservoirs have been subject to far more archaeological investigation than have community reservoirs, which are located in outlying residential areas of urban centers, hinterland, and rural areas. Community reservoirs tend to be smaller in size, though many exceptions exist. These reservoirs are typically embedded within the residential landscape, suggesting that their construction, use, and maintenance were directed by spatially adjacent residential groups. Many residential groups also collected water at the household level—household tanks. What we are calling community reservoirs and household tanks are open-air ponds that grade into one another in terms of size and are best distinguished subjectively by their association with multiple or individual residential groups.

Community Reservoirs

Good examples of community reservoirs have been documented at Turtle Pond Aguada and Aguada Lagunita Elusiva, both on the urban fringe of La Milpa. Turtle Pond Aguada originated as a natural aguada within a pocket bajo among the far eastern settlement zone of La Milpa (Chmilar 2005). Modifications included construction of a low berm, an inlet channel, and deepening resulting in a capacity of some 785 m^3, probably serving as a water supply for residential groups spread along a nearby ridge of higher ground. Aguada Lagunita Elusiva lies even further out on the eastern urban fringe of La Milpa but was significantly larger, with a capacity of at least 7,800 m^3 (Weiss-Krejci 2013) despite lying in an area of lesser population density. The area around this reservoir includes field walls indicative of intensive cultivation, an idea also supported by abundant maize pollen recovered in its sediments (Dunning and Beach 2010). There is no direct evidence that the reservoir was used for irrigation, such as by carrying pots of water to the fields, but that function remains a possibility.

Some other community reservoirs were much larger in size. The Xcoch South Aguada 1 had a capacity of about 12,000 m^3, seemingly far larger than sufficient for supplying the household needs in nearby areas on the urban fringe of Xcoch (Dunning, Weaver et al. 2014). The remains of two canals, now badly marled by modern agriculture, linking the reservoir with nearby farmland, suggest that the reservoir may have been used for agricultural production. Similarly, the Aguada Tintal, located in the hinterland of San Bartolo, was oversized for its low-population-density setting but could have been used to facilitate nearby cultivation (Dunning et al. 2008). In the densely settled, but distinctly nonurban landscape of the Río Bec region, reservoirs of varying size are a ubiquitous part of the landscape, perhaps serving both domestic and agricultural functions (Lemonnier and Vanniere 2013).

Household Tanks and Cisterns

Considerable interregional variation existed in domestic-scale water management strategies with the EIR from the Puuc Hills south to the Tikal area. In general, in the more northerly parts of the EIR, chultuns were most common, whereas in the south household tanks predominate, though examples of each

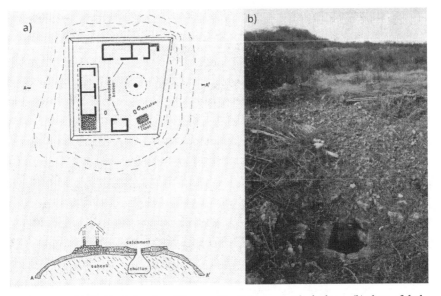

FIGURE 2.6. *(a) Idealized drawing of Puuc residential group with* chultun; *(b) photo of chultun with reinforced neck and sloping catchment (Yaxhom).*

type of feature can be found in both the north and south. Residential-scale tanks and chultuns have been less investigated than their larger, more visible, counterparts, but data from multiple sites within the region indicate that significant temporal variability was likely also found in household water features. The picture emerging from ongoing investigations across the Maya lowlands details the frequency and importance of household tanks and cisterns in providing for the daily water needs of the region's inhabitants. These features have been investigated at sites across multiple settlement scales within the EIR, from minor agricultural communities to highly developed urban centers (e.g., Becquelin and Michelet 1994; Brewer 2007; Brewer et al. 2017; Dunning 1992; McAnany 1990).

The regional surficial geology of the Puuc region was notably favorable for chultun construction, with abundant surface exposures of hard caprock with an underlying zone of softer sascab (Dunning 1992). After punching openings through the caprock, Maya people then excavated large, typically bell-shaped chambers made watertight with layers of plaster (figure 2.6a and b). Surfaces surrounding the opening were canted into the mouth and plastered to funnel rainfall into the cistern. Chultuns had capacities ranging from about 5 to as much as 90 m³. Chultuns are found in the majority of residential patio groups within Puuc communities, and their presence (or absence) can be used to help distinguish architectural groups with nonresidential functions (Dunning 1992). They are found in a relatively consistent ratio in relation to the number of presumed residential structures in ancient Puuc communities (Dunning, Weaver et al. 2014). Although highly dependent upon the extent and accuracy of mapping between sites, this spatial relationship is evident at other Puuc sites such as Sayil, Xuch, and Xculoc, among others, where significant numbers of both residential structures and chultuns have been documented. Despite the presence of sizable reservoirs at some of these sites, including Xcoch, the ratio of residential structures per chultun indicates that residential compounds were likely expected to satisfy their own water needs. However, chultun construction may have been restricted. Many rural hamlet sites in the Puuc lack chultuns, suggesting that these smallest of settlements represent seasonally occupied hamlets / farmsteads (Dunning 2004). Or was there an indentured rural population dependent on nearby minor or major centers for water?

Very few household tanks have been noted at Puuc region sites, though this may reflect a regional bias whereby archaeologists have not looked for these features given the ubiquity of chultuns. Several household tanks were identified and two excavated at Xcoch (Dunning, Weaver et al. 2014; Smyth et al. 2017). Both excavated examples proved to be Preclassic constructions, a finding consistent with the early dates from associated residential groups. Although the sample size is minuscule, data so far suggest that tanks may have been an early strategy in the Puuc that was later largely replaced by a preference for chultuns. Chultuns had the distinct advantage of being sealable, closed by stone or wooden lids to minimize evaporative loss and contamination.

Further south within the EIR, the evolution and sustainability of Yaxnohcah were dependent on significant hydraulic, agricultural, settlement, and landscape modification strategies that allowed the persistent occupation of the site from early in the Preclassic period, through the Preclassic "collapse" that engulfed some of its neighbors, and well into the Classic period (Anaya, Peuramaki-Brown, and Reese-Taylor 2016). At the household, or decentralized, scale, hydrologic modifications in the form of creating and maintaining small residential tanks took place in tandem with the community-wide, centralized investments in water management exhibited by the Middle and Late Preclassic Brisa and Fidelia Reservoirs, which are discussed above. Small reservoirs located adjacent to many of the household groups identified at Yaxnohcah would have provided an additional accessible water supply for the community (figure 2.7a, b, c).

Ongoing investigations through the Yaxnohcah Archaeological Project (YAP) have excavated five of these residential tanks, with excavations focused on understanding the chronology of their construction and the nature of their role in water management at the household level (Brewer 2016; Brewer 2018; Brewer and Carr 2017; Brewer et al. 2017). Each was determined to be a water storage feature based on a combination of physical and spatial characteristics (see figure 2.7a, b, c). Four of the depressions contained either a degraded plaster surface or thick layer of bajo

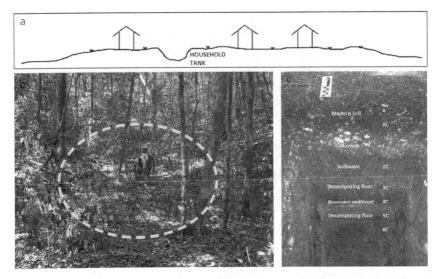

FIGURE 2.7. *(a) Idealized drawing of residential tank drawing; (b) photo of a residential tank at Yaxnohcah prior to excavation; (c). photo of excavation in YAX-3 Residential Group tank (Yaxnohcah).*

clay overlying their base, which would have functioned as a water retention sealant. The fifth fit the profile of a residential tank in terms of its surface area, depth, and location—adjacent to a residential complex in an area of the site lacking any visible water features—and was bordered by an extensive catchment area along its south, west, and southeast sides that would have been positioned to either receive outflow from or shed runoff into the reservoir, probably for agricultural purposes. Three of the five tanks also exhibited evidence of originating as limestone quarries, with either (or both) exposed limestone blocks visible around their rims or cut stone blocks forming their base. Similar depressions originating as quarries before being modified and used as small reservoirs have been identified elsewhere across the EIR (Folan 1982; Weiss-Krejci and Sabbas 2002). Analysis of recovered ceramic material and charcoal samples submitted for C^{14} dating was used to assess the chronology of the household tanks at Yaxnohcah. Dates for these features ranged from the Middle Preclassic to the Classic period, with each matching dates assigned to the nearest corresponding residential group (Peuramaki-Brow, Morton, and Castro 2016; Walker 2016). The creation and use of smaller aguadas and household tanks by a growing hinterland population fanning out from the urban core, combined with the continued exploitation of bajo areas as cultivated and managed wetland forests and agricultural zones, characterized residential-scale water management activities at Yaxnohcah from the Middle Preclassic into the Classic period (Brewer 2018; Brewer et al. 2017).

A series of household water management studies conducted at Medicinal Trail have revealed a multicomponent system of water features incorporated into a dispersed hinterland community engaged in agricultural production (Brewer 2007; Brewer, Hyde, and Stowe 2013; Chmilar 2005; Gill 2009; Hyde 2011; Lowe 2008; Percy 2009). Located on an escarpment edge, the site consists of multiple formal courtyard groups; numerous informal mound clusters; a series of landscape modifications geared toward domestic water collection and storage, including depressions, terraces, and berms; and the centrally located Medicinal Trail Reservoir (Hyde 2011). Extensive investigation of the reservoir revealed the presence of a degraded plaster floor located between a layer of clayey reservoir sediment and a lower clay-rich (Ab) horizon atop sascab. Combined with the tank's calculated capacity (153 m³) and its position adjacent to a residential structure (Structure A-7), the former plastered surface is a positive indicator that the reservoir functioned as a water storage feature. E. Weiss-Krejci and T. Sabbas (2002) report the presence of a similar hard gray layer, between 10 and 30 cm thick, overlaying white medium-hard, smooth bedrock at four excavated depressions near the neighboring Wari Camp and La Milpa East sites, which they also interpret as small water reservoirs. Visible cut marks and flattened edges on the limestone base of the depression and a recovered lithic inventory consisting of multiple tools ($N = 57$), including at least one intact midsized biface, support the notion that the reservoir may well have originated as a limestone quarry. The capacity of the Medicinal Trail Reservoir alone would have supplied the households in its immediate vicinity with a significant amount of water throughout much of the year. Combined with the additional supply provided by the other, smaller reservoirs, Medicinal Trail and its water supply would likely have functioned as a centralizing force for resource access among intercommunity members during the dry season and perhaps beyond.

Chultuns are also a common feature in the southern portion of the EIR, but the majority appear to have been used for purposes other than water storage as evident by their lack of interior plaster sealant and paved catchment areas around their openings (Dunning, Weaver et al. 2014; P. A. McAnany 1990; Scarborough 2003). However, a few examples of water storage chultuns have been noted around La Milpa and Yaxnohcah. Although none of these features have yet been excavated, their location within drainages or association with catchment rings strongly supports their hydrologic function.

DISCUSSION

The above discussion is limited to the capture and storage of water in tanks of variable size in the EIR. Reservoirs, tanks, and chultuns were also used to a lesser extent in ancient Maya communities outside of the EIR. A few areas outside of the EIR also faced severe seasonal water availability challenges and were dependent on rainfall capture, most notably the Vaca Plateau in east-central Belize, where the huge urban center of Caracol was dependent on reservoirs that were constructed at central and community scales (Chase 2016). We recognize that the Maya managed water for other purposes, most notably to manage soil moisture levels on hillslopes via terracing and in wetland setting via ditching (e.g., Beach, Luzzadder-Beach, and Krause 2015; Beach et al. 2002; Beach et al. 2009; Luzzadder-Beach, Beach, and Dunning 2012; Wyatt 2012, 2014; Lentz et al., chapter 3 in this volume).

Due to severe constraints posed by the natural environment in the EIR, the availability of water was a limiting factor for the human occupation of this region, which nevertheless developed into the well-populated heartland of Maya civilization. Water was most fundamentally needed for human consumption and sustenance, but other needs were also critical, including bathing, cooking, production of ceramics and plaster, and, where possible, localized irrigation. Water storage capacity has been proposed as a means of estimating ancient urban population numbers (e.g., P. A. McAnany 1990). However, this method is problematic, because normal human water needs go far beyond bare-minimum survival needs (see Becquelin and Michelet 1994). At best, water can be used as a constraining factor for archaeologically derived population estimates.

Rainwater capture and storage are evident as a fundamental aspect of urban development and design from the outset of population nucleation in the EIR at the beginning of the Middle Preclassic period (ca. 800 BCE). Urban design elements were of both a pragmatic (water collection and storage) and symbolic nature—reflecting the basic importance of water in the evolving cosmology of the ancient Maya and the increasingly intertwined nature of religious, political, and economic power in Preclassic and Classic period Maya culture and society. The importance of water for urban Maya society can be seen in the enormous amount of labor invested in its "harvest." In addition to examples discussed in the preceding text, there is an archaeological legacy of literally thousands of ancient reservoirs in the EIR, some of truly monumental proportions. For example, the main reservoir at Chactun is some 220 × 170 m (Šprajc 2015); Aguada Maya, near the site of Pozo Maya, is some 280 × 230 m in size (Culbert et al. 1996). The actual capacity and age of these reservoirs are not known, due to lack of excavation. Many larger reservoirs, especially those that continue to retain water for part of the year and are not overly obscured by tree canopy, are readily visible on multispectral satellite imagery, such as that regularly posted on Google Earth, but many are not. The introduction of LiDAR for mapping in Maya archaeology has the capability of revealing the full extent of reservoir construction (A. F. Chase et al. 2012). For example, at Yaxnohcah the acquisition of 25 km^2 of LiDAR centered over the site revealed eight previously unknown reservoirs in addition to the five already known (Anaya Hernández, Peuramaki-Brown, and

Reese-Taylor 2016; Dunning, Hernández, and Geovannini 2016; Reese-Taylor et al. 2016). LiDAR also has the capacity to reveal even small, closed depressions, many of which served as residential tanks, though excavation is needed to verify their nature and function (Brewer et al. 2017).

Evidence collected from geoarchaeological excavations in several EIR bajos suggests that some of these depressions were likely wetter, with some even holding shallow lakes, in the Preclassic, but progressively drying up into and through the Classic, exacerbating the water challenges for Maya occupation (Dunning, Beach, and Luzzadder-Beach 2006; Dunning et al. 2002; Hansen et al. 2002). The Maya lowlands were also beset with repeated episodes of severe or prolonged droughts, most notably in the Terminal Preclassic and Terminal Classic periods (e.g., Aimers and Hodell 2011; Douglas et al. 2015; Dunning, Wahl et al. 2014; Haug et al. 2003; Hodell, Brenner, and Curtis 2005; Kennett et al. 2012; Medina Elizade and Rohling 2012; Medina-Elizade et al. 2010). Over the centuries, Maya farmers and rulers alike became acutely aware of the propensity for drought in their environment and sought to intercede via religious ritual as well as the pragmatic response of increasing water collection and storage capacity (e.g., Lucero, Gunn, and Scarborough 2011). In the Late Preclassic period, San Bartolo and Xultun were rival centers only 8 km apart. San Bartolo was abandoned at the end of the Preclassic, while nearby Xultun rose to become one of the most preeminent and long-lived centers of the northeast Petén region. Only one small reservoir is known at San Bartolo, whereas there are at least six reservoirs at Xultun, suggesting that perhaps its rulers or populace responded more effectively to increasing water scarcity (Akpinar-Ferrand et al. 2012).

Tikal provides another example of a Preclassic urban center that adapted an elaborate system of reservoirs and emerged as a regional power in the Classic period. Analysis suggests that Classic Tikal was hydrologically "overbuilt," with its reservoirs potentially supplying more water than needed—at least as long as rainfall remained reasonably dependable (Lentz et al. 2014; Scarborough et al. 2012). Drought was not the only factor that could drive the Maya to increase investment in water storage. During a period of escalating regional warfare, the city of Tamarindito (outside of the EIR) chose to invest in a reservoir near the site center atop a defensible bluff rather than continue to rely only on several natural springs lying below the more easily defended terrain (Beach and Dunning 1997).

Over time in the Classic period, water storage features became increasingly complex, diverse, and redundant—perhaps reflecting lessons learned in the Terminal Preclassic droughts, or reflecting changing political, economic, or social organization. In addition to large central reservoirs, water storage was also developed at community and household levels. At Xcoch, spatial analysis indicates a positive correlation between chultun and reservoir locations—a relationship

FIGURE 2.8. *Space Shuttle photo of Uxmal showing some of the many* aguadas *at the site; inset photo showing Aguada ChenChan in the foreground and site center in the background.*

that suggests that the reservoirs may have functioned in part to allow chultuns to be refilled during the dry season. That is, the old Preclassic reservoirs, refurbished in the Classic period, became a backup system for household chultuns, perhaps giving some Puuc communities greater resilience to withstand drought (Dunning, Weaver et al. 2014). Nevertheless, in the Terminal Classic, droughts may have become too severe to survive, especially given the precariously high populations concentrated in many parts of the EIR (Isendahl, Dunning, and Sabloff 2014). There are more reservoirs located within the urban zone of Uxmal than at any other Puuc site, a fact that likely reflects a natural abundance of karst depressions, as well as a huge investment in labor in their modification for water storage (figure 2.8). Its locational advantages may have facilitated Uxmal's rise to regional prominence in the late ninth century CE (Dunning 1992). The apogee of monumental construction at Uxmal between 870 and 910 CE is marked by continued growth at the allied sites of Nohpat and Kabah but a suppression of construction at many surrounding sites. This suggests that Uxmal was siphoning away labor formerly bound to these other communities during a time of increasing environmental stress related to drought and declining agricultural output (Isendahl et al. 2015). Evidence suggests that Uxmal was a predatory state that expanded by military conquest, but that it met a violent end after 910 CE

(Carmean, Dunning, and Kowalski 2004). Uxmal, like almost all of the cities and towns in the EIR, was effectively abandoned by 1000 CE.

The question arises, Why did most of the EIR remain largely abandoned throughout the Postclassic? Among other reasons that may have made Postclassic resettlement of the Elevated Interior Region by large numbers of Maya difficult was the huge investment of time and labor required to revitalize infrastructure, especially for vital water collection and storage—systems that had grown incrementally over many generations and lay neglected and increasingly dysfunctional with each passing generation.

The Intergovernmental Panel on Climate Change has recommended expanding rainwater harvesting, improving water storage, conservation, and reuse among other strategies to offset negative impacts of climate change in Latin America (Intergovernmental Panel on Climate Change 2007). These are precisely many of the techniques that the ancient Maya honed while seeking sustainable occupation of the EIR and that could inform present-day population expansion in the region (Lucero, Gunn, and Scarborough 2011; van der Leeuw 2008). Today, the expansion of new towns and villages in many parts of the EIR relies on the pumping of groundwater from deep aquifers, both for domestic purposes and, increasingly, for irrigation agriculture. In some areas, tapped freshwater aquifers are already dropping and gypsic or saline aquifers are rising, threatening the long-term sustainability of this development strategy. Resurrecting the rain-harvesting adaptations pioneered by countless generations of Maya people offers an alternative model—either on its own, or in combination with groundwater-based development. In this way, the ancient Maya could perhaps aid their descendants, and other, non-Maya immigrants to enjoy a better future.

REFERENCES

Adams, R.E.W. 1991. "Nucleation of Population and Water Storage among the Ancient Maya." *Science* 251 (4994): 632.

Aimers, J. J., and D. Hodell. 2011. "Societal Collapse: Drought and the Maya." *Nature* 479 (7371): 44–45.

Akpinar-Ferrand, E., N. P. Dunning, D. L. Lentz, and J. G. Jones. 2012. "Use of *Aguadas* as Water Management Sources in Two Southern Maya Lowland Sites." *Ancient Mesoamerica* 23 (1): 85–101.

Anaya Hernández, A., M. Peuramaki-Brown, and K. Reese-Taylor. 2016. "Introducción." In *Proyecto Arqueológico Yaxnohcah, Informe de las 2014 y 2015 Temporadas de Investigaciones*, edited by A. Anaya Hernández, M. Peuramaki-Brown, and K. Reese-Taylor, 1–3. Report submitted to the Consejo de Arqueología del Instituto Nacional de Antropología e Historia, Mexico City.

Beach, T., and N. Dunning. 1997. "An Ancient Maya Reservoir and Dam at Tamarindito, El Peten, Guatemala." *Latin American Antiquity* 8 (1): 20–29.

Beach, T., S. Luzzadder-Beach, N. P. Dunning, J. Hageman, and J. Lohse. 2002. "Upland Agriculture in the Maya Lowlands: Ancient Maya Soil Conservation in Northwestern Belize." *Geographical Review* 92 (3): 372–397.

Beach, T., S. Luzzadder-Beach, N. Dunning, J. Jones, J. Lohse, T. Guderjan, S. Bozarth, S. Millspaugh, and T. Bhattacharya. 2009. "A Review of Human and Natural Changes in Maya Lowlands Wetlands over the Holocene." *Quaternary Science Reviews* 28 (17): 1710–1724.

Beach, T., S. Luzzadder-Beach, J. Flood, S. Houston, T, G. Garrison, E. Román, S. Bozarth, and J. Doyle. 2015. "A Neighborly View: Water and Environmental History of the El Zotz Region." In *Tikal: Paleoecology of an Ancient Maya City*, edited by D. L. Lentz, N. Dunning, and V. Scarborough, 258–279. Cambridge University Press, Cambridge.

Beach, T., S. Luzzadder-Beach, S. Krause, N. Brokaw, N. P. Dunning, J. Flood, T. Guderjan, Valdez, and S. Walling. 2015. "'Mayacene' Floodplain and Wetland Formation in the Rio Bravo Watershed, Northwestern Belize." *Holocene* 25 (10): 1612–1626.

Becquelin, P., and D. Michelet. 1994. "Demografía en la Zona Puuc: El recurso del método." *Latin American Antiquity* 5 (4): 289–311.

Brady, J. 2010. "Offerings to the Rain Gods: The Archaeology of Maya Caves." In *Fiery Pool: The Maya and the Mythic Sea*, edited by D. Finamore and S. D. Houston, 218–222. New Haven, CT: Yale University Press.

Brewer, J. L. 2007. "Understanding the Role of Small Depressions in Ancient Maya Water Management at the Medicinal Trail Site, Northwestern Belize." MA thesis, Department of Anthropology, University of Cincinnati.

Brewer, J. L. 2016. "Investigaciones en aguadas de escala residenciales." In *Proyecto Arqueológico Yaxnohcah, Informe de las 2014 y 2015 Temporadas de Investigaciones*, edited by A. Anaya Hernández, M. Peuramaki-Brown, and K. Reese-Taylor, 95–109. Report submitted to the Consejo de Arqueología del Instituto Nacional de Antropología e Historia, Mexico City.

Brewer, J. L. 2018. "Householders as Water Managers: A Comparison of Domestic-Scale Water Management Practices from Two Central Maya Lowland Sites." *Ancient Mesoamerica* 29 (1): 197–217.

Brewer, J. L., and C. Carr. 2017. "Operation 22: Continuing Household Water Management Investigations at Yaxnohcah." In *Proyecto Arqueológico Yaxnohcah, Informe de la 2016 Temporada de Investigaciones*, edited by K. Reese-Taylor and A. Anaya Hernández. Report submitted to the Consejo de Arqueología del Instituto Nacional de Antropología e Historia, Mexico City.

Brewer, J. L., C. Carr, N. P. Dunning, D. S. Walker, A. Anaya Hernández, M. Peuramaki-Brown, and K. Reese-Taylor. 2017. "Employing Airborne LiDAR and Archaeological

Testing to Determine the Role of Small Depressions in Water Management at the Ancient Maya Site of Yaxnohcah, Campeche, Mexico." *Journal of Archaeological Science: Reports* 13 (June): 291–302.

Brewer, J., D. M. Hyde, and M. Stowe. 2013. "Mapping Medicinal Trail: A Summary from 2004 to 2012." In *Research Reports from the Programme for Belize Archaeological Project*, Volume 7. Occasional Papers, Number 14, edited by J. Valdez F., 91–111. Austin: Mesoamerican Archaeological Research Laboratory, University of Texas.

Bullard, W. R., Jr. 1960. "Maya Settlement Pattern in Northeastern Peten, Guatemala." *American Antiquity* 25 (3): 355–372.

Carmean, K., N. Dunning, and J. K. Kowalski. 2004. "High Times in the Hill Country: A Perspective from the Terminal Classic Puuc Region." In *The Terminal Classic in the Maya Lowlands: Collapse, Transition, and Transformation*, edited by A. A. Demarest, P. M. Rice, and D. S. Rice, 424–449. University Press of Colorado, Boulder.

Chase, A. F., D. Z. Chase, C. Fisher, S. Leisz, and J. Weishampel. 2012. "The Geospatial Revolution in Mesoamerican Archaeology." *Proceedings of the National Academy of Sciences* 109 (32): 12916–12921.

Chase, A.S.Z. 2016. "Beyond Elite Control: Residential Reservoirs at Caracol, Belize." *WIREs Water* 3 (6): 885–897.

Chmilar, J. 2005. *Ancient Water Management: Archaeological Investigations at Turtle Pond, Northwestern Belize*. MA thesis, Department of Anthropology, University of Cincinnati.

Culbert, T. P., V. Fialko, B. McKee, L. Grazioso, and J. Kunen. 1996. "Investigación arqueológica en el Bajo La Justa: La temporada de 1996." In *X Simposio de Investigaciones Arqueológicas en Guatemala*, edited by J. P. Laporte and H. L. Escobedo, 367–371. Museo Nacional de Arqueología y Etnología de Guatemala, Guatemala City.

Dahlin, B. H., J. Foss, and M. E. Chambers. 1980. "Project Akalches: Reconstructing the Natural and Cultural History of a Seasonal Swamp. Preliminary Results." In *El Mirador, El Petén, Guatemala: An Interim Report. Papers of the New World Archaeological Foundation No. 45*, edited by R. T. Matheny, 37–58. Provo, UT: Brigham Young University.

Domínguez Carrazco, M., and W. J. Folan. 1996. "Calakmul, México: Aguadas, bajos, precipitación y asentamiento en el Petén Campechano." In *IX Simposio de Investigaciones Arqueológicas en Guatemala*, edited by J. P. Laporte and H. L. Escobedo, 171–193. Guatemala City: Museo Nacional de Antropología e Historia.

Douglas, P. M., M. Pagani, M. A. Canuto, M. Brenner, D. A. Hodell, T. I. Eglinton, and J. H. Curtis. 2015. "Drought, Agricultural Adaptation, and Sociopolitical Collapse in the Maya Lowlands." *Proceedings of the National Academy of Sciences* 112 (18): 5607–5612.

Dunning, N. P. 1992. *Lords of the Hills: Ancient Maya Settlement in the Puuc Region, Mexico*. Monographs in World Archaeology No. 15. Madison, WI: Prehistory Press.

Dunning, N. P. 2003. "Birth and Death of Waters: Environmental Change, Adaptation, and Symbolism in the Southern Maya Lowlands." In *Espacios mayas: Representaciones, usos, creencias*, edited by A. Breton, A. Monod-Becquelin, and M. H. Ruz, 49–76. Mexico City: Universidad Autónoma de México.

Dunning, N. P. 2004. "Down on the Farm: Classic Maya Houselots as Farmsteads." In *Ancient Maya Commoners*, edited by J. Lohse and F. Valdez, 96–116. Austin: University of Texas Press.

Dunning, N. P., E. Akpinar, C. Carr, R. Griffin, J. G. Jones, D. Lentz, A. Miller, and J. Prater. 2008. "Investigaciones geoarqueológicas y del medioambiente en los alrededores de San Bartolo, Petén: 2007." In *Proyecto Arqueológico San Bartolo: Informe Preliminar No. 6, Sexta Temporada 2007*, edited by M. Urquizú and W. Saturno, 57–71. Report submitted to Instituto Nacional de Antropología y Historia, Guatemala City.

Dunning, N. P., A. Anaya Hernández, and H. Geovannini. 2016. "Operaciones 13 y 19: Investigaciones en los reservorios." In *Proyecto Arqueológico Yaxnohcah, Informe de las 2014 y 2015 Temporadas de Investigaciones*, edited by A. Anaya Hernández, M. Peuramaki-Brown, and K. Reese-Taylor, 110–121. Report submitted to the Consejo de Arqueología del Instituto Nacional de Antropología e Historia, Mexico City.

Dunning, N. P., A. Anaya Hernández, A. Haggard, and C. Carr. 2017. "Investigaciones en el Reservorio Brisa." In *Proyecto Arqueológico Yaxnohcah, Informe de 2016 Temporada de Investigaciones*, edited by K. Reese-Taylor and A. Anaya Hernández, 93–122. Report submitted to the Consejo de Arqueología del Instituto Nacional de Antropología e Historia, Mexico City.

Dunning, N. P., and T. Beach. 2010. "Farms and Forests: Spatial and Temporal Perspectives on Ancient Maya Landscapes." In *Landscapes and Societies*, edited by I. P. Martini and W. Chesworth, 369–389. Berlin: Springer-Verlag.

Dunning, N. P., T. Beach, and S. Luzzadder-Beach. 2006. "Environmental Variability among Bajos in the Southern Maya Lowlands and Its Implications for Ancient Maya Civilization and Archaeology." In *Precolumbian Water Management: Ideology, Ritual, and Power*, edited by L. Lucero and B. Fash, 81–99. Tucson: University of Arizona Press.

Dunning, N. P., T. Beach, and S. Luzzadder-Beach. 2012. "Kax and Kol: Collapse and Resilience in Lowland Maya Civilization." *Proceedings of the National Academy of Sciences* 109 (10): 3652–3657.

Dunning, N. P., R. Griffin, J. Jones, R. Terry, Z. Larsen, and C. Carr. 2015. "Life on the Edge: Tikal in a Bajo Landscape." In *Tikal: Paleoecology of an Ancient Maya City*, edited by D. L. Lentz, N. Dunning and V. Scarborough, 95–123. Cambridge: Cambridge University Press.

Dunning, N. P., R. Griffin, T. Sever, W. Saturno, and J. Jones. 2017. "The Nature and Origin of Linear Features in the Bajo de Azúcar, Guatemala: Implications for Ancient Maya Adaptations to a Changing Environment." *Geoarchaeology* 32 (1): 107–129.

Dunning, N. P., and S. D. Houston. 2011. "Hurricanes as a Disruptive Force in the Maya Lowlands." In *Ecology, Power, and Religion in Maya Landscapes*, edited by C. Isendahl and B. L. Persson, 49–59Möckmühl, Germany: Verlag Anton Sauerwein.

Dunning, N. P., J. G. Jones, T. Beach, and S. Luzzadder-Beach. 2003. "Physiography, Habitats, and Landscapes of the Three Rivers Region." In *Heterarchy, Political Economy, and the Ancient Maya: The Three Rivers Region of the East-Central Yucatan Peninsula*, edited by V. Scarborough, F. Valdez, and N. P. Dunning, 14–24. Tucson: University of Arizona.

Dunning, N. P., J. Jones, J. Chmilar, and J. Blevins. 2006. "Investigaciones ambientales y geoarqueológicas in las alrededores de San Bartolo." In *Proyecto Arqueológico Regional San Bartolo, Informe Preliminar #3, Tercera Temporada 2005*, edited by W. Saturno and M. Urquizú, 610–624. Report submitted to Instituto Nacional de Antropología e Historia, Guatemala City.

Dunning, N. P., S. Luzzadder-Beach, T. Beach, J. G. Jones, V. L. Scarborough, and T. P. Culbert. 2002. "Arising from the Bajos: The Evolution of a Neotropical Landscape and the Rise of Maya Civilization." *Annals of the Association of American Geographers* 92 (2): 267–282.

Dunning, N. P., V. Scarborough, J. Valdez F., S. Luzzadder-Beach, T. Beach, and J. G. Jones. 1999. "Temple Mountains, Sacred Lakes, and Fertile Fields: Ancient Maya Landscapes in Northwestern Belize." *Antiquity* 73 (281): 650–660.

Dunning, N. P., D. Wahl, T. Beach, J. Jones, S. Luzzadder-Beach, and C. McCormick. 2014. "The End of the Beginning: Drought, Environmental Change, and the Preclassic to Classic Transition in the East-Central Yucatan Peninsula." In *The Great Maya Droughts in Cultural Context*, edited by G. Iannone, 107–129. Boulder: University Press of Colorado.

Dunning, N. P., and E. Weaver. 2015. "Final Thoughts: Space, Place, Ritual, and Identity in Ancient Mesoamerica." In *Memory Traces: Sacred Space at Five Mesoamerican Sites*, edited by L. Amrhein and C. Kristen-Graham, 203–218. Boulder: University Press of Colorado.

Dunning, N. P., E. Weaver, M. Smyth, and D. Ortegón. 2014. "Xcoch: Home of Ancient Maya Rain Gods and Water Managers." In *The Archaeology of Yucatan: New Directions and Data*, edited by T. Stanton, 65–80. Oxford: BAR International Series, Oxford.

Ebert, C., J. Awe, and J. A. Hogarth. 2016. "Classic Period Maya Water Management and Ecological Adaptation in the Belize River Valley." *Research Reports in Belizean Archaeology* 13 (January): 109–119.

Fialko, V. 2000. "Recursos hidráulicos en Tikal y sus periferias." In *XIII Simposio de Investigaciones Arqueológicas en Guatemala*, edited by J. P. Laporte, H. Escobedo, B. Arroyo, and A. C. Suasnavar, 556–565. Guatemala City: Museo Nacional de Arqueología y Etnología.

Fialko, V. 2005. "Diez años de investigaciones arqueológicas en la Cuenca del Río Holmul, Region Noreste del Petén." In *XVIII Simposio de Investigaciones Arqueológicas en*

Guatemala, edited by J. P. Laporte, B. Arroyo, and H. Mejía, 244–260. Guatemala City: Museo Nacional de Arqueología y Etnología.

Folan, W. J. 1982. "Mining and Quarrying Techniques of the Lowland Maya." *Anthropology* 6 (1–2): 149–174.

Ford, A. 1996. "Critical Resource Control and the Rise of the Ancient Maya." In *The Managed Mosaic: Ancient Maya Agriculture and Resource Use*, edited by S. L. Fedick, 297–303. Salt Lake City: University of Utah.

Frappier, A. B., J. Pyburn, A. D. Pinkey-Drobnis, X. Wang, D. R. Corbett, and B. H. Dahlin. 2014. "Two Millennia of Tropical Cyclone-Induced Mud Layers in a Northern Yucatán Stalagmite: Multiple Overlapping Climatic Hazards during the Maya Terminal Classic 'Megadroughts.'" *Geophysical Research Letters* 41 (14): 5148–5157.

Geovannini-Acuña, H. 2008. *Rain Harvesting in the Rainforest: The Ancient Maya Agricultural Landscape of Calakmul, Campeche, Mexico*. Oxford: BAR International Series.

Gill, E. 2009. "Operation 15: Berm Structures and Water Management at Medicinal Trail (RB 62), Belize." In *Research Reports from the Programme for Belize Archaeological Project, Volume 3. Occasional Papers, Number 10*, edited by R. Trachman and J. Valdez F., 121–126. Mesoamerican Archaeological Research Laboratory, University of Texas at Austin.

Gill, R. B. 2000. *The Great Maya Droughts: Water, Life, and Death*. Albuquerque: University of New Mexico Press.

Grazioso Sierra, L., and V. Scarborough. 2013. "Control de agua por los antiguos mayas: El sistema hidráulico de Tikal." *Contributions to New World Archaeology* 5: 39–56.

Hansen, R. D., S. Bozarth, J. Jacob, D. Wahl, and T. Schreiner. 2002. "Climatic and Environmental Variability in the Rise of Maya Civilization: A Preliminary Perspective from Northern Petén." *Ancient Mesoamerica* 13 (02): 273–295.

Harrison, P. D. 1993. "Aspects of Water Management in the Southern Maya Lowlands." In *Economic Aspects of Water Management in the Prehispanic New World*, edited by V. L. Scarborough and B. L. Isaac, 71–119. Research in Economic Anthropology, supplement No. 7. Greenwich, CT: JAI Press.

Haug, G. H., D. Gunther, L. C. Peterson, D. M. Sigman, K. A. Hughen, and B. Aeschliman. 2003. "Climate and the Collapse of Maya Civilization." *Science* 299 (5613): 1731–1735.

Hodell, D. A., M. Brenner, and J. H. Curtis. 2005. "Terminal Classic Drought in the Northern Maya Lowlands Inferred from Multiple Sediment Cores in Lake Chichancanab (Mexico)." *Quaternary Science Review* 24 (12–13): 1413–1427.

Houston, S. D. 2010. "Living Waters and Wondrous Beasts." In *Fiery Pool: The Maya and the Mythic Sea*, edited by D. Finamore and S. D. Houston, 66–79. New Haven, CT: Yale University Press.

Huchim Herrera, J., and I. Sánchez. 1990. El Sistema Hidráulico de Uxmal. *Boletín Académico de la Facultad de Ingeniería (Universidad Autónoma de Yucatán)* 13: 35–44.

Hyde, D. M. 2011. *Power Dynamics at a Commoner Hinterland Community in the Maya Lowlands: The Medicinal Trail Site, Northwestern Belize*. PhD diss., Department of Anthropology, University of Texas at Austin.

Intergovernmental Panel on Climate Change. 2007. *Summary for Policymakers of the Synthesis Report of the IPCC Fourth Assessment Report*. IPCC, Geneva. Accessed March 16, 2017. https://www.ipcc.ch/report/ar4/syr/.

Isendahl, C. 2011. "The Weight of Water: A New Look at Pre-Hispanic Puuc Maya Water Reservoirs." *Ancient Mesoamerica* 22 (1): 185–197.

Isendahl, C., N. Dunning, and J. Sabloff. 2014. "Growth Dependency and Decline in Classic Maya Puuc Political Economies." *Archaeological Papers of the American Anthropological Association* 24 (March): 43–55.

Isendahl, C., V. Scarborough, J. Gunn, N. Dunning, S. Fedick, G. Iannone, and L. Lucero. 2015. "Applied Perspectives on Pre-Columbian Maya Water Management Systems: What Are the Insights for Water Security?" In *The Oxford Handbook on Historical Ecology and Applied Archaeology*, edited by C. Isendahl and D. Stump, 1–14. Oxford: Oxford University Press.

Johnston, K. J. 2004. "Lowland Maya Water Management Practices: The Household Exploitation of Rural Wells." *Geoarchaeology* 19 (3): 265–292.

Kennett, D. J., S.F.M. Breienbach, V. V. Aquino, Y. Asmerom, J. Awe, J.U.L. Baldini, P. Bartlein, et al. 2012. "Development and Disintegration of Maya Political Systems in Response to Climate Change." *Science* 338 (6108): 788–791.

Kettunen, H., and C. Helmke. 2013. "Water in Maya Imagery and Writing." *Contributions to New World Archaeology* 5: 17–38.

Koszkul, W., and J. Žralka. 2013. "El manejo ritual y práctico del agua: El caso del Edificio 14 de Nakum, Guatemala." *Contributions to New World Archaeology* 5: 101–124.

Lemonnier, E., and B. Vanniere. 2013. "Agrarian Features, Farmsteads, and Homesteads in the Río Bec Nuclear Zone (Mexico)." *Ancient Mesoamerica* 24 (2): 397–413.

Lentz, D. L., N. P. Dunning, V. L. Scarborough, K. Magee, K. M. Thompson, E. Weaver, C. Carr, et al. 2014. "Farms, Forests, and the Edge of Sustainability at the Ancient Maya City of Tikal." *Proceedings of the National Academy of Sciences* 111 (52): 18513–18518.

Lentz, D. L., T. L. Hamilton, N. P. Dunning, V. Scarborough, T. Luxton, A. Vonderheide, E. Tepe, et al. 2020. "Molecular Genetic and Geochemical Assays Reveal Severe Contamination of Drinking Water Reservoirs at the Ancient Maya City of Tikal." *Scientific Reports* 10 (10316).

Lowe, J. D. 2008. *Excavations of Two Small Depressions at Group A, The Medicinal Trail Site RB 62, Belize*. MA thesis, Department of Anthropology, University of Texas at Austin.

Lucero, L. J. 1999. "Water Control and Maya Politics in the Southern Maya Lowlands." In *Complex Polities in the Ancient Tropical World*, edited by E. A. Bacus and L. J. Lucero, 35–49. Archaeological Papers of the American Anthropological Association Number 9. American Anthropological Association, Arlington, VA.

Lucero, L. J. 2002. "The Collapse of the Classic Maya: A Case for the Role of Water Control." *American Anthropologist* 104 (3): 814–826.

Lucero, L. J. 2006. *Water and Ritual: The Rise and Fall of Classic Maya Rulers*. Austin: University of Texas Press.

Lucero, L. J., J. D. Gunn, and V. L. Scarborough. 2011. "Climate Change and Classic Maya Water Management." *Water* 3 (2): 479–494.

Lundell, C. L. 1937. "The Vegetation of the Petén." In *Carnegie Institution of Washington Publication 478*. Washington, DC: Carnegie Institution.

Luzzadder-Beach, S., T. Beach, and N. P. Dunning. 2012. "Wetland Fields as Mirrors of Drought and the Maya Abandonment." *Proceedings of the National Academy of Sciences* 109 (10): 3646–3651.

Luzzadder-Beach, S., T. Beach, S. Hutson, and S. Krause. 2016. "Sky-Earth, Lake-Sea: Climate and Water in Maya History and Landscape." *Antiquity* 90 (350): 426–442.

McAnany, P. A. 1990. "Water Storage in the Puuc Region of the Northern Maya: A Key to Population Estimates and Architectural Variability." In *Precolumbian Population History in the Maya Lowlands*, edited by P. T. Culbert and D. Rice, 263–284. Albuquerque: University of New Mexico Press.

Matheny, R. T. 1978. "Northern Maya Lowland Water-Control Systems." In *Pre-Hispanic Maya Agriculture*, edited by P. D. Harrison and B. L. Turner II, 185–210. Albuquerque: University of New Mexico Press.

Matheny, R. T., D. Gurr, W. Forsyth, and R. Hauck. 1983. "Investigations at Edzná Campeche, Mexico." Vol. 1, pt. 1: The Hydraulic System. In *Papers of the New World Archaeological Foundation No. 46*, edited by R. T. Matheny, 239. Provo, Utah: Brigham Young University.

Matheny, R. T., R. D. Hansen, and D. Gurr. 1980. "Preliminary Field Report, El Mirador, 1979 Season." In *El Mirador, El Petén, Guatemala: An Interim Report. Papers of the New World Archaeological Foundation No. 45*, edited by R. T. Matheny, 1–23. Provo, UT: Brigham Young University.

Medina-Elizade, M., S. Burns, D. W. Lea, S. Asmerom, L. van Gunten, V. Polyak, M. Vuille, and A. Karmalkar. 2010. "High Resolution Stalagmite Climate Record from the Yucatan Peninsula Spanning the Maya Terminal Classic Period." *Earth and Planetary Science Letters* 298 (1–2): 255–262.

Medina-Elizade, M., J. M. Martín, F. Lases-Hernández, R. Bradley, and S. Burns. 2016. "Testing the 'Tropical Storm' Hypothesis of Yucatan Peninsula Climate Variability during the Maya Terminal Classic Period." *Quaternary Research* 86 (2): 111–119.

Medina-Elizade, M., and E. J. Rohling. 2012. "Collapse of Classic Maya Civilization Related to Modest Reduction in Precipitation." *Science* 335 (6071): 956–959.

Morales-Aguilar, C. A. 2009. *El sistema hidráulico de El Mirador, Peten, Guatemala: Una perspectiva general*. Proyecto Arqueológico Cuenca Mirador, Foundation for Archaeological Research and Environmental Studies (FARES).

Morley, S. G. 1938. *The Inscriptions of Petén*. Carnegie Institution of Washington, Publication 437, vol. 1. Carnegie Institution, Washington, DC.

Percy, M. 2009. "Excavation at the Medicinal Trail Site (2008): Operation 14." In *Research Reports for the Programme for Belize Archaeological Project, Volume 3. Occasional Papers, Number 10,* edited by R. Trachman and J. Valdez F., 143–144. Mesoamerican Archaeological Research Laboratory, University of Texas at Austin.

Peuramaki-Brown, M., S. G. Morton, and A. Castro. 2016. "Operación 17 en el Grupo Wo': Excavaciones de prueba en un lote doméstico peri-urbano." In *Proyecto Arqueológico Yaxnohcah, Informe de las 2014 y 2015 Temporadas de Investigaciones,* edited by A. Anaya Hernández, M. Peuramaki-Brown, and K. Reese-Taylor, 95–109. Report submitted to the Consejo de Arqueología del Instituto Nacional de Antropología e Historia, Mexico City.

Pohl, M. D., K. O. Pope, J. G. Jones, J. S. Jacob, D. R. Piperno, S. D. deFrance, D. L. Lentz, J. A. Gifford, M. E. Danforth, and J. K. Josserand. 1996. "Early Agriculture in the Maya Lowlands." *Latin American Antiquity* 7 (4): 355–372.

Rands, R. 1953. "The Water Lily in Maya Art: A Complex of Alleged Asiatic Origin." *Bulletin* 151 (34): 75–153. Bureau of American Ethnology, Smithsonian Institution, Washington, DC.

Reese-Taylor, K., and A. Anaya Hernández. 2013. *Proyecto Arqueológico Yaxnohcah, Informe de la Primera Temporada de Investigaciones.* Report submitted to the Consejo de Arqueología del Instituto Nacional de Antropología e Historia, Mexico City.

Reese-Taylor, K., and A. Anaya Hernández, eds. 2017. *Proyecto Arqueológico Yaxnohcah, Informe de 2016 Temporada de Investigaciones.* Report submitted to the Consejo de Arqueología del Instituto Nacional de Antropología e Historia, Mexico City.

Reese-Taylor, K., A. Anaya Hernández, A. Flores Esquival, K. Monteleone, A. Uriarte, C. Carr, H. Geovannini Acuña, J. C. Fernandez-Diaz, M. Peuramaki-Brown, and N. P. Dunning. 2016. "Boots on the Ground at Yaxnohcah: Ground-Truthing LiDAR in a Complex Tropical Landscape." *Advances in Archaeological Practice* 4 (3): 314–338.

Ringle, W. M. 2011. *The Yaxhom Valley Survey: Pioneers of the Puuc Region.* Research Grant 8913-11, National Geographic Society, Washington, DC.

Rosenmeier, M. F., D. A. Hodell, M. Brenner, J. H. Curtis, J. B. Martin, F. S. Anselmetti, D. Ariztegui, and T. P. Guilderson. 2002. "Influence of Vegetation Change on Watershed Hydrology: Implications for Paleoclimatic Interpretation of Lacustrine Records." *Journal of Paleolimnology* 27 (1): 117–131.

Saturno, W., D. Stuart, and B. Beltran. 2006. "Early Maya Writing at San Bartolo, Guatemala." *Science* 311 (5765): 1281–1283.

Scarborough, V. L. 1993. "Water Management in the Southern Maya Lowlands: An Accretive Model for the Engineered Landscape." In *Economic Aspects of Water Management in the Prehispanic New World,* edited by V. L. Scarborough and B. L. Isaac, 17–69. Research in Economic Anthropology, supplement No. 7. Greenwich, CT: JAI Press.

Scarborough, V. L. 1998. "Ecology and Ritual: Water Management and the Maya." *Latin American Antiquity* 9 (2): 135–159.

Scarborough, V. L. 2003. *The Flow of Power: Ancient Water Systems and Landscapes*. Santa Fe, NM: SAR Press.

Scarborough, V. L., R. Connelly, and S. Ross. 1994. "The Prehispanic Maya Reservoir System at Kinal, Peten, Guatemala." *Ancient Mesoamerica* 5 (1): 97–106.

Scarborough, V. L., N. P. Dunning, K. B. Tankersley, C. Carr, E. Weaver, L. Grazioso, B. Lane et al. 2012. "Water and Sustainable Land Use at the Ancient Tropical City of Tikal, Guatemala." *Proceedings of the National Academy of Sciences* 109 (31): 12408–12413.

Scarborough, V. L., and G. G. Gallopin. 1991. "A Water Storage Adaptation in the Maya Lowlands." *Science* 251 (4994): 658–662.

Scarborough, V. L., and L. Grazioso Sierra. 2015. "The Evolution of an Ancient Water-works System at Tikal." In *Tikal: Paleoecology of an Ancient Maya City*, edited by D. L. Lentz, N. P. Dunning, and V. L. Scarborough, 16–45. New York: Cambridge University Press.

Schele, L., and D. Friedel. 1990. *A Forest of Kings: The Untold Story of the Ancient Maya*. New York: Morrow.

Seefeld, N. 2013. "Public Provisions for Dry Seasons: The Hydraulic System of Uxul and Its Relevance for the Survivability of the Settlement." *Contributions to New World Archaeology* 5: 57–84.

Seefeld, N. 2018. *The Hydraulic System of Uxul: Origins, Functions, and Social Setting*. Oxford: Archaeopress.

Siemens, A. 1978. "Karst and the Pre-Hispanic Maya in the Southern Lowlands." In *Pre-Hispanic Maya Agriculture*, edited by P. D. Harrison and B. L. Turner II, 117–144. Albuquerque: University of New Mexico Press.

Smyth, M., N. P. Dunning, E. Weaver, P. van Beynen, and D. Ortegón Zapata. 2017. "The Perfect Storm: Climate Change and Ancient Maya Response in the Puuc Hills Region, Yucatan, Mexico." *Antiquity* 91 (356): 490–509.

Smyth, M. P., and D. Ortegón Zapata. 2008. "A Preclassic Center in the Puuc Region: A Report on Xcoch, Yucatan, Mexico." *Mexicon* 30: 63–68.

Šprajc, I. 2008. *Reconocimiento arqueológico en el sureste del estado de Campeche: 1996–2005*. Paris Monographs in American Archaeology 19. BAR International Series 1742, Archaeopress, Oxford.

Šprajc, I., ed. 2015. *Exploraciones arqueológicas en Chactún, Campeche, México*. Institute of Anthropological and Spatial Studies publication 7. Research Centre of the Slovenian Academy of Sciences and Arts, Ljubljana, Slovenia.

Stephens, J. L. 1841. *Incidents of Travel in Central America, Chiapas, and Yucatan*. Vol. 2. New York: Harper and Brothers.

Tokovinine, A. 2013. "Place and Identity in Classic Maya Narratives." In *Studies in Pre-Columbian Art and Archaeology 37*. Washington, DC: Dumbarton Oaks.

van der Leeuw, S. E. 2008. "Climate and Society: Lessons from the Past 10,000 Years." *Royal Swedish Academy of Science* 14 (November): 476–482.

Volta, B., R. González Heredia, L. F. Folan, W. J. Folan, and A. Morales López. 2013. "Los rasgos hidráulicos de Oxpemul, Campeche." *Los Investigadores de la Cultura Maya* 21: 265–278.

Wahl, D., T. Schreiner, R. Byrne, and R. Hansen. 2007. "A Paleoecological Record from a Late Classic Maya Reservoir in the North Petén." *Latin American Antiquity* 18 (2): 212–222.

Walker, D. S. 2016. "Apuntes sobre la secuencia cerámica de Yaxnohcah." In *Proyecto Arqueológico Yaxnohcah, Informe de las 2014 y 2015 Temporadas de Investigaciones*, edited by A. Anaya Hernández, M. Peuramaki-Brown, and K. Reese-Taylor, 144–171. Report submitted to the Consejo de Arqueología del Instituto Nacional de Antropología e Historia, Mexico City.

Weaver, E., C. Carr, N. Dunning, L. Florea, and V. Scarborough. 2015. "Examining Landscape Modifications for Water Management at Tikal Using 3-Dimensional Modeling with ArcGIS." In *Tikal: Paleoecology of an Ancient Maya City*, edited by D. Lentz, N. Dunning, and V. Scarborough, 87–94. Cambridge: Cambridge University Press.

Weiss-Krejci, E. 2013. "Ancient Maya Rainwater Reservoirs in Northwestern Belize." *Contributions to New World Archaeology* 5: 85–100.

Weiss-Krejci, E., and T. Sabbas. 2002. "The Potential Role of Small Depressions as Water Features in the Central Maya Lowlands." *Latin American Antiquity* 13 (3): 343–357.

Winemiller, T. L. 2003. "Water Resource Management by the Ancient Maya of Yucatan, Mexico." PhD diss., Louisiana State University, Department of Geography and Anthropology, Baton Rouge.

Wyatt, A. R. 2012. "Agricultural Practices at Chan: Farming and Political Economy in an Ancient Maya Community." In *Chan: An Ancient Maya Farming Community*, edited by C. Robin, 71–88. Gainesville: University Press of Florida.

Wyatt, A. R. 2014. "The Scale and Organization of Ancient Maya Water Management." *WIREs Water* 1 (5): 449–467.

3

Ancient Maya Intensive Agriculture and Water Management Practices

David Lentz, Nicholas Dunning, Payson Sheets,
Timothy Beach, Sheryl Luzzadder-Beach,
Andrew Wyatt, and Cynthia Robin

Just as the architecture, art, epigraphic representations, and astronomical observations of the Classic period Maya were evidence of a highly complex society, so were their approaches to agriculture and surface water hydrology. The purpose of this chapter is to provide an outline of the sophisticated land management practices that allowed the ancient Maya to develop large cities and sustain them for several centuries.

For many decades it had been presumed that the ancient lowland Maya practiced an extensive type of long fallow (fifteen to twenty years) swidden (slash-and-burn) or milpa agriculture that relied upon the regrowth of forests to replenish lost soil nutrients, thus creating a sustainable system of food production that could maintain the growth of urban centers. Recent studies have shown, however, that, while long fallow swidden approaches may have been adequate to meet the demands of inhabitants of sparsely populated portions of the neotropical forests, when areas became more densely populated, as in the Elevated Interior Region (EIR) (figure 3.1) during the Classic period, there was insufficient arable land to support the growth of emerging large polities

https://doi.org/10.5876/9781646422326.c003

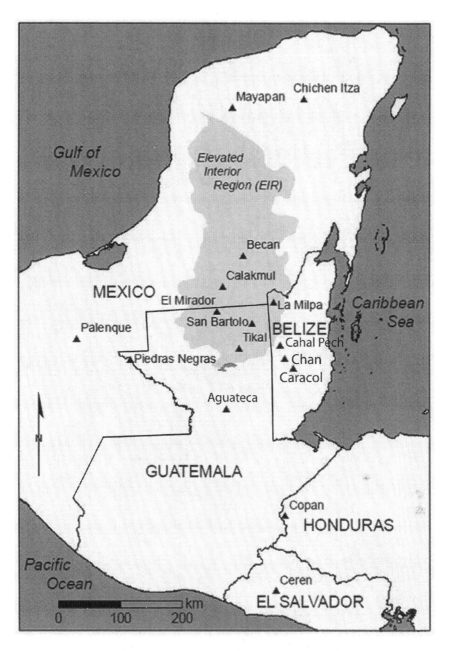

FIGURE 3.1. *Map of Mesoamerica showing the location of archaeological sites discussed in the text. The extent of the Elevated Interior Region (EIR), a karstic plateau in the Maya heartland, is illustrated.*

using long fallow swidden agriculture alone. Accordingly, agricultural strategies became much more diversified as populations expanded, and the adoption of a variety of intensive crop production techniques—such as short fallow systems, terracing, irrigated fields, drained fields, ridge and furrow techniques and the cultivation of dooryard gardens—became more commonplace. *Bajo*, karst depressions common in the EIR that range in size from as little as one or two to hundreds of square kilometers and contain a wide array of mostly seasonal wetland ecosystems (Dunning, Beach, and Luzzadder-Beach 2006), margins also became preferred areas for active cultivation. All of these intensive forms of agriculture were employed to enhance a food supply that allowed the dramatic Late Classic population growth.

MAYA LAND MANAGEMENT

The earliest evidence of agriculture in the lowlands of Mesoamerica came from the Grijalva River delta along the Gulf Coast of Tabasco at the San Andrés site where cultivated *Zea mays* L. (maize) pollen appeared along with evidence of forest clearance around 5000 BCE, followed soon thereafter by the appearance of *Manihot* (manioc) pollen at 4600 BCE (Pope et al. 2001). In the Maya region, early incipient cultivation was reported from scattered Archaic sites in the swampy areas of northern Belize. Observations of maize and manioc (*Manihot esculenta* Crantz) pollen recorded at Cob Swamp and Cobweb Swamp as early as 3000 BCE (Pohl et al. 1996) confirm the adoption of domesticated crops at this time. Considerable charcoal buildup in soil deposits dating to around 2500 BCE appeared shortly after evidence of plant domesticates in the pollen record, suggesting that extensive forest clearance occurred in conjunction with widespread plant cultivation. Agriculture was clearly beginning to become established at this time, but macroremains evidence for other Mesoamerican cultigens (maize, squash [*Cucurbita* spp.], cotton [*Gossypium hirsutum* L.], cacao [*Theobroma cacao* L.], chili peppers [*Capsicum annuum* L.], mamey [*Pouteria sapota* (Jacq.) H. E. Moore & Stearn], and avocado [*Persea americana* Mill.]) did not appear together until the Middle Preclassic horizons at the Cuello site (Miksicek et al. 1981), the Pulltrouser Swamp area (Miksicek 1983) in northern Belize, the Cahal Pech site in central Belize (Wiesen and Lentz 1999), and elsewhere in the Belize River Valley (Willey et al. 1965). Curiously, beans (*Phaseolus* spp.) do not appear in the Maya area until the early Late Preclassic period (300–100 BCE) at Cahal Pech (Powis et al. 1999; Wiesen and Lentz 1999). In fact, the earliest record of beans in Mesoamerica, from the Tehuacán Valley in Mexico, dates to around 350 BCE (Kaplan and Lynch 1999), just antecedent to the Cahal Pech find. Preclassic macrobotanical remains of manioc and sweet potatoes (*Ipomoea batatas* [L.] Lam.) were observed in northern Guatemala at San Bartolo (Santini 2016) and Tikal (Lentz et al. 2014), respectively. Thus, the paleoethnobotanical data reveal that the Mesoamerican agricultural plant assemblage was firmly entrenched by Late Preclassic times, and the food surpluses produced by this array of domesticates made possible the subsequent development of more dense populations and complex societies.

How these crops were grown and how the land was managed have long been together a topic for discussion among Mayanists (e.g., Dumond 1961; Flannery 1982; Harrison and Turner 1978; Turner 1974, 1983). The Spaniards observed contact-period Maya who practiced a form of swidden agriculture with a long-term cycle of cultivation episodes, followed by years of intermittent fallow (Jones 2000). Because of these observations and because this type of agricultural approach is still practiced in many areas of the Maya world today, archaeologists (e.g., J.E.S. Thompson 1954; Dumond 1961) assumed these same practices were followed by the ancient Maya, as well. Most of these observations, however, were recorded after the demographic collapse that followed the introduction of Old World diseases. The Spanish chroniclers were observing a diminished Maya population who had plenty of land to make long fallow swidden agricultural techniques function sustainably.

Indeed, it seems likely that the ancient Maya did practice extensive swidden agriculture, especially in the earliest settlements. For example, from the Tikal area there is pollen evidence from Lake Petén Itzá indicating extensive forest clearance during the Preclassic period (Hodell, Brenner, and Curtis 2000), as well as indications that sedimentation rates in the lake were highest in the Preclassic (Anselmetti et al. 2007). This observation coincides with data from bajos near Tikal, a city center located in present-day Guatemala, and elsewhere in the southern Maya lowlands that reveal considerable erosion from upland agricultural fields in the Preclassic period, before soil conservation practices became established (Beach et al. 2006; Beach et al. 2008; Beach, Luzzadder-Beach, Cook et al. 2015; Dunning and Beach 2000, 2010; Dunning et al. 2015). This widespread forest clearance coupled with soil erosion likely was the result of extensive swidden agriculture. This approach functioned adequately for many centuries, but soil loss remained an issue. Near the end of the Preclassic period, however, communities such as Tikal began to implement means of controlling soil and water loss.

The Tikal Maya responded to their erosion and concomitant sedimentation challenges by constructing earthworks, such as the Perdido and Corriental Reservoirs that were designed to slow and capture water moving downhill. The latter reservoir even appears to have employed sand purification filters at the ingress to reduce the sediment load of water flowing into the reservoir (Scarborough and Grazioso Sierra 2015). Evidence of Preclassic water management facilities, namely, canals and reservoirs, also appears at Cerros, Edzna, Yaxnohcah, and other centers (Dunning et al., chapter 2 in this volume; Hammond 2000). As the Classic period emerged at Tikal and elsewhere, the use of reservoirs, canals, and other means of controlling water flow and reducing erosion became more commonplace. Recent data from numerous sites in the last decade have brought to light the idea that agricultural activities of the ancient Maya, beginning by at least the Late Preclassic period and particularly in the larger centers, were anything but uniform. In fact, approaches to agriculture varied considerably from region to region and grew in sophistication from the earlier long fallow swidden applications (Beach 2017).

Land Management at Cerén

The archaeological site of Cerén in central El Salvador is an extraordinary example of a Classic period Maya farming village. The site was burned then rapidly smothered by several meters of volcanic ash around 660 CE as a result of the eruption of nearby Loma Caldera; thus it provides a unique data set, particularly regarding ancient Maya agricultural techniques and plant use practices. The villagers all managed to escape the conflagration but left behind most of their worldly possessions. Their houses, kitchens, storehouses, other buildings, and most of the artifacts abandoned by the fleeing farmers were preserved, more or less intact and in situ, as a result of the deep blanket of volcanic ash, or tephra, that covered the village just after the eruption.

Remarkably, the plants in the dooryards, storehouses, and fields were also preserved in a variety of ways. Some plant parts were partially burned as a result of the fires caused by lava bombs landing in the village, other plants in more protected areas were merely desiccated as a result of the hot ash, and still others were preserved for centuries as impressions or cavities in the ash holding the form of the disintegrated plants that produced them. Because of the painstaking excavations coupled with the use of dental plaster poured into each cavity in the ash encountered by archaeologists, household gardens and whole agricultural fields beyond the village could be identified, as well as the crops planted in them. This circumstance offers an extraordinary glimpse into the agricultural practices of the Classic Maya (Sheets 2002; Sheets et al. 2015).

One of the many surprising discoveries at Cerén was the revelation that the farmers used ridge and furrow techniques (figure 3.2), ostensibly to control erosion, maintain soil resources, and retain rainwater. Not only did they use the ridging technique, but they modified it to suit the plants being cultivated. For example, manioc, which has a broad cluster of thick roots that grow best in loose soil, was cultivated in a tall and wide planting ridge or bed. Cerén is toward the upper end of the range of precipitation for manioc, which is drought adapted, so it is not surprising that the manioc ridges run downhill to facilitate drainage. The manioc fields were extensive, largely monocrop, and just outside of the village. The large size of the manioc fields next to the village demonstrated that this was an important staple crop for the Cerén Maya, not one of marginal

FIGURE 3.2. *Ancient ridges and furrows in a maize field at the Cerén site in central El Salvador.*

utility. Maize, on the other hand, which has a much more compact root system, was planted in more narrow ridges with smaller furrows between. Maize fields were planted in rows perpendicular to the slope, undoubtedly an effort to retain runoff for thirsty maize plants and control erosion at the same time. Both maize and manioc were planted extensively at Cerén, attesting to their importance as Maya staple crops.

Inside the village, a different pattern of cultivation was observed. While there were small garden plots in which maize and other annual crops were grown in ridge and furrow style, there were also small orchards with numerous perennial crops and medicinal plants in plots between shaded areas. These plants could be carefully tended and fertilized with human feces or "night soil." Although most of the calories for the Cerén farmers likely came from the intensively mono-cropped fields surrounding the village, dooryard gardens and orchards provided important nutrients, spices, and medicine, not to mention shade from the hot tropical sun.

Because of the exceptional preservation at Cerén, our understanding of the array of plants used by the inhabitants of this humble Maya village is unparalleled. The most common crop plant by far was maize. The plants were found as plaster casts and carbonized macroremains. The variety of maize at Cerén appears to have been Chapalote-Nal Tel, a complex of races, well adapted to tropical heat, and widely used throughout the Maya lowlands. Other field crop plants included three species of beans that were unusually abundant (beans are rare at most Mesoamerican sites because they don't seem to preserve well), two species of squash, agave (*Agave* spp.), and cotton, with both seeds and fiber in evidence. Root crops were well represented at Cerén, with numerous plant casts of malanga (*Xanthosoma sagittifolium* [L.] Schott) and manioc that gave an extraordinarily clear picture of how significant these highly productive crops were to the ancient Maya (Lentz, Reyna de Aguilar et al. 1996; Lentz et al. 2002). Tree crops included avocado, cacao, calabash (*Crescentia cujete* L.), guava (*Psidium guajava* L.), hog plums (*Spondias* spp.), mamey, nance (*Brysonima crassifolia* [L.] H.B.K.) and others. Even the grass used to thatch houses (*Trachypogon spicatus* L. f.) was preserved throughout the village (Lentz, Beaudry-Corbett et al. 1996). Numerous charcoal samples were collected and identified, providing a detailed portrait of the rich natural history of Cerén and its ecological setting (Lentz and Ramirez-Sosa 2002).

Land Management at Aguateca

The agricultural pattern seen at Cerén has also been observed elsewhere in the Maya lowlands. Aguateca, in the Petén region of Guatemala, is another extraordinarily well-preserved Mesoamerican site—in this case, preservation is owed to the invasion of the site by enemies of the Aguateca polity, followed by burning and abandonment of the center. The fires, in particular, caused the carbonization and preservation of many plants that were produced at the site or were otherwise in some stage of consumption or storage. The usual field crops of maize, beans, squash, chili peppers, and cotton were in evidence, but also present were a striking number of fruit trees. Annona (*Annona* spp.), avocado, calabash, mamey, nance, cacao, and guava remains were all found in archaeological contexts. Also, there were remains from several useful palm trees, namely, huiscoyol (*Bactris major* Jacq.), cohune (*Attalea cohune* Mart.), and coyol (*Acrocomia aculeata* [Jacq.] Lodd. ex Mart.) (Lentz, Lane, and Thompson 2014).

To complement the paleoethnobotanical data, a survey of soil carbon isotopes was conducted around Aguateca to locate maize fields in the site core and its environs (Johnson, Wright, and Terry 2007; Wright, Terry, and Eberl 2009). The areas of $\delta^{13}C$ enrichment, indicating maize cultivation or the presence of other C_4 plants, were located chiefly along the margins of nearby wetlands. The areas adjacent to house compounds, however, showed no signs of enrichment, indicating that these areas were planted differently. Likely, the Maya planted the open spaces among the house compounds similar to the pattern seen at Cerén. Once again, the fields bearing the bulk of the crop production were away from the settlement while the areas within the settlement were planted with orchards and probably dooryard gardens.

Land Management at Tikal

At Tikal, we see how the approaches to agricultural subsistence observed at Cerén and Aguateca may have played out on a larger scale. With population growth over time, the agricultural system at Tikal needed to expand and gradually intensify to accommodate expanding populations during the Classic period. A recent study of agriculture at Tikal (Lentz et al. 2014; Lentz et al. 2015) began by describing a Voronoi diagram that approximated an extractive zone of the Late Classic Maya occupants as constrained by the adjacent contemporaneous communities. The extraction zone, approximately 1,100 km² of mostly upland soils, represented the land area from which the Tikal inhabitants produced most of their essential needs, aside from a few high-value trade items imported by human porters or possibly brought in by canoes during the wet seasons. Using pollen data, satellite imagery, and archaeological settlement data, researchers were able to define the amount of land inside the Voronoi polygon that was available for resource extraction. This zone encompassing the Tikal polity appears to have been divided into an upland forest reserve (350 km²), bajo land (235 km²), and land occupied by human settlement or the built environment (165 km²). What remained of the resource extractive zone was approximately 350 km² of relatively high-quality upland soils (Mollisols) used for agriculture. This land, which provided the bulk of the calories for a burgeoning populace, likely was devoted to some sort of short fallow cycle agriculture, possibly with ridge and furrow plantings (once again, as practiced at Cerén) and other strategies to reduce soil erosion. The "short fallow" part of this assessment comes from the observation that there was not enough land to feed 40,000–50,000 inhabitants and have twelve to fifteen years of land set aside in fallow. Evidently, the Maya could not rely solely on short fallow swidden agriculture, however, and developed several other kinds of intensive agriculture that were more productive and more sustainable.

AGRICULTURAL STRATEGIES

Terraces

Substantial evidence for the use of terracing by the ancient lowland Maya has recently come to light in many areas. Terracing of sloping terrain as a form of agricultural intensification has many benefits over a nonterraced landscape. Terraces reduce the amount of soil erosion, limit water runoff, improve the ability of the soil to retain moisture, increase the depth of soil, increase nutrient retention, and increase the amount of arable land when compared to a nonterraced landscape (Donkin 1979; Spencer and Hale 1961; Treacy and Denevan 1997). The only drawback to terracing is that it represents a huge overall labor investment when compared to simple swidden techniques, but that labor investment can be spread out over many generations and therefore is not onerous in a given year or decade. Nevertheless, terraces represent a means to substantially improve agricultural productivity in terms of the amount of food per area that can be produced vis-à-vis swidden techniques (A.S.Z. Chase and Weishampel 2016).

Accordingly, the use of terraces represents a basic means of intensifying agricultural production that has been documented in many urban and rural landscapes in the Maya lowlands, including the northern Maya Mountains and their adjacent foothills in west-central Belize (A. F. Chase and Chase 1998; Murtha 2002; Pollock 2003), the low hills of the Río Bec region in the northern Petén (Turner II 1983), the hills surrounding the Pasión River (Dunning and Beach 1994), the Petexbatún (Beach and Dunning 1995), the Three Rivers Region (Beach et al. 2002), and in the Belize River Valley, particularly in the area around Xunantunich (Ashmore et al. 1994; Neff et al. 1995; Yaeger and Connell 1993). We also find terraces throughout the Maya highlands, including a particular type of terrace called a *tablón* in the hills surrounding Lake Atitlán in Guatemala (Mathewson 1984).

The urban center of Caracol, in particular, made an extraordinary investment in terracing. While terracing has been known for decades to have formed the basis of urban agriculture at Caracol (A. F. Chase and Chase 1998; Healy et al. 1983), the application of LiDAR (Light Detection and Ranging) survey has revealed extensive efforts by the ancient Maya to construct tens of square kilometers of agricultural terraces in a densely settled polity (A. F. Chase et al. 2011; A.S.Z. Chase and Scarborough 2014; Chase and Weishampel 2016, Chase et al., chapter 7 in this volume). This form of agricultural intensification, along with a system of reservoirs, enabled the polity to support a large population in an area with no permanent bodies of water nearby.

While terraces appear to have been major investments in landesque capital, they were often constructed and managed at the local level. According to Robin Donkin, terraces were "undoubtedly constructed piecemeal by single families or small groups of families, and, unlike irrigation, their maintenance involved cooperation at a level no higher than that of the village community" (1979, 33). One of these small villages is the site of Chan in Belize, a small community similar in size to Cerén (Robin, Chase, and Chase 2012). At Chan, settlement surveys identified 1,223 terraces, grouped into 398 terrace sets, providing a density of 304 terraces per square kilometer, among the highest in the Maya lowlands (Wyatt 2012). Although the terraces at Chan were not centrally located, as seen at Caracol, the density of terracing, as well as the substantial height (up to 3 m) and length (as long as 300 m) of many of the terrace walls represented a considerable investment in agricultural infrastructure.

Paleoethnobotanical data from Chan terrace activity surfaces supported the hypothesis that the terraces were used for the cultivation of maize and the growth of orchards (Lentz et al. 2012). Notwithstanding the heavily modified landscape at the site, the identification of tropical hardwood charcoal indicates the continued presence of forested areas in the vicinity (Wyatt 2008a). The observation of archaeological pine charcoal on terrace beds further indicates that the soil was fertilized through the application of ash from domestic hearths (Wyatt 2008b). In his study of traditional Mexican and Central American farming practices, Gene Wilken noted that not only were ashes from the burning of fallow fields turned into the soil but, "even more deliberate than this procedure is the transfer of ash from domestic cooking and heating fires directly to the fields. Domestic ash is often carefully applied by hand around each plant, suggesting the high regard farmers have for this amendment" (Wilken 1987, 57). Wood ash provides significant amounts of phosphorus, calcium, magnesium, and potassium to the soils, as well as a number of valuable microelements, though its most apparent effect is the raising of soil pH, promoting plant growth and productivity (Demeyer, Voundi Nkana, and Verloo 2001). Raising the soil pH with wood ash can counteract aluminum and manganese toxicity (Demeyer, Voundi Nkana, and Verloo 2001, 290), a potential problem with continuously cultivated terrace soils (Healy et al. 1983). Terrace excavations also recovered a high density of *jute* shell (*Pachychilus* sp.) on planting surfaces, suggesting the application of different organic material as a soil amendment.

Terrace construction at Chan began in the Middle Preclassic and continued through the Terminal Classic period. The early terraces were associated with larger farmsteads and older households, indicating that construction and landscape modification began with the earliest settlers of the region. As populations grew, and particularly as the nearby urban center of Xunantunich became established as a political power in the valley, terrace construction continued and accelerated with more marginal terrain converted to agricultural land. In the process of modifying the landscape, Chan farmers also constructed extensive water management features, including small irrigation channels on terrace beds, small reservoirs to retain water specifically for watering terraces, and containment areas near natural springs to collect water in "spring houses."

Near the Aguada de Términos sector of Tikal, chert debris, ostensibly the flaked debitage from worked chert nodules quarried from the margins of the Bajo de Santa Fe, was used to create a system of terraces. Pollen data from the *aguada* suggest that the Maya farmers were using the terraces to grow maize and possibly the root crop *achira*, or arrowroot (*Canna indica* L.) (Dunning et al. 2015). Intriguingly, these are thus far the only agricultural terraces documented for Tikal despite an abundance of sloping terrain, suggesting that the Tikal Maya employed alternative methods to protect vulnerable slopes from erosion (Dunning et al. 2009) such as contour ridges, as at Cerén, and maintaining tree cover in orchards and managed forests (Lentz et al. 2014).

The use of terracing was widespread by the Classic period and undoubtedly served to increase agricultural productivity at a time when the Maya needed it most. Nevertheless, similar to Tikal, there are many sites and areas in the Maya lowlands with hilly topography where terracing was not widely used, again suggesting that other forms of slope stabilization were in use, or that land pressure was not as severe in all areas (Dunning and Beach 2010; Dunning et al. 1998).

Bajos

As early as the Middle Preclassic period, many Maya settlements began to position their communities adjacent to bajos, where rainwater runoff could be most readily captured and stored (Scarborough 2003; Dunning et al., chapter 2 in this volume). These basins underwent considerable environmental change over the course of Maya civilization, most commonly the accumulation of deep, colluvial soils on their margins as the result of erosion from adjacent uplands (Beach et al. 2006; Dunning, Beach, and Luzzadder-Beach 2006). As seen at Tikal, bajos were a valuable source of timber and agricultural products, particularly along the margins (Lentz and Hockaday 2009). Root crops, especially achira and malanga, are adapted to wetlands and can be planted in bajo margin soils (Lentz et al. 2015) as waters recede in the dry season. These crops would have done well in these situations, particularly if the bajo soils were augmented with colluvium from the uplands. Numerous large Maya polities—such as El Mirador (Hansen et al. 2002), Calakmul (Gunn et al. 2002), La Milpa (Dunning et al. 2002), Tikal (Dunning et al. 2015), and Yaxnohcah (Reese-Taylor et al. 2016)—are located adjacent to bajos, suggesting that the Maya regarded these seasonal wetlands as useful resource-laden areas. Indeed, these bajo margins, essentially ecotone areas, were rich in both floral and faunal diversity.

Raised or Drained Fields

In low-lying terrain around the margins of the EIR in the southern Maya lowlands, groundwater discharge feeds a number of perennial river systems. Associated perennial wetlands saw the development of raised or drained fields in locations with a high water table and a less permeable substrate. These areas undoubtedly were highly productive agricultural zones. Some of the earliest Maya drained field systems were identified at Pulltrouser (Turner and Harrison 1983) and Cob (Pohl et al. 1996) swamps in northern Belize starting around 1500–1300 BCE. Additional evidence of drained field agriculture was found in southeast Mexico, as well as northern Belize (Gliessman et al. 1983; Guderjan 2007; Harrison 1977, 1982, 1993; Harrison and Turner 1978; Scarborough 1983a, 1983b). Maize is generally cited as the likely crop planted in these fields, but pollen evidence for cotton, amaranth (*Amaranthus* spp.) (Turner and Harrison 1983), and manioc (Pohl et al. 1996) has also been identified. Cacao has been proposed as a suitable crop for drained fields (Hammond 1974), but clear pollen or macroremains evidence is lacking. Part of the problem with this scenario is that plant remains from the past do not preserve well in open field conditions in the wet-and-dry tropics. Also, many of the possible crops are zoophilous (animal pollinated) plants and do not produce much pollen; they are therefore less likely to be deposited into the context in which they would be recovered by archaeologists. Another issue is that we are unable to determine whether these fields were simply the result of wetlands being drained or were mounded areas built by Maya farmers to create "raised fields," as with the *chinampas* in the Valley of Mexico. Most of the published cases are drained fields, but at the Bird of Paradise, Chawak, and Sayap Ha sites in the Río Bravo watershed of northern Belize, there is convincing evidence that the Classic period Maya farmers were, with the help of floodplain sedimentation, building elevated planting beds in a wetland area (Beach, Luzzadder-Beach, Cook et al. 2015; Luzzadder-Beach and Beach 2009). A key aspect of wetland fields was the need to manage the high-sulfate water with water sourcing and crop types (Luzzadder-Beach and Beach 2008). Although these systems were highly productive, in the long run they were ephemeral and through the course of time, many of them were abandoned due to local changes in the water table or farmer desertion (Luzzadder-Beach, Beach, and Dunning 2012; Pohl et al. 1996).

Rejolladas

Rejolladas, or natural karst depressions that remain edaphically moist throughout the year, were used to grow specialty crops, especially fruit trees. Sometimes rejolladas (*k'oopob* in Yukatec Mayan) are referred to as "dry holes," but this is misleading. True, they don't generally have standing water, but because they are lower than the surrounding topography and tend to have deep soils, they accumulate moisture and retain it well. Modern rejolladas have been observed with numerous orchard trees such as papaya (*Carica papaya* L.), avocado, hog plums, mamey, guava, cotton, various palms, root crops and, importantly, cacao (Gómez-Pompa, Flores, and Fernández 1990). Cotton may seem like an odd inclusion here, but in pre-Columbian times it is likely that the Maya grew cotton as a shrub or small tree (Lentz 2000). Parenthetically, cotton was not only a source of fiber but also a source of oil for the ancient Maya. We know this because cottonseeds were being ground on a metate in Structure 4 at Cerén when the Loma Caldera erupted (Lentz and Ramírez Sosa 2002). Rejolladas with associated retaining walls have been found in northern Yucatán in the Chikinchel area (Kepecs and Boucher 1996). Similar features also have been identified at Cozumel (Friedel and Sabloff 1984), Chichen, and elsewhere in the northern lowlands (Andrews, Negrón, and Palma 1989; Dunning 1991; Roys 1965; Schmidt 1981; R. Thompson 1956). In the southern lowlands, rejolladas were reported at Aguateca, where these depressions were apparently exploited for cacao cultivation because of their ability to retain soil moisture (Dunning, Beach, and Rue 1997). Cacao is a tree that is intolerant of dry conditions, so in the Petén with its extended dry season, the Maya would have had to find microhabitats, such as rejolladas, that would stay moist to successfully grow cacao.

At Tikal, the so-called Inscriptions Reservoir was apparently not a reservoir at all (it lacks an impermeable floor and other water management features), resembling instead a natural rejollada, possibly used for the cultivation of cacao. Although it was previously thought that Tikal was too hot in the dry season to grow cacao, which has been described as a "finicky" tree that requires constant shade and consistent moisture, cacao charcoal was identified among the ancient plant remains at Tikal (figure 3.3) and, therefore, must have been growing there (Lentz et al. 2014). It is easy to imagine that the seeds of cacao, as a valued commodity and one that is not especially heavy, might have been imported into the city. Transportation of the wood of cacao, however, which has no special qualities, seems highly unlikely. The rejollada hypothesis answers the question of where cacao could have been grown at Tikal because the Inscriptions Reservoir depression would have served as a large, deep basin where the soils remain sufficiently moist in the dry season. In addition, the wood of two of cacao's most frequently used shade tree symbionts, *Gliricidia sepium* [Jacq.] Steud. (madre de cacao) and *Erythrina* sp., also was found among the plant remains at Tikal. Cacao was an important crop to the ancient Maya, and rejolladas were places where it could be grown, even when the trees were moved outside the range of their natural habitat.

Chich Mounds

Chich mounds were a localized form of agricultural intensification (Kepecs and Boucher 1996). They were comprised of clusters of small rocks, gravel, or pot

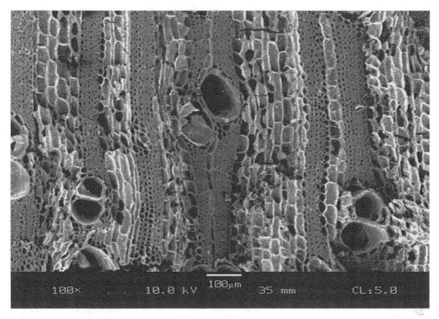

FIGURE 3.3. *Scanning electron micrograph of cacao (*Theobroma cacao*) wood from the Tikal site.*

sherds piled up around the base of a cultivated plant, often orchard trees. These small mounds served a variety of purposes: they could act as a kind of mulch that would help retain water around the roots of the plant with the added benefit that the chich material would not blow away or decay. Also, the chich mounds would have helped to anchor plants, especially small trees, making them less likely to blow over or "lodge" during a storm. These features have been reported from a variety of northern Maya lowlands sites (Killion et al. 1989; Ringle and Andrews 1988; Ringle, Bey III, and Peraza L. 1991; Sabloff et al. 1985).

Irrigation

Irrigation systems were another means utilized by the Maya to enhance agricultural productivity. A notable example of an irrigation system was recently investigated at Classic period Tikal. The Perdido Reservoir, one of the larger bajo-margin tanks surrounding the perimeter of the city, was observed to contain an unusual amount of debris as compared to other reservoirs, indicating that inflowing water was not filtered and the tank likely did not serve as a source of drinking water and may have had another purpose. It may well have functioned, perhaps exclusively, as a source of irrigation water (Scarborough and Grazioso Sierra 2015). The Perdido Reservoir was supplied with water largely from the drainage of the Mundo Perdido Plaza area of the site core. The water from the plaza was directed to the ingress gate of the Perdido Reservoir by a series of steep channels or canals. The egress of the reservoir was located just above a large flat "pocket *bajo*." A soil profile from a test pit excavated into the pocket bajo indicated that the typical bajo vertisol, clay-rich soil with significant vertical cracking as it dries, was interrupted around 400–570 CE by a series of stratified alluvial deposits (Dunning et al. 2015). Moreover, a series of carbon isotope profiles were taken within the pocket bajo, and $\delta^{13}C$ values indicated several periods of enrichment from C_4 plants (figure 3.4). This represents what was almost certainly maize cultivation because modern plant surveys revealed no C_4 plants there today (K. Thompson et al. 2015), and paleoethnobotanical analysis of thousands of charred plant parts from Tikal revealed only one cultivated C_4 plant, maize (Lentz et al. 2015). Furthermore, maize was by far the most common plant remain found at Tikal, so it would be odd if the Maya there were not growing maize, at least occasionally, in an irrigated field. In short, all of this points to the Perdido Reservoir being a component of a highly engineered irrigation system that was likely under elite control (Lentz et al. 2014). This irrigation system would have increased the productivity of the pocket bajo area, and the overall agricultural productivity of the Tikal resource extraction zone, as well, through the possibility of double cropping (both in wet and dry seasons) and the added insurance that harvests would be less susceptible to unexpected dry periods.

The construction of this kind of irrigation system would have greatly enhanced the prestige and power of the ruling elite, because its members would have had the power to solve a problem farmers fear the most: not having enough rainfall for crops when it was developmentally required. This was a powerful innovation in terms of food production, particularly as populations grew at Tikal in the Late Classic period. Elsewhere in Mesoamerica, reservoir-based irrigation systems have been found at Xoxocotlán in Oaxaca (W. E. Doolittle 1990), but otherwise they appear to be scarce in the ancient Maya area.

DISCUSSION

Perhaps no subject has generated as much discussion among generations of Maya scholars as the manner by which the ancient Maya provided sustenance to their communities. As populations grew over time, the systems of food production appeared to expand and intensify. One of the most significant aspects of the niche construction activities of the ancient Maya relates to their agricultural methods. The Maya population density increased and the Maya's economic underpinnings became more diversified as people moved from their Archaic antecedents into the Preclassic and ultimately into the Classic period. As these demographic changes progressed, so did their agricultural and water management capabilities. They began with small-scale horticulture of just a few crops such as maize and

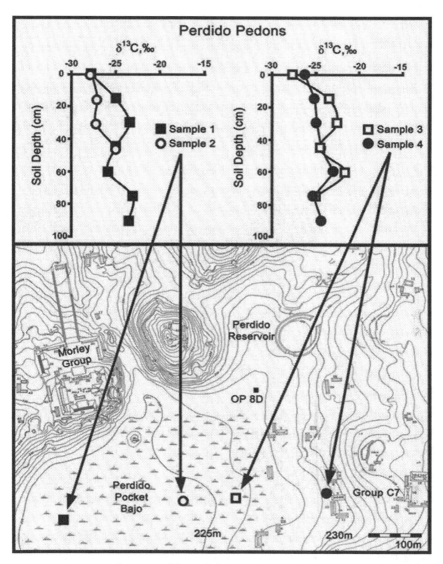

FIGURE 3.4. *Topographic image of the Perdido Reservoir at the Tikal site showing the location of a pocket bajo that was repeatedly flooded to enhance crop production. Maize was likely one of the crops grown as seen in the episodic enrichment of stable carbon isotopes.*

manioc, then added crops that could provide a full spectrum of dietary nutrition as well as the ability to exploit different microhabitats, such as upland areas, bajo fringes, and intermediate zones. The full array, more or less, of Mesoamerican crops was assembled by the Late Preclassic period if not earlier. The coalescing of these cultigens was significant both for its dietary impact and for the overall sustainability of the cropping system as a whole. Beans were an essential part of the complex of domesticates because they are high in protein content, they produce essential amino acids (lysine and tryptophane) lacking in maize, and they add nitrogen to the soil through nitrogen-fixing bacterial symbionts (*Rhizobium* spp.) housed in their root nodules (Kaplan 1973). Squash was important because of the oils in its seeds. Our society denigrates anything related to fat content, but in fact we need fat in our diet to absorb some nutrients, such as the vitamin E complex. The Maya had few animal sources of fat, so this critical need had to be met through agricultural production. This fat requirement was bolstered by some other crops with high oil content, such as avocado, mamey, cacao, cotton seeds and, perhaps most prominent in terms of oil production, various palms, for example, coyol and cohune. Maize and the root crops supplied most of the calories and a plethora of field crops, such as chili peppers, chayote (*Sechium edule* [Jacq.] Sw.), and numerous tree crops, added variety and other essential vitamins.

As these domesticates were brought together in the Preclassic period, agriculture was practiced extensively, most likely using long fallow swidden techniques. Initially these methods may have worked well, as populations were low and well dispersed and there was plenty of undisturbed forest to exploit, but as populations increased, less undisturbed forest was available, and problems with soil erosion began to emerge around the end of the Late Preclassic period. The Maya responded with earthworks to control the flow of water and with it, in many cases, the flow of soil. They also responded with other techniques to control erosion, such as terracing, the use of check dams, and ridge and furrow agriculture. As communities continued to grow in the Classic period, their boundaries began to collide, resulting in restrictions on the amount of land per capita available for long fallow systems. These limiting factors forced the Maya to shorten fallow cycles and intensify their approaches to agriculture with terracing, the use of raised or drained fields, the exploitation of bajo margins, and, as seen at Tikal, the development of reservoir-fed irrigation systems.

These agricultural adaptations sustained the polities of the Late Classic Maya for several centuries during a time of above-average rainfall. A series of well-documented, multidecadal droughts in the mid-ninth century (e.g., Douglas et al. 2015; Kennett et al. 2012; Wahl, Byrne, and Anderson 2014), however, proved to be a catastrophic tipping point for the Late Classic Maya in the EIR. They had maximized their agricultural and forest extraction potential, while ultimately they were dependent on rainwater to fill their reservoirs and grow crops (Dunning, Beach, and Luzzadder-Beach 2012; Turner and Sabloff 2012). Without regular seasonal rainfall, their fields became parched, the reservoirs ceased to contain potable water, and the Maya were forced to abandon their magnificent cities. These conditions was more than simply bad fortune. As recent studies have shown in other neotropical areas, when a major portion of a tropical forest is cleared, it affects the hydrological cycle by reducing evapotranspiration (Cook et al. 2012; Griffin et al. 2014; Oglesby et al. 2010). This turn of events, ultimately, will reduce the regional rainfall. It now seems likely that the agricultural practices and extensive forest clearance of the ancient Maya of the EIR contributed to their demise.

REFERENCES

Andrews, A. P., Tomas Gallareta Negrón, and Rafael Cobos Palma. 1989. "Preliminary Report of the Cupul Survey Project." *Mexicon* 11: 91–95.

Anselmetti, Flavio S., David A. Hodell, Daniel Ariztequi, Mark Brenner, and Michael F. Rosenmeier. 2007. "Quantification of Soil Erosion Rates Related to Ancient Maya Deforestation." *Geology* 35 (10): 915–918. https://doi.org/10.1130/G23834A.1.

Ashmore, Wendy, Samuel V. Connell, Jennifer J. Ehret, Chad H. Gifford, L. Theodore Neff, and Jon C. Vandenbosh. 1994. "The Xunantunich Settlement Survey." In *Xunantunich Archaeological Project: 1994 Field Season*, edited by Richard M. Leventhal and Wendy Ashmore, 248–290. Report submitted to the Institute of Archaeology, Belmopan, Belize.

Beach, Timothy. 2017. "Morals to the Story of the 'Mayacene' from Geoarchaeology and Paleoecology." In *Exploring Frameworks for Tropical Forest Conservation: Managing Production and Consumption for Sustainability*, edited by Nuria Sanz, 108–137. Paris: UNESCO.

Beach, Timothy, and Nicholas P. Dunning. 1995. "Ancient Maya Terracing and Modern Conservation in the Petén Rain Forest of Guatemala." *Journal of Soil and Water Conservation* 50 (2): 138–145.

Beach, Timothy, Nicholas Dunning, Sheryl Luzzadder-Beach, Duncan Cook, and Jon Lohse. 2006. "Impacts of the Ancient Maya on Soils and Soil Erosion in the Central Maya Lowlands." *CATENA* 65 (2): 166–178. https://doi.org/10.1016/j.catena.2005.11.007.

Beach, Timothy, Sheryl Luzzadder-Beach, Duncan Cook, Nicholas Dunning, Douglas Kennett, Samantha Krause, Richard Terry, Debora Trein, and Fred Valdez. 2015. "Ancient Maya Impacts on the Earth's Surface: An Early Anthropocene Analog?" *Quaternary Science Reviews* 124 (September): 1–30.

Beach, Timothy, Sheryl Luzzadder-Beach, Nicholas Dunning, and Duncan Cook. 2008. "Human and Natural Impacts on Fluvial and Karst Depressions of the Maya Lowlands." *Geomorphology* 101 (1–2): 308–331. https://doi.org/10.1016/j.geomorph.2008.05.019.

Beach, Timothy, Sheryl Luzzadder-Beach, Nicholas Dunning, Jon Hageman, and Jon Lohse. 2002. "Upland Agriculture in the Maya Lowlands: Ancient Maya Soil Conservation in Northwestern Belize." *Geographical Review* 92 (3): 372–397. https://doi.org/10.1111/j.1931-0846.2002.tb00149.x.

Beach, Timothy, Sheryl Luzzadder-Beach, Samantha Krause, Stanley Walling, Nicholas Dunning, Jonathan Flood, Thomas Guderjan, and Fred Valdez. 2015. "'Mayacene' Floodplain and Wetland Formation in the Rio Bravo Watershed of Northwestern Belize." *The Holocene* 25 (10): 1612–1626.

Chase, Adrian S.Z., and John Weishampel. 2016. "Using LiDAR and GIS to Investigate Water and Soil Management in the Agricultural Terracing at Caracol, Belize." *Advances in Archaeological Practice* (Cambridge University Press) 4 (3): 357–370. https://doi.org/10.1007/s10814-016-9101-z.

Chase, Arlen F., and Diane Z. Chase. 1998. "Scale and Intensity in Classic Maya Agriculture: Terracing and Agriculture in the 'Garden City' of Caracol, Belize." *Culture and Agriculture* 20 (2–3): 60–77.

Chase, Arlen F., Diane Z. Chase, John F. Weishampel, Jason B. Drake, Ramesh L. Shrestha, K. Clint Slatton, Jaime J. Awe, and William E. Carter. 2011. "Airborne LiDAR, Archaeology, and the Ancient Maya Landscape at Caracol, Belize." *Journal of Archaeological Science* 38 (2): 387–398. https://doi.org/10.1016/j.jas.2010.09.018.

Chase, Arlen F., and Vernon L. Scarborough. 2014. "The Resilience and Vulnerability of Ancient Landscapes: Transforming Maya Archaeology through IHOPE." *Archeological Papers of the American Anthropological Association*. Hoboken, NJ: Wiley Periodicals.

Cook, B. I., K. J. Anchukaitis, J. O. Kaplan, M. J. Puma, M. Kelley, and D. Gueyffier. 2012. "Pre-Columbian Deforestation as an Amplifier of Drought in Mesoamerica." *Geophysical Research Letters* 39 (16). https://doi.org/10.1029/2012GL052565.

Demeyer, Alex, J. C. Voundi Nkana, and M. G. Verloo. 2001. "Characteristics of Wood Ash and Influence on Soil Properties and Nutrient Uptake: An Overview." *Bioresource Technology* 77 (3): 287–295.

Donkin, Robin Arthur. 1979. *Agricultural Terracing in the Aboriginal New World*. No. 56. Tucson: University of Arizona Press.

Doolittle, William E. 1990. "Terrace Origins: Hypotheses and Research Strategies." In *Yearbook. Conference of Latin Americanist Geographers*, 16: 94–97. University of Texas Press, Austin.

Douglas, Peter M. J., Mark Pagani, Marcello A. Canuto, Mark Brenner, David A. Hodell, Timothy I. Eglinton, and Jason H. Curtis. 2015. "Drought, Agricultural Adaptation, and Sociopolitical Collapse in the Maya Lowlands." *Proceedings of the National Academy of Sciences* 112 (18): 5607–5612. https://doi.org/10.1073/pnas.1419133112.

Dumond, D. E. 1961. "Swidden Agriculture and the Rise of Maya Civilization." *Southwestern Journal of Anthropology* (University of Chicago Press) 17 (4): 301–316. https://doi.org/10.1086/soutjanth.17.4.3628942.

Dunning, Nicholas P. 1991. "Soils and Settlement in the Sayil Valley: A Preliminary Assessment." In *The Ancient Maya City of Sayil: The Mapping of a Puuc Region Center*, Publication 60, edited by J. A. Sabloff and G. Tourtellot, 20–27. New Orleans: Middle American Research Institute, Tulane University.

Dunning, Nicholas P., and Timothy Beach. 1994. "Soil Erosion, Slope Management, and Ancient Terracing in the Maya Lowlands." *Latin American Antiquity* 5 (1): 51–69.

Dunning, Nicholas P., and Timothy Beach. 2000. "Stability and Instability in Prehispanic Maya Landscapes." In *An Imperfect Balance: Landscape Transformations in the*

Precolumbian Americas, edited by David Lentz, 179–202. New York: Columbia University Press.

Dunning, Nicholas P., and Timothy Beach. 2010. "Farms and Forests: Spatial and Temporal Perspectives on Ancient Maya Landscapes." In *Landscapes and Societies*, edited by Peter I. Martini and Ward Chesworth, 369–389. Dordrecht: Springer Netherlands. https://doi.org/10.1007/978-90-481-9413-1_23.

Dunning, Nicholas P., Timothy Beach, Pat Farrell, and Sheryl Luzzadder-Beach. 1998. "Prehispanic Agrosystems and Adaptive Regions in the Maya Lowlands." *Culture Agriculture* (Blackwell Publishing Ltd.) 20 (2–3) 87–101. https://doi.org/10.1525/cag .1998.20.2-3.87.

Dunning, Nicholas P., Timothy Beach, and Sheryl Luzzadder-Beach. 2006. "Environmental Variability among Bajos in the Southern Maya Lowlands and Its Implications for Ancient Maya Civilization and Archaeology." *Precolumbian Water Management: Ideology, Ritual, and Politics*, edited by Lisa J. Lucero and Barbara Fash, 81–99. Tucson: University of Arizona Press.

Dunning, Nicholas P., Timothy P. Beach, and Sheryl Luzzadder-Beach. 2012. "Kax and Kol: Collapse and Resilience in Lowland Maya Civilization." *Proceedings of the National Academy of Sciences* 109 (10): 3652–3657. https://doi.org/10.1073/pnas.1114838109.

Dunning, Nicholas P., Timothy Beach, Sheryl Luzzadder-Beach, and John G. Jones. 2009. "Creating a Stable Landscape: Soil Conservation among the Ancient Maya." In *The Archaeology of Environmental Change: Socionatural Legacies of Degradation and Resilience*, edited by Christopher Fisher, James Hill, and Gary Feinman, 85–105. Tucson: University of Arizona Press.

Dunning, Nicholas P., Timothy Beach, and David Rue. 1997. "The Paleoecology and Ancient Settlement of the Petexbatun Region, Guatemala." *Ancient Mesoamerica* 8 (2) (Cambridge University Press): 255–266. https://doi.org/10.1017/S0956536100001711.

Dunning, Nicholas P., Robert E. Griffin, John G. Jones, Richard E. Terry, Zachary Larsen, and Christopher Carr. 2015. "Life on the Edge: Tikal in a Bajo Landscape." In *Tikal: Paleoecology of an Ancient Maya City*, edited by David Lentz, Nicholas Dunning, and Vernon Scarborough, 95–123. New York: Cambridge University Press.

Dunning, Nicholas P., Sheryl Luzzadder-Beach, Timothy Beach, John G. Jones, Vernon Scarborough, and T. Patrick Culbert. 2002. "Arising from the Bajos: The Evolution of a Neotropical Landscape and the Rise of Maya Civilization." *Annals of the Association of American Geographers* 92 (2): 267–283.

Flannery, Kent V. 1982. *Maya Subsistence: Studies in Memory of Dennis Puleston*. New York: Academic Press.

Friedel, David A., and Jeremy A. Sabloff. 1984. *Cozumel: Late Maya Settlement Patterns*. Orlando, FL: Academic Press.

Gliessman, S. R., B. L. Turner, F. J. Rosado May, and M. F. Amador. 1983. "Ancient Raised Field Agriculture in the Maya Lowlands of Southeastern Mexico." In *Drained*

Field Agriculture in Central and South America, BAR International Series No. 189, edited by J. P. Darch, 91–110. Oxford: British Archaeological Reports.

Gómez-Pompa, Arturo, José Salvador Flores, and Mario Aliphat Fernández. 1990. "The Sacred Cacao Groves of the Maya." *Latin American Antiquity* (Cambridge University Press) 1 (3): 247–257. https://doi.org/10.2307/972163.

Griffin, Robert, Robert Oglesby, Thomas Sever, and Udaysankar Nair. 2014. "Agricultural Landscapes, Deforestation, and Drought Severity." In *The Great Maya Droughts in Cultural Context*, edited by G. Iannone, 71–86. Boulder: University Press of Colorado.

Guderjan, Thomas H. 2007. *The Nature of an Ancient Maya City: Resources, Interaction, and Power at Blue Creek, Belize*. Tuscaloosa: University of Alabama Press.

Gunn, Joel D., John E. Foss, William J. Folan, Maria del Rosario Domínguez Carrasco, and Betty B. Faust. 2002. "Bajo Sediments and the Hydraulic System of Calakmul, Campeche, Mexico." *Ancient Mesoamerica* (Cambridge University Press) 13 (2): 297–315.

Hammond, Norman. 1974. *Mesoamerican Archaeology: New Approaches*. Austin: University of Texas Press.

Hammond, Norman. 2000. "The Maya Lowlands: Pioneer Farmers to Merchant Princes." In *The Cambridge History of Native Peoples of the Americas: Mesoamerica*, Vol. 2 (part 1), edited by R.E.W. Adams and M. J. Macleod, 197–249. Cambridge: Cambridge University Press.

Hansen, Richard D., Steven Bozarth, John Jacob, David Wahl, and Thomas Schreiner. 2002. "Climatic and Environmental Variability in the Rise of Maya Civilization: A Preliminary Perspective from Northern Peten." *Ancient Mesoamerica* (Cambridge University Press) 13 (2): 273–295. https://doi.org/10.1017/S0956536102132093.

Harrison, Peter D. 1977. "The Rise of the Bajos and the Fall of the Maya." In *Social Process in Maya Prehistory*, edited by Norman Hammond, 469–508. New York: Academic Press.

Harrison, Peter D. 1982. "Subsistence and Society in Eastern Yucatan." In *Maya Subsistence: Studies in Memory of Dennis E. Puleston*, edited by K. Flannery, 119–130. New York: Academic Press.

Harrison, Peter D. 1993. "Aspects of Water Management in the Southern Maya Lowlands." *Research in Economic Anthropology* 7: 71–119.

Harrison, Peter D., and Billie L. Turner. 1978. *Pre-Hispanic Maya Agriculture*. Albuquerque: University of New Mexico Press.

Healy, Paul F., John D.H. Lambert, J. T. Arnason, and Richard J. Hebda. 1983. "Caracol, Belize: Evidence of Ancient Maya Agricultural Terraces." *Journal of Field Archaeology* (Routledge) 10 (4): 397–410. https://doi.org/10.1179/009346983791504200.

Hodell, David A., Mark Brenner, and Jason H. Curtis. 2000. "Climate Change in the Northern American Tropics and Subtropics since the Last Ice Age: Implications for Environment and Culture." In *Imperfect Balance: Landscape Transformations in the Precolumbian Americas*, edited by David Lentz, 13–38. New York: Columbia University Press.

Johnson, Kristofer D., David R. Wright, and Richard E. Terry. 2007. "Application of Carbon Isotope Analysis to Ancient Maize Agriculture in the Petexbatún Region of Guatemala." *Geoarchaeology* (Wiley Subscription Services, Inc., A Wiley Company) 22 (3): 313–336. https://doi.org/10.1002/gea.20155.

Jones, Grant D. 2000. "The Lowland Mayas: From the Conquest to the Present." In *The Cambridge History of Native Peoples of the Americas*. Vol. 2, *Mesoamerica*, pt. 2, edited by R.E.W. Adams and M. J. Macleod. Cambridge: Cambridge University Press.

Kaplan, Lawrence. 1973. "Ethnobotanical and Nutritional Factors in Domestication of American Beans." In *Man and His Foods*, edited by C. Earle Smith Jr., 75–85. Tuscaloosa: University of Alabama Press.

Kaplan, Lawrence, and Thomas F. Lynch. 1999. "Phaseolus (Fabaceae) in Archaeology: AMS." *Economic Botany* 53 (3): 261–272. https://doi.org/10.1007/BF02866636.

Kennett, Douglas J., Sebastian F.M. Breitenbach, Valorie V. Aquino, Yemane Asmerom, Jaime Awe, James U. L. Baldini, Patrick Bartlein et al. 2012. "Development and Disintegration of Maya Political Systems in Response to Climate Change." *Science* 338 (6108): 788 LP-791.

Kepecs, Susan, and Sylviane Boucher. 1996. "The Pre-Hispanic Cultivation of Rejolladas Stone-Lands: New Evidence from Northeast Yucatan." In *The Managed Mosaic*, edited by S. Fedick, 69–91. Salt Lake City: University of Utah Press.

Killion, Thomas W., Jeremy A. Sabloff, Gair Tourtellot, and Nicholas P. Dunning. 1989. "Intensive Surface Collection of Residential Clusters at Terminal Classic Sayil, Yucatan, Mexico." *Journal of Field Archaeology* (Routledge) 16 (3).: 273–294. https://doi.org/10.1179/jfa.1989.16.3.273.

Lentz, David L. 2000. *Imperfect Balance: Landscape Transformations in the Precolumbian Americas*. New York: Columbia University Press.

Lentz, David L., Marilyn P. Beaudry-Corbett, Maria Luisa Reyna de Aguilar, and Lawrence Kaplan. 1996. "Foodstuffs, Forests, Fields, and Shelter: A Paleoethnobotanical Analysis of Vessel Contents from the Ceren Site, El Salvador." *Latin American Antiquity* (Cambridge University Press) 7 (3): 247–262. doi:10.2307/971577.

Lentz, David L., Nicholas Dunning, Vernon Scarborough, Kevin Magee, Kim Thompson, Eric Weaver, Christopher Carr, et al. 2014. "Forests, Fields, and the Edge of Sustainability at the Ancient Maya City of Tikal." *Proceedings of the National Academy of Sciences* 111 (52): 18513–18518.

Lentz, David L., L. Haddad, S. Cherpelis, H. J. Mary Joo, and M. Potter. 2002. "Long-Term Influences of Ancient Maya Agroforestry Practices on Tropical Forest Biodiversity in Northwestern Belize." In *Ethnobiology and Biocultural Diversity*, edited by J. R. Stepp, F. S. Wyndham, and R. Zarger, 431–442. Athens: University of Georgia Press.

Lentz, David L., and Brian Hockaday. 2009. "Tikal Timbers and Temples: Ancient Maya Agroforestry and the End of Time." *Journal of Archaeological Science* 36 (7): 1342–1353. https://doi.org/10.1016/j.jas.2009.01.020.

Lentz, David L., B. Lane, and K. Thompson. 2014. "Food, Farming and Forest Management at Aguateca." In *Life and Politics at the Royal Court of Aguateca: Artifacts, Analytical Data, and Synthesis*, edited by T. Inomata and D. Triadan. Monographs of the Aguateca Archaeological Project First Phase, vol. 3, 203–217. Provo: University of Utah Press.

Lentz, David L., Kevin Magee, Eric Weaver, John Jones, Kenneth B. Tankersley, Angela Hood, Gerald Islebe, Carlos Ramos, and Nicholas Dunning. 2015. "Agroforestry and Agricultural Practices of the Ancient Maya at Tikal." In *Tikal: Paleoecology of an Ancient Maya City*, edited by David Lentz, Nicholas Dunning, and Vernon Scarborough, 152–185. Cambridge: Cambridge University Press.

Lentz, David L., and Carlos R. Ramírez-Sosa. 2002. "Cerén Plant Resources: Abundance and Diversity." In *Before the Volcano Erupted: The Cerén Village in Central America*, edited by P. D. Sheets, 33–42. Austin: University of Texas Press.

Lentz, David L., Maria Luisa Reyna de Aguilar, Raul Villacorta, and Helen Marini. 1996. "Trachypogon Plumosus (Poaceae, Andropogoneae): Ancient Thatch and More from the Ceren Site, El Salvador." *Economic Botany* 50 (1): 108–114. https://doi.org/10.1007/BF02862115.

Lentz, David L., Sally Woods, Angela Hood, and Marcus Murph. 2012. "Agroforestry and Agricultural Production of the Ancient Maya at the Chan Site." In *Chan: An Ancient Maya Farming Community*, edited by Cynthia Robin, 89–109. Gainesville: University Press of Florida.

Luzzadder-Beach, Sheryl, and Timothy P. Beach. 2008. "Water Chemistry Constraints and Possibilities for the Ancient and Contemporary Maya Lowlands." *Journal of Ethnobiology* 28 (2): 211–230.

Luzzadder-Beach, Sheryl, and Timothy P. Beach. 2009. "Arising from the Wetlands: Mechanisms and Chronology of Landscape Aggradation in the Northern Coastal Plain of Belize." *Annals of the Association of American Geographers* 99 (1): 1–26.

Luzzadder-Beach, Sheryl, Timothy P. Beach, and Nicholas P. Dunning. 2012. "Wetland Fields as Mirrors of Drought and the Maya Abandonment." *Proceedings of the National Academy of Sciences* 109 (10): 3646–3651. https://doi.org/10.1073/pnas.1114919109.

Mathewson, Kent. 1984. *Irrigation Horticulture in Highland Guatemala: The Tablón System of Panajachel*. Boulder, CO: Westview Press.

Miksicek, Charles H. 1983. "Macrofloral Remains of the Pulltrouser Area: Settlements and Fields." In *Pulltrouser Swamp: Ancient Maya Habitat, Agriculture and Settlement in Northern Belize*, edited by Billie L. Turner and Peter D. Harrison, 94–104. Austin: University of Texas Press.

Miksicek, Charles H., Robert McK. Bird, Barbara Pickersgill, Sara Donaghey, Juliette Cartwright, and Norman Hammond. 1981. "Preclassic Lowland Maize from Cuello, Belize." *Nature* 289 (5793): 56–59. https://doi.org/10.1038/289056a0.

Murtha, Timothy M. 2002. "Land and Labor: Classic Maya Terraced Agriculture at Caracol, Belize." Unpublished PhD diss., Pennsylvania State University, State College.

Neff, Theodore L., Cynthia Robin, Kevin Schwarz, and Mary K. Morrison. 1995. "The Xunantunich Settlement Survey." In *Xunantunich Archaeological Project: 1995 Field Season*, edited by Richard M. Leventhal and Wendy Ashmore, 139–163. Los Angeles: UCLA.

Oglesby, Robert J., Thomas L. Sever, William Saturno, David J. Erickson, and Jayanthi Srikishen. 2010. "Collapse of the Maya: Could Deforestation Have Contributed?" *Journal of Geophysical Research* 115 (D12): D12106. https://doi.org/10.1029/2009 JD011942.

Pohl, Mary D., Kevin O. Pope, John G. Jones, John S. Jacob, Dolores R. Piperno, Susan D. deFrance, David L. Lentz, John A. Gifford, Marie E. Danforth, and J. Kathryn Josserand. 1996. "Early Agriculture in the Maya Lowlands." *Latin American Antiquity* (Cambridge University Press) 7 (4): 355–372. https://doi.org/10.2307/972264.

Pollock, Adam. 2003. "Summary of Ancient Maya Terrace Operations in the Southern Periphery of Minanhá." In *Archaeological Investigations in the North Vaca Plateau, Belize: Progress Report of the Sixth (2004) Field Season*, edited by G. Iannone and J. E. Herbert, 85–101. Peterborough, ON: Social Archaeology Research Program, Department of Anthropology, Trent University.

Pope, Kevin O., Mary E. D. Pohl, John G. Jones, David L. Lentz, Christopher von Nagy, Francisco J. Vega, and Irvy R. Quitmyer. 2001. "Origin and Environmental Setting of Ancient Agriculture in the Lowlands of Mesoamerica." *Science* 292 (5520): 1370–1373. http://science.sciencemag.org/content/292/5520/1370.abstract.

Powis, Terry G., Norbert Stanchly, Christine D. White, Paul F. Healy, Jaime J. Awe, and Fred Longstaffe. 1999. "A Reconstruction of Middle Preclassic Maya Subsistence Economy at Cahal Pech, Belize." *Antiquity* 73 (280): 364–76. https://doi.org/10.1017 /S0003598X00088311.

Reese-Taylor, Kathryn, Armando Anaya Hernández, F. C. Atasta Flores Esquivel, Kelly Monteleone, Alejandro Uriarte, Christopher Carr, Helga Geovannini Acuña, Juan Carlos Fernandez-Diaz, Meaghan Peuramaki-Brown, and Nicholas Dunning. 2016. "Boots on the Ground at Yaxnohcah: Ground-Truthing LiDAR in a Complex Tropical Landscape." *Advances in Archaeological Practice* (Cambridge University Press) 4 (3): 314–38. DOI: https://doi.org/10.7183/2326-3768.4.3.314.

Ringle, William M., and E. Wyllys Andrews. 1988. "Formative Residences at Komchen, Yucatan, Mexico." In *Household and Community in the Mesoamerican Past*, edited by R. R. Wilk and W. Ashmore, 171–197. Albuquerque: University of New Mexico Press.

Ringle, William M., George J. Bey III, and C. Peraza L. 1991. "Preliminary Report of the Ek Balam Project, 1989 Field Season." Submitted to the National Geographic Society.

Robin, Cynthia, Diane Z. Chase, and Arlen F. Chase, eds. 2012. *Chan: An Ancient Maya Farming Community*. Gainesville: University Press of Florida.

Roys, Ralph L. 1965. "Lowland Maya Native Society at Spanish Contact." In *Handbook of Middle American Indians*. Vol. 3, edited by R. Wauchope, 659–678. Austin: University of Texas Press.

Sabloff, Jeremy A., Gair Tourtellot, Bernd Fahmel-Beyer, Patricia A. McAnany, Diana Christensen, Sylviane Boucher, and Thomas R. Killion. 1985. "Settlement and Community Patterns at Sayil, Yucatan, Mexico: The 1984 Season." *Research Paper Series* No. 17. Albuquerque: Latin American Institute, University of New Mexico.

Santini, Lauren M. 2016. "The Fabricated Forest." PhD diss., Harvard University, Cambridge, MA.

Scarborough, Vernon L. 1983a. "A Preclassic Maya Water System." *American Antiquity* (Cambridge University Press) 48 (4): 720–44. https://doi.org/10.2307/279773.

Scarborough, Vernon L. 1983b. "Raised Field Detection at Cerros, Northern Belize." In *Drained Field Agriculture in Central and South America*, edited by J. P. Darch, 123–136. Proceedings of the 44th International Congress of Americanists, British Archaeological Research International Series 189. Oxford.

Scarborough, Vernon L. 2003. *The Flow of Power: Ancient Water Systems and Landscapes.* Santa Fe, NM: School of American Research Press.

Scarborough, Vernon L., and Liwy Grazioso Sierra. 2015. "The Evolution of an Ancient Waterworks System at Tikal." In *Tikal: Paleoecology of an Ancient Maya City*, edited by David Lentz, Nicholas Dunning, and Vernon Scarborough, 16–45. Cambridge: Cambridge University Press.

Schmidt, Peter J. 1981. "La Producción agrícola prehistórica de los Mayas." *Yucatán: Historia y Economía 4* (23): 38–54.

Sheets, Payson D., ed. 2002. *Before the Volcano Erupted: The Cerén Village in Central America.* Austin: University of Texas Press.

Sheets, Payson, Christine Dixon, David Lentz, Rachel Egan, Alexandria Halmbacher, Venicia Slotten, Rocío Herrera, and Celine Lamb. 2015. "The Sociopolitical Economy of an Ancient Maya Village: Cerén and Its Sacbe." *Latin American Antiquity* (Cambridge University Press) 26 (3): 341–361. https://doi.org/10.7183/1045-6635 .26.3.341.

Spencer, Joseph E., and Gary A. Hale. 1961. "The Origin, Nature, and Distribution of Agricultural Terracing." *Pacific Viewpoint* 2 (1): 1–40.

Thompson, J.E.S. 1954. *The Rise and Fall of Maya Civilization.* Civilization of the American Indian Series. Norman: University of Oklahoma Press.

Thompson, Kim M., Angela Hood, Dana Cavallaro, and David L. Lentz. 2015. "Connecting Contemporary Ecology and Ethnobotany to Ancient Plant Use Practices of the Maya at Tikal." In *Tikal: Paleoecology of an Ancient Maya City*, edited by David Lentz, Nicholas Dunning, and Vernon Scarborough, 124–151. Cambridge: Cambridge University Press.

Thompson, Raymond H. 1956. "The Subjective Element in Archaeological Inference." *Southwestern Journal of Anthropology* (University of Chicago Press:) 12 (3): 327–332. https://doi.org/10.1086/soutjanth.12.3.3629088.

Treacy, John M., and William M. Denevan. 1997. "The Creation of Cultivable Land through Terracing." In *The Archaeology of Garden and Field*, edited by N. F. Miller and K. L. Gleason, 91–110. Philadelphia: University of Pennsylvania Press.

Turner, Billie L. 1974. "Prehistoric Intensive Agriculture in the Mayan Lowlands." *Science* 185 (4146): 118 LP-124. http://science.sciencemag.org/content/185/4146/118.abstract.

Turner, Billie L. 1983. *Once beneath the Forest: Prehistoric Terracing in the Rio Bec Region of the Maya Lowlands*. Boulder, CO: Westview Press.

Turner, Billie L., and Peter D. Harrison. 1983. *Pulltrouser Swamp: Ancient Maya Habitat, Agriculture, and Settlement in Northern Belize*. Austin: University of Texas Press.

Turner, Billie L., and Jeremy A. Sabloff. 2012. "Classic Period Collapse of the Central Maya Lowlands: Insights about Human–Environment Relationships for Sustainability." *Proceedings of the National Academy of Sciences* 109 (35): 13908–13914. https://doi.org/10.1073/pnas.1210106109.

Wahl, David, Roger Byrne, and Lysanna Anderson. 2014. "An 8700 Year Paleoclimate Reconstruction from the Southern Maya Lowlands." *Quaternary Science Reviews* 103 (November): 19–25. https://doi.org/10.1016/j.quascirev.2014.08.004.

Wiesen, Ann, and David L. Lentz. 1999. "Floral Remains from Cahal Pech and Surrounding Sites." In *Belize Valley Preclassic Maya Project*, edited by P. F. Healy and J. J. Awe, 53–68. Trent University Occasional Papers in Anthropology. Peterborough, Canada.

Wilken, Gene C., ed. 1987. *Good Farmers: Traditional Agricultural Resource Management in Mexico and Central America*. Berkeley: University of California Press.

Willey, Gordon R., William R. Bullard, John B. Glass, James C. Gifford, and Orville Elliot. 1965. *Prehistoric Maya Settlements in the Belize Valley*. Vol. 54. Cambridge, MA: Peabody Museum of Archaeology and Ethnology, Harvard University.

Wright, David R., Richard E. Terry, and Markus Eberl. 2009. "Soil Properties and Stable Carbon Isotope Analysis of Landscape Features in the Petexbatún Region of Guatemala." *Geoarchaeology* (Wiley Subscription Services, Inc., A Wiley Company) 24 (4).: 466–491. https://doi.org/10.1002/gea.20275.

Wyatt, Andrew R. 2008a. "Gardens on Hills: The Archaeology of Ancient Maya Terrace Agriculture at Chan, Belize." PhD diss., University of Illinois at Chicago.

Wyatt, Andrew R. 2008b. "Pine as an Element of Household Refuse in the Fertilization of Ancient Maya Agricultural Fields." *Journal of Ethnobiology* 28 (2): 244–258.

Wyatt, Andrew R. 2012. "Agricultural Practices at Chan: Farming and Political Economy in an Ancient Maya Community." In *Chan: An Ancient Maya Farming Community*, edited by Cynthia Robin, 71–88. Gainesville: University Press of Florida.

Yaeger, J., and S. V. Connell. 1993. "Settlement Archaeology at Xunantunich." In *Xunantunich Archaeological Project: 1993 Field Season*, edited by R. M. Leventhal and W. Ashmore, 172–202. Report submitted to the Institute of Archaeology, Belmopan.

4

Many Visions of Water

Wendy Ashmore

> *To attract a permanent, loyal support population to principal centers, elite managers*
> *would have appropriated everyday ritual activity, especially water ritual, to manipulate*
> *deeply held traditional formulas relating to water use.—Scarborough (2003, 115)*

Water is life, as Vernon Scarborough reminds us in the epigram. Conflicts over water and other resources are not new, of course. I am among those who remember well the long gasoline lines of 1970s United States, drivers waiting their turns at the gas pump. Then and now, patience was often in short supply. At the time, however, I also remember conversations with a number of people about gas not being a central need for daily life: wait, they said, until the competition for *water*, truly requisite for life. That dire situation has arrived, as confirmed repeatedly in the title and chapters of this book.

The chapter title, "Many Visions of Water," recognizes the multiplicity of research goals and findings applied to understanding "Adam's ale" worldwide. Not surprisingly, much current research focuses on sustainability and, in archaeology,

https://doi.org/10.5876/9781646422326.c004

on how ancient hydrological technologies can inform on water procurement, storage, and use options today (A. Chase and Scarborough 2014a, 2014b; Scarborough et al. 2012). Maya scholars have joined in the goals and aims of the interdisciplinary and international project Integrated History and Future of People on Earth (IHOPE), to examine how the Maya past can best inform the present and future for the Maya and other societies. Clearly, these contributions are critical to humankind as a whole, and the IHOPE-Maya project is notable for the richness of its findings and potentials for application.

This brief chapter offers one view of how interpreters' ideas about ancient Maya water have expanded in recent decades. It is far from an exhaustive review. My particular theme is attention to meanings and rituals related to water, highlighting contributions by Scarborough and others, and reinforcing the tenet that many factors—political, economic, ecological, ritual, and more—shape how water is conceived and used, in culture-specific ways.

CONTEXTS FOR UNDERSTANDING WATER AND ITS IMPORTANCE

As other chapters in this volume show, studies of Maya water uses, management, and meanings reflect quite varied topical, disciplinary, and theoretical perspectives. That variety stems, at least in part, to changes in prevailing social, political, and ecological conditions. In 1985, for example, Richard Wilk pointed to the dual nature of archaeology, in that "it simultaneously engages in a fairly rigorous pursuit of objective facts about the past and an informal and sometimes hidden dialogue on contemporary politics, philosophy, religion, and other important subjects" and that "like other social sciences, *always* draws on current events and politics as a source of general orientation" (Wilk 1985, 308, 311; emphasis in original). Wilk provisionally relates interest in ancient Maya warfare, ecology, and religion to a succession of then-current phenomena including the war in Vietnam, the official advent of Earth Day, and the growth of religious fundamentalism in the United States. His aim is less a critique of these interpretive domains than it is a call for "acknowledge[ing] that there is no neutral, value-free, or non-political past" (1985, 319; see also Coe 2011). Similarly, Andrew Sherratt (1996) proposes cyclical changes in British archaeologists' characterizations of human spatial perspectives as "settlement patterns" or "landscapes," correlating these with times of, respectively, enlightenment views during stable economic prosperity and contextual, relativistic views in times of economic uncertainty. As summary, he draws on "a botanical metaphor: we can either pick our flowers and mount them, suitably pressed, in Linnaean taxonomies, in the manner of the Enlightenment: or we can follow the arch-theoretician of the Romantic movement, Johann Gottfried Herder, in 'leaving each flower in place and contemplating it there just as it is, according to time and kind'" (156).

One could argue that a parallel shift is attested in the United States, in the contrast and complementarity of processual archaeology in the 1960s and after, and more humanistic perspectives emerging in the 1970s (Paddayya 1990; Patterson 1990, 1995; Willey and Sabloff 1993). Processual archaeology came to light in contexts of post–World War II prosperity; concentration on large-scale, globally pertinent questions (e.g., origins of food production, or of state societies); systems and evolutionary models; strong positivist confidence of scientific pursuits as optimal for addressing those questions; and, to provide evidence for analysis, the rise in computer capacities to handle increasingly large data sets. Humanistic archaeological challenges and complements included more attention to history and historical contingencies, to diversity among society's members in those large data sets, and to the potential heterogeneity of interpretive models (Brumfiel 1992; Crumley 1979, 1987).

For example, reports from the Quirigua Project (1974–1979) documented three distinct kinds of water features: (1) geomorphic evidence for the changing course of the Río Motagua; (2) a docking facility linking the river and the civic center, or Site Core (Ashmore 1984a, 381; Sharer 1978, 1988); and (3) a series of ceramic-lined wells associated with residences in the floodplain adjoining the Site Core (Ashmore 1984b, 2007). Interpretations of all three features were based in functional-processual models of social, political, and economic systems thriving in the still-heady times since World War II (Ashmore 2007; Sharer and Coe 1979). Interpretations of the three findings were that (1) unlike today, the eighth- and ninth-century Río Motagua course was immediately adjacent to the civic core; (2) the docking facility eased transport of people and goods via the river; and (3) residents with wells had direct access to cleaner, more filtered water than the river ever provided. *No significant research pursued water's meanings or rituals.*

Authors of the project's earliest publications gave little attention to more humanistic interpretations, of water features or otherwise at Quirigua. Exceptions are epigraphers and art historians, who advanced understanding of the history and styles of stone stelae and other major Quirigua sculptures (Jones 1983; Looper 2003; Stone 1983). Later, my own approaches to civic planning proposed that the basis for the latter lay in Maya concepts of the cosmos (Ashmore 1989, 1991). James Brady is more specific about microcosmic recognition at Dos Pilas, directly linking water to the arrangement of civic buildings and spaces: thunderous surges of water announced the rainy season each year, and the physical sources of that multisensory spectacle were a cave and springs at the base of the king's palace (Brady 1997; Brady and Ashmore 1999). Indeed, the ancient name for that palace complex, K'inalha', acknowledged explicitly its location with the springs (Stuart and Houston 1994, 84–85). The royal occupant was thereby credited with success in the crucial matter of providing a new year of rain. Elsewhere, place-names identify whole polity centers with local physiographic features: at Palenque, the Maya place-name, Lakamha', embodies the wide waters that adjoin and run through the settlement (Stuart 2010; Stuart and Houston 1994). Indeed, Evon Vogt and David Stuart (2005, 163) note that Classic Maya place-names were identified most often with caves and springs.

Attention to water-related iconography and ritual emerged as a complement to economic, ecological, and political concerns, as in Dennis Puleston's (1977) prescient "The Art and Archaeology of Hydraulic Agriculture in the Maya Lowlands." In that chapter, Puleston introduces this complementary perspective: he infers that the ancient Maya perceived water lily pads afloat on still water as an expression of cosmic order; the lily pads stood for the nonoverlapping scutes on the back of a crocodile, individual scutes denoting individual raised agricultural fields, on the crocodilian earth, the terrestrial domain set appropriately atop a watery underworld. Of course, Puleston is best known for his productive engagement with settlement patterns, ecologies, and subsistence strategies of the ancient Maya, and this contribution furthered that work. In addition, however, the 1977 essay expanded the range of data he considered pertinent, to include epigraphic and iconographic sources (McLeod and Puleston 1978). In an account of Puleston's life for a volume in his memory, the late Gordon R. Willey called that 1977 essay "one of the most seminal and brilliant papers in Maya archaeology" (1982, 9).

In subsequent decades, many scholars have strongly linked water and its management to economic, political, and symbolic aspects of ancient (and modern) life, Maya or otherwise (Fash 2005, 2010; Freidel 1975; Kettunen and Helmke 2013). Elsewhere in the world, the effects of colonization can yield contrasting views about the values and treatment of water. For example, David Biggs (2010) writes of precolonial and French colonial conceptualizations of the Mekong River delta in Vietnam and how the colonizers brought dredges and other heavy equipment to reshape the delta more to their liking. As I write this chapter, the Standing Rock Sioux and their supporters are battling corporate and government aims to complete the Dakota Access Pipeline (DAPL), connecting western North Dakota with southern Illinois. Among the supporters is the Sierra Club, which joined the efforts to stop the pipeline (Sierra Club n.d.). Protesting the oil pipeline draws on politicoeconomic as well as religious grounds: Forcing pipeline construction would violate long-established treaties, as well as current federal regulations (National Environmental Policy Act [NEPA]; National Historic Preservation Act [NHPA]). Not only would potential pipeline leaks contaminate the water supply; the pipeline itself would disrupt sacred ground (Imbler 2017; Worland 2016). These are matters of sustainability in multiple ways, and involving multiple shareholders, often with mutually conflicting goals and reasons. *Oil and gasoline are important to many, but for everyone, water is life.*

MAYA WATER MEANINGS, SYMBOLISM, AND RITUALS

Meanings and Symbolism

Not all water is or ever was the same. In the United States today, for example, people commonly distinguish potable from nonpotable varieties (when given the opportunity to choose). For the Maya, distinctions include water "dripping in a cave [as] extremely pure," thereby restricted in use to "ritual drinks and healing potions" (Fash and Davis-Salazar 2006, 138). Harri Kettunen and Christophe Helmke (2013, 19–20) note that while the term for water (**HA'**) is fairly uniform across, different words exist for "ocean," "lake," and "river" in at least some Mayan languages.

At a larger scale, Karl Taube (1988, 199; 2010; see also Miller 1982) describes divergent meanings the Maya attributed to the seas flanking and underlying the Yucatán Peninsula: the eastern sea is where the sun rises and the western sea where the sun plunges into the watery milieu of the Underworld.

The daily circular route implied in Taube's remarks is echoed in other Indigenous American cultures, such as relayed in Gary Urton's *At the Crossroads of the Earth and the Sky: An Andean Cosmology* (1981), in which he contends that at the Quechua-speaking village of Misminay, Peru, the Vilcanota River "is the main artery for the movement of water collected from smaller tributaries of the earth back to the cosmic sea, from where it is taken up into the Milky Way and recycled through the universe. The Milky Way is itself thought to be the celestial reflection of the Vilcanota" (1981, 38). Similarly, in discussing Inca irrigation canals, Jeanette Sherbondy remarks that "a basic concept in Andean cosmology in general, is that the sea surrounds the world and lies under it" (1982, 121).

Karl Taube writes of Flower Mountain, central to Maya and other Mesoamerican societies, as a "place of gods, ancestors and celestial ascent" (2004, 92), where "rain-making moisture entered the sky." Its location is the axis for the sun's daily circuit, and also gives access to the watery underworld, an axis mundi linking the earth to both water and the sky (93). The famed sixteenth-century *Popol Vuh* was first transcribed and translated to Spanish in the eighteenth century. The anonymous authors of the document relate the origins of earth and sky: "First the earth was created, the mountains and the valleys. The waterways were divided, their branches coursing among the mountains. For thus was created the earth . . . The sky was set apart. The earth was also set apart within the waters. Thus was conceived the successful completion of the work when they thought and when they pondered" (Christenson 2007, 62–63). Once again, the Indigenous structure of the cosmos links celestial, terrestrial, and watery levels in daily, annual, and other circuits. Water is key.

Local or regional water shortages, especially droughts, call for rainmaking rituals and sometimes pilgrimages to regain water stability (Brady 1989; Iannone,

Yaeger, and Hodell 2014; Ishihara 2008; Lucero 1999, 239; Lucero and Kinkella 2015; Lucero et al. 2016; Moyes et al. 2009; Patel 2005; Schaafsma and Taube 2006). Joel Palka (2014) describes, with or without water shortages, pilgrimage and ritual landscapes of the Maya, among the Lacandon of today, their neighbors, and ancestors of all. Drawing on archaeology, history, and ethnography, he notes that such ritual practices have prevailed from deep time to the modern day. He studies "ritual landscapes," an active term he prefers to sacred landscapes, the elements of which he singles out as "mountains, cliffs, boulders, *caves*, ruins, *bodies of water, and islands*, which have always been important in Mesoamerican cultures" (2014, 9; emphasis added). Shankari Patel (2005) argues that the island of Cozumel was a place of pilgrimage to caves and cenotes to celebrate, thank, and petition the Maya goddess Ix Chel. Citing evidence from her own and earlier work, she noted the *sacbe* (causeway) system linking shrines built at those landscape features in a pilgrim circuit of the island's water features (Freidel 1975). James Brady (1989, 413–414) contends that Maya pilgrimages were oriented most commonly to water deities, with the extraordinary cave of Naj Tunich being a prominent destination for these goals, in antiquity and today.

Studies of water and other landscape components continue to merge iconographic and epigraphic study with archaeological research. The tremendous growth in cave archaeology has greatly expanded exploration of the watery underworld, including abundant evidence for ritual activities (Brady 2010; Brady and Prufer 2005; McLeod and Puleston 1978). Mesoamerican mountains are often thought to be filled with water, with access by caves (Fash and López Lujan 2009). Not surprisingly, water was prominent in reenactments of creation. In the extraordinary murals of San Bartolo, 100 BCE, the North Wall depicts "a zoomorphic mountain bearing an ancient and bent tree, flowering plants, and wild beasts. . . . The mountain exhales a massive plumed serpent, a widespread symbol of breath and wind in ancient Mesoamerica. . . . The scene probably constitutes a version of the emergence myth of Mesoamerica and the American Southwest, *here with the maize god and humans conveying food and water out of the ancestral cave of origin*" (Taube 2013, 100; emphasis added).

Water was critical for ritual acts and reenactments of more local creations, as well, insofar as the combination of water and mountain is crucial to establishing a new civic center. At Maya Tikal, Vernon Scarborough (1998; see also Scarborough and Gallopin 1991) notes that the largest reservoirs were positioned at approximately cardinal points and thereby helped define a landscape structured by the four appropriate corners. Like cenotes farther north, and water-filled caves elsewhere, the Tikal *aguadas* (reservoirs) also were portals to the watery underworld. Five cenotes at Preclassic T'isil, Quintana Roo, likewise might have provided settlement structure and underworld portals (Fedick, Mathews, and Sorensen 2012).

Rituals and offerings at such water places are clear in archaeological evidence from Chichén Itzá to Copán (Coggins 1984; Fash and Davis-Salazar 2006; Martos López 2010) and were significant landscape nodes for asserting social order among neighbors and political control by rulers (Scarborough 1998). Indeed, Lisa Lucero (1999, 44) argues that it "was ideological association with water purification, in addition to the control of reservoirs, that provided Maya rulers the foundation on which to build and maintain their power." In the same vein, William Walker and Lucero (2000) argue for the roots of community-wide rituals in everyday life of ordinary families: "Often public events are successful because leaders incorporate familiar ritual practices in them, which is why household rituals are embedded in the ancestral rites of lineages" (132).

Moreover, the shimmering mirror-like surface of *still* water plausibly lent itself to divination: Taube (1992, 2016) describes mirrors as implements for divination and goes on to note that in Mesoamerica and the US Southwest, mirrors are widely equated with supernatural caves. Mirrors and caves are linked metaphorically *through water*: all have characteristics of visual or physical transition, and reflection. For the foregoing reasons, then, reservoirs and other bodies of water were arguably potent liminal features of the landscape.

Nicholas Dunning and colleagues (1999) write eloquently of the anciently engineered landscape at the juncture of northern Belize, Mexico, and Guatemala. Within their study area, the interdisciplinary team explores evidence of "intentional and unintentional environmental changes. Intentional changes included the centrally directed erection of monumental architecture as well as the accretional engineering of the landscape by generations of farmers. Unintentional effects included sometimes devastating soil loss and *hydrological changes*. Both the intentional and unintentional must be read for the landscape to provide a more comprehensive picture of Maya civilization" (650; emphasis added). Dunning and colleagues also specifically consider water and hydraulic features on the land, creation of dams, terracing, and reservoirs to acknowledge the growing populace and need for more reliable resources, including water. They give special attention to "sacred *cenotes*," and the role of each as "a transformative boundary, simultaneously separating and connecting cosmic planes" (657).

Ritual

Recognizing ritual remains in the archaeological record can be challenging, fraught with ambiguities in critically establishing material correlates for past ritual behavior. Some turn to stratigraphic evidence of recurring materialized behavior, especially in relation to events in building, rebuilding, and termination of architecture (D. Chase and A. Chase 1998; Lucero 2003, 526; Mock 1998; Walker and Lucero 2000). The life history approach for buildings also works for objects, whose life span may be transformed by their "killing," such as perforated ceramic plates. Although the perforation ruins them for mundane uses, they become ready for deposition in caches, burials, and such contexts (Bell 2007, 341). Other analysts look for objects and traces found in what Mayanists have long considered ritual contexts, such as caches or burials (e.g., burned censers; exotic preciosities such as jade and marine shell; symbolic arrangement of cache contents, often forming a scene and, in others, a cosmogram) (Becker 1992; D. Chase 1988; D. Chase and A. Chase 1998). The key, of course, is to look for evidence of ritual *activities*, rather than simply objects. A "performative approach to ritual" has seemed an apt avenue for exploration (Inomata 2003; Inomata and Coben 2006).

Performance related to water includes water in caves. For the Yalahau region of Quintana Roo, Dominique Rissolo concludes that while cave water was not essential for sustenance (see Fash and Davis-Salazar 2006), the "presence of water in a cave was of paramount importance. Water sources were the focus of ritual activity even where long, arduous crawls were required to reach very modestly sized pools" (Rissolo 2005, 365). The crawling, whatever its length and difficulty, animated the importance of the rituals performed at the end.

In the same vein, Lucero and Andrew Kinkella (2015) consider Cara Blanca, Belize, a unique east-west line of twenty-five freshwater pools, in an area of remarkably sparse habitation settlements. The spatial juxtaposition suggests to the authors that Cara Blanca was a Maya sacred place, and plausibly a destination of pilgrimage. The abundance of water lilies in the pools today indicates clean, still water, whose cosmological significance has been noted earlier. Visible to the south for several kilometers, the stark white façade of Cara Blanca requires pilgrims to cross difficult terrain to reach the pools, and then, as they came closer to the pools, a cool breeze would welcome them (2015, 28). Whether drawn to the place to make ritual offerings to water deities or to venerate the pools, it was intentional movement, including its sometimes arduous nature, that bonded pilgrims and place more strongly.

Writing of finds in the Grieta Principal (Main Chasm) of Aguateca, Reiko Ishihara-Brito finds that significant portions of this roofless cave relate to rain making, with finds of musical instruments, miniature vessels, and child sacrifices (Ishihara 2008). At a portion nicknamed "Chill Hill," billowing clouds of mist form and rise, easily matching the long-standing Mesoamerican belief that clouds—which bring rain—originate in caves. In Western views, the underlying phenomenon is geothermal, but the Aguateca king took advantage of the location, building the palace complex on the ground next to Chill Hill. Ishihara envisions rainmaking rituals, with musical performers and possibly dancers, the sounds of their performance rising to areas beyond the *grieta*. At times of drought and/or political crisis, the frequency and intensity of such rituals may well have intensified. Again, the performances implied from finds at the Grieta Principal are what activate the water rituals and ensure that they will be effective.

CONCLUSIONS

The foregoing pages portray one view of how ideas about conceptions and uses of water among the ancient Maya have expanded in recent decades, with emphasis here on roles of meaning, symbolism, and ritual. As described earlier, times of confidence, political stability, and economic prosperity favor Maya water studies focused generally on documentation and scientific explanations for the technologies and their water yield (Lansing 2007; Lucero 2003; Scarborough 2003). Political aspects of water control and allocation are staples in interpretations. In the uncertain political and economic milieu of today, water symbolism, meaning, and ritual have grown.

What differs, in my view, from the transitions cited earlier with regard to processual and more humanistic approaches, is the increasingly collaborative nature of archaeology in many parts of the world. Through this collaboration, authority for the research comes from a much more diverse set of stakeholders. These all have positive implications for sustainability and longer-term social justice. The Native American Graves Protection and Repatriation Act (NAGPRA) in the United States and the global work of the World Archaeological Congress (WAC) and IHOPE recognize and foment respect between Indigenous and Western parties—if perhaps not as rapidly or extensively as many would wish. Research findings from IHOPE-Maya investigators relate eloquently how the past can inform the present, while respecting historically contingent cultural goals and values.

Ongoing conflict between the Standing Rock Sioux and federal and corporate agencies exemplifies the profundity of firmly held belief systems, on both sides: this, too, is in part a case of the past informing on the present. In short, cumulative research yields ever-more acute insights about not only sustainable water programs but also about meanings, management, and rituals attached to water in ancient Maya society. Vernon L. Scarborough is a leader in these pursuits, resolute in the search for ever-more thorough understanding. Water *is* life.

ACKNOWLEDGMENTS

I am grateful to editors Jean T. Larmon, Lisa Lucero, and Fred Valdez Jr. for the opportunity to contribute to this volume. Doing so would not have been possible without the critical work on the subject of water by Vern Scarborough and other researchers, cited or not. As always, I thank Tom Patterson for his insightful feedback and relentless encouragement.

REFERENCES

Ashmore, Wendy. 1984a. "Quirigua Archaeology and History Revisited." *Journal of Field Archaeology* 11 (4): 365–386.

Ashmore, Wendy. 1984b. "Classic Maya Wells at Quirigua, Guatemala: Household Facilities in a Water-Rich Setting." *American Antiquity* 49 (1): 147–153.

Ashmore, Wendy. 1989. "Construction and Cosmology: Politics and Ideology in Lowland Maya Settlement Patterns." In *Word and Image in Maya Culture: Explorations in Language, Writing, and Representation*, edited by William F. Hanks and Don S. Rice, 272–286. Salt Lake City: University of Utah Press.

Ashmore, Wendy. 1991. "Site-Planning Principles and Concepts and Concepts of Directionality among the Ancient Maya." *Latin American Antiquity* 2 (3): 199–226.

Ashmore, Wendy. 2007. *Settlement Archaeology at Quiriguá, Guatemala. Quiriguá Reports IV*. University Museum Monograph 126. Philadelphia: University of Pennsylvania Museum.

Becker, Marshall J. 1992. "Burials as Caches, Caches as Burials: A New Interpretation of Ritual Deposits among the Classic Period Lowland Maya." In *New Theories on the Ancient Maya*, edited by Elin C. Danien and Robert J. Sharer, 185–196. University Museum Monograph 77. Philadelphia: University of Pennsylvania Museum.

Bell, Ellen E. 2007. "Early Classic Ritual Deposits within the Copan Acropolis: The Material Foundations of Political Power at a Classic Period Maya Center." PhD diss., University of Pennsylvania.

Biggs, David. 2010. *Quagmire: Nation-Building and Nature in the Mekong Delta*. Seattle: University of Washington Press.

Brady, James E. 1989. "An Investigation of Maya Ritual Cave Use, with Special Reference to Naj Tunich, Guatemala." PhD diss., University of California, Los Angeles.

Brady, James E. 1997. "Settlement Configuration and Cosmology: The Role of Caves at Dos Pilas." *American Anthropologist* 99 (3): 602–618.

Brady, James E. 2010. "Offerings to the Rain Gods: The Archaeology of Maya Caves." In *Fiery Pool: The Maya and the Mythic Sea (Peabody Essex Museum)*, edited by Daniel Finamore and Stephen Houston, 220–222. New Haven CT: Yale University Press.

Brady, James E., and Wendy Ashmore. 1999. "Mountains, Caves, Water: Ideational Landscapes of the Ancient Maya." In *Archaeologies of Landscape: Contemporary Perspectives*, edited by Wendy Ashmore and A. Bernard Knapp, 124–145. Malden, CT: Blackwell.

Brady, James E., and Keith M. Prufer, eds. 2005. *In the Maw of the Earth Monster: Mesoamerican Ritual Cave Use*. Austin: University of Texas Press.

Brumfiel, Elizabeth M. 1992. "Breaking and Entering the Ecosystem: Gender, Class, and Faction Steal the Show." *American Anthropologist* 94 (3): 551–556.

Chase, Arlen F., and Vernon L. Scarborough, eds. 2014a. *The Resilience and Vulnerability of Ancient Landscapes: Transforming Maya Archaeology through IHOPE*. Archeological Papers of the American Anthropological Association, 24. Arlington VA: American Anthropological Association, and Hoboken NJ: Wiley.

Chase, Arlen F., and Vernon L. Scarborough. 2014b. "Diversity, Resiliency, and IHOPE-Maya: Using the Past to Inform the Present." In *The Resilience and Vulnerability of*

Ancient Landscapes: Transforming Maya Archaeology through IHOPE. Archeological Papers of the American Anthropological Association, 24, edited by Arlen F. Chase and Vernon L. Scarborough, 1–10. Arlington, VA: American Anthropological Association; Hoboken, NJ: Wiley.

Chase, Diane Z. 1988. "Caches and Censerware: Meaning from Maya Pottery." In *A Pot for All Reasons: Ceramic Ecology Revisited*, edited by Charles C. Kolb and Louana M. Lackey, 81–104. Philadelphia: Temple University Press.

Chase, Diane Z., and Arlen F. Chase. 1998. "The Architectural Context of Caches, Burials, and Other Ritual Categories for the Classic Period Maya (as Reflected at Caracol, Belize)." In *Function and Meaning in Classic Maya Architecture*, edited by Stephen D. Houston, 299–332. Washington, DC: Dumbarton Oaks Research Library and Collection.

Christenson, Allen J. 2007. *Popol Vuh: Sacred Books of the Quiché Maya People*. Mesoweb. Accessed January 24, 2015. www.mesoweb.com/publications/Christenson/populvuh.pdf.

Coe, Michael D. 2011. "The Cold War and the Maya Decipherment." In *Their Way of Writing: Scripts, Signs, and Pictographs in Pre-Columbian America*, edited by Elizabeth Hill Boone and Gary Urton, 9–20. Washington, DC: Dumbarton Oaks Research Library and Collection.

Coggins, Clemency Chase. 1984. "The Cenote of Sacrifice: A Catalogue." In *Cenote of Sacrifice: Maya Treasures from the Sacred Well at Chichén Itzá*, edited by Clemency Chase Coggins and Orrin C. Shane III, 23–165. Austin: University of Texas Press.

Crumley, Carole L. 1979. "Three Locational Models: An Epistemological Assessment for Anthropology and Archaeology." In *Advances in Archaeological Method and Theory*. Vol. 2, edited by Michael B. Schiffer, 141–173. Tucson: University of Arizona Press,

Crumley, Carole L. 1987. "A Dialectical Critique of Hierarchy." In *Power Relations and State Formation*, edited by Thomas C. Patterson and Christine W. Gailey, 155–169. Washington, DC: American Anthropological Association, Archeology Section.

Dunning, Nicholas P., Vernon Scarborough, Fred Valdez Jr., Sheryl Luzzadder-Beach, Timothy Beach, and John G. Jones. 1999. "Temple Mountains, Sacred Lakes, and Fertile Fields: Ancient Maya Landscapes in Northern Belize." *Antiquity* 73 (281): 650–660.

Fash, Barbara W. 2005. "Iconographic Evidence for Water Management and Social Organization at Copán." In *Copán: The History of an Ancient Maya Kingdom*, edited by E. Wyllys Andrews and William L. Fash, 103–138. Santa Fe, NM: School of American Research Press.

Fash, Barbara W. 2010. "Symbols of Water Management at Copan, Honduras." In *Fiery Pool: The Maya and the Mythic Sea (Peabody Essex Museum)*, edited by Daniel Finamore and Stephen Houston, 80–82. New Haven, CT: Yale University Press.

Fash, Barbara W., and Karla L. Davis-Salazar. 2006. "Copan Water Ritual and Management: Image and Sacred Place." In *Precolumbian Water Management: Ideology, Ritual, and Power*, edited by Lisa J. Lucero and Barbara W. Fash, 129–143. Tucson: University of Arizona Press.

Fash, William, and Leonardo López Luján. 2009. "Introduction." In *The Art of Urbanism: How Mesoamerican Kingdoms Represented Themselves in Architecture and Imagery*, edited by William L. Fash and Leonardo López Luján, 1–20. Washington, DC: Dumbarton Oaks Research Library and Collection.

Fedick, Scott L., Jennifer P. Mathews, and Kathryn Sorensen. 2012. "Cenotes as Conceptual Markers at the Ancient Maya Site of T'isil, Quintana Roo, Mexico." *Mexicon* 34 (5): 118–123.

Freidel, David. 1975. "The *Ix Chel* Shrine and Other Temples of Talking Idols." In *A Study of Changing Pre-Columbian Commercial Systems: The 1972–1973 Seasons at Cozumel, Mexico*, edited by Jeremy A. Sabloff and William L. Rathje, 60–87. Monographs of the Peabody Museum, 3. Cambridge, MA: Peabody Museum of Archaeology and Ethnology.

Iannone, Gyles, Jason Yaeger, and David Hodell. 2014. "Assessing the Great Maya Droughts: Some Critical Issues." In *The Great Maya Droughts: Case Studies in Resilience and Vulnerability*, edited by Gyles Iannone, 51–70. Boulder: University Press of Colorado.

Imbler, Sabrina. 2017. "Here's How the Standing Rock Sioux Will Keep Fighting Dakota Access—in Court." *Grist*. http://grist.org/climate-energy/the-standing-rock-sioux -could-still-beat-the-dakota-access-pipeline-in-court/.

Inomata, Takeshi. 2003. "Comment on Lucero's 'The Politics of Ritual.'" *Current Anthropology* 44 (4): 546–547.

Inomata, Takeshi, and Lawrence S. Coben, eds. 2006. *Archaeology of Performance: Theaters of Power, Community, and Politics*. Lanham, MD: AltaMira / Rowman and Littlefield.

Ishihara, Reiko. 2008. "Rising Clouds, Blowing Winds: Late Classic Maya Rain Rituals in the Main Chasm, Aguateca, Guatemala." *World Archaeology* 40 (2): 169–189.

Jones, Christopher. 1983. "Monument 26, Quiriguá, Guatemala." In *Quiriguá Reports, II*, edited by Robert J. Sharer, Edward M. Schortman, and Patricia A. Urban, Paper No. 13, 118–128. University Museum Monograph 49. Philadelphia: University of Pennsylvania.

Kettunen, Harri, and Christophe Helmke. 2013. "Water in Maya Imagery and Writing." *Contributions in New World Archaeology* 5: 17–38.

Lansing, Stephen J. 2007. *Priests and Programmers: Technologies of Power in the Engineered Landscape of Bali*. Princeton, NJ: Princeton University Press.

Looper, Matthew G. 2003. *Lightning Warrior: Maya Art and Kingship at Quiriguá*. Austin: University of Texas Press.

Lucero, Lisa J. 1999. Water Control and Maya Politics in the Southern Maya Lowlands. In *Complex Polities in the Ancient Tropical World*, edited by E. A. Bacus and L. J. Lucero, pp. 34–49. Archeological Papers of the American Anthropological Association Number 9. American Anthropological Association, Arlington, VA.

Lucero, Lisa J. 2003. "The Politics of Ritual: The Emergence of Early Classic Maya Rulers." *Current Anthropology* 44 (4): 523–558.

Lucero, Lisa J., Jessica Harrison, Jean Larmon, Zachary Nissen, and Erin Benson. 2016. "Prolonged Droughts, Short-Term Responses, and Diaspora: The Power of Water and Pilgrimage at the Sacred *Cenotes* of Cara Blanca, Belize." WIREs Water 2016. https://doi.org/10.1002/wat2.1148.

Lucero, Lisa J., and Andrew Kinkella. 2015. "A Place for Pilgrimage: The Ancient Maya Sacred Landscape of Cara Blanca, Belize." In *Of Rocks and Water: Towards an Archaeology of Place*, edited by Ömür Harmansah, 13–39. Joukowsky Institute Publication 5. Oxford: Oxbow Books.

Martos López, Luis Alberto. 2010. "Objects Cast into Cenotes." In *Fiery Pool: The Maya and the Mythic Sea (Peabody Essex Museum)*, edited by Daniel Finamore and Stephen Houston, 223–225. New Haven, CT: Yale University Press.

McLeod, Barbara, and Dennis E. Puleston. 1978. "Pathways into Darkness: The Search for the Road to Xibalbá." In *Tercera Mesa Redonda de Palenque*. Vol. 4. edited by Merle Greene Robertson and Donnan Call Jeffers, 71–77. Monterey, CA: Pre-Columbian Art Research Institute.

Miller, Arthur G. 1982. *On the Edge of the Sea: Mural Painting at Tancah-Tulum, Quintana Roo, Mexico*. Washington, DC: Dumbarton Oaks Research Library and Collection.

Mock, Shirley Boteler, ed. 1998. *The Sowing and the Dawning: Termination, Dedication, and Transformation in the Archaeological and Ethnographic Record of Mesoamerica*. Albuquerque: University of New Mexico Press.

Moyes, Holley, Jaime J. Awe, George A. Brook, and James W. Webster. 2009. "The Ancient Maya Drought Cult: Late Classic Cave Use in Belize." *Latin American Antiquity* 20 (1): 175–206.

Paddayya, K. 1990. *The New Archaeology and Aftermath: A View from Outside the Anglo-American World*. Pune, India: Ravish Publishers.

Palka, Joel W. 2014. *Maya Pilgrimage to Ritual Landscapes: Insights from Archaeology, History, and Ethnography*. Albuquerque: University of New Mexico Press.

Patel, Shankari. 2005. "Pilgrimage and Caves on Cozumel." In *Stone Houses and Earth Lords: Maya Religion in the Cave Context*, edited by Keith M. Prufer and James E. Brady, 91–112. Boulder: University Press of Colorado.

Patterson, Thomas C. 1990. "Some Theoretical Tensions with and between the Processual and Postprocessual Archaeologies." *Journal of Anthropological Archaeology* 9 (2): 189–200.

Patterson, Thomas C. 1995. *Toward a Social History of Archaeology in the United States*. Fort Worth, TX: Harcourt Brace and Company.

Puleston, Dennis E. 1977. "The Art and Archaeology of Hydraulic Agriculture in the Maya Lowlands." In *Social Process in Maya Prehistory*, edited by Norman Hammond, 449–467. London: Academic Press.

Rissolo, Dominique. 2005. "Beneath the Yalahau: Emerging Patterns of Cave Use from Northern Quintana Roo, Mexico." In *In the Maw of the Earth Monster: Mesoamerican Ritual Cave Use*, edited by James E. Brady and Keith M. Prufer, 342–372. Austin: University of Texas Press.

Scarborough, Vernon L. 1998. "Ecology and Ritual: Water Management and the Maya." *Latin American Antiquity* 8 (2): 135–159.

Scarborough, Vernon L. 2003. *The Flow of Power: Ancient Water Systems and Landscapes*. Albuquerque: University of New Mexico Press.

Scarborough, Vernon L., Nicholas P. Dunning, Kenneth Tankersley, Christopher Carr, Eric Weaver, Liwy Grazioso, Brian Lane et al. 2012. "Water and Sustainable Land Use at the Ancient Tropical of Tikal, Guatemala." *Proceedings of the National Academy of Sciences* 109 (31): 12408–12413.

Scarborough, Vernon L., and Gary G. Gallopin. 1991. "A Water Storage Adaptation in the Maya Lowlands." *Science* 251 (4994): 658–662.

Schaafsma, Polly, and Karl A. Taube. 2006. "Bringing the Rain: An Ideology of Rain Making in the Pueblo Southwest and Mesoamerica." In *A Precolumbian World: Searching for a Unitary Vision of Ancient Mesoamerica*, edited by Jeffrey Quilter, 231–285. Washington, DC: Dumbarton Oaks Research Library and Collection.

Sharer, Robert J. 1978. "Archaeology and History at Quirigua, Guatemala." *Journal of Field Archaeology* 5 (1): 51–70.

Sharer, Robert J. 1988. "Quiriguá as a Classic Maya Center." In *The Southeast Classic Maya Zone*, edited by Elizabeth H. Boone and Gordon R. Willey, 31–65. Washington, DC: Dumbarton Oaks Research Library and Collection.

Sharer, Robert J., and William R. Coe. 1979. "The Quirigua Project: Origins, Objectives, and Research in 1973 and 1974." In *Quirigua Reports I: Papers 1–5*, edited by Robert J. Sharer and Wendy Ashmore, 1–11. Museum Monograph 37. Philadelphia: University of Pennsylvania Museum.

Sherbondy, Jeannette. 1982. "The Canal System of Hunan Cuzco." PhD diss., University of Illinois at Urbana-Champaign.

Sherratt, Andrew. 1996. "'Settlement Patterns' or 'Landscape Studies'? Reconciling Reason and Romance." *Archaeological Dialogue* 3 (2): 140–159.

Sierra Club. n.d. "Dakota Access Pipeline." Accessed May 19, 2017. https://www.sierraclub.org/iowa/dakota-access-pipeline.

Stone, Andrea J. 1983. The "Zoomorphs of Quiriguá," PhD diss., University of Texas, Austin.

Stuart, David. 2010. "The Wide Waters of Palenque." In *Fiery Pool: The Maya and the Mythic Sea (Peabody Essex Museum)*, edited by Daniel Finamore and Stephen Houston, 41–43. New Haven, CT: Yale University Press.

Stuart, David, and Stephen D. Houston. 1994. *Classic Maya Place Names*. Studies in Pre-Columbian Art and Archaeology, 33. Washington, DC: Dumbarton Oaks Research Library and Collection.

Taube, Karl. 1988. "A Prehispanic Maya Katun Wheel." *Journal of Anthropological Research* 44 (2): 183–203.

Taube, Karl. 1992. "The Iconography of Mirrors at Teotihuacan." In *Art, Ideology, and the City of Teotihuacan*, edited by Janet C. Berlo, 169–204. Washington, DC: Dumbarton Oaks Research Library and Collection.

Taube, Karl. 2004. "Flower Mountain: Concepts of Life, Beauty, and Paradise among the Classic Maya." *RES* 45 (Spring): 69–98.

Taube, Karl. 2010. "Where Earth and Sky Meet: The Sea in Ancient and Contemporary Maya Cosmology." In *Fiery Pool: The Maya and the Mythic Sea (Peabody Essex Museum)*, edited by Daniel Finamore and Stephen Houston, 202–219. New Haven, CT: Yale University Press.

Taube, Karl. 2013. "The Classic Maya Temple: Centrality, Cosmology, and Sacred Geography in Ancient Mesoamerica." In *Heaven on Earth: Temples, Ritual, and Cosmic Symbolism in the Ancient World*, edited by Deena Ragavan, 89–125. University of Chicago Oriental Institute Seminars, No. 9. Chicago: Oriental Institute of the University of Chicago.

Taube, Karl. 2016. "Through a Glass, Brightly: Recent Investigations Concerning Mirrors and Scrying in Ancient and Contemporary Mesoamerica." In *Manufactured Light: Mirrors in the Mesoamerican Realm*, edited by Emiliano Gallaga M. and Marc G. Blainey, 285–314. Boulder: University Press of Colorado.

Urton, Gary F. 1981. *At the Crossroads of the Earth and the Sky: An Andean Cosmology*. Austin: University of Texas Press.

Vogt, Evon Z., and David Stuart. 2005. "Some Notes on Ritual Caves among the Ancient and Modern Maya." In *In the Maw of the Earth Monster: Mesoamerican Ritual Cave Use*, edited by James E. Brady and Keith M. Prufer, 155–185. Austin: University of Texas Press.

Walker, William H., and Lisa J. Lucero. 2000. "The Depositional History of Ritual and Power." In *Agency in Archaeology*, edited by Marcia-Anne Dobres and John H. Robb, 130–147. London: Routledge.

Wilk, Richard R. 1985. "The Ancient Maya and the Political Present." *Journal of Anthropological Research* 41 (3): 307–326.

Willey, Gordon R. 1982. "Dennis Edward Puleston (1940–1978): Maya Archaeologist." In *Maya Subsistence: Studies in Memory of Dennis E. Puleston*, edited by Kent V. Flannery, 1–15. New York: Academic Press.

Willey, Gordon R., and Jeremy A. Sabloff. 1993. *A History of American Archaeology*. 3rd ed. New York: W. H. Freeman.

Worland, Justin. 2016. "What to Know about the Dakota Access Pipeline Protests." *Time*. http://time.com/4548566/dakota-access-pipeline-standing-rock-sioux/.

5

Three Tropical Thoughts

The Migration to Tropical Ecology

Joel D. Gunn

The last twenty years have seen numerous attempts at every kind of model and method to plumb Maya occupation of the Yucatán Peninsula. In the end, however, for most archaeologists and casual readers of history, the ultimate goal is a flowing narrative of what transpired. Such narratives may be regarded as mere overviews or, even worse, inaccurate with regard to details. They do, however, serve as useful entrées to the subject of Maya cultural evolution and a bridge to the details and doubts that form the underlying corpus of leading-edge research into past events. Using three ideas espoused by Vernon Scarborough and colleagues, this chapter attempts to formulate a narrative about tropical urban settlements that integrates ideas concerning the Maya lowlands on the one hand and those of tropical, complex societies worldwide, on the other. They are not the only ideas that underpin a current narrative, but they also serve in starring roles.

For the Maya, now the largest extant Indigenous ethnic group in North and Central America, the historical narrative can be briefly summed in a sentence. The Maya rose from watery origins thousands of years ago and evolved to discover engineered solutions to the contradictions between tropical ecology and

https://doi.org/10.5876/9781646422326.c005

human communications systems. An even briefer summary: how the Maya got themselves into trouble, and how they fixed it. These topics are covered in detail in previous publications (Gunn et al. 2017; Gunn, Folan et al. 2014; Gunn et al. 2019; Volta and Gunn 2012, 2016).

CHAPTER FRAMEWORK

The narrative of the Maya is not a short story. It is a novel with many chapters, twists, turns, reverses, and victories. For the casual reader, the central point of interest is frequently the ninth century CE, cataclysmic collapse of one of the world's great civilizations. At a more detailed level, it is now understood that "The Collapse" was one of several such reversals over three millennia. This reversal did engender a major reorganization of the economic and social structure of the Maya community of cultures and languages, eventually bringing it into the modern world economy through/with the Spanish Empire.

I should mention that my perspective is weighted toward the western central Maya lowlands, essentially the state of Campeche around Calakmul and Edzna. This emphasis largely results from analytical and soils experiences in the Candelaria and Champoton-Desempeño River systems, and some ethnographic observation directly and indirectly with Betty B. Faust, William J. Folan, and Lynda Flory Folan (Gunn et al. 2002, 2019). I have tried to make the east-west treatment as balanced as possible by reading up on the eastern peninsula and assisting the Integrated History and Future of People on Earth (IHOPE)–Maya working group in a peninsular-wide study of information systems (Gunn et al. 2017). That said, it is probably time given the looming importance of Calakmul and El Mirador in the overall Maya narrative and the history of world civilizations that a reweighting be made.

The three main chapters of intervening social development covered here involve origins based on controlling natural water passages, the evolution of settlement in a tropical environment, and, eventually, great engineering achievements in the conquest of water control. Like all good stories, this one has a conflict: the lack of fit between the demands of the tropical environment and the increased interpersonal communications demanded by growing, complex economies. Table 5.1 outlines this evolution along with some of the supporting ideas introduced in the course of thinking about Maya developmental issues. As we shall see, all three themes fit comfortably within the scope of intensive water management.

CIVILIZED LIFE CAME FROM THE SEA:
THE WATERY ORIGINS OF MAYA CULTURE

More than one line of evidence indicates that "Maya-land" was more a water world than a terrestrial world, as has been generally supposed. A key element

TABLE 5.1. Thought guide to Maya historical narrative. The proposed linear narrative is outlined in this table. It is based on three hypotheses proposed by Scarborough and colleagues during the last three decades. I have added some supporting ideas that aid in tying the three central themes together into an infoecological system spanning the last 3,000 years.

Sections and Topics	Literature Sources	Phenomena
MANAGING NATURAL WATER HIGHWAYS (SCARBOROUGH 1985, 1993A, 1993B)		
Sea Level Stabilization baselines	(Day et al. 2007; Day et al. 2012)	Two maxima of civilization formation worldwide
Human origins	(Broadhurst et al. 2002; Marean et al. 2007)	From the sea
Linguistic time clocks	(Josserand 2011; Malmström 1978)	Minimums of time
Mythic environments	(Freidel, Schele, and Parker 1993; Milbrath 1999)	Rivers
External trade relations	(Lohse 2010)	Stones and ceramics
Transpeninsular trade routes	(Adams 1978; Scholes and Roys 1968)	Cortés Road
MANAGING WATERY LANDSCAPE (SCARBOROUGH AND VALDEZ 2009)		
Tropical diversity	(Denevan 1996; Hannah et al. 2002)	Dispersions
MANAGING WATER GRADIENTS (SCARBOROUGH AND BURNSIDE 2010)		
Urban thresholds	(Cowgill 2004)	Utility of cities
Urban networks	(van der Leeuw 2007)	Hierarchies of cities
Energy gradients	(Tainter et al. 2003)	Extending the year
Perched water tables	(Gunn et al. 2002)	Protected water storage
Reservoirs	(Dunning, chapter 2 in this volume; Scarborough and Valdez 2009)	Somewhat protected water

in this perspective is that water played an integral role in the Maya worldview. My fascination with the Maya began thirty years ago in Acalan (the "land of the canoe" in the lower Candelaria River valley of southern Campeche, Mexico; Gunn and Adams 1981), the capital of the Chontal sea traders, and continues to the present with an ever-deepening belief that the Maya and other great civilizations around the world were inextricably bound to the seas and lands near the seas. Perhaps less empirical than Hernán Cortés's and Bernal Díaz del Castillo's writings on Acalan, but nevertheless a great insight, is the Maya foundation myth of the Paddler Gods. It serves as just warning of the watery origins of the over- and underworlds through which the Paddler Gods (figure 5.1, upper panel) conveyed the chiefly Maize God and several animal companions. A painted vase shows the Paddlers transporting the Maize God through watery, fishy realms (figure 5.1, lower panel). Susan Milbrath (1999, 127–130) reports that the Milky Way was viewed as a river in the sky along which the Paddlers transported the Maize God in the dry season when the sun and the moon crossed the Milky Way. In

FIGURE 5.1. *(Upper panel) Paddler Twins conveying the Maize God, various hand holds may signal attitudes (D. Reents-Budet, personal communication, 2014), moving to the right, inscribed on a bone from Tikal. (Lower panel) Paddler Twins conveying the Maize God under water, moving to the left, nude women dress the god for his journey under water, fish nibbles face of dead man at bottom, from a Guatemalan vase (adapted from Freidel, Schele, and Parker 1993, Schele sketches, downloaded from http://ancientamericas.org/collection/ aa010559 and http://ancientamericas.org/collection/aa010108, accessed June 9, 2017).*

addition to moving the Maize God and his animal companions about in eternal waters—the sources of life, death, and resurrection for the Maya—the Paddlers appear to control the long-term changes in time, the turning of the nearly 400-year *bak'tun* periods (Freidel, Schele, and Parker 1993). Many myths worldwide involve twins, beginning with Gilgamesh, probably around 2800 BCE; many involve time, like the European Janus, keeper of the doorway of the year—but few involve water.

On a wider and more empirical scale, anatomically modern humans are increasingly seen as evolving near fishy waters (Broadhurst et al. 2002; Marean et al. 2007). Scarborough (1991, 3) speculated some time ago that the Maya were of marine coastal origin, perhaps from along the Caribbean coast of Belize. However, the earliest well-dated evidence from coastal areas comes from the Gulf Coasts of Campeche and Tabasco in Mexico (Gunn, Day et al. 2014; Gunn et al. 2019; Pope et al. 2001; Siemens 2009). This evidence may be available because the Campeche Bank along the southern and eastern Gulf Coast offers an archaeologically more accessible continental margin. A linguistic hypothesis implies that Proto-Mayan speakers occupied the Gulf Coast 4,000 or more years ago. They seem to have occupied the areas more focused in the southwestern Yucatán Peninsula while the Zoque linguistic family was more to the west (Hopkins 2011; Josserand 1975; Josserand 2011; Malmström 1978). Estuary and lake sediment evidence in these areas indicates that as early as 7,000 years ago, humans were burning vegetation and consuming fish, manatee, and shellfish along the Gulf Coast of Tabasco (Pope et al. 2001). The same practices can be said for the area around the lower Candelaria River in Campeche (Gunn, Day et al. 2014; Siemens 2009). Today, these areas remain Mexico's most productive marine habitats.

In worldwide perspectives, there are compelling reasons why civilizations should have appeared by seas 7,000 years ago; at that time, the rise of the sea from much lower Pleistocene levels was completed. Global, near relative-stabilization of the seas high on the continental margins created wide, new estuarine areas that produced ten times the fish and wildlife as those of the Ice Ages (Day et al. 2007; Day et al. 2012; Gunn, Day et al. 2014). Not surprisingly, these vast reserves of protein—and, more important, omega-3 fats from which all animal nervous systems have been constructed since the earliest complex organism—attracted human populations and incubated basic building blocks of civilizations: concentrated, ethnically diverse populations with complex, stratified social organizations.

Sea level stabilization also precipitated the infilling of lower river valleys and facilitated the creation of rich agricultural lands therein. A spectacular example is the lower Nile River valley that turned from a barren, 100 m deep canyon, to the rich, swampy fishing and hunting reserves depicted in early Egyptian paintings, replete with hippopotamuses and aquatic birds. As the coasts became overcrowded, nascent complex societies expanded into lower river valleys. There they learned how to amplify the production of Neolithic domesticated plants and animals through irrigation and other water control measures. This process was repeated most notably in the desert regions of the world, including Egypt, Mesopotamia, the northern Great Central Plain of China, and the north coast of Peru (see Day et al. 2012). The lower river valley settlements tended to supply carbohydrates and fabrics, while fishy links to the coasts were maintained for protein and essential fats.

Urbanization is especially evident, in Mesopotamia for example, where the center of complex society reseated from coastal towns at the head of the Persian Gulf to the lower Euphrates River valley. An important example of such an urban couplet was Eridu, generally recognized as the biblical Tower of Babel, and its lower valley descendant Uruk, one of the world's first great cities by 3200 BCE. At that time, the goddess Innana was formally moved from Eridu to Uruk, where a great temple precinct had been prepared to receive her.

One has to wonder how this urbanization played out in moister tropical areas, such as the lower Candelaria, Grijalva, and Usumacinta River systems of Mexico and Guatemala. It appears that wetter areas, such as the southern Gulf Coast, reached this development along a different path—a later, second wave of civilizations (Gunn, Folan et al. 2014). The southern Gulf Coast is a good example, with some of the earliest dates for the domestication of maize and other Mesoamerican cultigens between 6,000 and 7,000 years ago. As would be expected after sea level stabilization, population appears to have increased, as indicated by an influx of carbon into coastal swamps about 7,000 years ago (Pope et al. 2001, 1371). However, like other wet regions, they appear to have increased population without elaboration of the social organization and urbanization (Day et al. 2012; Gunn, Day et al. 2014). Southern China, like the Gulf Coast, was similarly populous but nonelaborating (Liu 2004).

This second wave was probably delayed because tropical coasts and coastal plains at their best, during global warm periods, support large populations without the social structure necessary under seasonally droughty conditions to maintain large, dense, year-around populations (Ford 1996; Ford and Nigh 2009). The infilling of lower river valleys would only have augmented this process. As a result of the ecological richness of tropical coasts and coastal plains, most tropical regions developed complex social organizations a millennium later than arid regions (Gunn, Day et al. 2014). The reason for this was probably a notable global cooling around 4,500 years ago (the early Late Holocene) that resulted in lowering of sea levels by about a meter; less precipitation; lowered river discharge, especially in the tropics; and other conditions that called for more attention to a hierarchical social organization that dry regions like Mesopotamia already possessed. This second worldwide wave of civilizations appeared following this climatic alteration. As we shall see, the second wave followed the rules of tropical ecology rather than those of the deserts, with examples appearing in southern China, the lower Mekong, Sri Lanka, and the lower Mississippi, and among the Olmecs (1400–400 BCE) (see Fletcher 2009; Penny and Fletcher, chapter 9 in this volume).

WATER AND THE ORIGIN OF MAYA CIVILIZATION

Understanding the rise of the Olmecs and their relationships to the early Maya is still a work in progress and important in this context because they appear to have sparked the entry of Maya hunter-gatherers into a Mesoamerican, region-wide economy involving jade that comes exclusively from the Motagua River valley in Honduras. It is clear that human populations began to build around 7,000 years ago in the Olmec homeland around the Grijalva-Bari river system in Veracruz, Mexico (Pope et al. 2001), as well as in the lower Candelaria River (Siemens 2009). Linguistic analyses suggest that Maya speakers originally occupied the southern Gulf Coast before 3,400 years ago and then were displaced by the Zoque-speaking Olmecs who appeared from the Pacific coast (Clark 1993; Josserand 1975; Malmström 1978). However, evident continuities between the cultures before 3,400 years ago and those after raised questions about this relationship. Pool (2007, 189) posits there is room for influence from the Pacific coast but little support for a substantial population intrusion.

Given the extremely rich marine resources that appeared along the southern/southeastern Gulf Coast on the Campeche Bank after 7,000 years ago, it would not be surprising to find multiple, ethnically diverse populations developing in a relatively limited area, in this case around the Laguna de Términos with the Olmecs to the west and the Maya to the east. Day and colleagues (2012) think that increases in populations among multiethnic populations after sea level stabilization may be one of the key elements in the origins of complex societies. Before the early Late Holocene, both developed increasing populations but little in the way of complex society for the simple reason that rich resources could support large populations without the need for much organizational complexity (see Graeber and Wengrow 2021). However, in the increasingly dry early Late Holocene, Olmec Zoque speakers developed and/or imported stratified social organization and architectural methods previously foreign to the Zoque and Maya populations. In this regard, one cannot but be impressed by the fact that there must have been huge populations resident in the San Lorenzo area before the mobilization of the tremendous labor force for this construction.

Approximately 3,000 years ago, the Maya followed this development, possibly first in the lower Grijalva River basin, and then into the highlands and the Yucatán Peninsula (Adams 2005; Hopkins 2011; Pool 2007; Sullivan 2015). The Olmec homeland remained a center of civilization for about a millennium and then returned to its former, diversely stratified self after 400 BCE as the Maya of the Lake District, in the cities of Nakbe and El Mirador, began to dominate trade relations in a great florescence of commerce, learning, and architecture beginning in the Middle Preclassic (~1000–400 BCE). In the Classic period, the center of Zoque-speaking society moved westward to Tres Zapotes in the Tuxtla Mountains (Pool 2007). This migration placed them in the travel ways between the developing Mexican highlands and the Maya lowlands. Like the Chontal Maya, as observed by the Spanish in the Postclassic and Historical periods, they seem to have developed a distributed political economy rather than the highly hierarchical social organizations of cities in the Lake District (Wade 2017).

MAYA, WATER, TRADE, AND MOVEMENT

Like all mountains facing subducted coasts, as in the Pacific coast of Guatemala, the uplifting of the mountains on one side of a landmass creates depressions on the opposite side (Pope and Dahlin 1989; Siemens and Puleston 1972). Such depressions, for example, the Sub-Andean Depression along the east side of the Andes in Peru and the Hercynian Depression on the north side of the Alps in Austria, usually manifest as lines of lakes and swamps, as is found across the southern Maya lowlands. Those lines of swamps and lakes frequently nurture second-wave civilizations.

Into this landscape came the first extensive act of water management by the Maya: making waterways into highways. They linked the Gulf Coast sea along this depression to the only sources of jade in Guatemala (Josserand 2011; Seitz et al. 2001). By whatever means Olmec complexity developed, either troublesome or cooperatively with the Maya, it apparently did not inhibit the Maya from supplying the Olmecs with much-prized jade in great quantities. Around 1000 BCE, the Cholan-speaking Maya, then resident in the Pasión River watershed halfway along the depression, took on this task and the spread of jade is clearly documented through linguistic relationships. At that time the Cholan language spread across the Lake District from the Gulf Coast to beyond the Motagua River in Honduras. The city of Ceibal in Guatemala seems to have been the center of this linguistic efflorescence (Inomata et al. 2015; Josserand 2011).

Exactly how the jade trade was organized on these watery highways is not clear. By 950 BCE, however, jade and all other forms of imported goods, including obsidian, became common across the southern Maya lowlands (Estrada-Belli 2011; Inomata et al. 2015; Lohse 2010). Agriculture and ceramic vessels, previously absent from the peninsular interior, also appeared. The pathways along which trade flowed were evidently diverse and not limited to these watery landscapes—there are a number of possible portages across the peninsula (Adams 1978; Chase and Chase 2011; Laporte, Adánez, and Mejía 2008; Volta and Gunn 2012, 2020), as well as some overland possibilities.

An interesting candidate for a hybrid overland/water route is that taken by Cortés in his transpeninsular entrada of 1524 and 1525 (Scholes and Roys 1968, appendix B). Cortés brought an army from the Mexican highlands that included Spanish men and horses, as well as Indigenous military. At Jonuta on the Usumacinta River, local men roughed out a map for crossing the peninsula and

FIGURE 5.2. (facing page) *Approximate route of Cortés 1524–1525 across the Yucatán Peninsula. The expedition would have avoided the many wetlands and swamps mapped by Kenneth Pope and Bruce Dahlin (1989) but chained together parallel wetlands to carry cross-peninsular traffic (Adams 1978). See text for identifiable details. The Usumacinta / San Pedro Mártir segment of Cortés's route is shown to emphasize the proximity of the two watersheds. One of Cortés's possible routes from the San Pedro to the Candelaria could have been traversed in canoes except for a short portage. During the middle years of the Classic conflicts between Calakmul and Tikal, this route would have been interrupted, NW-SE movement being blocked by a no-cities buffer between the combatants (Adams 2005) and replaced by two routes, one through Calakmul and the other through Tikal, both on SW to NE trajectories through the central Mesoplano (see Gunn, Folan, et al. 2014 for details). This buffer would have included El Mirador, perhaps explaining in part El Mirador's decline at that time. (Route is plotted on Scholes and Roys 1968, map 1.)*

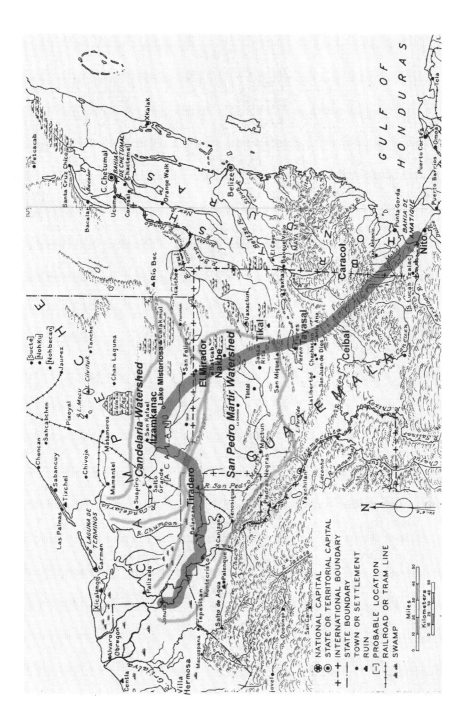

sent him on to Great Acalan on the Candelaria River, where the Chontal Maya could fill in the details because they traded with the east coast (Scholes and Roys 1968, 435). From Jonuta, Cortés trekked up the Usumacinta–San Pedro system to Tenosique (figure 5.2). Then, by building a bridge across the San Pedro Mártir, they crossed over into the Candelaria River farmlands of Acalan. At Acalan, Cortés was instructed by "merchants" on how to proceed to Nito in Honduras (now Guatemala). Paxbolonacha, king of Acalan, gave him 600 porters (Scholes and Roys 1968, 461). As they were leaving Acalan territory, Cortés requisitioned a couple of unsuspecting merchants as guides. From the city of Itzamkanac at the junction of the Candelaria River and its tributaries, the army carved a road eastward through Cehache farmlands toward Lake Misteriosa, then southeastward through forest toward Tayasal on Lake Petén. Up until Tayasal, the journey had been over dry, forested territory, much of it uninhabited. Then, after a more arduous traverse of the Maya Mountains with many horses lost, they arrived at the Dulce River and Nito.

One of the intriguing characteristics of this route is that it passes within a few kilometers of many great, Preclassic cities of the Maya: Itzamkanac, Calakmul, Uxul, Yaxnohkah, El Mirador, Nakbe, Tintal, El Peru or Waka (Freidel, Escobedo, and Guenter 2007), Tikal, Uaxactun, Ceibal, and Caracol. It is unclear if the route passed along the Transversal at the foot of the Sierra Madre Oriental, as described by Arthur Demarest (2007). The problems with the route may have been that while the Acalan merchants were familiar with traveling through the Maya Mountains by foot, the terrain proved devastating to horses (Laporte, Adánez, and Mejía 2008).

Yet, the fact that the Spanish traveled to Honduras with horses indicates that there was an overland path. Rivers also paralleled the route, including the Candelaria (Siemens and Puleston 1972) and Pasión (Demarest 2007) rivers, which could have been and were used for much more efficient canoe transportation (Adams 1978). The route also avoided the most impassable sections of the Usumacinta River system (Aliphat Fernandez 1994; Golden et al. 2012; Gunn and Folan 2000; Schele and Freidel 1990), corresponds in part to a least-cost overland route calculated by Beniamino Volta and Joel D. Gunn (2012, 2020), and corresponds in part to a relatively well-understood transportation route from Cancuen through Corona referred to as the "Calakmul royal road" (Canuto, Baron, and Desailly-Chanson 2012; Demarest et al. 2014; Freidel, Escobedo, and Guenter 2007). It is relevant that the royal road was still used in part, or at least known, in postcontact times.

TROPICAL ECOLOGY AND URBAN FOOTPRINTS

The Maya began to build cities along the Royal/Cortés Road from the Gulf of Mexico to Honduras (see figure 5.2) and other portages in the Middle Preclassic

(1000–400 BCE). Through the middle decades of the twentieth century, there was a great debate about whether the Maya were really urbanized or they just built great ritual monuments that were visited during ritual seasons. This issue was finally resolved as the realization crept through archaeological scholarship that urbanization as it was understood then was a figment of Eurocentric, Medieval imaginations. Cities were visualized as highly concentrated human populations that served as trading centers starting with Venice in the Early Middle Ages and eventually shifting to Florence, Lyon, London, and so on (Braudel 1979). However, as tropical ecology came to be understood, this understanding changed. Tropical ecologists discovered that the tropics are highly bioactive and species diverse (Denevan 1996; Lovejoy and de Padua 1980; Scarborough and Burnside 2010). As the number of species increases, the density of any given species per unit area necessarily declines. Also, in a highly bioactive environment, dense human populations would quickly pollute their environment and expose themselves to pathogens at devastating levels. For these and other reasons, tropical human populations tend to "mimic" biological patterns (Scarborough and Burnside 2010, 335). This set of tropical ecology relationships devastated archaeologists' urban imaginings as Eurocentric preconceptions gave way to thinking about alternative urban designs.

Vernon Scarborough and Fred Valdez (2009) found applications of the idea in a concept of aggregations of communities with diverse functions, all summing to the necessary social functions of a complex society, such as trade; a trading community where markets were held; diplomacy, where issues with other communities were resolved in the presence of ball games; and religion, where matters of ritual were dealt with and executed to coordinate social activities and insure correct planting times of crops. Perhaps the term "conurbation" as used by Anne Pyburn (2008, 255) applies here—"a number of cities or towns that form one continuous settlement area"—and one could add, sociocultural function. This structure dispersed the population over a landscape enough so that in a well-watered climate the environment could purify itself of adverse microbial activity simultaneously with habitation by human extended families. In addition to explaining the low densities of tropical societies, this concept might enable understanding of the upper bounds of human population densities given varying precipitation quantities and microbial species (Lucero, Gunn, and Scarborough 2011). Study of microbial outputs in sediments may enable species-density quantification in water supplies (White et al. 2018). The additional population densities enriched communications and facilitated trade in a manner characteristic of urban settlements.

Once recognized, these dispersed tropical urban footprints became evident in other tropical habitats, such as the Amazon River basin (Heckenberger et al. 2008) and Southeast Asia (Penny and Fletcher, chapter 9 in this volume), and probably remains to be appreciated in other regions, such as the Congo River basin. One has to also ask if nontropical, nonurban, or sparsely populated landscapes, such as that of the Celts of pre-Roman Europe (Crumley 1987), might have operated on similar principles.

China is an interesting case parallel to the Maya lowlands. The Great Central Plain, one of China's cradles of civilizations, is located on the interface between the tropics and subtropics much as is the Yucatán Peninsula but at a much larger scale. Large populations developed there in the Middle Holocene, when the area was tropical because of a warmer global climate that expanded the tropics toward the poles. In the change from Middle to Late Holocene about 4,500 years ago, the Great Central Plain shifted from being tropical to subtropical, which is to say seasonally dry. Global cooling contracted the tropics equatorward. Since the 1930s, the Central Plain Middle Holocene is generally identified as being "Neolithic" while the Late Holocene is "civilized." However, Li Liu's (2004) analysis of the settlement patterns indicates that the Middle Holocene was socially stratified with a tropical urban footprint like the southern, lowland Maya. The Chinese Late Holocene was civilized in a fashion more like the Medieval, European, urban stereotype.

The dispersed, tropical urban footprint of the Maya lowlands, and the need for competitive, higher aggregation of populations imposed by trade relations and communications, brings out the essential conflict between habitat and economic objectives in Maya history. One of the essential rules of commerce is that the closer people are together, the less time it takes to seal commercial agreements and focus on transporting goods (Cowgill 2004; Gunn, Folan et al. 2014; Gunn et al. 2017; van der Leeuw 2007). Taken to extremes in the modern era, such principles engender the straightening of fiber optics between Chicago and New York to speed up trading by milliseconds. In Classic Maya times, shortening communications lines was at the level of assembling populations in earshot. The southern lowland Maya achieved this by moving their primary cities out of potentially fetid swampy lowlands in the Lake District on to promontories in the elevated interior Mesoplano. They were wedged between the rivers of the central lowlands and the cenotes of the northern lowlands, so no resident groundwater was available (see Dunning et al., chapter 2 in this volume). The only water solution was to equip them with rain-catching reservoirs. Each rainy season, the cities were flushed clean and the reservoirs refilled. Both Calakmul and Tikal are located about 40 km from permanent water, perhaps pointing to some sort of underlying, active principle relative to departure from permanent water. More on this later.

To review efforts to scale up the Maya economy, initial steps to place communities on the Royal/Cortés Road took place in watery environments at Ceibal on the Pasión River (Inomata et al. 2015) and Nakbe on a lake in the Middle

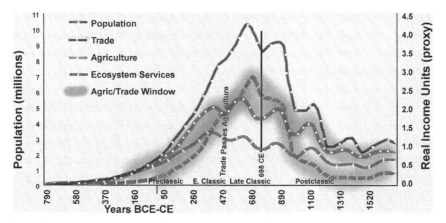

FIGURE 5.3. *Simulation of the Classic economy estimates that trade became the most valuable activity in the economy in the middle of the Classic period. Dates are approximate, but it is worth noting that a simulation based almost entirely on geographic and social dynamics internal to the peninsula could convincingly approximate the historical record. Trade is very low in the Postclassic because the simulation only represents intrapeninsular trade, not extrapeninsular trade, which was probably substantial (adapted from Heckbert, Costanza, and Parrott 2014, figure 2).*

Preclassic (Hansen 1991). This was at the time the Olmec Homeland was being deurbanized in favor of El Tajin on the path to highland Mexico and commerce with the Maya lowlands. At that time in the Late Preclassic, the growing trading ambitions of the Maya and their communications systems' needs must have come into conflict with their wet environments. A simulation of the Preclassic and Classic economies (figure 5.3) suggests that trade began to expand dramatically in the Late Preclassic, around 50 CE (Heckbert, Costanza, and Parrott 2014, 58–59). Probably the first efforts to overcome the trade/information/water conflict were taken in the Late Preclassic as the focus of command moved from Nakbe to a less fetid location and a much grander city building design at El Mirador—it involved modest landscape modifications to control water with dams blocking down slop water flows (see Dunning et al., chapter 2 in this volume; Matheny and Matheny 2011, pocket map). However modest, it facilitated the largest-ever Indigenous city. Some of the sustainability of this situation was probably supported by a moister environment that helped with both watering and cleansing (Wahl et al. 2006; see Freidel and colleagues, chapter 6 in this volume for additional discussion of climate changes). This design proved to be an intermediate effort to meet the communications demands of trade relations through seasonal water management. As can be seen in figure 5.3, trade values surpassed combined agriculture and ecosystem services in the early Late Classic, around 550 CE under the Kaan kings. Following that time, a water control project of great scale was constructed at Calakmul (Folan et al. 1995; Gunn et al. 2002), Calakmul's golden age. In the next section, I will discuss a perspective on a cascade of calamity this final solution eventually precipitated, and the Maya system's sustainable resolution to it.

WATERY CITIES: HOW THE INTERIOR CITIES GOT THEMSELVES INTO TROUBLE AND HOW THE MAYA FIXED IT

Maya urbanization went through stages of development in terms of how water was managed (Lucero, Gunn, and Scarborough 2011; Scarborough 1993a, 1993b). During the early stage, in the Middle and Late Preclassic, cities relied on natural water basins as sources of their water, referred to as "concave watersheds," a stage of landscape development originally outlined by Vernon Scarborough (1993a, 1993b; see also Dunning et al., chapter 2 in this volume). In the Calakmul/ Mirador region this stage is clear at Middle Preclassic Nakbe, noted above. There, the city was built around a natural lake (Jacob 1995). The lake not only supplied water, but also highly organic bottom sediments that were a source of fertilizer for terrace gardens (Hansen et al. 2002). Interestingly, the Nakbe period appears to have been wetter than the subsequent Classic period (Torrescano and Islebe 2009; Wahl et al. 2006). Perhaps the city achieved some amount of longevity because it was regularly flushed out by stronger tropical rains. Although it became a source of elaborate ceramics in the Classic period (Reents-Budet et al. 2011), Nakbe never matched the size and splendor of its successor El Mirador (Hansen 1998). El Mirador represented a slight adjustment of the concave water resource design; it was built on a westward-sloping land surface (Domínguez Carrasco et al. 2011) upon which dams could be constructed to retain water. El Mirador represents the most energetic architectural period of the Maya lowlands, as indicated by the sheer volume of construction. Even after its population was much diminished in the Classic period, it remained an elaborate pilgrimage destination (Hansen 2004). Remnant cities rechristened as pilgrimage destinations are a frequent feature of long-term cultures worldwide such as in Mesopotamia, where Kish was abandoned in favor of Baghdad (Yoffee 2016, 6–7).

The next stage in Scarborough's landscape evolution idea is that of the convex water microcatchments, the construction of cities on promontories or at the heads of watersheds in the Mesoplano, as Dunning and colleagues point out (Dunning, Beach, and Luzzadder-Beach 2012; Dunning et al. 2013). Calakmul, Caracol (see Chase et al., chapter 7 in this volume), and Tikal are the exemplars of this design. Calakmul is only 37 km north of El Mirador and represents the next stage in the evolution, after Nakbe and El Mirador. Under gradually drying conditions of the later first millennium CE, the El Mirador design, and certainly the Nakbe design, would have become untenable for large populations because of disease. By then the Maya trading economy must have been

FIGURE 5.4. *Visual simulation of Classic period Calakmul, 3D Fly Through. See Scarborough et al. (2012) for a map of the Tikal water city (adapted from Winemiller et al. 2011 simulation; Gunn, Folan, et al. 2014, figure 8.6).*

huge (Heckbert, Costanza, and Parrott 2014; Masson 2012; Masson and Freidel 2012). The most likely reason for the location of Calakmul is that its promontory overlooks El Laberinto Bajo, a 10 km wide gap through the Elevated Interior Region or Mesoplano of the peninsula, and therefore the most engineerable of the transpeninsular portages (Gunn, Folan et al. 2014; Volta and Gunn 2012, 2020). The other possible portages are narrow valleys that would have been impassable in the rainy season. The Calakmul engineers could have built dams and canals at El Laberinto, making year-round water transportation possible. It may be the reason El Mirador was such an ideal location and accommodated support for such a large population—it controlled both the Royal/Cortés Road mentioned above and El Laberinto Bajo; thus it was the crossroads of two important trading avenues. During the Calakmul golden age, Calakmul became the terminus of the Royal Road.

During its golden age, Calakmul represents the convex water management design. Two large reservoirs were constructed in a water district near the ritual precinct of the city to collect water (figure 5.4) (Domínguez Carrasco 1991; Folan et al. 1995; Winemiller et al. 2011), apparently for consumption. Water was collected from the hills to the southeast along canals flanked by temples and from the plaster-covered architecture and courtyards (Folan et al. 1995; Gunn, Folan, et al. 2014). Large reservoirs were built, all masonry lined, in the bajo below the promontory, apparently to collect gray water for irrigation of bajo-edge agricultural fields (Geovannini Acuña 2008; Gunn et al. 2002). All of the reservoirs had to be masonry lined to keep rainwater from coming into contact with an underlying gypsum veneer emplaced over the peninsula by the Chicxulub impact 65 million years ago (Gunn et al. 2009; Perry, Velazquez Oliman, and Wagner 2011).

Calakmul's promontory ritual precinct contained large pyramids, markets, and palaces that would have allowed for close packing of many citizens important to the Calakmul state, the largest of the Maya polities (Adams 2005). Not only was the center of the city a great concentration of administrative personnel, but there were at least ten additional palace complexes (Fletcher and Gann 1994). Administrative subunits were distributed around hydrological subsections of the city, each dependent on and responsible for a local *aguada* (reservoir) and its surrounding barrio (Gunn et al. 2002). Like the main promontory, each would have been self-sanitizing and self-watering, as long as there was sufficient precipitation. This conurbation of barrios would have supplied the personnel for various administrative tasks and some surplus food to support the bureaucracy. The bureaucracy would have been organized into three departments—policy, military, and religion (Folan, Gunn, and Domínguez Carrasco 2001)—a long-standing Maya sociopolitical pattern (Freidel et al. 2017).

The advantages and disadvantages of such an urban design are many. Most important, the design allowed for the concentration of an administrative bureaucracy at the peak of the Maya lowlands' Late Classic trading surge (Heckbert, Costanza, and Parrott 2014). Evidence from murals in the promontory marketplace indicate a wide range of everyday comestible market items (Carrasco Vargas, Vázquez López, and Martin 2009); it seems likely that the transpeninsular trade in highly valued minerals, such as jade and granite, continued (Braswell et al. 2004). However, by some means or for some reason, the trade in obsidian was either of little interest or not accessible to the Calakmul elites (Braswell 2013; Braswell et al. 2004).

From an information exchange point of view, Calakmul would have provided a dense menu of exchange possibilities to traders and elites dependent on controlling traders. Such hubs are generally regarded as consisting of about 10,000 or more information personnel and supporting populations (Cowgill 2004; van der Leeuw 2007). Clearly the city easily contained that many persons, estimated at minimally 50,000 based on current mapping of the central 30 km² of the city (Folan et al. 1995; May Hau et al. 1990).

Two main liabilities are evident. For one, the construction, and even more so the maintenance, of such an infrastructure would have been very demanding in terms of labor inputs, creating a very high annual energy gradient (Tainter et al. 2003) that had to be supplied by human labor, particularly for the restoration of the water by the wet season. In other words, the city was engineered to control water gradients so that available water declined slowly enough to last through the dry season. Second, the population would have been totally dependent on precipitation for critical water supplies. The first of these points, the ability to supply labor, would have been strongly dependent on a sustainable bureaucracy with good potential to provide administrative guidance year after year. Of course, the second, regular and predictable precipitation, was dependent on global climate and its highly sensitive variations typical of the boundary between the tropics and the subtropics (Gunn and Folan 2000; Gunn, Folan, and Robichaux 1995).

By the time that Calakmul rose to its golden age between 500 and 700 CE, the peak of the transpeninsular Maya trading economy, the utility of the Royal/ Cortés Road had been compromised by conflicts with Tikal. An early battle between the two is recorded at Naachtun in 486 CE (Martin and Grube 2008, 39). In fact, the period of Calakmul's prominence corresponds to an episode when an alliance between Calakmul and Caracol managed to subdue the ambitions of the Tikal elites (Robichaux 2010; see Chase et al., chapter 7, in this volume for further discussion of Caracol). During this time, Calakmul was able to maintain open access to the Royal Road by military action against distant cities such as Palenque (Martin and Grube 2008), and by establishing a trading colony at Cancuen (Demarest et al. 2014). When the alliance folded to Tikal's growing balance of power in the early 700s CE, Calakmul lost its prominence in the interior lowlands. It would also have been subjected to serious, long-term droughts in the late 700s and 800s CE, during which it was abandoned by its former rulers, apparently in favor of the growing economic importance of coastal cities. Thus, Calakmul's two main liabilities were challenged. Soon after, Calakmul and El Mirador were occupied by groups from the north, possibly Oxpemul in alliance with Tikal (Robichaux 2010).

Similar tales of water city evolution can probably be constructed for Caracol and Tikal. Ceibal could have served as concave-stage antecedent for Caracol judging by proximity and the distribution of E-Groups between the cities (Chase and Chase 2017). Uaxactun and/or Cival (Estrada-Belli 2011) might be concave antecedents for Tikal. This suggests that Scarborough's model is extensible and productive, in that it applies to much else besides the Calakmul state.

How Maya society fixed the problems created by the ninth-century droughts is not complex. By the Late Classic, coastal cities had been developing marine transportation, navigation, and commerce for a millennium (Gunn et al. 2017). Thanks to the much-reduced costs of transporting goods by sea, not to mention the more dependable water resources of the coastal plains and coastal zones, by the Late Classic the interior cites must have been at a great disadvantage because of their portaging. There are signs, in fact, that by the Late Classic, the great interior cites were economically moribund. Among them, the hegemonic capital of the central and southern lowlands, Tikal, had pulled in its perimeter to little more than the city itself and by doing so sacrificed its supporting hinterlands and clients (Lentz et al. 2014; Lentz et al., chapter 3 in this volume; Martin and Grube 2008). In at least one case, that of the Kaan rulers of Calakmul during its golden age, they appear to have fled to a coastal plain town, Calkini, and continued as part of the administrative structure of that city (Folan, Bolles, and Ek 2016). Ruling families appear to have been flexible in their headquarters' locations in the Classic, so it would not be surprising to find all the great interior families reordering their business plans toward efficient transportation by sea. Why did they leave the magnificent architecture behind? A question for another day.

CONCLUSIONS

Taken as a whole, these three ideas—watery origins, tropical footprints, and water cities—stitch together a historical narrative of the shape and evolution of water management practices among the Maya polities. They also, as foundational concepts, serve as an explanation of much of the underpinnings of the Maya civilization, since, as Scarborough (see also Ford 1996) pointed out, water management is essential for complex society, especially those sitting on the edge of the dynamic, tropical edge of the subtropics. Of course, there are other components to that model that require attention, such as why writing was developed and why an elaborate agricultural ritual system, represented by E-Groups, is so evident in the Mayas' astronomical system (Milbrath 1999; Šprajc 2004).

A concept that Scarborough has added to the mix in recent years is the idea of the past informing the future. With anthropogenic global warming accelerating at an alarming rate in the last decade, the modern global economic system needs all the advice it can get in terms of understanding and implementing solutions. The "past informing" concept must surely be exploited in understanding and resolving this problem. The Intergovernmental Panel on Climate Change (IPCC) recently issued a report estimating that the world economy has about a quarter century to reverse the impacts of global warming. One can hope that the Maya narrative will be a part of this resolution. Of special importance in this analogy is that the Maya society of the first millennium CE was, like the modern world, not a hierarchical state but a diverse league founded on common cultural principles. The commonality in the modern world is more economic than cultural, though that commonality seems to be lending to a new worldwide cultural commonality but not a global, hierarchical government.

REFERENCES

Adams, Richard E.W. 1978. *Routes of Communication in Mesoamerica: The Northern Guatemalan Highlands and the Peten*. Paper read at Mesoamerican Routes and Contacts and Cultural Contacts, at Brigham Young University, Provo, Utah.

Adams, Richard E.W. 2005. *Prehistoric Mesoamerica*. 3rd ed. Norman: University of Oklahoma Press.

Aliphat Fernandez, Mario M. 1994. *Classic Maya Landscape in the Upper Usumacinta River Valley*. Calgary: Department of Archaeology, University of Calgary.

Braswell, Geoffrey E. 2013. "Ancient Obsidian Procurement and Production in the Peten Campechano: Uxul and Calakmul during the Early Classic to Terminal Classic Periods." *Indiana* 30: 149–171.

Braswell, Geoffrey E., Joel D. Gunn, María del Rosario Domínguez Carrasco, William J. Folan, Laraine A. Fletcher, Abel Morales Lopez, and Michael D. Glascock. 2004. "Defining the Terminal Classic at Calakmul, Campeche." In *The Terminal Classic in the Maya Lowlands: Collapse, Tradition, and Transformation*, edited by A. A. Demarest, P. M. Rice, and D. S. Rice, 162–194. Boulder: University Press of Colorado.

Braudel, Fernand. 1979. *The Perspective of the World: Civilization and Capitalism 15th–18th Century*. Vol. 3. New York: Harper and Row, Publishers.

Broadhurst, C. L., Y. Wang, M. A. Crawford, S. C. Cunnane, J. E. Parkington, and W. F. Schmidt. 2002. "Brain-Specific Lipids from Marine, Lacustrine, or Terrestrial Food Resources: Potential Impact on Early African Homo Sapiens." *Comparative Biochemistry and Physiology—Part B: Biochemistry & Molecular Biology* 131 (4): 653–673.

Canuto, Marcello, Joanne Baron, and Yann Desailly-Chanson. 2012. *La Corona and Calakul's "Royal Road."* Memphis: Society for American Archaeology.

Carrasco Vargas, Ramón, Verónica A. Vázquez López, and Simon Martin. 2009. "Daily Life of the Ancient Maya Recorded on Murals at Calakmul, Mexico." *Proceedings of the National Academy of Sciences* 106 (46): 19245–19249.

Chase, Arlen F., and Diane Z. Chase. 2011. *Belize Red Ceramics and Their Implications for Trade and Exchange in the Eastern Maya Lowlands*. Paper read at 9th Belize Archaeology Symposium, San Ignacio, Cayo, Belize.

Chase, Arlen F., and Diane Z. Chase. 2017. "E Groups and the Rise of Complexity in the Southeastern Maya Lowlands." In *Maya E Groups: Calendars, Astronomy, and Urbanism in the Early Lowlands*, edited by D. A. Freidel, A. F. Chase, A. S. Dowd, and J. Murdock, 31–74. Gainesville: University Press of Florida.

Clark, John E. 1993. "Quiénes fueron los olmecas." Paper read at Segundo y Tercer Foro de Archeología de Chiapas, Tuxtla Gutiérrez, Chiapas, Mexico.

Cowgill, George L. 2004. "Origins and Development of Urbanism: Archaeological Perspectives." *Annual Review of Anthropology* 33: 525–549.

Crumley, Carole L. 1987. "Celtic Settlement before the Conquest: The Dialectics of Landscape and Power." In *Regional Dynamics: Burgundian Landscapes Historical Perspective*, edited by Carole L. Crumley and William H. Marquardt, 403–429. Academic Press, San Diego.

Day, John W., Jr., Joel D. Gunn, William J. Folan, and Alejandro Yáñez-Arancibia. 2012. "The Influence of Enhanced Post-glacial Coastal Margin Productivity on the Emergence of Complex Societies." *Journal of Island and Coastal Archaeology* 7 (1): 23–52.

Day, John W., Jr., Joel D. Gunn, William J. Folan, Alejandro Yáñez-Arancibia, and Benjamin P. Horton. 2007. "Emergence of Complex Societies after Sea Level Stabilized." *EOS Transaction, American Geophysical Union* 88 (15): 169–170.

Demarest, Arthur A. 2007. *The Great Western Trade Route and the Development and Decline of Classic Maya Civilization*. Paper read at Society for American Archaeology, Austin.

Demarest, Arthur A., Chloé Andrieu, Paola Torres, Mélanie Forné, Tomás Barrientos, and Marc Wolf. 2014. "Economy, Exchange, and Power: New Evidence from the Late Classic Maya Port City of Cancuen." *Ancient Mesoamerica* 25 (1): 187–219.

Denevan, William M. 1996. "A Bluff Model of Riverine Settlement in Prehistoric Amazonia." *Annals of the Association of American Geographers* 86 (4): 654–681.

Domínguez Carrasco, María del Rosario. 1991. "El sistema hidráulico de Calakmul, Campeche." *Información* 15: 51–83.

Domínguez Carrasco, María del Rosario, William J. Folan, Gary Gates, Beniamino Volta, Raymundo González Heredia, Joel D. Gunn, Abel Morales López, and Hubert Robichaux. 2011. *Oxpemul, su altiplanicie Kárstica Ondulada-Calakmul y su Cuenca: El Preclásico*. Paper read at XXV Simposio de Investigaciones Arqueológicas en Guatemala, Ciudad de Guatemala, Guatemala.

Dunning, Nicholas P., Timothy Beach, Liwy Grazioso Sierra, John Jones, David L. Lentz, Sheryl Luzzadder Beach, Vernon L. Scarborough, and Michael P. Smyth. 2013. "A Tale of Two Collapses: Environmental Variability and Cultural Disruption in the Maya Lowlands." *Diálogo Andino* 41: 171–183.

Dunning, Nicholas P., Timothy P. Beach, and Sheryl Luzzadder-Beach. 2012. "Kax and Kol: Collapse and Resilience in Lowland Maya Civilization." *Proceedings of the National Academy of Sciences* 109 (10): 3652–3657.

Estrada-Belli, Francisco. 2011. *The First Maya Civilization: Ritual and Power before the Classic Period*. New York: Routledge.

Fletcher, Laraine A., and James A. Gann. 1994. "Análisis gráfico de patrones de asentamiento: El caso Calakmul." In *Campeche maya colonial*, edited by W. J. Folan Higgins, 84–121. Campeche: Universidad Autónoma de Campeche.

Fletcher, Roland. 2009. "Low-Density, Agrarian-Based Urbanism: A Comparative View." *Insights* 2 (4): 2–20.

Folan, William J., David D. Bolles, and Jerald D. Ek. 2016. "On the Trail of Quetzalcoatl/Kukulcan: Mythic Trade Routes, Interaction Networks, and Interpolity Connections in the Maya Lowlands." *Ancient Mesoamerica* 27 (2): 293–318.

Folan, William J., Joel D. Gunn, and María del Rosario Domínguez Carrasco. 2001. "Triadic Temples, Central Plazas, and Dynastic Palaces: A Diachronic Analysis of the Royal Court Complex, Calakmul, Campeche, Mexico." In *Royal Courts of the Ancient Maya: Data and Case Studies*, edited by T. Inomata and S. D. Houston, 223–265. Boulder: Westview.

Folan, William J., Joyce Marcus, Sophia Pincemin, María del Rosario Domínguez Carrasco, Laraine Fletcher, and Abel Morales López. 1995. "Calakmul: New Data from an Ancient Maya Capital in Campeche, Mexico." *Latin American Antiquity* 6 (4): 310–334.

Ford, Anabel. 1996. "Critical Resource Control and the Rise of the Classic Period Maya." In *The Managed Mosaic: Ancient Maya Agriculture and Resource Use*, edited by S. Fedick, 297–303. Salt Lake City: University of Utah Press.

Ford, Anabel, and Ronald Nigh. 2009. "Origins of the Maya Forest Garden: Maya Resource Management." *Journal of Ethnobiology* 29 (2): 213–236.

Freidel, David A., Arlen F. Chase, Anne S. Dowd, and Jerry Murdock. 2017. *Maya E Groups: Calendars, Astronomy, and Urbanism in the Early Lowlands.* Gainesville: University Press of Florida.

Freidel, David A., Hector L. Escobedo, and Stanley P. Guenter. 2007. "A Crossroads of Conquerors: Waka' and Gordon Willey's 'Rehearsal for the Collapse' Hypothesis." In *Gordon R. Willey and American Archaeology: Contemporary Perspectives*, edited by J. A. Sabloff and W. L. Fash, 187–208. Norman: University of Oklahoma Press.

Freidel, David, Linda Schele, and Joy Parker. 1993. *Maya Cosmos: Three Thousand Years on the Shaman's Path.* New York: W. Morrow.

Geovannini Acuña, Helga. 2008. *Rain Harvesting in the Rainforest: The Ancient Maya Agricultural Landscape of Calakmul, Campeche, Mexico.* Vol. 1879, BAR International Series. Oxford: Archaeopress.

Golden, Charles, Andrew Scherer, A. René Muñoz, and Zachary Hruby. 2012. "Polities, Boundaries and Trade in the Classic Period Usumacinta River Basin." *Mexicon* 34 (1): 11–19.

Graeber, David, and David Wengrow. 2021. *The Dawn of Everything: A New History of Humanity.* Farrar, Straus and Giroux, New York.

Gunn, Joel D., and R.E.W. Adams. 1981. "Climatic Change, Culture, and Civilization in North America." *World Archaeology* 13 (1): 85–100.

Gunn, Joel D., John W. Day, Alejandro Yáñez-Arancibia, Alfred H. Siemens, and Betty B. Faust. 2014. "The Maya in Global Perspective: The Dawn of Complex Societies, the Beginning of the Anthropocene, and the Future of the Earth System." Paper presented at the Annual Conference of the SAA, Austin, TX.

Gunn, Joel D., and William J. Folan. 2000. "Three Rivers: Subregional Variations in Earth System Impacts in the Southwestern Maya Lowlands (Candelaria, Usumacinta, and Champoton Watersheds)." In *The Way the Wind Blows: Climate, History, and Human Action*, edited by R. Mcintosh, J. Tainter and S. Mcintosh, 223–270. New York: Columbia University Press.

Gunn, Joel D., William J. Folan, Christian Isendahl, María del Rosario Domínguez Carrasco, Betty B. Faust, and Beniamino Volta. 2014. "Calakmul: Agent Risk and Sustainability in the Western Maya Lowlands." In *The Resilience and Vulnerability of Ancient Landscapes: Transforming Maya Archaeology through IHOPE*, edited by A. F. Chase and V. L. Scarborough. Toronto, ON: American Anthropological Association.

Gunn, Joel D., William J. Folan, María del Rosario Domínguez Carrasco, and Frank Miller. 2009. "Explicando la sustentabilidad de Calakmul, Campeche: Eslabones interiores en El Sistema de Energía del Estado Regional de Calakmul." In *Encuentro Internacional de Los Investigadores de La Cultura Maya*, XVIII, Toma 1: 13–40. Campeche: Universidad Autónoma de Campeche.

Gunn, Joel D., William J. Folan, Nuria Torrescano Valle, Betty B. Faust, Helga Geovannini Acuña, and Alfred H. Siemens. 2019. "From Calakmul to the Sea: A Holistic Perspective on Calakmul and the Candelaria / Champoton Watershed Systems Historical Ecologies." In *Ecology of the Southern Yucatan Peninsula*, edited by Nuría Torrescano Valle, 209–248. Springer.

Gunn, Joel, William J. Folan, and Hubert R. Robichaux. 1995. "A Landscape Analysis of the Candelaria Watershed in Mexico: Insights into Paleoclimates Affecting Upland Horticulture in the Southern Yucatan Peninsula Semi-Karst." *Geoarchaeology* 10 (1): 3–42.

Gunn, Joel D., John E. Foss, William J. Folan, Ma del Rosario Domínguez Carrasco, and Betty B. Faust. 2002. "Bajo Sediments and the Hydraulic System of Calakmul, Campeche, Mexico." *Ancient Mesoamerica* 13 (2): 297–315.

Gunn, Joel D., Vernon L. Scarborough, William J. Folan, Christian Isendahl, Arlen F. Chase, Jeremy A. Sabloff, and Beniamino Volta. 2017. "A Distribution Analysis of the Central Maya Lowlands Ecoinformation Network: Its Rises, Falls, and Changes." *Ecology and Society* 22 (1): 20. https://doi.org/10.5751/ES-08931-220120.

Hannah, L., G. F. Midgley, T. Lovejoy, W. J. Bond, M. Bush, J. C. Lovett, D. Scott, and F. I. Woodward. 2002. "Conservation of Biodiversity in a Changing Climate." *Conservation Biology* 16:264–268.

Hansen, R. D. 1991. "The Maya Rediscovered: The Road to Nakbe." *Natural History* 5 (91): 8–14.

Hansen, Richard D. 1998. "Continuity and Disjunction: The Pre-Classic Antecedents of Classic Maya Architecture." In *Function and Meaning in Classic Maya Architecture*, edited by S. D. Houston, 49–122. Washington, DC: Dumbarton Oaks.

Hansen, Richard D. 2004. "El Mirador, Guatemala: El apogeo del Preclásico en el área maya." *Arqueología Mexicana* 11 (66): 28–33.

Hansen, R. D., S. Bozarth, J. Jacob, D. Wahl, and T. Schreiner. 2002. "Climatic and Environmental Variability in the Rise of Maya Civilization: A Preliminary Perspective from the Northern Peten." *Ancient Mesoamerica* 13 (2): 273–295.

Heckbert, Scott, Robert Costanza, and Lael Parrott. 2014. "Achieving Sustainable Societies: Lessons from Modelling the Ancient Maya." *Solutions* 5 (5): 55–64.

Heckenberger, Michael J., J. Christian Russell, Carlos Fausto, Joshua R. Toney, Morgan J. Schmidt, Edithe Pereira, Bruna Franchetto, and Afukaka Kuikuro. 2008. "Pre-Columbian Urbanism, Anthropogenic Landscapes, and the Future of the Amazon." *Science* 321 (5893): 1214–1217.

Hopkins, Nicholas A. 2011. *The Origin of the Southern Mayan Languages*. Paper read at Society for American Archaeology, Annual Meeting.

Inomata, Takeshi, Jessica MacLellan, Daniela Triadan, Jessica Munson, Melissa Burham, Kazuo Aoyama, Hiroo Nasu, Flory Pinzon, and Hitoshi Yonenobu. 2015. "Development of Sedentary Communities in the Maya Lowlands: Coexisting Mobile Groups and Public Ceremonies at Ceibal, Guatemala." *Proceedings of the National Academy of Sciences* 112 (14): 4268–4273.

Jacob, John S. 1995. "Archaeological Pedology in the Maya Lowlands." In *Special Publication 44*. Madison, WI: Soil Science Society of America.

Josserand, Katheryn. 1975. *Archaeological and Linguistic Correlations for Mayan Prehistory*. Paper read at Actas del XII Congreso Internacional de Americanistas, at Mexico, September 2 to 7, 1974.

Josserand, J. Kathryn. 2011. "Languages of the Preclassic Period along the Pacific Coastal Plains of Southeastern Mesoamerica." In *The Southern Maya in the Late Preclassic; The Rise and Fall of an Early Mesoamerican Civilization*, edited by M. Love and J. Kaplan, 141–174. Boulder: University Press of Colorado.

Laporte, Juan Pedro, Jesús Adánez, and Héctor H. Mejía. 2008. "Entre cayucos y caites: Una ruta de interacción entre el mar Caribe y el río Pasión." In *XXI Simposio de Arqueología en Guatemala, 2007*. Digital version, edited by J. P. Laporte, B. Arroyo and H. Mejía. Museo Nacional de Arqueología y Etnología, Guatemala City.

Lentz, David L., Nicholas P. Dunning, Vernon L. Scarborough, Kevin S. Magee, Kim M. Thompson, Eric Weaver, Christopher Carr et al. 2014. "Forests, Fields, and the Edge of Sustainability at the Ancient Maya City of Tikal." *Proceedings of the National Academy of Sciences* 111 (52): 18513–18518.

Liu, Li. 2004. *The Chinese Neolithic: Trajectories to Early States*. New Studies in Archaeology, edited by W. Ashmore, C. Gamble, J. O'Shea, and C. Renfrew. Cambridge: Cambridge University Press.

Lohse, Jon C. 2010. "Archaic Origins of the Lowland Maya." *Latin American Antiquity* 21 (3): 312–352.

Lovejoy, T. E., and M.T.J. de Padua. 1980. "Scientific Help towards Saving Amazonian Species?" *Environmental Conservation* 7 (4): 288.

Lucero, Lisa J., Joel D. Gunn, and Vernon L. Scarborough. 2011. "Climate Change and Classic Maya Water Management." *Water International* 3 (2): 1-x.

Malmström, Vincent H. 1978. "A Reconstruction of the Chronology of Mesoamerican Calendrical Systems." *Journal for the History of Astronomy* 9: 105–116.

Marean, Curtis W., Miryam Bar-Matthews, Jocelyn Bernatchez, Erich Fisher, Paul Goldberg, Andy I. R. Herries, Zenobia Jacobs et al. 2007. "Early Human Use of Marine Resources and Pigment in South Africa during the Middle Pleistocene." *Nature* 449 (October): 905–907. https://doi.org/doi:10.1038/nature06204.

Martin, Simon, and Nikolai Grube. 2008. "Chronicle of the Maya Kings and Queens: Deciphering the Dynasties of the Ancient Maya." 2nd ed. London: Thames and Hudson.

Masson, Marilyn A. 2012. Maya Collapse Cycles. *Proceedings of the National Academy of Sciences* 109 (45): 18237–18238.

Masson, Marilyn A., and David A. Freidel. 2012. "An Argument for Classic Era Maya Market Exchange." *Journal of Anthropological Archaeology* 31 (4): 455–484.

Matheny, Ray T., and Deanne G. Matheny. 2011. *Introduction to Investigations at El Mirador, Petén, Guatemala*. El Mirador Series, Part 1. Papers of the New World Archaeological Foundation, Number Fifty-Nine. Provo, UT: New World Archaeological Foundation, Brigham Young University.

May Hau, J., Rogelio Couoh Muñoz, R. González Heredia, and W. J. Folan. 1990. *Mapa de Calakmul, Campeche, México*. Campeche: CIHS, Universidad Autónoma de Campeche.

Milbrath, Susan. 1999. *Star Gods of the Maya: Astronomy in Art, Folklore, and Calendars*. Austin: University of Texas Press.

Perry, Eugene, Guadalupe Velazquez Oliman, and Niklas Wagner. 2011. "Preliminary Investigation of Groundwater and Surface Water Geochemistry in Campeche and Southern Quintana Roo." In *Water Resources in Mexico*, edited by U. Oswald Spring, 87–97. Heidelberg, Germany: Springer.

Pool, Christopher A. 2007. *Olmec Archaeology and Early Mesoamerica, Cambridge World Archaeology*. New York: Cambridge University Press.

Pope, Kevin O., and Bruce H. Dahlin. 1989. "Ancient Maya Wetland Agriculture: New Insights from Ecological and Remote Sensing Research." *Journal of Field Archaeology* 16 (1): 87–106.

Pope, Kevin O., Mary E. D. Pohl, John G. Jones, David L. Lentz, Christopher von Nagy, Francisco J. Vega, and Irvy R. Quitmyer. 2001. "Origin and Environmental Setting of Ancient Agriculture in the Lowlands of Mesoamerica." *Science* 292 (5520): 1370–1373.

Pyburn, K. Anne. 2008. "Pomp and Circumstance before Belize: Ancient Maya Commerce and the New River Conurbation." In *The Ancient City: New Perspectives on Urbanism in the Old and New World*, edited by J. Marcus and J. A. Sabloff, 247–272. Santa Fe, NM: School for Advanced Research Press.

Reents-Budet, Dorie, Sylviane Boucher Le Landais, Yoly Palomo Carrillo, Ronald L. Bishop, and M. James Blackman. 2011. *Cerámica del estilo códice: Nuevos datos de producción y patrones de distribución*. Paper read at XXIV Simposio de Investigaciones Arqueológicas en Guatemala, July 19–24, 2010, Guatemala City.

Robichaux, Hubert R. 2010. *The Ancient Maya Monuments at Oxpemul, Campeche, México*. Mesoweb. http://www.mesoweb.com/publications/Oxpemul.pdf.

Scarborough, Vernon L. 1985. "Resourceful Landscaping: A Maya Lesson." *Archaeology* 38: 58–59.

Scarborough, Vernon L. 1991. *Archaeology at Cerros, Belize, Central America.* Vol. 3: *The Settlement System in a Late Preclassic Maya Community.* Dallas: Southern Methodist University Press.

Scarborough, Vernon L. 1993a. "Water Management in the Southern Maya Lowlands: An Accretive Model for the Engineered Landscape." *Research in Economic Anthropology* 7: 17–69.

Scarborough, Vernon L. 1993b. "Water Management in the Southern Maya Lowlands: An Accretive Model for the Engineered Landscape." In *Economic Aspects of Water Management in the Prehistoric New World*, edited by V. L. Scarborough and B. L. Isaac, 17–69. Greenwich: JAI Press.

Scarborough, Vernon L., and William R. Burnside. 2010. "Complexity and Sustainability: Perspectives from the Ancient Maya and the Modern Balinese." *American Antiquity* 75 (2): 327–363.

Scarborough, Vernon L., Nicholas P. Dunning, Kenneth B. Tankersley, Christopher Carr, Eric Weaver, Liwy Grazioso, Brian Lane, John G. Jones, Palma Buttles, Fred Valdez, and David L. Lentz. 2012. "Water and Sustainable Land Use at the Ancient Tropical City of Tikal, Guatemala." *Proceedings of the National Academy of the Sciences* 109 (31): 12408–12413.

Scarborough, Vernon L., and Fred Valdez Jr. 2009. "An Alternative Order: The Dualistic Economies of the Ancient Maya." *Latin American Antiquity* 20 (1): 207–227.

Schele, Linda, and David Freidel. 1990. *A Forest of Kings: The Untold Story of the Ancient Maya.* New York: William Morrow and Company, Inc.

Scholes, France V., and Ralph L. Roys. 1968. *The Maya Chontal Indians of Acalan-Texchell: A Contribution to the History and Ethnography of the Yucatan Peninsula.* Norman: University of Oklahoma Press.

Seitz, R., G. E. Harlow, V. B. Sisson, and Karl A. Taube. 2001. "'Olmec Blue' and Formative Jade Sources: New Discoveries in Guatemala." *Antiquity* 75 (290): 687–688.

Siemens, Alfred H. 2009. "Un Río en tierra maya." Paper read at Los Investigadores de la Cultura Maya, Campeche.

Siemens, Alfred H., and Dennis E. Puleston. 1972. "Ridged Fields and Associated Features in Southern Campeche: New Perspectives on the Lowland Maya." *American Antiquity* 37 (2): 228–239.

Šprajc, Ivan. 2004. "More on Mesoamerican Cosmology and City Plans." *Latin American Antiquity* 16 (2): 209–216.

Sullivan, Timothy D. 2015. "Shifting Strategies of Political Authority in the Middle through Terminal Formative Polity of Chiapa de Corzo, Chiapas, Mexico." *Latin American Antiquity* 26 (4): 452–472.

Tainter, Joseph A., T.F.H. Allen, Amanda Little, and Thomas W. Hoekstra. 2003. "Resource Transitions and Energy Gain: Contexts of Organization." *Ecology and Society* 7 (3): 4.

Torrescano, Nuria, and G. A. Islebe. 2009. *Palynological and Chronological Evidence of Drought in the Yucatan Maya Lowlands during the Late Holocene.* In preparation.

Torrescano-Valle, Nuria, and G. A. Islebe. 2015. "Holocene Paleoecology, Climate History and Human Influence in the Southwestern Yucatan Peninsula." *Review of Palaeobotany and Palynology* 217:1–8.

van der Leeuw, Sander E. 2007. "Information Processing and Its Role in the Rise of the European World System." In *Sustainability or Collapse? An Integrated History and Future of People on Earth*, edited by R. Costanza, L. J. Graumlich, and W. Steffen, 213–241. Cambridge, MA: MIT Press.

Volta, Beniamino, and Joel D. Gunn. 2012. *Análisis de costo mínimo de posibles rutas de intercambio transpeninsulares en el Petén campechano.* Paper read at 54th International Congress of Americanists, July 15–20, Vienna, Austria.

Volta, Beniamino, and Joel D. Gunn. 2016. *The Political Geography of Long-Distance Trade in the Maya Lowlands: Comparing Proxies for Power Structure and Exchange Networks.* Paper read at Abstracts of the Society for American Archaeology 81st Annual Meeting, Washington, DC.

Volta, Beniamino, Joel D. Gunn, Lynda Florey Folan, William J. Folan, and Geoffrey E. Braswell. 2020. "The Political Geography of Long-Distance Exchange in the Elevated Interior Region of the Yucatán Peninsula." In *The Real Business of Ancient Maya Economies: From Farmers' Fields to Rulers' Realms*, edited by Marilyn A. Masson, David A. Freidel, and Arthur A. Demarest, pp. 352–367. 1st ed. University Press of Florida.

Wade, Lizzie. 2017. "Kings of Cooperation: The Olmec City of Tres Zapotes May Have Owed Its Longevity to a New Form of Government." *Archaeology* 70 (3): 26–29.

Wahl, David, Roger Byrne, Thomas Schreiner, and Richard Hansen. 2006. "Holocene Vegetation Change in the Northern Petén and Its Implications for Maya Prehistory." *Quaternary Research* 65 (3): 380–389.

White, A. J., Lora R. Stevens, Varenka Lorenzi, Samuel E. Munoz, Carl P. Lipo, and Sissel Schroeder. 2018. "An Evaluation of Fecal Stanols as Indicators of Population Change at Cahokia, Illinois." *Journal of Archaeological Science* 93 (May): 129–34. https://doi.org/10.1016/j.jas.2018.03.009.

Winemiller, Terance L., William J. Folan, Jacinto May Hau, Raymundo González H., Fletcher Loraine, L. Florey Folan, Abel Morales L., and Joel D. Gunn. 2011. *Modelos 3d y los sistemas de información geográfica: Descubriendo nueva información en el manejo de los recursos hidrológicos prehistóricos del sitio de Calakmul, Campeche.* Paper read at XXI Encuentro Los Investigadores de La Cultura Maya, Dirección de Difusión Cultural y Centro de Investigaciones Históricas y Sociales, Campeche, Mexico.

Yoffee, Norman. 2016. "The Evolution of Fragility: The Resistible Rise and Irresistible Fall of Early States." In *State Formation and State Decline in the Near and Middle East*, edited by Rainer Kessler, Walter Sommerfeld, and Leslie Tramontini, 6–13. Wiesbaden, Germany: Harrassowitz Verlag.

6

Water Trails and Water Mountains

The View from Northwest Petén

David Freidel, Mary Jane Acuña, Carlos R. Chiriboga, and Michelle Rich

Lisa Lucero and Barbara Fash (2006) and their contributors demonstrate, and Wendy Ashmore (chapter 4 in this volume) underscores, the inextricable bonds between the practical exigencies of water management in pre-Columbian Mesoamerican societies and the sacred and ritual qualities of water to those peoples and their rulers. Already in the Early Preclassic period, by 1600 BCE, Laguna Manatí and its adjacent hill in the heartland of Olman received votive offerings clearly documenting that it was a water mountain, a portal to the supernatural world of gods and ancestors, a symbol of the place of creation (Ortíz Ceballos and Rodríguez 2000). Richard Townsend (1992), in a cogent and seminal essay on the sacred landscape of the Aztecs, describes the royal pilgrimage to Mount Tlaloc to propitiate the seasonal rains. The Aztecs regarded mountains as containers of water (Townsend 1992, 181), with rivers flowing from their feminine divine embodiment in Chalchiuhtlicue (Jade Skirt), wife of the Storm God, Tlaloc. Townsend rightly observed that the water mountain idea was deeply ancient in Mesoamerica, represented in the Preclassic at Chalcatzingo in Morelos and in the Classic at Yaxchilan, the Maya city built into a mountainside framed

https://doi.org/10.5876/9781646422326.c006

by a great oxbow in the Usumacinta River. He related the water mountain trope universal in Mesoamerica to the central Mexican Aztec notion of settlements or dominions as Atl Tepetl, or water and hill places, usually rendered Altepetl in our literature. Here, we use the premises of mountains as containers of water and pyramids as representations of mountains (Freidel, Escobedo, and Melendez 2013; Vogt and Stuart 2005, 157 and figure 2) to discuss the identification of the water mountain at El Perú-Waka'. We further explore the prospect that islands like the one that forms around the site of El Achiotal in the rainy season also manifested the mountainous land that first emerged from the primordial waters and, in this case, was conceived of as the cosmic turtle. The seasonal water trail linking El Perú-Waka' to El Achiotal, and onward to the city of El Tintal to the east, was likely a pilgrimage route as well as a trade route, much like the coastal routes linking Cozumel in trade and commerce at the time of the Conquest (Freidel and Sabloff 1984).

In this chapter, we explore the significance of these concepts at the ancient Maya site of El Perú-Waka', specifically discussing its water mountain and water trail connections to El Achiotal and El Tintal. We hope to respond in this way to Wendy Ashmore's call for explicit contemplation of water symbolism in Maya studies (chapter 4 in this volume). The site's water mountain, called the Mirador locally, is a large natural hill ritually dedicated, and terraformed, at the beginning of the city's history to literally be such a place. In its buildings and offerings, it possesses a symbolic significance that relates it to important aspects of political authority and legitimation in the Wak dynasty realm and the Maya southern lowland world (Freidel 2014). With a more practical function, water trails refer to the network of rivers and streams that flow through northwestern Petén, connecting El Perú-Waka' with other sites, such as El Achiotal and distant El Tintal in the Central Karstic Uplands (CKU), among others. As Gunn (chapter 5 in this volume) illustrates, interior riverine water transport and communication routes played a vital role in Preclassic and Classic period civilization of the central and southern lowlands. Vernon Scarborough (1991) was well aware of this reality regarding the location of Cerro Maya (Cerros) near the mouth of the New River. While Joel Gunn (chapter 5 in this volume) looks principally to the coastal canoe routes as driving the development of social complexity in broad theoretical terms, we are sure that he will take the interior routes into consideration going forward. As the present study of water trails is in progress, we introduce the preliminary results of regional hydraulic models to demonstrate the probability of the water trails branching into northern Petén and provide evidence for the identification of water mountains at El Perú-Waka'. This study has significant implications for enhancing our understanding of the geopolitical landscape, as well as the Indigenous knowledge of water management and symbolism from the Preclassic through the Classic periods.

We begin with a description of the geographical setting of El Perú-Waka' pertaining to the overall theme, followed by a summary of the supporting evidence for the existence of water trails associated with it and for the identification of water mountains at that site. Our supporting evidence for the proposed water trail linking El Perú-Waka' with El Achiotal and El Tintal relies on archaeological and iconographic evidence, as well as the application of geographic information system (GIS) techniques to create hydrological models of streams.

SETTING

Northwestern Petén, Guatemala, is a land of dramatic contrasts that includes the 3,000 km^2 Laguna del Tigre National Park. The swampy flat country of the western part of this park is now thoroughly compromised, having been invaded and developed by oil companies, cattle ranchers, and farmers. This part contrasts with the eastern sector of the park, where hills rise to escarpments marking the southwestern edge of the CKU, still under wilderness and mature rainforest. Water captured in the CKU slowly drains underground to the west, feeding springs and rivers—such as the San Juan, Chocop, and Xucub—that flow into the San Pedro Mártir River, a placid major artery linking central Petén to the western part of Maya lowland country. Archaeological projects in northwestern Petén stand ground with government agencies and nongovernmental organizations (NGOs) against invaders intent on moving west to east, destroying the rain forest and seizing the public lands. The ancient inhabitants of El Perú-Waka', a regional royal capital from the Late Preclassic until the Terminal Classic periods (ca. 150 BCE–1000 CE) were also standing ground against adversaries, for their city on top of a 100 m tall escarpment commanded the San Juan River, a water trail linking the CKU to the San Pedro Mártir River, and eventually to the Gulf of Mexico. Rising 45 m majestically above this compact city, one of the densest in the southern Maya lowlands, is a natural hill that the founders terraced into a massive pyramid. Called the Mirador Hill, it allowed observers on it or on one of the three temple complexes of the Mirador Group built atop it to see as far west as the Sierra Lacandon range that marks the edge of the Usumacinta River drainage. Conversely, travelers moving up the San Pedro Mártir River very likely could have seen the plastered and painted Mirador Group pyramids and temples from many days distance while paddling great dugout canoes. Examination of new Light Detection and Ranging (LiDAR) data confirms the presence of a stairway descending 30 m from the first terrace of the Mirador Hill to its base and the beginning of a causeway connecting it with Structure M13-1, the city temple and fire shrine. Flanking this causeway at the base of the Mirador Hill are artificial reservoirs. When filled in the rainy season, these reservoirs transformed the Mirador Hill into a water mountain (figure 6.1).

The city of El Perú-Waka' was defended by its steep south-side escarpment, and it commanded a wide rainy season lagoon and port facility on the San Juan

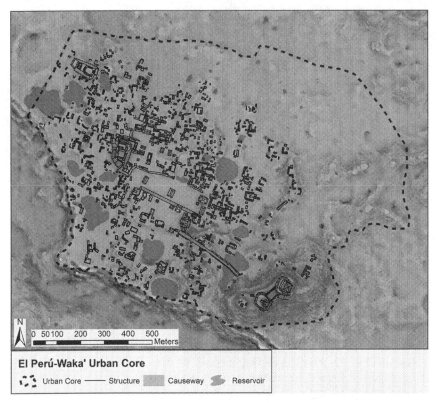

FIGURE 6.1. *LiDAR DEM of El Perú-Waka' urban core with adjusted and rotated Proyecto Arqueológico Waka' (PAW) structure map. The Mirador Hill is located in the lower right area of the map. Damien B. Marken and Matthew C. Ricker (n.d.), data courtesy of Pacunam LiDAR Initiative (PLI), generated by National Center for Airborne Laser Mapping (NCALM), map by Damien B. Marken, courtesy of PAW.*

River 5 km above its confluence with the San Pedro Mártir River. It seems very likely that the city was established to control canoe traffic on the San Juan River, which, we argue, provided access during flood tide to the port town or way-station of El Achiotal to the northeast and, possibly even to the great city of El Tintal in the CKU (Chiriboga et al. 2017). El Tintal was further connected by several causeways to other cities in the CKU, including El Mirador, and no doubt its strategic location gave it an important role in Preclassic geopolitics. The water trails connecting El Tintal with El Perú-Waka' via the San Juan River drainage would have established an extensive fluvial network linking the Maya regional core to the Gulf of Mexico and the Olmec heartland of Tabasco and Veracruz in the Middle Preclassic and Late Preclassic periods. El Perú-Waka's location at the confluence of the San Juan and San Pedro Mártir Rivers strengthens its position as a city of water trails starting in the Late Preclassic and, as we explore below, as a water mountain. This positioning seems to have been relevant during an important moment in Classic Maya history known as the entrada, also discussed below, as the discovery of an early fifth-century stela at El Achiotal that has been associated with Sihyaj K'ahk' and the installment of New Order kings (Auld-Thomas, Montejo, and Parris 2016, 223–224) highlights the significance of the route.

NORTHWESTERN WATER TRAILS IN PETÉN

While the lowland Maya inhabited a world of rivers, seasonally inundated lands, and extensive coastlines, they are usually excluded from the comparative literature on the hearths of ancient civilizations where rivers and seas played vital roles in transportation: Egypt, Mesopotamia, the Indus, China, and Greece. The role of coastal canoe trade in Maya civilization has had its long-term champions (Andrews 1983). In general, however, the southern lowlands have been regarded, like coeval societies in pre-Hispanic Mexico to the west, to be a landlocked world of human porters, challenging to the successful and expedient transport of bulk commodities over any distance. That perception is now changing significantly, at least among students of the lowland Maya. For example, the contributors to a recent book on the archaeology of Chetumal Bay, edited by Debra Walker (2016), regard the bay as a hub of waterborne communication and transportation with historical and economic connections deep into the interior of the peninsula. Not only do these archaeologists see rivers such as the New and Hondo Rivers as conduits of canoe traffic but also seasonally flooded *bajos* (natural depressions that seasonally fill with water) in Quintana Roo, as well as adjacent permanent bodies of water such as Laguna Bacalar (Guderjan 2016; see also Gunn, chapter 5 in this volume).

T. Patrick Culbert and his colleagues carried out survey and reconnaissance in bajo settings in northeastern Petén (1997). While they were primarily interested in the prospects of habitation and subsistence farming in bajo settings, their findings suggest that the Maya used canoe transportation through extensive areas during seasonal flooding. Settlement in bajos could not be reasonably accessed by any other means of transportation for nearly half the year. From our experience in seasonally inundated areas of northwestern Petén, it seems highly likely that footpaths through forest and bush would be canals for shallow draft canoes during the flood tide. Christopher Jones (1996), in his study of the Tikal market, envisioned this city as a trading center and saw the geographic importance within the southern lowlands of this regionally pivotal city with the reasonable implication that in addition to footpaths, east-west commerce could have moved across inundated land, flanking the city by means of canoe transport.

The western escarpment zone of the CKU is not as dramatically defined as the eastern escarpment zone. Instead, it gradually descends with wide stretches of seasonally inundated land to the west continuing toward Laguna del Tigre

National Park. The rivers and springs of this area drain some of the rains that pour down on the CKU, and these saturated lowlands west of the escarpment experience months of seasonal inundation during the rainy season. This area feeds the great San Pedro Mártir River on its journey toward the Gulf of Mexico. We think that some sites in this region participated in canoe transport and commerce linking the Mirador state to westward regions during the Preclassic period, certainly El Achiotal adjacent to the escarpment near the Mirador zone, and El Perú-Waka' on a commanding rise overlooking the tributary San Juan River just north of its confluence with the San Pedro Mártir River.

Historical documents from the fifteenth century (Scholes and Roys 1968) reveal that canoe travel was a preferred mode of transportation, not only for trade but also for basic mobility in the region of the Candelaria River basin and its tributaries in southern Campeche, Mexico. These historical accounts also include references to the use of seasonal drainages to reach certain centers by canoe, as they were located on "islands" and "raised headlands" (Scholes and Roys 1968, 50–51). This observation is the reason the region was known as Acalan, the "Place of Canoes." Hernán Cortés reported on extensive canoe use on the great rivers and marshes, which were also used to travel from one sea to the other (Finamore 2010, 146–147).

The site of El Achiotal is located on an island, much like those referenced in the historical documents, in the ecotone along the western edge of the CKU (Acuña 2011, 2013; Acuña and Chiriboga 2010; Acuña et al. 2010). The small ceremonial center sits atop an elongated karstic platform rising some 40 m above the surrounding bajos (figure 6.2). A large pyramidal structure, 5C-01, dominates the settlement at the southern end of the ridge and is characterized by a long construction sequence, from the Preclassic into the Classic periods. Phase–sub 4, a Late Preclassic building, was decorated with stylistically unique and ideologically sophisticated murals that relate to the important connection between ancient Maya political economy and the institution of divine kingship (Acuña 2013). The archaeological and iconographic evidence from Structure 5C-01, combined with the site's location and geographical setting, suggest El Achiotal was a port town at the juncture of seasonal, wetland canoe transportation and overland routes on which goods were likely transported in and out of the large ceremonial centers in northern Petén.

When El Achiotal hill became an island in the rainy season, it took on the appearance of the first land emerging from placid waters, the primordial turtle. Mary Jane Acuña describes the turtle iconography of Structure 5C-01–sub 4 this way:

> In addition to the murals, the small mask on the upper steps of the staircase
> was a performance platform for an individual, certainly a ruler. With the temple

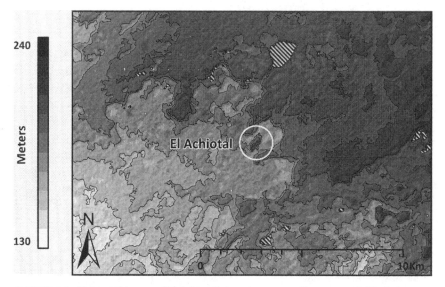

FIGURE 6.2. *Topographic map of El Achiotal's location over a ridge surrounded by* bajos *(map by C. R. Chiriboga).*

as backdrop, decorated in dark red over a cream plaster, the divine king could perform in front of the crowd gathered below. As seen from the plaza, the king would stand on the head of what I interpret as a turtle . . . The black band painted on the staircase risers would be seen from below as connecting the turtle with the earth. In Maya mythology, the turtle represents the earth from where life emerges and it is materialized metaphorically with the image of the Maize God performing in and emerging from the carapace of the turtle. There are examples of this in the Preclassic period on the murals at San Bartolo (Taube, et al. 2010, figure 46) and painted on a Codex-style vessel from the Classic period (K1892), as well as other examples. As a metaphor for fertility, life, and the foundation for divine kinship, rulers performing at the top of the staircase on Structure 5C-01-sub 4, on the head of the turtle, equated themselves with the Maize God. Perhaps, among the multiple meanings embedded in the symbolism of this building, it also represented a turtle effigy. Thus, ritual ceremonies of the king validating and justifying his divine status that took place in the building would be like the Maize God performing inside the turtle carapace. (2013, 345–346)

The cosmic turtle was the place of resurrection of the Maize God following death, sometimes depicted as emerging from his own skull as on K1892. On K1181 that skull is depicted explicitly as resting inside a mortuary bundle. The royal bundle house, Structure 5C-01, was likely an effigy symbolic of the island site as a whole. Downstream at El Péru-Waka', the royal palace acropolis—burial place of an early third-century bundled king, and probably many others—was perched on the hill above the San Juan River. It symbolized turtle mountain for the famous seventh-century royal couple K'inich Bahlam II and his queen Kaloomte' K'abel who stand upon turtle effigies on El Péru Stelae 33 and 34.

Radiocarbon dates recovered from ash lenses outside the building suggest El Achiotal Structure 5C-01–sub 4 was in use in the Late to Terminal Preclassic periods (89 BCE–217 CE, total range of dates) (Acuña 2013, 334), nicely corresponding to chronological assessment based on iconographic style and pottery types. In her analysis of the iconography, Acuña (2013) identified the main theme of the murals as representations of bundles. Mural 1 depicts a bundle mask, which is conceptually related to ancestry and kingship. Mural 2 was painted with symbolism of value and power, perhaps metaphoric representations of currency, as expressed with profile polymorphs. Vertically positioned J-scroll and bracket motifs framed all nine murals, most of which were destroyed in antiquity. Following Julia Guernsey's (2006) proposition that this motif represents cloth, Acuña argued that these murals metaphorically "wrapped" or "bundled" the building. This is the first bundle house found archaeologically in the Maya lowlands, although Debra Walker (2013) now identifies a bundle house at Late Preclassic Cerro Maya. A bundle house is proposed to have been a place where bundling events likely took place, and where bundles were brought, kept/stored, or exchanged, maybe even charged with ritual power (Acuña 2013). The combined symbolism embedded in the iconographic program of the murals at El Achiotal sheds light on the ideological and practical associations between divine kingship and the political economy. Bundle houses were important for ritual and politics, as illustrated in Classic period depictions of buildings and representations of rulers receiving tribute in the forms of bundles, or a combination of both (e.g., rollout K8075 of the Kerr Maya Vase photo collection available on http://research.mayavase.com/kerrmaya_list.php?_allSearch=&hold_search=&x=31&y=12&vase_number=8075&date_added=&ms_number=&site=).

In the Late Preclassic period, El Mirador and other large centers on the CKU were at their first cultural peak (Chiriboga et al. 2017; Hansen 1998), expending enormous amounts of energy and labor on monumental architecture projects. Richard Hansen has proposed that the population relied on agricultural gardens created with rich bajo mud. There is no clear understanding of population size for these cities in the Preclassic, as the archaeological footprint represents a palimpsest of over a millennium of occupation. But we doubt this strategy was sufficient to supply the large population inhabiting the region year round. Instead, they surely relied simultaneously on the importation of bulk commodities from outside the region during periods of prodigious civic-religious construction programs when self-sufficiency was not possible (cf. Chase and Chase 2016). Based on the discovery of long-distance exchange goods found in archaeological contexts at sites on the CKU (Chiriboga et al. 2017), and the political and economic implications of the Preclassic iconography at El Achiotal, in addition to the extensive network of causeways connecting major settlements, we know that the population was well connected locally and regionally. We propose that the water trail connecting El Perú-Waka' with El Achiotal, and perhaps farther north, was one access point for the transport of bulk items and other commodities, including knowledge.

THE SAN JUAN RIVER WATERSHED

In order to further evaluate our El Achiotal–El Perú-Waka' water-route hypothesis, we have applied GIS techniques to define the San Juan River and its watershed, and to identify areas of water accumulation that may have enabled the proposed seasonal transportation route. Utilizing a Shuttle Radar Topography Mission (SRTM) 30 meter resolution digital elevation model, coauthor Chiriboga was able to generate a preliminary hydrologic model of the region using ArcHydro toolset in ArcGis 10.2. Chiriboga generated a synthetic stream network representing an idealized model of the region's surface drainage, which then helped to delineate the San Juan River's watershed (figure 6.3). Areas prone to inundation were identified through the mapping of sections with internal drainage (sinks) and of low topographic prominence, through the application of the Topographic Position Index (TPI) algorithm, a moving window algorithm which quantifies a point's topographic position relative to the surrounding region (Weiss 2001).

The output of the model provided the delineation of the San Juan River Watershed, which represents the total contributing area of surface drainage that ultimately flows into the San Juan River, and indicated the areas prone to seasonal inundation. In addition to the region's surface hydrology, most of the San Juan watershed lies atop a karst landscape composed mostly of evaporites, which constitute an important source of groundwater. This geologic unit, known as the Buena Vista Formation in Guatemala and the Icaiche Formation in Campeche and Quintana Roo, is composed of alternating layers of gypsum, chalks, limestones and dolomites, and clay beds (López Ramos 1975; Vinson 1962), constituting the Xpujil Aquifer on the Mexican side of the formation (CONAGUA 2009). Its base, consisting of a layer of at least 200 m of scarp-forming gypsum evaporites, is exposed along the northern bank of the San Pedro Mártir River in the region east of the town of Paso Caballos, and along multiple escarpments found across the region. This complex geology suggests the presence of both perched and confined aquifers, which have been identified along the eastern CKU (Bauer-Gottwein et al. 2011; Gondwe et al. 2010). The aquifers can also be inferred by the presence of a host of other characteristic features of karsts, such as sinking streams and swallow holes (known as *xuch* in southern Campeche and Quintana Roo), blind valleys, poljes (also known as

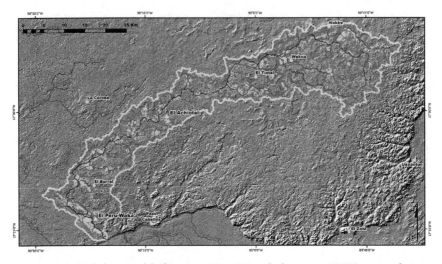

FIGURE 6.3. *Hydrologic model of San Juan River Watershed using an SRTM 30 m resolution DEM (map by C. R. Chiriboga).*

bajos or *akalches*), and so on. Although not directly applied to our model, previous studies of groundwater flow across the Yucatán Peninsula (Bauer-Gottwein et al. 2011) have characterized the regional subsurface water flow as following generalized surface topography for the western CKU, so it is expected that a significant amount of additional water is supplied to the San Juan River by karst springs and groundwater base flow originating in the regional gypsum aquifer.

The San Juan River Watershed can be further divided into three sections based on the geomorphology of the region. The Upper San Juan Watershed consists of a highland plateau of residual *mogotes* (karst hills) interspaced by seasonally inundated low-lying bajos or akalches. This area constitutes an important aquifer recharge zone and presents slow surface runoff due to the presence of an extensive bajo system. The Middle San Juan Watershed presents a stepped landscape formed by erosional dissolution of the underlying karst geology, which has left at least two well-defined escarpments that provide important points of aquifer outflow. The Lower Watershed can be characterized by a less-pronounced slope and a surface geology with sections of quaternary alluvium that provide the substrate for the San Juan River's current channel course.

Recent paleoenvironmental research from the region also provides interesting evidence to reinforce our position. In 2001, a team led by David Wahl extracted a lake core from Laguna Puerto Arturo, located 4 km from the site of El Achiotal (Wahl, Byrne, and Anderson 2014; Wahl, Schreiner, and Byrne 2005; Wahl et al. 2007). Continued analysis has provided an environmental history of the immediate region through the interpretation of both paleoclimate and paleoenvironmental proxy data. Paleoenvironmental data, primarily from pollen and soil erosion studies, identified two moments of vegetation recovery corresponding to the Middle Preclassic (520–330 Cal yr BCE) and to the transition from Late Preclassic to Early Classic (Cal yr 110–230 CE), during which time the land cover shifted from one of agricultural activity to one of forest cover (Wahl et al. 2007).

Additionally, in their palaeoclimatological reconstruction, Wahl and his team identified multiple regime shifts toward wetter conditions (Wahl, Byrne, and Anderson 2014). The periods spanning from 2325–2125 Cal yr BP (375–225 Cal yr BCE) and from 875–625 Cal yr BP (1075–1325 Cal yr CE) were found to represent abrupt shifts from a dry regime to a significantly wetter one, with a third, though not as pronounced, shift occurring during the Classic period, from 1625–1250 Cal yr BP (325–700 Cal yr CE). Such changes would have significantly increased both surface and groundwater availability in the region. Investigations at El Tintal, located in the Upper San Juan Watershed, reveal that cultural peaks and artificial hydraulic features appear to correlate with evidence of more humid periods found in the paleoenvironmental data (Chiriboga et al. 2017). It is too early to tell, but we can speculate that the three sections of the watershed were affected differently by humid-dry periods based on characteristics of their microenvironments and geology.

MAYA WATER MOUNTAINS

Scarborough has focused our attention on water mountains, or Altepetl, among the Aztec and extrapolated by Nawa Sugiyama (2014) to the Pyramid of the Moon at the highland Classic city of Teotihuacan. Scarborough's (1998) seminal article on Tikal illuminated the enormous and enduring significance of water mountains to the Maya. Earlier, Scarborough spent a fair amount of time studying water dynamics at Cerro Maya while conducting settlement survey at the site, and he wrote cogently of the essential landscaping fact that quarrying material to raise sacred mountains and plazas demanded careful drainage systems to move rainwater to the surrounding reservoir ponds framing the core area (Scarborough 1983, 1991). Quite literally, the Cerro Maya center, a trading port on Chetumal Bay in Belize, was indeed a water mountain. Maya water mountain settlements, as he has noted throughout his career, are ubiquitous in the southern lowlands and we can now include El Tintal in the CKU (Acuña and Matute 2017b; Chiriboga et al. 2017).

The water mountain at El Perú-Waka' is the Mirador Hill, with water reservoirs at its base on the northwestern side flanking the main stairway and giving access to the summit temples (Freidel 2014). As previously described, it is a partially terraced natural hill rising some 45 m above the main plaza, and it looms over the city (see figure 6.1). Supporting evidence for its identification as a water

FIGURE 6.4. *Vaulted corridor into the artificial cave in Structure P13-5, researched by Michelle Rich, being photo-documented by Francisco Castañeda (l), and the interior view of the same corridor (r). Photographs by Michelle Rich and Francisco Castañeda, courtesy of the Proyecto Arqueológico Regional El Perú-Waka', Ministry of Culture, Guatemala City.*

mountain has been found during the broader mapping project, in which Damien Marken and colleagues investigate the water systems at El Perú-Waka' in order to define the relationship between water and land (Marken, Maxson, and Pérez Dueñas 2016; Ricker, Marken, and Rivas 2017). Additionally, excavations in Structure P13-5 (Rich 2013), located at the north side base of the Mirador Hill, revealed the presence of an artificial masonry cave with an elaborate stepped vaulted entryway (figure 6.4). Evidently, the structure was constructed over a gray flowstone formation packed with what appears to be yellow crystalline calcite precipitate, a possible fossil spring. The cave gave open access to a wall at the far southern end of the yellow matrix. The masonry platform was constructed and used during the Late Preclassic and Early Classic periods, according to ceramic assemblages found in construction fill and burial contexts and supported a perishable superstructure (Rich 2013, 195). Based on the architectural context and ceramic assemblages, it is likely the people of the community used this platform for feasting and rituals, eventually completely burying this evident fossil spring under it. Combined, the evidence supports the identification of the Mirador Hill as a water mountain, not only because of the spring-like feature, but also due to the major tanks or bajos flanking its northern and western sides. However, as described below, we argue that it was not just a water mountain in the long-standing Maya sense, but also may have been a dominion mountain, an Altepetl, in the highland Mexican sense.

EL PERÚ-WAKA' AND THE WINTE' NAAH

El Perú-Waka' was the first place in the Maya lowlands where the central Mexican warrior Sihyaj K'ahk' established a new government in 378 CE as documented on El Perú Stela 15 (Freidel, Escobedo, and Guenter 2007; Guenter 2005; Stuart 2000). The arrival of this statesman into lowland history is called the entrada in Maya studies and it heralds the advent of a century-long period, called the New Order, during which Teotihuacan styles of dress, regalia, and religious cult symbolism were celebrated at Tikal, Copan, and El Perú-Waka', among other lowland Maya capitals. The religious cult introduced by Sihyaj K'ahk' features a kind of shrine called a Winte' Naah. This term remains elusive in decipherment but generally appears to refer to "foundation" or "origin" metaphysically. In iconographic terms, a major feature is the presence of fire ritual. Principal deities of the Winte' Naah Fire Shrine cult in the Maya lowlands include the goggle-eyed and fanged Storm God, the Feathered Serpent, and the Maya Sun God, conflating Central Mexican and Maya symbolism. At El Perú-Waka' the tutelary gods of the city were the Moon Goddess (Three Moon), the death god Akan, and the Sun God. These gods, along with the aforementioned Mexican gods, presided over the Winte' Naah Fire cult at El Perú-Waka'. In the context of this political change, Sihyaj K'ahk' made the Wak dynasty king K'inich Bahlam

I his vassal, and he evidently founded a Winte' Naah Fire Shrine of the lowland Maya New Order era (Freidel, Escobedo, and Guenter 2007). In reference to the original Altepetl at Teotihuacan, Sugiyama and colleagues (2014) identify that mountain as a place of powerful animal spirits, including of raptor birds, water, darkness, and the feminine divine. We find these characteristics in the evidence from the Mirador Hill.

At the summit of the Mirador Hill at El Perú-Waka' is one of two pyramids. Structure O14-04 is a pyramid with a *adosada* (frontal platform) built in the Early Classic period. Along with the proposed Winte' Naah Fire Shrine in the city center, this is one of two documented Teotihuacan-inspired adosadas in the Maya lowlands. A seventh-century masonry shrine built on this Early Classic platform over an important tomb, Burial 39, described below, contained fragments of stucco effigies, including a larger-than-life size stucco head of a Teotihuacano from central Mexico wearing the goggles of the Storm God in his hair (Rich 2011; Rich, Piehl, and Matute 2006). The archaeological evidence, architectural features, and chronology favor the association of this place with the Entrada of Sihyaj K'ahk'.

Rich and colleagues (Rich, Piehl, and Matute 2006) discovered two Early Classic burials beneath the adosada platform, both possibly sacrificial offerings. Burial 25 was placed directly into construction fill under an early plaster floor and contained the remains of a mature woman. The offerings included a jadeite bead, which was probably placed in her mouth; large fragments of *Spondylus spp.* shell over her face; and two ceramic vessels, one of which was an unslipped striated water jar, suggesting the woman was associated with water (figure 6.5). The other vessel, decorated with a macaw motif, is similar to a coeval plate discovered at Tikal in Burial PNT-062, possibly another sacrificial offering (Laporte and Fialko 1995, figure 31). The macaw portrayed on the Waka' vessel has a body that is distinctively trapezoidal in shape, evoking a pyramid at the heart of the bird. The pyramid features half of a quatrefoil motif represented at the center, establishing the bird and the pyramid as a portal to the supernatural world of gods and ancestors. The quatrefoil portal has a long history in Mesoamerica and was also depicted on the back of the Olmec-style figurine (Rich et al. 2010) found in Burial 39, a later tomb intrusive into the adosada. This half-quatrefoil is flanked on either side by a dangling, sectioned body of a centipede, representing the kingdom of Wak'. The vessel's presence in the foundational burial, therefore, marks Structure O14-04 and its adosada as a deeply sacred place. Macaws—the animal inspiration for the Principal Bird Deity—are a pervasive animal at Waka' to this day, in spite of modern depredations, and an appropriate animal spirit for this proposed Altepetl.

The second interment, Burial 24, was a small tomb chamber cut into bedrock located east of Burial 25. It was stratigraphically under the same plaza floor as Burial 25 and both were positioned beneath the subsequent adosada. Burial 24

FIGURE 6.5. *Dos Arroyos Polychrome basal flange bowl and Triunfo Striated water jar from Burial 25 in Structure O14-04. Photograph by Michelle Rich, courtesy of the El Perú-Waka' Regional Archaeological Project, Ministerio de Cultura y Deportes de Guatemala.*

contained the remains of two young women interred in a tableau macabre, one on top of the other—indeed, perhaps in what Andrew Scherer and colleagues (2014) identify as a *danse macabre*, as one women had her arms positioned in a possible dance pose. The ceramic offering vessels included elaborate scutate lid dishes. The number 3, associated with the hearth of creation, is echoed in the lid of one of the vessels that depicts three masks of the god of the number 13 according to Stephen Houston (personal communication, 2007), the god who is also *witz'* (water spray) (Stuart 2007). In sum, we see significant symbolism in these offerings appropriate for the dedication of this adosada shrine platform as the summit of an Altepetl established in the time of the Sihyaj K'ahk's Entrada in the Maya area (Freidel 2014). As mentioned earlier, recent analysis of LiDAR imagery provided by the Pacunam LiDAR Initiative (PLI) (see Marken and Pérez Dueñas 2017 for a summary and synthesis of this information in light of existing survey data) shows a possible grand stairway on the northwestern side of this hill flanked by a reservoir. This reservoir was already recorded on the 2015 site map (Marken, Maxson, and Pérez Dueñas 2016), but confirmation of this pattern lends further support to the water mountain hypothesis.

Recent discoveries at El Achiotal are also relevant to the entrada. Taking over after Acuña, as part of the La Corona Regional Archaeological Project's research at the site, Luke Auld-Thomas discovered a remarkable early fifth-century stela that references the era of the entrada (Auld-Thomas, Montejo, and Parris 2016). This revered stone monument possibly memorializes Sihyaj K'ahk's interest in the ancient water path leading from El Perú-Waka' into the heartland of the Mirador state. We believe that the El Perú-Waka' Mirador Hill remained similarly charged with memories of the entrada, as shown in the effigy Teotihuacano mentioned above. The tomb intrusive into the existing adosada in the mid-seventh century, known as Burial 39, is being thoroughly studied by Rich. It contained a complex ritual deposit surrounding and adorning the deceased, including the now well-known narrative figurine scene at the foot of the deceased, posited by Rich and colleagues to be a funerary ceremony being conducted for a deceased king. It is possible that the reigning, living king figurine portrayed in this ceremony may be the overlord of the Wak dynasty, the Kaanul king Yuknoom Ch'een the Great. In the Late Classic, the site of Calakmul, Mexico, was seat to the Kaanul dynasty, which was in frequent antagonistic relationships with Tikal for regional power and control and which established strategic alliances with sites such as El Perú-Waka'. What is certain is that this presiding figurine king wears a giant limpet shell pectoral, what the highland Mexicans called an Oyohualli, a reference to the sea and to female genitalia (Coe 2009). The Hunal tomb at Copan, resting place of the dynastic founder and New Order lord K'inich Yax K'uk' Mo' (Bell et al. 2004), contained such a pectoral and the inscribed text, according to David Stuart (2004), identifies it as a Winte' "thing." On a looted, lidded offering cup, Kaanul king Yuknoom Ch'een the Great is portrayed along with a spouse, evidently in celebration of the K'atun jubilee of 672 CE (Prager 2004). The text on the lid refers to an enigmatic lord who is titled Wak Chan K'awiil, stood-up mountain spirit. Christian Prager (2004) suggests that this epithet refers to a Kaanul king nicknamed "sky raiser." This king occurs on Late Classic Codex–style painted vases at the beginning of a series of Kaanul kings (Martin 1997). However, successors to Yuknoom Ch'een also referred to him as K'awiil, equivalent to "founder" (Martin 2005, 8). Following Stanley Guenter (personal communication 2011), we identify this as another reference to Yuknoom Ch'een the Great, but here as lord of a great mountain. We suggest that the mid-seventh-century interment of the Wak ruler in Burial 39, under the auspices of the Kaanul king Yuknoom Ch'een, inside a centuries-old symbol of Teotihuacan, points to the Mirador Hill as an Altepetl water mountain established by Sihyaj K'ahk' at El Perú-Waka'. Such a view of Maya history makes this geographically peripheral and modest water mountain a strategic place in lowland regional politics. Its importance no doubt also derived significantly from its location on and near vital water transport routes since the Preclassic period.

DISCUSSION

Water mountains and water routes surely helped to define the lowland Maya world as it evolved. The human management of these features likely figured prominently in Maya political geography for both practical and ideological purposes (Lucero 2006; Scarborough 1998). Combined, the archaeological evidence from El Achiotal and the regional survey associated with it support the hypothesis of a westward route through the San Juan River Watershed toward the San Pedro Mártir River. The location of El Perú-Waka' at the confluence of these two rivers likely increases the possibility of its role as a port city. However, it must be noted that in present-day conditions, the confluence of the San Juan with the San Pedro Rivers has so silted up that the latter only flows into the former during the height of the flood tide and most of the time the San Juan drains underground before it reaches the San Pedro. There is still a San Juan channel at the confluence, but it is a decidedly narrow one as observed by Roan McNab of Wildlife Conservation Society (personal communication, 2017). McNab further observed the presence of ancient platforms along the northern shore of the San Pedro River south of El Perú-Waka' and near this confluence. Additional research may help to determine the prospect that the narrow channel was maintained in antiquity as open to canoe traffic, a highly defensible route linking the postulated port facility at Laguna El Perú to the main river. Ongoing research at this location, carried out by Alex Rivas as a component of the settlement pattern survey directed by Damien Marken, promises further results. The recent discovery of another sizeable settlement, El Peruito, northwest of El Perú-Waka' some 8 km on the San Pedro River (Pérez 2017) reinforces the prospect that it was a canoe transport route. Acuña proposed that the waning of El Achiotal in the Early Classic period resulted from the cessation in the use of a seasonal route to supply the core cities from the west, which were suffering from a dramatic demographic decline in the Late to Terminal Preclassic period. However, the discovery by Auld-Thomas of an Early Classic stela at El Achiotal commemorating the Entrada of Sihyaj K'ahk' in the fourth century CE suggests that this old route into the Mirador heartland was still known and revered. More important, the data we present here are suggestive of the need to reevaluate the models explaining how the ancient Maya population moved themselves, as well as goods, across the landscape.

More generally, interior state frontiers and water routes linking core area states to periphery frontier zones, some following natural features, as in this case, must have helped define the political geography of the Maya lowlands from the Preclassic onward. By the Late Preclassic period, the CKU was the geographical heartland of the lowlands and home to El Mirador and a constellation of related sites, such as El Tintal, which is now being contextualized archaeologically

(Acuña 2014; Acuña and Matute 2016, 2017a, 2017b; Chiriboga et al. 2017). This area probably constitutes the core of the earliest lowland regional state. Freidel is on record (2018) as siding with the argument that this was the original Kaanul state that would later reemerge as the dominant power in the Late Classic lowlands (Hansen and Guenter 2005; Martin 1997). Simon Martin and Eric Velásquez García (2016) now believe that Ichkabal near Dzibanche in Quintana Roo was the Preclassic capital of Kaanul. Whatever the outcome of that debate, the Mirador zone cities must have been a formidable dominant presence economically and politically. Late Preclassic El Achiotal in northwestern Petén was, in our view, an interior frontier center between the Mirador area and the swampy riverine country to the west during the Late Preclassic state-level organization centered in northern Petén (Acuña 2013). This regional state fostered not only interior frontier gateway centers but also salient entrepôt centers well beyond its reach and situated to participate in strategic trade and commerce. Late Preclassic Cerro Maya, near the confluence of the New River and Chetumal Bay, was a trading port on the natural frontier of the peninsula (Robertson 2016; Walker 2016). The Caribbean littoral, and material culture such as ceramics as analyzed by Reese-Taylor, Walker, and Robertson (see Walker 2016; chapters 2, 3, and 7 in this volume), suggests it was established by northern lowland Maya and served as a salient of interior states of the era. On both the eastern and western side of the southern Maya lowlands, water trails helped define transport routes and water mountains helped define centers. To paraphrase Levi-Strauss and salute Vernon Scarborough, for the Maya like most other peoples in the ancient world, water was good to think as well as to drink.

REFERENCES

Acuña, Mary Jane. 2011. "Investigaciones en el sitio arqueológico El Achiotal." In *Proyecto Arqueológico La Corona. Informe Final: Temporada 2010*, edited by Tomás Barrientos, Marcello Canuto, and Mary Jane Acuña, 43–45. Report submitted to the Institute of History and Anthropology of Guatemala.

Acuña, Mary Jane. 2013. "Art, Ideology, and Politics at El Achiotal: A Late Preclassic Frontier Site in Northwestern Petén, Guatemala." PhD diss., Washington University in St. Louis, St. Louis, MO.

Acuña, Mary Jane. 2014. *Proyecto Arqueológico El Tintal. Informe No. 1: Resultados de la primera temporada de Campo, 2014*. Report submitted to the Dirección General del Patrimonio Cultural y Natural, Guatemala.

Acuña, Mary Jane, and Carlos Chiriboga. 2010. "Investigación arqueológica en el sitio El Achiotal." In *Proyecto Arqueológico La Corona. Informe Final: Temporada 2009*, edited by Marcello Canuto and Tomás Barrientos, 201–245. Report submitted to the Institute of History and Anthropology of Guatemala.

Acuña, Mary Jane, Carlos Chiriboga, Marcello Canuto, and Tomás Barrientos. 2010. "El Período Preclásico en la región noroccidental de Petén: Datos recientes y modelos interpretativos." In *XXIII Simposio de Investigaciones Arqueológicas en Guatemala, 2009*, Vol. 1, edited by Bárbara Arroyo, Adriana Linares, and Lorena Paiz, 39–52. Guatemala City: Asociación Tikal.

Acuña, Mary Jane, and Varinia Matute, eds. 2016. *Proyecto Arqueológico El Tintal. Informe No. 2: Resultados de la segunda temporada de campo, 2015*. Report submitted to the Dirección General del Patrimonio Cultural y Natural, Guatemala City.

Acuña, Mary Jane, and Varinia Matute, eds. 2017a. *Proyecto Arqueológico El Tintal. Informe No. 3: Resultados de la tercera temporada de campo, 2016*. Report submitted to the Dirección General del Patrimonio Cultural y Natural, Guatemala City.

Acuña, Mary Jane, and Varinia Matute, eds. 2017b. *Proyecto Arqueológico El Tintal. Informe No. 4: Resultados de la cuarta temporada de campo, 2017*. Report submitted to the Dirección General del Patrimonio Cultural y Natural, Guatemala, Guatemala City.

Andrews, Anthony P. 1983. *Maya Salt Production and Trade*. Tucson: University of Arizona Press.

Auld-Thomas, Luke, Mauro Montejo, and Caroline Parris. 2016. "Investigaciones arqueológicas en El Achiotal, Temporada 2015." In *Proyecto Arqueológico La Corona. Informe Final: Temporada 2015*, edited by Tomás Barrientos, Marcello Canuto, and Eduardo Bustamante, 189–252. Report submitted to the Dirección General del Patrimonio Cultural y Natural, Guatemala City.

Bauer-Gottwein, P., B.R.N. Gondwe, G. Charvet, L. E. Marín, M. Rebolledo-Vieyra, and G. Merediz-Alonso. 2011. "Review: The Yucatán Peninsula Karst Aquifer, Mexico." *Hydrogeology Journal* 19 (3): 507–524.

Bell, Ellen E., Robert J. Sharer, Loa P. Traxler, David W. Sedat, Christine W. Carrelli, and Lynn A. Grant. 2004. "Tombs and Burials in the Early Classic Acropolis at Copan." In *Understanding Early Classic Copan*, edited by Ellen E. Bell, Marcello Canuto, and Robert J. Sharer, 131–158. Philadelphia: University of Pennsylvania Museum of Archaeology and Anthropology.

Chase, Arlen F., and Diana Z. Chase. 2016. "The Ancient Maya City: Anthropogenic Landscapes, Settlement Archaeology, and Caracol, Belize." *Research Reports in Belizean Archaeology* 13: 3–14.

Chiriboga, Carlos R., Mary Jane Acuña, Varinia Matute, Arlen F. Chase, and Diana Z. Chase. 2017. "Investigaciones recientes en El Tintal y su paisaje arqueológico." Paper presented at the XXXI Simposio de Investigaciones Arqueológicas en Guatemala, Guatemala City.

Coe, Michael D. 2009. "The Kislak Oyohualli Pendant: Eroticism and War among the Toltec." Third Jay Kislak Lecture, Library of Congress, Washington, DC.

CONAGUA. 2009. "Determinación de la disponibilidad de agua en el acuífero Xpujil, Estado de Campeche." Gerencia de Aguas Subterráneas, Subdirección General Técnica, Comisión Nacional del Agua.

Culbert, T. Patrick, Vilma Fialko, Brian McKee, Liwy Grazioso, Julie Kunen, and Leonel Páez. 1997. "Investigaciones arqueológicas en el Bajo La Justa, Petén." In *X Simposio de Investigaciones Arqueológicas en Guatemala, 1996*, edited by Juan Pedro Laporte and Héctor L. Escobedo, 367–371. Guatemala City: Museo Nacional de Arqueología y Etnología.

Finamore, Daniel. 2010. "Navigating the Maya World." In *Fiery Pool: The Maya and the Mythic Sea*, edited by Daniel Finamore and Stephen Houston, 144–159. Salem, MA: Peabody Essex Museum.

Freidel, David A. 2014. "La Montaña Sagrada de *Waka'*: Paisaje e Historia." In *Proyecto Regional Arqueológico El Perú-Waka'. Informe No. 12: Temporada 2014*, edited by Juan Carlos Pérez, Griselda Pérez, and David A. Freidel, 9–17. Report submitted to the Dirección General del Patrimonio Cultural y Natural, Guatemala. Available on Mesoweb.com.

Freidel, David A. 2018. "Maya and the Idea of Empire." In *Pathways to Complexity*, edited by Kathryn Brown and George Bey, 363–386. Gainesville: University of Florida Press.

Freidel, David A., Héctor L. Escobedo, and Stanley P. Guenter. 2007. "A Crossroads of Conquerors: Waka' and Gordon Willey's 'Rehearsal for the Collapse' Hypothesis." In *Gordon R. Willey and American Archaeology: Contemporary Perspectives*, edited by Jeremy A. Sabloff and William Fash, 187–208. Norman: University of Oklahoma Press.

Freidel, David A., Héctor L. Escobedo, and Juan Carlos Melendez. 2013. "Mountains of Memories, Structure M12–32 at El Peru." In *Millenary Maya Societies: Past Crises and Resilience*, edited by M.-Charlotte Arnauld and Alain Breton, 235–247. Mesoweb On Line Publications. http://www.mesoweb.com/publications/MMS/index.html.

Freidel, David A., and Jeremy A. Sabloff. 1984. *Cozumel, Late Maya Settlement Patterns*. New York: Academic Press.

Gondwe, Bibi R. N., Simon Stisen, Mario Rebolledo-Vieyra, Peter Bauer-Gottwein, Sara Lerer, Luis Marín, and Gonzalo Merediz-Alonso. 2010. "Hydrogeology of the South-Eastern Yucatan Peninsula: New Insights from Water Level Measurements, Geochemistry, Geophysics and Remote Sensing." *Journal of Hydrology* 389 (1–2): 1–17.

Guenter, Stanley. 2005. "Informe preliminar de la epigrafía de El Perú." In *Proyecto Arqueológico El Perú-Waka'. Informe No. 2: Temporada 2004*, edited by Héctor L. Escobedo and David A. Freidel, 359–400. Report submitted to the Instituto de Antropología e Historia, Guatemala City.

Guernsey, Julia. 2006. "Late Formative Period Antecedents for Ritually Bound Monuments." In *Sacred Bundles*, edited by Julia Guernsey and F. Kent Reilly III, 22–39. Barnardsville, BC: Boundary End Archaeology Research Center.

Hansen, Richard D. 1998. "Continuity and Disjunction: The Pre-Classic Antecedents of Classic Maya Architecture." In *Function and Meaning in Classic Maya Architecture*, edited by Stephen D. Houston, 49–122. Washington, DC: Dumbarton Oaks Research Library and Collection.

Hansen, Richard D., and Stanley Guenter. 2005. "Early Social Complexity and Kingship in the Mirador Basin." In *Lords of Creation: The Origins of Sacred Maya Kingship*, edited by Virginia Fields and Dorie Reents-Budet, 60–61. London: Scala Publishers Limited.

Jones, Christopher. 1996. *Excavations in the East Plaza of Tikal*. Tikal Report 16. Vols. 1 and 2. Philadelphia: University of Pennsylvania Museum of Archaeology and Anthropology.

Laporte, Juan Pedro, and Vilma Fialko. 1995. "Un Reencuentro con mundo perdido, Tikal, Guatemala." *Ancient Mesoamerica* 6 (1): 41–94.

López Ramos, E. 1975. "Geological Summary of the Yucatan Peninsula." In *The Gulf of Mexico and the Caribbean: Ocean Basins and Margins*, edited by A.E.M. Nairn and F. G. Stehli, 257–282. New York: Plenum Press.

Lucero, Lisa J. 2006. "The Political and Sacred Power of Water in Ancient Maya Society." In *Precolumbian Water Management: Ideology, Ritual, and Politics*, edited by Lisa J. Lucero and Barbara Fash, 116–128. Tucson: University of Arizona Press.

Lucero, Lisa J., and Barbara W. Fash, eds. 2006. *Precolumbian Water Management: Ideology, Ritual, and Politics*. Tucson: University of Arizona Press.

Marken, Damien B., Erika Maxson, and Douglas Pérez Dueñas. 2016. "Mapeo topográfico en El Perú-Waka', 2015: Documentando el centro urbano de la ciudad y su transición hacia la Periferia." In *Proyecto Arqueológico El Perú-Waka'. Informe No. 13: Temporada 2015*, edited by Juan Carlos Pérez, Griselda Pérez, and David A. Freidel, 170–191. Fundación de Investigación Arqueológica Waka', Guatemala. Available on Mesoweb.com.

Marken, Damien, and Douglas Pérez Dueñas. 2017. "LiDAR en El Perú (Polígono 12): Análisis preliminar y comprobación sobre el terreno 2017." In *Proyecto Arqueológico Waka'. Informe No. 25: Temporada 2017*, 222–274. Informe entregado a la Dirección General del Patrimonio Cultural y Natural, Guatemala City.

Marken, Damien B., and Matthew C. Ricker. n.d. "Fire, Earth and Water: Urban Settlement, Soils and Hydrology at El Perú-Waka'." In *Kingdom of the Centipede: New Archaeological Perspectives on the Classic Maya Center of El Perú-Waka'*, edited by Keith Eppich, Damien B. Marken, and David Freidel. Gainesville: University Press of Florida.

Martin, Simon. 1997. "The Painted King List: A Commentary on Codex-Style Dynastic Vases." In *The Maya Vase Book*. Vol. 5, edited by Barbara Kerr and Justin Kerr, 846–867. New York: Kerr Associates.

Martin, Simon. 2005. "Of Snakes and Bats: Shifting Identities at Calakmul." *PARI* 6 (2): 5–13.

Martin, Simon, and Eric Velásquez García. 2016. "Polities and Places: Tracing the Top-onyms of the Snake Dynasty." *PARI* 17 (2): 23–33.

Ortiz Ceballos, Ponciano, and María del Carmen Rodríguez. 2000. "The Sacred Hill of El Manatí: A Preliminary Discussion of the Site's Rigual Paraphernalia." In *Olmec Art and Archaeology in Mesoamerica*, edited by John E. Clark and Mary E. Pye, 75–93. Studies in the Visual Arts, Symposium Papers 35. Washington, DC: National Gallery of Art, distributed by Yale University Press.

Pérez, Juan Carlos. 2017. Sitio *arqueológico El Peruito, Parque Nacional Laguna del Tigre*. Proyecto Arqueológico El Perú-Waka'. Report submitted to the Ministry of Culture and Sports, Guatemala, City.

Prager, Christian M. 2004. A "Classic Maya Ceramic Vessel from the Calakmul Region in the Museum zu Allerheiligen, Schaffhausen, Switzerland." *Human Mosaic* 35 (1): 31–40.

Rich, Michelle. 2011. "Ritual, Royalty and Classic Period Politics: The Archaeology of the Mirador Group at El Perú-Waka', Petén, Guatemala." PhD diss., Department of Anthropology, Southern Methodist University, Dallas.

Rich, Michelle. 2013. "Operación WK-15: Excavaciones en la estructura P13-5." In *Proyecto Arqueológico El Perú-Waka'. Informe No. 10: Temporada 2012*, edited by Juan Carlos Pérez, 175–198. Report submitted to the Dirección General del Patrimonio Cultural y Natural, Guatemala. Available on https://www.mesoweb.com/resources/informes/Waka2014.pdf.

Rich, Michelle, David A. Freidel, F. Kent Reilly III, and Keith Eppich. 2010. "An Olmec-Style Figurine from El Perú-Waka', Petén, Guatemala: A Preliminary Report." *Mexicon* 17 (5): 115–122.

Rich, Michelle, Jennifer Piehl, and Varinia Matute. 2006. "WK-11A: Continuación de las excavaciones en el complejo El Mirador, Estructura O14-04." In *Proyecto Arqueológico El Perú-Waka'. Informe No. 3: Temporada 2005*, edited by Héctor L. Escobedo and David A. Freidel, 225–261. Report submitted to the Dirección General del Patrimonio Cultural y Natural, Guatemala. Available on https://www.mesoweb.com/resources/informes/ElPeru-WK-11-2006.pdf.

Ricker, Matthew C., Damien B. Marken, and Alexander Rivas. 2017. "WK20: Transectos para extracción de núcleos del suelo en rasgos de superficies de agua: Reservorios de Xucub, Tanque y Plaza 1." In *Proyecto Arqueológico Waka'. Informe No. 14: Temporada 2016*, edited by Juan Carlos Pérez, 161–221. Report submitted to the Dirección General del Patrimonio Cultural y Natural, Guatemala.

Robertson, Robin. 2016. "Red Wares, Zapatista, Drinking Vessels, Colonists, and Exchange at Cerro Maya." In *Perspectives on the Ancient Maya of Chetumal Bay*, edited by Debra S. Walker, 125–148. Gainesville: University Press of Florida.

Scarborough, Vernon L. 1983. "A Late Preclassic Water System." *American Antiquity* 48 (4): 720–744.

Scarborough, Vernon L. 1991. *The Settlement System in a Late Preclassic Maya Community. Archaeology at Cerros, Belize, Central America.* Vol. 3. Dallas: Southern Methodist University Press.

Scarborough, Vernon L. 1998. "Water Management and the Maya." *Latin American Antiquity* 9 (2): 135–159.

Scherer, Andrew K., Charles Golden, Ana Lucía Arroyave, and Griselda Pérez. 2014. "Danse Macabre: Death, Community, and Kingdom at El Kinel, Guatemala." In *The Bioarchaeology of Space and Place: Ideology, Power, and Meaning in Maya Mortuary Contexts*, edited by G. Wrobel, 193–224. New York: Springer.

Scholes, France V., and Ralph L. Roys. 1968. *The Maya Chontal Indians of Acalan-Tixchel: A Contribution to the History and Ethnography of the Yucatan Peninsula.* Norman: University of Oklahoma Press.

Stuart, David. 2000. "'The Arrival of Strangers': Teotihuacan and Tollan in Classic Maya History." In *Mesoamerica's Classic Heritage: From Teotihuacan to the Aztecs*, edited by David Carrasco, Lindsay Jones, and Scott Sessions, 465–513. Boulder: University Press of Colorado.

Stuart, David. 2004. "The Beginning of the Copan Dynasty: A Review of the Hieroglyphic and Historical Evidence." In *Understanding Early Classic Copan*, edited by Ellen E. Bell, Marcello Canuto, and Robert J. Sharer, 215–247. Philadelphia: University of Pennsylvania Museum of Archaeology and Anthropology.

Stuart, David. 2007. "Reading the Water Serpent as Witz." https://mayadecipherment.com/2007/04/13/reading-the-water-serpent/#:~:text=The%20%E2%80%9CWater%20Serpent%E2%80%9D%20is%20a,a%20nibbling%20fish%20or%20two.

Stuart, David. 2008. "A Childhood Ritual on the Hauberg Stela." March. http://decipherment.wordpress.com/2008/03/27/a-childhood-ritual-on-the-hauberg-stela.

Sugiyama, Nawa, Gilberto Pérez, Bernardo Rodríguez, Fabiola Torres, and Raúl Valadez. 2014. "Animals and the State: The Role of Animals in State-Level Rituals in Mesoamerica." In *Animals and Inequality in the Ancient World*, edited by Sue Ann McCarty and Benjamin Arbuckle, 11–31. Boulder: University Press of Colorado.

Townsend, Richard. 1992. "The Renewal of Nature at the Temple of Tlaloc." In *The Ancient Americas, Art from Sacred Landscapes*, edited by Richard Townsend, 171–185. Chicago: Art Institute of Chicago; Munich: Prestel Verlag.

Vinson, G. L. 1962. "Upper Cretaceous and Tertiary Stratigraphy of Guatemala." *Bulletin of the American Association of Petroleum Geologists* 46 (4): 425–456.

Wahl, David, Roger Byrne, and Lysanna Anderson. 2014. "An 8700 Year Paleoclimate Reconstruction from the Southern Maya Lowlands." *Quaternary Science Reviews* 103 (November): 19–25.

Wahl, David, Roger Byrne, Thomas Schreiner, and Richard Hansen. 2007. "Palaeolimnological Evidence of late-Holocene Settlement and Abandonment in the Mirador Basin, Peten, Guatemala." *Holocene* 17 (6): 813–820.

Wahl, David, Thomas Schreiner, and Roger Byrne. 2005. "La secuencia paleo-ambiental de la Cuenca Mirador en Petén." In *XVIII Simposio de Investigaciones Arqueológicas en Guatemala, 2004*, edited by Juan Pedro Laporte, Bárbara Arroyo, and Héctor Mejía, 49–54. Guatemala City: Museo Nacional de Arqueología y Etnología, Guatemala.

Walker, Debra S. 2013. "Caching in Context at Cerros, Belize." Cerros Research Online Catalog. www.academia.edu/2965645/Caching_in_Context_at_Cerros_Belize.

Walker, Debra S. 2016. *Perspectives on the Ancient Maya of Chetumal Bay*. Gainesville: University Press of Florida.

Weiss, Andrew. 2001. "Topographic Position and Landforms Analysis." Poster session presented at the ESRI User Conference, San Diego, July 9.

7

Caracol, Belize, and Tikal, Guatemala

Ancient Maya Human-Nature Relationships and Their Sociopolitical Context

Arlen F. Chase, Diane Z. Chase, and Adrian S.Z. Chase

A comparison of the ancient sites of Tikal, Guatemala, and Caracol, Belize, provides insight into the variability that existed among neighboring ancient Maya polities during the Late Classic period (550–900 CE) in the southern lowlands of the Yucatán Peninsula. This comparison underscores the alternative human-environment trajectories that are possible even among neighboring polities. Significant differences in water management and agricultural sustainability exist at these two sites. While some of these characteristics may be related to micro-environmental differences, others are likely due to variability in past human decision-making and the resultant adaptations. The ancient cities of Caracol and Tikal, located some 76 km apart from each other, are two of the largest and most important cities of the Maya southern lowlands during the Late Classic period. However, there are marked differences in their natural settings that may have contributed to their varying trajectories of development. Compared to Caracol, Tikal is located in a relatively low and flat karst environment that is surrounded by *bajos* (natural depressions that seasonally fill with water) on two of its sides. In contrast, Caracol is located in an elevated region in the foothills of the Maya

https://doi.org/10.5876/9781646422326.c007

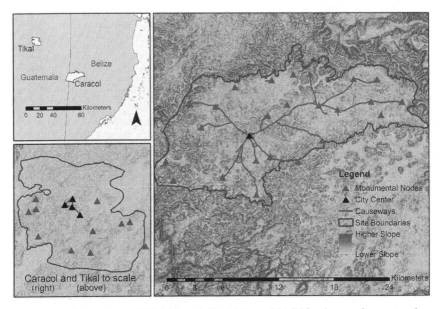

FIGURE 7.1. *Comparison of Tikal (lower left) and Caracol (right) landscapes showcasing the difference in slope between both cities (slope derived from JPL NASA STRMdata).*

Mountains, where there are many hills with fairly steep slopes separated by deep valleys but not the extensive bajo areas found at Tikal (figure 7.1). Particularly distinctive are their differences in approaches to water management—Tikal focused on the central control of water, while, in contrast, Caracol focused on the widespread dispersion of water storage facilities among residential groups. Differences also appear in agricultural strategies and site organization, potentially related to microenvironmental variations (e.g., soils, elevation, rainfall) associated with the two locations. Both cities had the benefit of being venues of long-term archaeological projects and we have a detailed understanding of both of these urban areas over time.

Both places also have fairly extensive hieroglyphic records that provide Maya written histories for their elite rulers over time, suggesting an intertwined history between the two cities. Once within Tikal's sphere of influence, Caracol overcame Tikal through ritual warfare and gained its independence at the onset of the Late Classic period (562 CE) (A. F. Chase 1991). The archaeology at Tikal further suggests that Caracol directly impacted Tikal during the first half of the Late Classic period, following Caracol's takeover of that center. Thus, a comparison of these two places yields striking information about the interconnectedness of Late Classic sites during the apogee of Maya civilization. Yet, while Tikal and Caracol had an intertwined history, they varied in other aspects of social and ritual organization and provide two very different expressions of ancient Maya city planning and urban culture. How much these different urban forms and organizations were influenced by their landscapes and environmental settings (e.g., A. F. Chase and Scarborough 2014) remains an open question and one of great significance for understanding the evolutionary trajectories of the ancient Maya in the Southern lowlands.

Looking first at their environmental settings, it is possible to see some significant differences between the two sites. Tikal is located on a relatively flat terrain, albeit with some "higher slopes" (Murtha 2015, 91) and is situated approximately 200 m above sea level. It is bounded to its east and west by areas of extensive bajo, or swamp, that were seasonally inundated with water. While the margins of some bajos were agriculturally productive (Culbert, Levi, and Cruz 1990; Kunen et al. 2000), precisely how and when these features were exploited by the ancient Maya are not clear (Dunning et al. 2015, 122); however, when filled with water the bajos could have been traversed by canoes, facilitating trade and the transport of bulk goods (especially to the east of Tikal; e.g., Dunning et al. 2017). Canopy in the upland areas of Tikal consists of broadleaf trees with a canopy height approaching 40 m; the canopy height in the Caracol area only approaches 25 m (A. F. Chase, Lucero et al. 2014, 18, 20). Caracol is located in a very karstic, hilly environment that ranges from approximately 450 to over 600 m above sea level. Because of the broken limestone, most water percolates down into deep caves; thus, bajos are not at all common at Caracol. The differences in absolute elevation also mean that Caracol is cooler (ranging from as low as 6°C to as high as 39°C, with an average temperature of 26°C) than Tikal (an average temperature of 30°C and a maximum of 39°C). Both sites were dependent on rainfall for their primary water sources, but Caracol generally receives 25 percent more rain than Tikal—an average of 2,400 mm per year as compared to 1,800 mm per year at Tikal; Vernon Scarborough and Gary Gallopin (1991, 659) report a range of 1,350 to 2,000 mm per year at Tikal. Caracol's position in the western foothills of the Maya Mountains also afforded ready access to metamorphic rock resources that were exported to other parts of the Maya area in the form of groundstone manos and metates (A. F. Chase, D. Chase et al. 2014).

ARCHAEOLOGICAL RESEARCH AT TIKAL AND CARACOL

Both Caracol and Tikal have been the focus of long-term archaeological research projects that have resulted in substantial on-the-ground surveyed maps for the two sites (figure 7.2).

Tikal

The University Museum of the University of Pennsylvania began a long-term excavation project at Tikal in 1956, which continued through 1969 (Coe and Haviland 1982; Sabloff 2003), at which point work was continued by Guatemalan

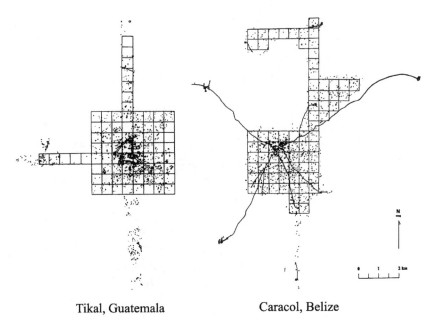

Tikal, Guatemala   Caracol, Belize

FIGURE 7.2. *Mapped areas of Tikal (after Carr and Hazard 1961 and Puleston 1983) and Caracol (after A. F. Chase and D. Chase 2001) compared for scale (see also A. F. Chase, D. Chase, and Smith 2009).*

researchers (Laporte and Fialko 1995). The University Museum Project resulted in the production of the first extensive map of a Maya site and its settlement, eventually covering a total of 23 km² (Carr and Hazard 1961; Puleston 1983). The University Museum excavations at Tikal investigated 4 main architectural complexes intensively (North Acropolis / Great Plaza; Central Acropolis; West Plaza; and East Plaza), 29 residential groups intensively (examining 83 structures), 17 residential groups with minor excavations, and 89 other residential groups with test pits. In addition, several other central architectural groups were tested for "recurrent layouts" (e.g., Twin-Pyramid Groups) and "structural peculiarities" (e.g., sweat baths) (Coe and Haviland 1982, 28–39; Haviland 2003, 114). As a result of the University Museum investigations, some 207 burials (177 minor burials; 11 crypt; 19 chamber) (Moholy-Nagy 2008, 17), 209 caches (Moholy-Nagy 2008, 17), and 223 problematical deposits (Moholy-Nagy 2008, 68) were recovered at Tikal. These totals have been increased substantially by subsequent Guatemalan Projects (e.g., Laporte 2003; Laporte and Fialko 1995).

Caracol

From 1950 through 1953 Caracol was an opportune location for research by the University Museum. Its investigations led to the acquisition of a series of Maya stelae and altars for display in Philadelphia (Beetz and Satterthwaite 1981). A subsequent program of investigation and excavation by the Caracol Archaeological Project (CAP) began at Caracol in 1985 and has continued on an annual basis to this day (A. F. Chase and D. Chase 1987; D. Chase and A. F. Chase 1994, 2015, 2017). This program has resulted in the transit mapping of some 23 km² of the site (A. F. Chase and D. Chase 2001), now augmented by Light Detection and Ranging (LiDAR) data to demonstrate that the city of Caracol covered more than 200 km² (A.S.Z. Chase 2016b, 2021; A. F. Chase, D. Chase, and Weishampel 2010; A. F. Chase et al. 2011; A. F. Chase, D. Chase et al. 2014). As of the conclusion of the 2020 field season, CAP has excavated in all of the "downtown" architectural groups as well as in 153 residential groups (54 of these groups intensively), resulting in the recovery of 398 interments containing 803 individuals (associated with 1,419 pottery vessels) and 363 formal caches (associated with 808 pottery vessels). An additional 356 reconstructible pottery vessels were recovered from the floors of plazas and structures (along with substantial use-related remains). Crafting areas have been identified throughout the site (minimally 33 for lithic production, 5 for working conch shell, 2 for working bone, 31 for textile production, 2 potential spondylus production areas).

Tikal and Caracol Time Lines

The archaeological data from both Tikal and Caracol are overlapping and complementary. Occupation of both sites began in the Middle Preclassic period, with initial occupation at Tikal slightly predating Caracol with a projected origin date based on ceramics of approximately 800 BCE (Culbert 2003, 54) as opposed to approximately 600 BCE for Caracol (A. Chase and D. Chase 2006). Both sites appear to have had contact with peoples across and beyond the Maya area. In the middle of the Early Classic period (between 300 CE and 450 CE), individuals from the Mexican site of Teotihuacan in central Mexico were likely among the city inhabitants at both Tikal (see Iglesias Ponce de León 2003) and Caracol (A. F. Chase and D. Chase 2011). Both sites florescence in the Late Classic period, becoming sizeable urban centers, though they were somewhat divergent in their internal socioeconomic structures and urban organization, as will be discussed below. Tikal supported anywhere from 40,000 to upward of 80,000 people (Haviland 2003; Murtha 2015) and Caracol supported over 100,000 people (A. F. Chase and D. Chase 1994; D. Chase and A. F. Chase 2017). Both cities were largely abandoned by 900 CE, though Tikal has evidence for Postclassic visitations probably from populations living in the Lake Petén area (Culbert 2003, 64–65). Changes in the structure and functioning of Caracol are apparent at the end of the Classic period.

Caracol has evidence of status-linked ceramic subcomplexes in the Terminal Classic period (A. F. Chase and D. Chase 2004, 2007), just before its collapse, and it is possible that a similar phenomenon also existed at Tikal during Eznab times (A. F. Chase and D. Chase 2008, 27–29). At Caracol, it is clear that the palace elites were using a different ceramic subcomplex from that used by the rest of the population; this high-status palace ceramic subcomplex employs vessel types, such as modeled-carved pedestalled vases, that are widely distributed in the eastern lowlands at the time of the collapse. There is also evidence of rapid abandonment in the Caracol epicenter, presumably due to conflict (A. F. Chase and D. Chase 2020a). At Tikal, similar vessel types were included within the Eznab Ceramic Complex, the distribution of which correlated with stone buildings located in epicentral locations. At Caracol, this late subcomplex also occurs within epicentral stone buildings, but extensive excavation in residential groups was able to demonstrate that the more localized Late Classic ceramics continued in use alongside the high-status subcomplex outside the epicenter. At Tikal, however, the association of Eznab ceramics with stone buildings and not in residential groups was interpreted to mean that there was a significant reduction in population (Culbert 1973; 1974, 107; 1988). We, instead, suggest that the situation at Caracol and Tikal was similar.

During the Terminal Classic period, the high-status groups at both centers most likely differentiated themselves from the rest of the population through the use of status-linked ceramics (see A. F. Chase and D. Chase 2004, 2005). This interpretation means that it is difficult to identify the Terminal Classic period outside of high-status contexts (A. F. Chase and D. Chase 2008, 27–29), implying that there likely was not as significant a reduction in population at Tikal during this era as has been previously argued. (Culbert et al. [1990, 120] suggest only 14.2 percent of the population in Central Tikal and 21.4 percent of the total population was present in Eznab times based on ceramic assessment; for comparative purposes, almost all epicentral contexts at Caracol have produced Terminal Classic ceramics, and at least 39.4 percent of the residential groups were occupied.) The nature of the final occupations for these two sites clearly has significant impact on interpretations of depopulation and lack of agricultural sustainability relative to the Classic Maya collapse.

HIEROGLYPHIC HISTORY

In combination with the archaeological data, epigraphic records provide the strongest confirmation that the histories of Caracol and Tikal were intertwined. Tikal emblem glyphs appear in the early monuments of Caracol and indicate that Caracol was under the sway of Tikal during the end of the Early Classic period (Martin and Grube 2000). Caracol gained its independence from Tikal in 562 CE by means of a star-war (A. F. Chase 1991; D. Chase and A. F. Chase 2003), at which time the dominating relationship shifted to Caracol. Caracol maintained a complicated relationship with Tikal until Naranjo bested Caracol with a star-war in 680 CE.

Both sites have long dynastic records. Tikal's goes back to at least 292 CE, and Caracol's goes back to 331 CE; based on ruler counts, Tikal had at least thirty-two rulers and Caracol had at least twenty-nine (Martin and Grube 2000). An argument has also been advanced for the instillation of an individual from Teotihuacan as an Early Classic ruler at Tikal in 379 CE, following the execution of the previous dynastic ruler by the interlopers (Stuart 2000). The 562 CE star-war had similarly severe implications for Tikal. We have provided multiple, reinforcing lines of evidence that two Caracol rulers assumed rulership at Tikal and were interred in the North Acropolis after this event during Tikal's epigraphic hiatus (A. F. Chase and D. Chase 2020b; D. Chase and A. F. Chase 2017; see also Moholy-Nagy 2016 for a general discussion of monuments and hiatuses). The latest-known monumental dates from the two sites are 869 CE at Tikal (Martin 2003) and 884 CE at Caracol (D. Chase and A. F. Chase 2017, 2021).

However, while both Caracol and Tikal have extensive dynastic histories, these histories are not equivalent; in fact, the hieroglyphs themselves suggest differences between the two sites. Caracol uses a variant emblem glyph that is often portrayed without the traditional water affix, which is translated as the Maya word *chulel* and believed to have signified divinity or holiness. The lack of this prefix at Caracol may have been associated with the attempts to lessen the distinctions between elite and others at the site, intentional patterns identified in the archaeological record (A. F. Chase and D. Chase 2009). Just as the hieroglyphs suggest differences between the two sites, the ability to compare and contrast these two sites in terms of their spatial layouts, their archaeological records, and their human-nature relationships permits significant insights into the sociopolitical variability that existed among the ancient Maya.

AGRICULTURE

Although the inhabitants of both sites were rainfall dependent, the agricultural systems for the inhabitants at Tikal and Caracol differed. While households at both sites may have engaged in kitchen gardens, it would appear that Tikal focused more on extensive agriculture with possibly some intensive agriculture at the edges of its bajos (see Dunning, Beach, and Luzzadder-Beach 2006). Residential groups at Tikal are distributed in "fragmented clusters" that resulted in "less space around each household" but that left "large tracts of uninhabited areas interspersed between settlement clusters" (Murtha 2015, 91). Because there are no (or minimal) agricultural terraces at Tikal, this implies a different agricultural strategy than Caracol's for supporting that site's population, one that likely focused on "cooperative labor exchanges meeting the maintenance demands of weeding and harvesting" (Murtha 2015, 92). While Tikal's households may have had kitchen gardens immediately surrounding them, no phosphorus (P) tests exist to confirm these.

In contrast to Tikal, Caracol focused on terraforming the landscape with agricultural terraces (figure 7.3) to carry out more intensive agriculture, and the extent of Caracol's agricultural terracing (over 160 km2; D. Chase and A. F. Chase 2014a, 2017) is reflective of a fully anthropogenic and managed landscape that incorporated agriculture into an urban framework (A. F. Chase and D. Chase 2016a, 2016b). Further, at Caracol, P tests suggest that "the landscape surrounding houses was substantially enriched with household wastes" (Murtha 2015, 86). While probably initially prompted by the need to manage soil loss and water flow in hilly terrain to be agriculturally sustainable, the ancient Maya at Caracol used their technological prowess to completely modify the landscape. Given the care that the ancient Maya gave to constructing the agricultural terraces at Caracol directly on bedrock (A. F. Chase and D. Chase 1998), which permitted them to manage the flow of water over the landscape (A.S.Z. Chase and Weishampel 2016), it is likely that the Caracol Maya provided the same care to managing plants and trees throughout the site (in accord with the tenets of Ford and Nigh's [2009] "forest garden").

Both Caracol and Tikal practiced rain-dependent agriculture. Both were located in environments lacking permanent bodies of standing or flowing water, but the two sites approached their landscapes differently. Caracol aggressively terraformed its environment, while Tikal was more passive, with the possible exception of water flow into its large centrally constructed reservoirs. As noted above, Caracol also received more rain. Thus, while both sites engaged in maize agriculture, Caracol's terracing, in combination with an increased rainfall total, likely permitted more than one crop per season (with crops being cycled or mixed for nitrogen fixation), indicating that the site was agriculturally self-sustaining (Murtha 2009, 2015). This may not have been the case with Tikal, which likely imported agricultural products into its confines during the rainy season by using its associated bajos as canoe transit highways (Dahlin and Chase 2014).

WATER

Discussion of water in the Maya area has largely focused on the lack of permanent natural bodies of water within the confines of many of the largest sites of the Classic period; this emphasis is true for both Tikal and Caracol. Because these sites were dependent on rainfall, some researchers have focused on large epicentral reservoirs and argued that elite power in Classic period society was embedded in the control of water and water rituals (Lucero 2006; Lucero and Fash 2006), while others recognized that the full monopolization of this kind of power was unlikely (Johnston 2004, 266; Scarborough 2003, 113). An examination of strategies of water control and management at Caracol and Tikal reveals different approaches to capturing and distributing potable water, probably because of differences in the environmental settings of both sites (A.S.Z. Chase and Cesaretti 2019).

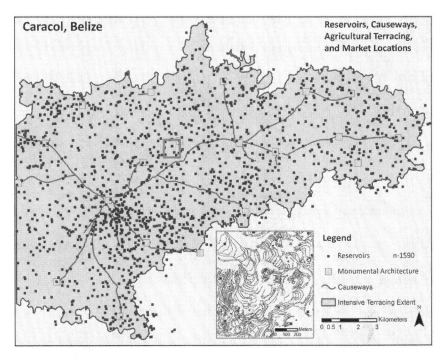

FIGURE 7.3. *Map of the areal extent of Caracol, showing reservoir distribution, monumental architecture and public plaza distribution, extent of the intensive agricultural terracing, and the causeway system at the site (after A.S.Z. Chase 2016a).*

Scarborough and Gallopin (1991, 659) defined three kinds of reservoirs for Tikal (figure 7.4): large central precinct reservoirs, residential reservoirs, and bajo-margin reservoirs. While it is implied that the majority of these were constructed and modified, it is crucial to distinguish between constructed reservoirs and naturally occurring *aguadas* (small body of natural water) (see Gallopin 1990, 19). Gallopin (1990, 19) followed the typology established by the Tikal mappers (Carr and Hazard 1961, 13), which established six types of reservoirs: deep-dug or constructed, modified aguadas, natural aguadas, quarry pits, *pozas* (small constructed household reservoir), and special cases. Within the three-division schema used for Tikal, 9 reservoirs (6 central-precinct and 3 residential) were deep-dug or constructed, and four bajo-margin reservoirs were modified aguadas; 47 small pozas were associated with structures and were likely constructed; 15 natural aguadas and "other small reservoirs" were not associated with structures (Scarborough and Gallopin 1991, 661). Whereas Tikal's noncentral reservoirs include a mix of constructed reservoirs and natural (nonconstructed) aguadas, the vast majority—if not all—of Caracol's minimally 1,590 residential reservoirs (see figure 7.3) are formally constructed features (A.S.Z. Chase

2016a). Because of the extensive modification of Caracol's landscape by the construction of agricultural terraces (A. F. Chase and D. Chase 1998; A.S.Z. Chase and Weishampel 2016; D. Chase and A. F. Chase 2014a, 2017), naturally occurring aguadas were minimized and completely bounded within the agricultural fields, often being modified like those at Tikal (see Crandall 2009). It is clear that Caracol's anthropogenic landscape (A. F. Chase and D. Chase 2016b) was different from the bajo-dominated landscape of Tikal (see A.S.Z. Chase and Cesaretti 2019; Lentz, Dunning, and L. Scarborough 2015a). It has also become evident that a spectrum of water management strategies existed throughout the Maya lowlands, which are not always as easy to define as the Caracol example (see, e.g., Brewer et al. 2017 for the difficulty in defining natural versus constructed features in the region of Yaxnohcah, Mexico; see also Dunning et al., chapter 2 in this volume).

By far the largest and most important reservoirs at Tikal were those located in the central precinct of the site amidst the large public architecture and broad causeways (see figure 7.4). These six reservoirs held the bulk of Tikal's water and were extensively engineered to direct water flow and filter potable water (Harrison 2012; Scarborough et al. 2012). The concentration of water in the center of Tikal has led to an argument for the centralization of power. "At Tikal water management allowed resource control and therefore political control by a central-precinct elite" (Scarborough and Gallopin 1991, 661). At Caracol, water management also allowed resource control but did not imply complete political control, as reservoirs were also located within residential settlement (A.S.Z. Chase 2016a). Built reservoirs occur at both Tikal and Caracol, but at Tikal they tend to be fairly large and to contain the bulk of the water needed by the site's inhabitants (Scarborough and Gallopin 1991; Scarborough et al. 2012). At Caracol, the situation is inverted. While eight large reservoirs are associated with widely dispersed public architecture at Caracol (see A.S.Z. Chase 2016b, figs. 3 and 4, table 2), there is a far more extensive body of constructed household reservoirs; as previously mentioned, minimally 1,590 built reservoirs are distributed over the landscape along with four natural aguadas.

The distribution of water features at these two sites is significant in identifying how their populations were organized and governed. As noted above, Scarborough (2003) would argue that there was centralized management of water through Tikal's large reservoir system; Lisa J. Lucero (2006) would argue that this and water ritual were the source of elite power. At Caracol, although there is usually one large reservoir associated with each older major architectural concentration, the distribution of reservoirs throughout the landscape in association with residential groups strongly suggests that a different governing strategy and source of elite power existed (A.S.Z. Chase 2019). At Caracol, large bodies of water in the epicenter could demonstrate elite ability to harness

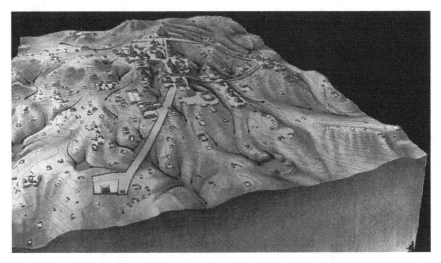

FIGURE 7.4. *Reconstruction of central Tikal showing the articulation of reservoirs with the landscape and the central architectural features (after Scarborough, Chase, and Chase 2012).*

valuable water resources, but individual households also controlled their own water resources. The residential settlement at Caracol is distributed amidst a continuous landscape of agricultural terracing, and at least one-sixth of the residential groups at the site were associated with constructed reservoirs. This arrangement suggests that control of both of these resources, agricultural land and water, was more localized at Caracol; while there may have been centralized input in disputes, the placement of these features on the landscape is suggestive of a less-centralized strategy regarding land and water than is seen at Tikal.

CITY FORM AND FUNCTION

There were also significant differences in lifestyles between Tikal and Caracol.

Households

These differences can be seen primarily in the physical layouts of residential groups, but also in the material culture and burial patterns associated with these residential groups. Only 14 percent of the residential groups at Tikal contained an eastern shrine, known as a Plaza Plan 2 arrangement (Becker 2003, 259). At Caracol some 70 percent of the residential groups include an eastern shrine containing interments and caches (A. F. Chase and D. Chase 2009; D. Chase and A. F. Chase 2017); many of these structures are also associated with centrally located stairway niches or with centrally placed architectural stair balks, indicative of ritual activity areas. While Tikal sees eastern shrine groups as being somewhat special, the Caracol data instead suggest that ritual was incorporated into the majority of that site's residential units (D. Chase and A. F. Chase 2017). The burials that are associated with the eastern shrines at both sites have been interpreted as representing a focus on "ancestor" veneration; yet, the archaeological contexts from Caracol suggest that the ritual focus was actually one that commemorated cyclical time (A. F. Chase and D. Chase 2013; D. Chase and A. F. Chase 2011, 2017, 2023). At Tikal, most burials contained a single extended individual with head to the north; at Caracol, at least half of the burials contain multiple individuals in varying degrees of articulation, and extended burials are found with head to both the south and north. While the majority of the tombs known from Tikal are associated with public architecture in the site center, Caracol tombs are also located in most residential groups (25 tombs in the site epicenter; 105 tombs in 75 different residential groups). Formal caches in specially made pottery containers also commonly occur in residential groups at Caracol (recovered in 81 different residential groups outside of the site epicenter through the 2020 field season) but are not generally found in residential groups at Tikal; rather, formal pottery cache containers at Tikal are correlated with the large central architecture (e.g., Culbert 1993, 2003). These data can be used to infer that social differences and inequality were more ingrained at Tikal, with a Gini coefficient of 0.62 (Kohler et al. 2018, table 11.3), than at Caracol, with a Gini of 0.34 (A.S.Z. Chase 2017, table 2), again having ramifications for the organization of society. Caracol appears to have focused on more collective decisions for the good of the broader population, whereas Tikal appears to have focused on the prerogatives of the elite. Based on the available archaeological data, household crafting appears at both sites but appears to be more widespread at Caracol (Becker 1983; A. F. Chase and D. Chase 2015).

Architecture

There are also significant architectural differences between the two sites that can be used to infer broader city organization. The causeway system at Tikal links the epicenter of the site together, whereas the causeway system at Caracol integrates the full extent of the urban area. At Tikal the causeways formed a closed system, integrating the central architecture of the site with three different temples (figure 7.5). At Caracol the causeway system unites the landscape, integrating the site epicenter with a series of large open plazas with nonpermanent range building substructures that served administrative and market purposes (see figure 7.3); the Caracol causeways also integrated previously independent early sites into Caracol's metropolitan area. The difference in market locations and access is also striking. At Tikal, there was a single built market in the site epicenter complete with stone vaulted rooms (Becker 2015; Jones 2015); while goods were clearly made available to the populace (e.g., Masson and Freidel 2012), the built environment implies rigid control by the central Tikal elite. There is a

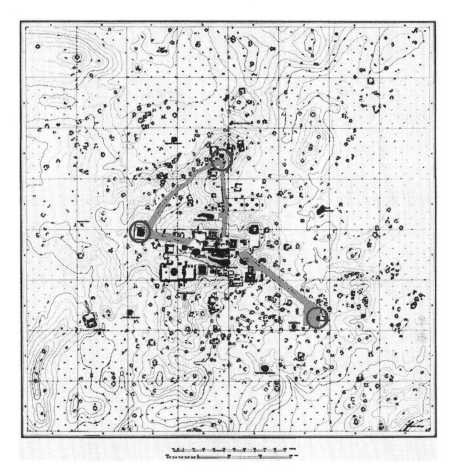

FIGURE 7.5. *The central 16 km² of Tikal (from Carr and Hazard 1961), showing the integration of broad causeways (shaded) and temples (circled) in the site epicenter (map of the ruins of Tikal used with permission of the University of Pennsylvania Museum of Archaeology and Anthropology).*

possibility that there were markets at a series of minor centers located outside of the Tikal epicenter (see A. F. Chase and D. Chase 2003), but these were not formally integrated into a single system by causeways, as at Caracol. Robert Fry (2003) argues that there were local markets at Tikal based on the distribution of utilitarian pottery. At Caracol, foreign goods were probably widely available in its local markets (A. F. Chase et al. 2015; D. Chase and A. F. Chase 2014b).

Two other architectural assemblages speak to differences between the two cities: E Groups and Twin-Pyramid Groups. Some nine Twin-Pyramid Groups are known from Tikal (Jones 1969); three others are known from Yaxha, Uolantun, and Chalpate (Becker 2003, 258); none occurs at Caracol. These are highly standardized structural arrangements and consist of two radial temples located on the eastern and western sides of large plazas. No structures crowned these pyramids, and plain stelae and altars were set in a row in front of the eastern pyramid. A vaulted range building with nine doorways defines the southern extent of the plaza, and an unroofed walled enclosure, holding a carved stelae and altar that celebrate the current *k'atun* (a unit of time in the Maya calendar equal to 19.713 years), is located on the northern side of the plaza. These unique architectural complexes were constructed to celebrate k'atun endings at Tikal minimally from 9.10.0.0.0 (633 CE) through 9.18.0.0.0 (790 CE). Hattula Moholy-Nagy (2016, 264) notes that these complexes "were probable venues for elaborate ceremonies that linked the ruler's place in social history with the great cosmic cycles of time." Caracol also commemorated cyclical time but in different ways—marking larger periods of time in E Groups, an architectural assemblage that defines the earliest public architecture in the Maya area (Freidel et al. 2017; see also Inomata et al. 2021) and shorter periods of time with *k'atun* altars or ritual interments of burials and caches (A. F. Chase and D. Chase 2013; D. Chase and A. F. Chase 2011).

Both Caracol and Tikal had E Groups. At Caracol, the E Group continued to be utilized in recognizable form from the Late Preclassic through the Terminal Classic period (A. F. Chase and D. Chase 2017a). In the Early Classic period, the Caracol E Group was augmented with northern and southern pyramids. No formal buildings occur atop the southern or western pyramids in Caracol's E Group, whereas the northern pyramid supports a vaulted building. At the end of the Early Classic, tombs are associated with the E Group eastern platform and its lateral buildings but not directly with the core central building in the E Group, which continues in unmodified architectural form through the time of the site's collapse.

At Tikal, the eastern E Group platform morphs into a platform supporting three vaulted buildings that house a series of dynastic tombs and burials (Laporte 2003; Laporte and Fialko 1995). The three eastern structures in Tikal's E Group are all converted into dynastic temples in the Protoclassic period, likely being the venue of that site's royal burials for that era. In the Early Classic, there is a venue shift back to the North Acropolis for royal interments and the Main Plaza at Tikal, and the architectural temples located here are used to house dynastic burials through the Late Classic period. That there was a Late Classic focus on dynasty at Tikal is clear from the monuments lined up in the Main Plaza of Tikal in front of the North Acropolis temples. Tikal manifests a greater fusion of public ritual focusing on dynasty than is found at Caracol. The distribution of both Twin-Pyramid Groups and tall freestanding temples at Tikal in the Late Classic period—and their clear focus as dynastic symbols—differs from what is found at Caracol and is presumably reflective of a different governmental strategy focusing on the ruler in the late Late Classic period (after 680 CE).

FIGURE 7.6. *Photograph of Tikal Temple 1 on the eastern side of the Great Plaza, looking southeast.*

Layout

Temples at Tikal vary significantly in their placement from those at Caracol during the Late Classic period. At Tikal the temple structure carries over into the Plaza Plan 2 residential groups and the eastern shrine sometimes is a temple building (e.g., Tikal Structure 5G-8). While vaulted buildings on eastern pyramids do exist at Caracol (e.g., Caracol Structure K19), most eastern structures had flatter summits containing perishable buildings. At Tikal the public fusion of dynasty and architectural plan is seen in Temple 1, which functions as an exceedingly visible eastern shrine building (figure 7.6). This is significantly different from Caracol, where Late Classic temples are ensconced within relatively private locations that did not emphasize public access. For instance, although visible to some degree, the Late Classic temples associated with the summit of Caana (figure 7.7; see also A. F. Chase and D. Chase 2017b), the summit of the Central Acropolis, and the summit of the Northeast Acropolis are not publicly accessible. Thus, unlike the highly accessible public temples of Tikal, the ones at Caracol are all integrated into residential households. Again, these data are relevant to the differences observed at the two sites; the architectural data from Tikal would support an interpretation of an integrated state religion focused on dynasty, something also suggested by the *incensario* (censer) distribution at that site (Rice 1999) and by the elaborateness of Late Classic royal tombs (e.g., Burial 116 and 196; see Coggins 1975 and Harrison 1999).

FIGURE 7.7. *Photograph of Caana, Caracol's central architectural complex, looking north.*

Caracol presents a different situation. Overall, material items and goods are more equally distributed throughout residential groups at the site, with most residential groups focused on their own shrine and not on royal temples. Late Classic royal tombs found in Caracol's epicentral buildings are not ostentatious; in fact, burials in residential groups often contain items as elaborate as those found in epicentral tombs, albeit sometimes with the remains of a larger number of individuals. Thus, there also appear to be significant differences in ritual practices between the two sites.

DISCUSSION

So, how does this all fit together? We feel that the data demonstrate that different practices and adaptations were present at the two sites, guided not only by variations in their environmental settings, but also by human choices. The distribution of the residential settlement, constructed agricultural fields, and constructed reservoirs at Caracol demonstrates a focus on long-term sustainability that represents a different strategy from the one used at Tikal. The two landscapes were used in different ways. Caracol's Late Classic environment is almost completely anthropogenic (or human made); the agricultural terraces constituted landesque capital and were used year after year, requiring maintenance to keep their fertility and usefulness (D. Chase and A. F. Chase 2014a); the site's abundant constructed reservoirs must have also required similar attention.

Both Caracol and Tikal were focused on water drainage; at Tikal, this took the form of channeling the water into large catchment areas so that it could be used both for drinking and other purposes, with only a secondary interest on smaller constructed reservoirs (Scarborough et al. 2012; Scarborough and Gallopin 1991); at Caracol, while water was drained into larger reservoirs in areas of public architecture, there was a greater focus on channeling the flow of rainfall and dispersing water over the agricultural terraces to maximize water and soil retention (A.S.Z. Chase and Weishampel 2016) as well as the dispersed collection of potable water in some 1,600 constructed reservoirs (A.S.Z. Chase 2016a). At Tikal, while there may have been intensive cropping at the bajo margins (Dunning et al. 2015), there was not the same focus on agricultural production in the vicinity of the residential groups that is seen at Caracol; in fact, given the arguments regarding carrying capacity at Tikal (e.g., Lentz et al. 2015b), sustainability at Tikal may have been dependent in the Late Classic period on the importation of food across flooded bajos during the rainy season, presumably under centralized control. This practice also would accord with the more centralized focus on water seen at Tikal.

Thus, at Tikal, monumental architecture, reservoirs, and causeways focus on elite order and interests. The landscape was not significantly transformed for agriculture. The reservoirs were centrally located and larger in capacity; while some smaller ones occur in the landscape, they are nowhere near the number that are found at Caracol. Given its central location, size, and permanent structures, the central market at Tikal may also have been utilized as a source of power to control the economic distribution of goods at the site. Late Classic Tikal temples were the focal architectural points, visibly signifying both elite power and probably a state religious focus. In contrast, at Caracol there was a focus on top-down collective action, with the elites seemingly promoting the public good in terms of the distribution of goods and resources. Ritual and religion likewise were not narrowly focused on the dynastic line but rather on the temporal order of which all were a part. Agricultural intensification was widely practiced. Landscape modification provided agricultural sustainability with reservoirs also benefiting the broader population. Markets may have had central oversight but offered access to goods throughout greater Caracol. Thus, the sociopolitical organizations of Late Classic period Tikal and Caracol were significantly different from each other and speak to the extent of cultural diversity in the Maya region. While hieroglyphs, iconography, and symbolism may at the surface appear to have been similar at the two centers, the archaeological record provides evidence that significantly different social customs and practices were followed at the two sites, which partially explains both the broader human-nature relationships that are evident and the differences in their societal trajectories.

The differences in site practices are especially surprising given the control of both cities by the Caracol elite in the early part of the Late Classic period. At the same time that Caracol "usurpers" (Haviland 1992, 73) ritually transformed the center of Tikal through the appropriation of Tikal Structures 5D32 and 5D33 for the interment of two of its rulers (A. F. Chase and D. Chase 2020b; D. Chase and A. F. Chase 2017), the broader populations at the two sites enjoyed very different access to resources, wealth, and ritual. The fact that little else changed within Tikal society may suggest that Caracol used Tikal as an extractive economy for its own purposes during the early part of the Late Classic period, much as Caracol may have been an extractive economy for Tikal during the late part of the Early Classic period (D. Chase and A. F. Chase 2020), that primary urban revenue sources at both city centers differed (sensu Blanton and Fargher 2008), or that a mix of various factors existed.

Caracol's impact on the landscape of Tikal is primarily seen in the ritual transformation of that site. The tall Late Classic temples that came to dominate Tikal started with the construction of Tikal Structure 5D-33-1st for the interment of Caracol ruler K'an II. Also introduced were Twin-Pyramid Groups. These large standardized architectural complexes aligned well with the focus on cyclical time seen throughout Caracol's residential groups (A. F. Chase and D. Chase 2013; D. Chase and A. F. Chase 2017) but represent an architectural elaboration not found at Caracol. That the "three earliest groups, constructed during the long hiatus, were partially demolished later" (Moholy-Nagy 2016, 264) suggests yet another ritual act. These Twin-Pyramid Groups would have been constructed by K'an II, and their ritual destruction would have been appropriate once Tikal was again independent. The fact that the new Tikal ruler, Jasaw Chan K'awiil, erected his first monuments in Caracol style (e.g., a Giant Ahau altar) within the Twin-Pyramid Group built for the 9.13.0.0.0 k'atun ceremony (Jones and Satterthwaite 1982, 62)—and ritually defaced and destroyed the earlier examples of this architectural form—symbolically placed him within the cosmic cycles of time as the new and independent ritual overlord of Tikal. Yet, the broader population of Tikal was far removed from the standards of wealth and ritual found in his Late Classic tomb (e.g., Coe 1990, 604–609).

CONCLUSION

Given the interconnectedness and proximity of these two sites, the extant variability is striking. Both Tikal and Caracol were founded in landscapes lacking natural, permanent bodies of water. Thus, both populations were forced to adapt the terrain to their subsistence needs. In terms of potable water, two different strategies were followed. At Tikal, there was the formal capture of large bodies of water in huge holding tanks adjacent to public architecture, seemingly augmented by the terrain. At hillier Caracol, while larger reservoirs were constructed in association with public architecture, many smaller reservoirs were also constructed throughout the landscape, thus lending a modicum of independence to the site's population in terms of this resource. Regarding agriculture, the residents of Caracol began to terraform the landscape by the Late Preclassic period, eventually constructing an almost continuous web of agricultural terraces. This did not happen at Tikal. Because of the early and continuous human labor poured into the fertility of Caracol's agricultural terraces, these features provided greater productivity and likely led to surpluses that could be exported elsewhere. While the bajo margins may have been similarly productive at Tikal, it is less likely that they yielded huge surpluses that could be exported outside of Tikal; it is more likely that some of Tikal's bulk food items came from some distance, possibly being transported in the rainy season when the bajos were full of water and canoe travel was a possibility. Ritual at Tikal seemed to center on the elite and the royal dynasty; the economic market was also centralized and controlled. The opposite was the case at Caracol, where markets were distributed over the landscape and most residential groups partook of their own rituals. Thus, the human-nature relationships at these two sites differed dramatically and were reflected both in the broader organization of the sites and in their social patterns.

There were unintended consequences in each of these paths. At Caracol, the terrace construction and independently constructed reservoirs, in combination with a system of distributed market locales all dendritically connected to the site epicenter by causeways, defined residential and agricultural space and helped the site to expand outward. At Tikal, the bajos constrained settlement expansion and probably productivity; yet, the site focus on centrality—as evinced in the placement of reservoirs, temples, causeways, and its single marketplace—also implied more direct control over its population. Thus, the two sites were idiosyncratic in their approaches to sustainability and social policy. More than any other aspects of their societies, however, access to and control of water defined their distinct trajectories: at Tikal, water was a resource that could be centrally controlled, much like that site's people and central architecture; at Caracol, water was a local resource that could be accessed and controlled by individual residential groups, reflecting the structural differences that existed among Classic era polities.

ACKNOWLEDGMENTS

The archaeological work that we have undertaken at Caracol over the past thirty-six years has been undertaken in conjunction with the Belize Institute of Archaeology and has involved five universities (University of Central Florida; University of Nevada, Las Vegas; Claremont Graduate University; Pomona College; and, Arizona State University) with sponsorship derived from a host of foundations and funding agencies, including the Alphawood Foundation; the

Ahau Foundation; the Dart Foundation; the Foundation for the Advancement of Mesoamerican Studies, Inc.; the Geraldine and Emory Ford Foundation; the Government of Belize; the Harry Frank Guggenheim Foundation; the NASA Space Archaeology Program; the National Science Foundation; the Stans Foundation; UCF-UF—Space Research Initiative; the United States Agency for International Development; the Trevor Colbourn Endowment from the University of Central Florida; and private donations to the foundations at UCF, UNLV, and Pomona College. We would also like to note that the long-term archaeological work undertaken at Tikal was both an inspiration and a database for the research that we have done at Caracol—especially as two of us did both our undergraduate and graduate work at the University of Pennsylvania and were very familiar with the "Tikal Room." Besides our own familiarity with Tikal and its archaeological history, part of the stimulus for comparing and contrasting Tikal and Caracol was the extensive work that Vern Scarborough has undertaken on water management and reservoirs at Tikal; his exploration of the Tikal system has led us to define a very different expression of water management for Caracol that expands our knowledge of ancient Maya technical prowess.

REFERENCES

Becker, Marshall J. 1983. "Indications of Social Class Differences Based on the Archaeo-logical Evidence for Occupational Specialization among the Classic Maya at Tikal, Guatemala." *Revista Española de Antropología Americana* 13: 29–46.

Becker, Marshall J. 2003. "Plaza Plans at Tikal." In *Tikal: Dynasties, Foreigners, and Affairs of State*, edited by J. A. Sabloff, 253–280. Santa Fe, NM: School of American Research Press.

Becker, Marshall J. 2015. "Ancient Maya Markets: Architectural Grammar and Market Identifications." In *The Ancient Maya Marketplace: The Archaeology of Transient Space*, edited by E. King, 90–110. Tucson: University of Arizona Press.

Beetz, Carl P., and Linton Satterthwaite. 1981. *The Monuments and Inscriptions of Caracol, Belize.* University Museum Monograph 45. Philadelphia: University of Pennsylvania.

Blanton, Richard E., and Lane F. Fargher. 2008. *Collective Action in the Formation of Pre-Modern States.* New York: Springer.

Brewer, Jeffrey L., Christopher Carr, Nicholas P. Dunning, Debra S. Walker, Armando Anaya Hernandez, Meaghan Peuramaki-Brown, and Kathryn Reese-Taylor. 2017. "Employing Airborne LiDAR and Archaeological Testing to Determine the Role of Small Depressions in Water Management at the Ancient Maya Site of Yaxnohcah, Campeche, Mexico." *Journal of Archaeological Science: Reports* 13 (1): 291–302.

Carr, Robert E., and James E. Hazard. 1961. *Map of the Ruins of Tikal, El Peten, Guate-mala.* Tikal Report 11. Philadelphia: University of Pennsylvania.

Chase, Adrian S.Z. 2016a. "Beyond Elite Control: Residential Reservoirs at Caracol, Belize." *WIREs Water* 3 (6): 885–897.

Chase, Adrian S.Z. 2016b. "Districting and Urban Services at Caracol, Belize: Intrasite Boundaries in an Evolving Maya Cityscape." *Research Reports in Belizean Archaeology* 13: 15–28.

Chase, Adrian S.Z. 2017. "Residential Inequality among the Ancient Maya: Operationalizing Household Architectural Volume at Caracol, Belize." *Research Reports in Belizean Archaeology* 14: 31–39.

Chase, Adrian S.Z. 2019. "Water Management among the Ancient Maya: Degrees of Latitude." *Research Reports in Belizean Archaeology* 16: 101–109.

Chase, Adrian S.Z. 2021. "Urban Life at Caracol, Belize: Neighborhoods, Inequality, Infrastructure, and Governance." PhD dissertation, School of Human Evolution and Social Change, Arizona State University, Tempe.

Chase, Adrian S.Z., and Rudolf Cesaretti. 2019. "Diversity in Ancient Maya Water Management Strategies and Landscapes at Caracol, Belize, and Tikal Guatemala." *WIREs Water* 6 (2): e1332.

Chase, Adrian S.Z., and John F. Weishampel. 2016. "Using LiDAR and GIS to Investigate Water and Soil Management in the Agricultural Terracing at Caracol, Belize." *Advances in Archaeological Practice* 4 (3): 357–370.

Chase, Arlen F. 1991. "Cycles of Time: Caracol in the Maya Realm." In *Sixth Palenque Round Table, 1986, Vol. VII*, edited by M. G. Robertson, 32–42. Norman: University of Oklahoma Press.

Chase, Arlen F., and Diane Z. Chase. 1987. *Investigations at the Classic Maya City of Caracol, Belize: 1985–1987*. Monograph 3. San Francisco: Pre-Columbian Art Research Institute.

Chase, Arlen F., and Diane Z. Chase. 1994. "Details in the Archaeology of Caracol, Belize: An Introduction." In *Studies in the Archaeology of Caracol, Belize*, edited by D. Z. Chase and A. F. Chase, 1–11. Monograph 7. San Francisco: Pre-Columbian Art Research Institute.

Chase, Arlen F., and Diane Z. Chase. 1998. "Scale and Intensity in Classic Period Maya Agriculture: Terracing and Settlement at the 'Garden City' of Caracol, Belize." *Culture and Agriculture* 20 (2): 60–77.

Chase, Arlen F., and Diane Z. Chase. 2001. "Ancient Maya Causeways and Site Organization at Caracol, Belize." *Ancient Mesoamerica* 12 (2): 273–281.

Chase, Arlen F., and Diane Z. Chase. 2003. "Minor Centers, Complexity, and Scale in Lowland Maya Settlement Archaeology." In *Perspectives on Ancient Maya Rural Complexity*, edited by G. Iannone and S. Connell, 108–118. Cotsen Institute of Archaeology Monograph 49. Los Angeles: University of California.

Chase, Arlen F., and Diane Z. Chase. 2004. "Terminal Classic Status-Linked Ceramics and the Maya 'Collapse': *De Facto* Refuse at Caracol, Belize." In *The Terminal Classic in the Maya Lowlands: Collapse, Transition, and Transformation*, edited by A. Demarest, P. Rice, and D. Rice, 342–366. Boulder: University Press of Colorado.

Chase, Arlen F., and Diane Z. Chase. 2005. "Contextualizing the Collapse: Hegemony and Terminal Classic Ceramics from Caracol, Belize." In *Geographies of Power:*

Understanding the Nature of Terminal Classic Pottery in the Maya Lowlands, edited by S. Lopez Varella and A. Foias, 73–91. BAR Monograph S1447. Oxford: British Archaeological Reports.

Chase, Arlen F., and Diane Z. Chase. 2007. " 'This is the End': Archaeological Transitions and the Terminal Classic Period at Caracol, Belize." *Research Reports in Belizean Archaeology* 4: 13–27.

Chase, Arlen F., and Diane Z. Chase. 2008. "Methodological Issues in the Archaeological Identification of the Terminal Classic and Postclassic Transition in the Maya Area." *Research Reports in Belizean Archaeology* 5: 23–36.

Chase, Arlen F., and Diane Z. Chase. 2009. "Symbolic Egalitarianism and Homogenized Distributions in the Archaeological Record at Caracol, Belize: Method, Theory, and Complexity." *Research Reports in Belizean Archaeology* 6: 15–24.

Chase, Arlen F., and Diane Z. Chase. 2011. "Status and Power: Caracol, Teotihuacan, and the Early Classic Maya World." *Research Reports in Belizean Archaeology* 8: 3–18.

Chase, Arlen F., and Diane Z. Chase. 2013. "Temporal Cycles in the Archaeology of Maya Residential Groups from Caracol, Belize." *Research Reports in Belizean Archaeology* 10: 13–23.

Chase, Arlen F., and Diane Z. Chase. 2015. "The Domestic Economy of Caracol, Belize: Articulating with the Institutional Economy in an Ancient Maya Urban Setting." *Research Reports in Belizean Archaeology* 12: 15–23.

Chase, Arlen F., and Diane Z. Chase. 2016a. "The Ancient Maya City: Anthropogenic Landscapes, Settlement Archaeology, and Caracol, Belize." *Research Reports in Belizean Archaeology* 13: 3–14.

Chase, Arlen F., and Diane Z. Chase. 2016b. "Urbanism and Anthropogenic Landscapes." *Annual Review of Anthropology* 45: 361–376.

Chase, Arlen F., and Diane Z. Chase. 2017a. "E Groups and the Rise of Complexity in the Southeastern Maya Lowlands." In *Maya E-Groups: Calendars, Astronomy, and Urbanism in the Early Lowlands*, edited by D. Freidel, A. Chase, A. Dowd, and J. Murdoch, 31–71. Gainesville: University Press of Florida.

Chase, Arlen F., and Diane Z. Chase. 2017b. "Ancient Maya Architecture and Spatial Layouts: Contextualizing Caana at Caracol, Belize." *Research Reports in Belizean Archaeology* 14: 13–22.

Chase, Arlen F., and Diane Z. Chase. 2020a. "Final Moments: Contextualizing On-Floor Archaeological Materials from Caracol, Belize." *Ancient Mesoamerica* 31 (1): 77–87.

Chase, Arlen F., and Diane Z. Chase. 2020b. "The Materialization of Classic Period Maya Warfare: Caracol Stranger-Kings at Tikal." In *A Forest of History: The Maya after the Emergence of Divine Kingship*, edited by T. Stanton and M. K. Brown, 20–48. Boulder: University Press of Colorado.

Chase, Arlen F. and Diane Z. Chase. 2021. The Transformation of Maya Rulership at Caracol, Belize. In *Maya Kingship: Rupture and Transformation from Classic to Postclassic*

Times, edited by Tsubasa Okoshi, Arlen F. Chase, Philippe Nondedeo, and M. Charlotte Arnauld, 349-356. University Press of Florida, Gainesville.

Chase, Arlen F., Diane Z. Chase, Jaime J. Awe, John F. Weishampel, Gyles Iannone, Holley Moyes, Jason Yaeger et al. 2014. "Ancient Maya Regional Settlement and Inter-Site Analysis: The 2013 West-Central Belize LiDAR Survey." *Remote Sensing* 6 (9): 8671–8695.

Chase, Arlen F., Diane Z. Chase, and Michael E. Smith. 2009. "States and Empires in Ancient Mesoamerica." *Ancient Mesoamerica* 20 (2): 175–182.

Chase, Arlen F., Diane Z. Chase, Richard Terry, Jacob M. Horlacher, and Adrian S. Z. Chase. 2015. "Markets among the Ancient Maya: The Case of Caracol, Belize." In *The Ancient Maya Marketplace: The Archaeology of Transient Space*, edited by E. King, 226–250. Tucson: University of Arizona Press.

Chase, Arlen F., Diane Z. Chase, and John F. Weishampel. 2010. "Lasers in the Jungle: Airborne Sensors Reveal a Vast Maya Landscape." *Archaeology* 63 (4): 27–29.

Chase, Arlen F., Diane Z. Chase, John F. Weishampel, Jason B. Drake, Ramesh L. Shrestha, K. Clint Slatton, Jaime J. Awe, and William E. Carter. 2011. "Airborne LiDAR, Archaeology, and the Ancient Maya Landscape at Caracol, Belize." *Journal of Archaeological Science* 38 (2): 387–398.

Chase, Arlen F., Lisa J. Lucero, Vernon L. Scarborough, Diane Z. Chase, Rach Cobos, Nicholas Dunning, Joel Gunn et al. 2014. "Tropical Landscapes and the Ancient Maya: Diversity in Time and Space." In *The Resilience and Vulnerability of Ancient Landscapes: Transforming Maya Archaeology through IHOPE*, edited by A. F. Chase and V. L. Scarborough, 11–29. AP3A Paper 24 (1). Arlington, VA: American Anthropological Association.

Chase, Arlen F., and Vernon L. Scarborough. 2014. *The Resilience and Vulnerability of Ancient Landscapes: Transforming Maya Archaeology through IHOPE.* AP3A Paper 24 (1). Arlington, VA: American Anthropological Association.

Chase, Diane Z., and Arlen F. Chase. 1994. *Studies in the Archaeology of Caracol, Belize.* Monograph 7. Pre-Columbian Art Research Institute, San Francisco.

Chase, Diane Z., and Arlen F. Chase. 2003. "Texts and Contexts in Classic Maya Warfare: A Brief Consideration of Epigraphy and Archaeology at Caracol, Belize." In *Ancient Mesoamerican Warfare*, edited by M. K. Brown and T. W. Stanton, 171–188. Walnut Creek, CA: Alta Mira Press.

Chase, Diane Z., and Arlen F. Chase. 2011. "Ghosts amid the Ruins: Analyzing Relationships between the Living and the Dead among the Ancient Maya at Caracol, Belize." In *Living with the Dead: Mortuary Ritual in Mesoamerica*, edited by J. L. Fitzsimmons and I. Shimada, 78–101. Tucson: University of Arizona Press.

Chase, Diane Z., and Arlen F. Chase. 2014a. "Path Dependency in the Rise and Denouement of a Classic Maya City: The Case of Caracol, Belize." In *The Resilience and Vulnerability of Ancient Landscapes: Transforming Maya Archaeology through IHOPE*, edited by A. F. Chase and V. L. Scarborough, 142–154. AP3A Paper 24 (1). Arlington, VA: American Anthropological Association.

Chase, Diane Z., and Arlen F. Chase. 2014b. "Ancient Maya Markets and the Economic Integration of Caracol, Belize." *Ancient Mesoamerica* 25 (1): 239–250.

Chase, Diane Z., and Arlen F. Chase. 2015. "Thirty Years of Archaeology at Caracol, Belize: Retrospective and Prospective." *Research Reports in Belizean Archaeology* 12: 3–14.

Chase, Diane Z., and Arlen F. Chase. 2017. "Caracol, Belize, and Changing Perceptions of Ancient Maya Society." *Journal of Archaeological Research* 25 (3): 185–249.

Chase, Diane Z., and Arlen F. Chase. 2020. "The Economic Landscape of Caracol, Belize." In *Nuts and Bolts of the Real "Business" of Ancient Maya Exchange*, edited by M. Masson, D. Freidel, and A. Demarest, 132–148. Gainesville: University Press of Florida.

Chase, Diane Z., and Arlen F. Chase. 2023. "The Materialization of Time in the Maya Archaeological Record: Examples from Caracol and Santa Rita Corozal, Belize." In *The Materialization of Time in the Ancient Maya World: Mythic History and Ritual Order*, edited by D. Freidel, A. Chase, A. Dowd, and J. Murdock. Gainesville: University Press of Florida.

Coe, William R. 1990. *Excavations in the Great Plaza, North Terrace, and North Acropolis of Tikal.* 6 vols. Tikal Report 14. Philadelphia: University of Pennsylvania Museum.

Coe, William R., and William A. Haviland. 1982. *Introduction to the Archaeology of Tikal, Guatemala.* Tikal Report 12. Philadelphia: University of Pennsylvania Museum.

Coggins, Clemency C. 1975. "Painting and Drawing Styles at Tikal: An Historical and Iconographic Reconstruction." PhD diss., Harvard University, Cambridge, MA.

Crandall, James. 2009. "Water and Mountains: Maya Water Management at Caracol, Belize." MA thesis, Department of Anthropology, University of Central Florida, Orlando.

Culbert, T. Patrick. 1973. "The Maya Downfall at Tikal." In *The Classic Maya Collapse*, edited by T. P. Culbert, 63–92. Albuquerque: University of New Mexico Press.

Culbert, T. Patrick. 1974. *The Lost Civilization: The Story of the Classic Maya.* New York: Harper and Row.

Culbert, T. Patrick. 1988. "The Collapse of Classic Maya Civilization." In *The Collapse of Ancient States and Civilizations*, edited by N. Yoffee and G. Cowgill, 69–101. Tucson: University of Arizona Press.

Culbert, T. Patrick. 1993. *The Ceramics of Tikal: Vessels from the Burials, Caches, and Problematical Deposits.* Tikal Report 25A. Monograph 81. Philadelphia: University Museum, University of Pennsylvania.

Culbert, T. Patrick. 2003. "The Ceramics of Tikal." In *Tikal: Dynasties, Foreigners, and Affairs of State*, edited by J. A. Sabloff, 47–81. Santa Fe, NM: School of American Research Press.

Culbert, T. Patrick, Laura J. Kosakowsky, Robert E. Fry, and William A. Haviland. 1990. "The Population of Tikal, Guatemala." In *Precolumbian Population History in the Maya Lowlands*, edited by T. P. Culbert and D. Rice, 103–121. Albuquerque: University of New Mexico Press.

Culbert, T. Patrick, Laura J. Levi, and Luis Cruz. 1990. "Lowland Maya Wetland Agriculture: The Rio Azul Agronomy Program." In *Vision and Revision in Maya Studies*, edited by F. Clancy and P. Harrison, 115–124. Albuquerque: University of New Mexico Press.

Dahlin, Bruce H., and Arlen F. Chase. 2014. "A Tale of Three Cities: Effects of the CE 536 Event in the Lowland Maya Heartland." In *The Great Maya Droughts in Cultural Context: Case Studies in Resilience and Vulnerability*, edited by G. Iannone, 127–155. Boulder: University Press of Colorado.

Dunning, Nicholas P., Timothy Beach, and Sheryl Luzzadder-Beach. 2006. "Environmental Variability among *Bajos* in the Southern Maya Lowlands and Its Implications for Ancient Maya Civilization and Archaeology." In *Precolumbian Water Management: Ideology, Ritual, and Power*, edited by L. Lucero and B. Fash, 81–99. Tucson: University of Arizona Press.

Dunning, Nicholas P., Robert E. Griffin, John G. Jones, Richard E. Terry, Zachary Larsen, and Christopher Carr. 2015. "Life on the Edge: Tikal in a *Bajo* Landscape." In *Tikal: Paleoecology of an Ancient Maya City*, edited by D. Lentz, N. Dunning, and V. Scarborough, 95–123. Cambridge: Cambridge University Press.

Dunning, Nicholas P., Robert E. Griffin, Thomas L. Sever, William A. Saturno, and John G. Jones. 2017. "The Nature and Origins of Linear Features in the *Bajo* de Azúcar, Guatemala: Implications for Ancient Maya Adaptation to a Changing Environment." *Geoarchaeology: An International Journal* 32 (1): 107–129.

Ford, Anabel, and Ronald Nigh. 2009. "Origins of the Maya Forest Garden: Maya Resource Management." *Journal of Ethnobiology* 29 (2): 213–236.

Freidel, David A., Arlen F. Chase, Anne Dowd, and Jerry Murdock. 2017. *Maya E Groups: Calendars, Astronomy, and Urbanism in the Early Lowlands*. Gainesville: University Press of Florida.

Fry, Robert E. 2003. "The Peripheries of Tikal." In *Tikal: Dynasties, Foreigners, and Affairs of State*, edited by J. A. Sabloff, 143–170. Santa Fe, NM: School of American Research Press.

Gallopin, Gary G. 1990. "Water Storage Technology at Tikal, Guatemala." MA thesis, Department of Anthropology, University of Cincinnati.

Harrison, Peter D. 1999. *The Lords of Tikal: Rulers of an Ancient Maya City*. London: Thames and Hudson.

Harrison, Peter D. 2012. "A Marvel of Maya Engineering: Water Management at Tikal." *Expedition* 54 (2): 19–26.

Haviland, William A. 1992. "From Double-Bird to Ah Cacao: Dynastic Troubles and the Cycle of the *K'atuns* at Tikal, Guatemala." In *New Theories on the Ancient Maya*, E. C. Danien and R. J. Sharer, 71–80. Philadelphia: University Museum, University of Pennsylvania.

Haviland, William A. 2003. "Settlement, Society, and Demography at Tikal." In *Tikal: Dynasties, Foreigners, and Affairs of State*, edited by J. A. Sabloff, 111–142. Santa Fe, NM: School of American Research Press.

Iglesias de Ponce de León, María J. 2003. "Problematic Deposits and the Problem of Interaction: The Material Culture of Tikal during the Early Classic Period." In *The Maya and Teotihuacan: Reinterpreting Early Classic Interaction*, edited by G. E. Braswell, 167–198. Austin: University of Texas Press.

Inomata, Takeshi, Daniela Triadan, Rodrigo Liendo, and Keiko Teranishi. 2021. "Spatial and Temporal Standardization in Southern Mesoamerica during the Preclassic Period: New Discoveries from the Middle Usumacinta Region, Mexico." In *The Materialization of Time: Mythic History and Ritual Order in the Ancient Maya World*, edited by D. Freidel, A. Chase, A. Dowd, and J. Murdock. Gainesville: University Press of Florida.

Johnston, Kevin J. 2004. "Lowland Maya Water Management Practices: The Household Exploitation of Rural Wells." *Geoarchaeology* 19 (3): 265–292.

Jones, Christopher. 1969. "The Twin-Pyramid Group Pattern: A Classic Maya Architectural Assemblage at Tikal, Guatemala." PhD diss., Department of Anthropology, University of Pennsylvania, Philadelphia.

Jones, Christopher. 2015. "The Marketplace at Tikal." In *The Ancient Maya Marketplace: The Archaeology of Transient Space*, edited by E. King, 67–89. Tucson: University of Arizona Press.

Jones, Christopher, and Linton Satterthwaite. 1982. *The Monuments and Inscriptions of Tikal: The Carved Monuments*. University Museum Tikal Report 33A. University of Pennsylvania, Philadelphia.

Kohler, Timothy A., Michael E. Smith, Amy Bogaard, Christian E. Peterson, Alleen Betzenhauser, Gary M. Feinman, Rahul C. Oka et al. 2018. "Deep Inequality: Summary and Conclusions." In *Ten Thousand Years of Inequality: The Archaeology of Wealth Differences*, edited by Timothy A. Kohler and Michael E. Smith, 289–317. Tucson: University of Arizona Press.

Kunen, Julie L., T. Patrick Culbert, Vilma Fialko, B. R. McKee, and Liwy Grazioso. 2000. "*Bajo* Communities: A Case Study from the Central Peten." *Culture and Agriculture* 22 (3): 15–31.

Laporte, Juan Pedro. 2003. "Thirty Years Later: Some Results of Recent Investigations in Tikal." In *Tikal: Dynasties, Foreigners, and Affairs of State*, edited by J. A. Sabloff, 281–318. Santa Fe, NM: School of American Research Press.

Laporte, Juan Pedro, and Vilma Fialko. 1995. "Un Reencuentro con Mundo Perdido, Tikal, Guatemala." *Ancient Mesoamerica* 6 (1): 41–94.

Lentz, David L., Nicholas P. Dunning, and Vernon L. Scarborough. 2015a. *Tikal: Paleoecology of an Ancient Maya City*. Cambridge: Cambridge University Press.

Lentz, David L., Devin Magee, Eric Weaver, John G. Jones, Kenneth B. Tankersley, Angela Hood, Gerald Islebe, Carmen E. Ramos Hernandez, and Nicholas P. Dunning. 2015b. "Agroforestry and Agricultural Practices of the Ancient Maya at Tikal." In *Tikal: Paleoecology of an Ancient Maya City*, edited by D. Lentz, N. Dunning, and V. Scarborough, 152–189. Cambridge: Cambridge University Press.

Lucero, Lisa J. 2006. *Water and Ritual: The Rise and Fall of Classic Mayan Rulers*. Austin: University of Texas Press.

Lucero, Lisa J., and Barbara Fash. 2006. *Precolumbian Water Management: Ideology, Ritual and Power*. Tucson: University of Arizona Press.

Martin, Simon. 2003. "In Line of the Founder: A View of Dynastic Politics at Tikal." In *Tikal: Dynasties, Foreigners, and Affairs of State*, edited by J. A. Sabloff, 3–45. Santa Fe, NM: School of American Research Press.

Martin, Simon, and Nikolai Grube. 2000. *Chronicle of the Maya Kings and Queens: Deciphering the Dynasties of the Ancient Maya*. London: Thames and Hudson.

Masson, Marilyn A., and David A. Freidel. 2012. "An Argument for Classic-Era Maya Market Exchange." *Journal of Anthropological Archaeology* 31 (4): 455–484.

Moholy-Nagy, Hattula. 2008. *The Artifacts of Tikal: Ornamental and Ceremonial Artifacts and Unworked Material*. Tikal Report 27A. Philadelphia: University of Pennsylvania Museum of Archaeology and Anthropology.

Moholy-Nagy, Hattula. 2016. "Set in Stone: Hiatuses and Dynastic Politics at Tikal, Guatemala." *Ancient Mesoamerica* 27 (2): 255–266.

Murtha, Timothy. 2009. *Land and Labor: Maya Terraced Agriculture. An Investigation of the Settlement Economy and Intensive Agricultural Landscape of Caracol, Belize*. Saarbrucken, Germany: DM Verlag Dr. Muller.

Murtha, Timothy. 2015. "Negotiated Landscapes: Comparative Settlement Ecology of Tikal and Caracol." In *Classic Maya Polities of the Southern Lowlands: Integration, Interaction, Dissolution*, edited by D. Marken and J. Fitzpatrick, 75–98. Boulder: University Press of Colorado.

Puleston, Dennis E. 1983. *The Settlement Survey of Tikal*. Tikal Report 13. Philadelphia: University Museum, University of Pennsylvania.

Rice, Prudence. 1999. "Rethinking Classic Lowland Maya Pottery Censers." *Ancient Mesoamerica* 10 (1): 25–50.

Sabloff, Jeremy A. 2003. *Tikal: Dynasties, Foreigners, and Affairs of State*. Santa Fe, NM: School of American Research Press.

Scarborough, Vernon L. 2003. *The Flow of Power: Ancient Water Systems and Landscapes*. Santa Fe, NM: School of American Research Press.

Scarborough, Vernon L., Arlen F. Chase, and Diane Z. Chase. 2012. "Low Density Urbanism, Sustainability, and IHOPE-Maya: Can the Past Provide More than History?" *UGEC Viewpoints* 8: 20–24.

Scarborough, Vernon L., Nicholas P. Dunning, Kenneth B. Tankersley, Christopher Carr, Eric Weaver, Liwy Grazioso, Brian Lane, et al. 2012. "Water and Sustainable Land Use at the Ancient Tropical City of Tikal, Guatemala." *Proceedings of the National Academy of Sciences* 109 (31): 12408–12413.

Scarborough, Vernon L., and Gary G. Gallopin. 1991. "A Water Storage Adaptation in the Maya Lowlands." *Science* 251 (4994): 658–662.

Stuart, David. 2000. "'The Arrival of Strangers': Teotihuacan and Tollan in Classic Maya History." In *Mesoamerica's Classic Heritage: From Teotihuacan to the Aztecs*, edited by Davíd Carrasco, Lindsay Jones, and Scott Sessions, 465–513. Boulder: University Press of Colorado.

Stuart, David. 2004. "The Beginning of the Copan Dynasty: A Review of the Hieroglyphic and Historical Evidence." In *Understanding Early Classic Copan*, edited by Ellen E. Bell, Marcello Canuto, and Robert J. Sharer, 215–247. Philadelphia: University of Pennsylvania Museum of Archaeology and Anthropology.

Stuart, David. 2007. "Reading the Water Serpent as Witz." http://decipherpment .wordpress.com/2007/04/13/reading-the-water-serpent.

Stuart, David. 2008. "A Childhood Ritual on the Hauberg Stela." March 2008, http:// decipherment.wordpress.com/2008/03/27/a-childhood-ritual-on-the-hauberg-stela.

Stuart, David. 2014. "Animals and Sacred Mountains: How Ritualized Performances Materialized State-Ideologies at Teotihuacan, Mexico." PhD dissertation, Department of Anthropology, Harvard University, Cambridge, MA.

Taube, Karl A. 2010. "Where Earth and Sky Meet: The Sea and the Sky in Ancient and Contemporary Maya Cosmology." In *Fiery Pool: The Maya and the Mythic Sea*, edited by Daniel Finamore and Stephen D. Houston, 202–219. New Haven, CT: Peabody Essex Museum and Yale University Press.

Townsend, Richard. 1992. "The Renewal of Nature at the Temple of Tlaloc." In *The Ancient Americas: Art from Sacred Landscapes*, edited by Richard Townsend, 171–185. Chicago and Munich: The Art Institute of Chicago and Prestel Verlag.

Vinson, G. L. 1962. "Upper Cretaceous and Tertiary Stratigraphy of Guatemala." *Bulletin of the American Association of Petrolium Geologists* 46 (4): 425–456.

Wahl, David, Roger Byrne, and Lysanna Anderson. 2014. "An 8700 Year Paleoclimate Reconstruction from the Southern Maya Lowlands." *Quaternary Science Reviews* 103: 19–25.

Wahl, David, Roger Byrne, Thomas Schreiner, and Richard Hansen. 2007. "Palaeolimnological Evidence of Late-Holocene Settlement and Abandonment in the Mirador Basin, Peten, Guatemala." *The Holocene* 17 (6): 813–820.

Wahl, David, Thomas Schreiner, and Roger Byrne. 2005. "La Secuencia Paleo-Ambiental de la Cuenca Mirador en Petén." In *XVIII Simposio de Investigaciones Arqueológicas en Guatemala, 2004*, edited by Juan Pedro Laporte, Bárbara Arroyo, and Héctor Mejía, 49–54. Guatemala: Museo Nacional de Arqueología y Etnología.

Walker, Debra S. 2013. "Caching in Context at Cerros, Belize." www.academia.edu/296 5645/Caching_in_Context_at_Cerros_Belize, Cerros Research Online Catalog.

Walker, Debra S. 2016. *Perspectives on the Ancient Maya of Chetumal Bay*. Gainesville: University Press of Florida.

Weiss, Andrew. 2001. "Topographic Position and Landforms Analysis." Poster session presented at the ESRI User Conference, San Diego, CA, July 9, 2001.

8

From "Preclassic" to "Classic" and "Postclassic" among the Maya

The Role of Information Processing and Socioenvironmental-economic Values in the Emergence and Decline of "Watery" Cities

Sander van der Leeuw

PREFACE

The reader be warned: I am not a Mayanist, and although I began my career as an archaeologist, I essentially gave up that profession in the mid 1990s to focus on what is now called "sustainability scholarship." In my confrontation with Maya archaeology,[1] I learned how little I knew about the Maya, and in return confronted my esteemed colleagues and friends with some more general, systemic and at one point even "complex adaptive systems" ideas about the evolution of societies. Inevitably, I will be short on specific details concerning the Maya, but I hope that the overall perspective presented here may resonate sufficiently to be interesting to my colleagues in various parts of the world.

. . .

The history of humankind is the history of the coevolution of its cognition with its actions, its organization, and its natural environment. Or in other words, it

---

[1] This essay was written to honor Vern Scarborough for his important role in Maya archaeology and his innovative ideas about it, as well as his friendship.

https://doi.org/10.5876/9781646422326.c008

is the history of human discovery and implementation of "tools for thought and action." In a number of papers (van der Leeuw and Aschan-Leygonie 2005; van der Leeuw 2007, 2012), I have argued that the driver of this process is the interaction between phenomena, information, and knowledge, which could in a nutshell be described as follows:

> Problem solving structures knowledge—> more knowledge increases the information-processing capacity—> that in turn allows the cognition of new problems—> creates new knowledge—> knowledge creation involves more and more people in processing information—> increases the size of the group involved and its degree of aggregation—> creates more problems—> increases need for problem solving—> problem solving structures more knowledge . . . etc.

I am here taking this feedback loop, and its evolution, as a dynamic that can—for lack of another more general one—serve as an *ultimate* explanation of the changes humans and their societies have gone through from the Pleistocene to the recent "Great Acceleration" in societal complexity, technology, environmental impact, and so on (Rockström et al. 2009; Steffen et al. 2015).

From circa 50,000 BCE or thereabouts, collective information processing involves larger and larger groups of people. As long as these groups are ambulant, one of the main constraints in such collective solving of challenges is the time involved in finding, over wide spaces and without means of distance-bridging communication, the partners with whom to devise solutions. Hence, around 10,000 BCE we witness the emergence of the first villages. In these, one's discussion partners could be approached much more easily, without losing time in searching for them. That layout set in motion an acceleration of innovation that inevitably involved more and more people, in larger and larger settlements, the largest of which we can call "towns."

The central question raised in this chapter is how this process might have played out in the Yucatán Peninsula, with its tropical ecology, highly varied geography, and challenges in water management as the Maya evolved from a rural, agriculture-focused society into an urban one that still had an agricultural base but also developed a wide range of other activities such as crafts, exchange, and environmental management. In other words, *I will be developing elements of a proximate explanation of the emergence of Maya urban society that instantiates the evolution of human cognitive, technological, societal, and environmental coevolution that is my ultimate explanation for the emergence of human complex societies.* In doing so, I will lean on the work of the other authors in this volume, as well as the work of the source of our inspiration: Vern Scarborough.

As I have previously argued (van der Leeuw 2014), our Western scientific tradition has in many disciplines, but especially in archaeology, focused on searching for the origins of phenomena that we are acquainted with and in many cases have defined in the present. In the true sense of the word, the archaeologist has for a long time been "a prophet turned backward," imputing past developments based on present observations and the remains of human activities dating back to the past. If we are to improve our understanding of the dynamics that drove the emergence of the present, however, we have to argue *from the past to the present*, focusing on how the new dynamics emerged at different times in history. That will be, as far as possible, the approach followed here (see also Costanza et al. 2012; Dearing, van der Leeuw, and Costanza 2012; van der Leeuw et al. 2011).

THE CONTEXT OF EMERGENCE

One of the interesting issues raised by Scarborough and G. Gallopin (1991) is whether the Maya actually "emerged from the sea" (i.e., initially developed their culture and societal organization on coastal sites) and then moved inward along the main rivers in the peninsula, adapting their relationship to the changing availability of water in the process. I am not in a position to argue this either way; Gunn's (chapter 5 in this volume) comparison with other societies (Egypt, Near East), however, certainly has an inherent logic when one considers that the sea level stabilized around 7000 BCE at a height that implied the flooding of low-lying river mouths and therefore the creation of large estuaries in many places on Earth. Such estuaries are many times more fertile than either land or deep sea and are thus likely to have attracted populations in search for subsistence.

From the "emergence" perspective that we need to apply if we are to understand the evolutionary dynamics of Maya (and all other) societies, it is important to emphasize that the early Maya area and its societies should not be treated as an entity, as has been the case in many studies. Rather, as many Mayanists would now agree, the long-term Maya dynamic is one of growing interaction between a number of different regional societies, in very different natural environments, in different parts of the area now covered by Guatemala, Belize, and the Yucatán Peninsula (e.g., Chase et al., chapter 7 in this volume).

The thrust of my argument is focused on the transition from the Preclassic to the Classic Maya, from essentially rural agricultural societies, to locally aggregated societies with many urban characteristics (though not the high population densities of many towns in temperate and subtropical zones), and then to a highly interactive regional sociocultural sphere involving much long-distance exchange and trade, communication, and information sharing. In my 2014 paper (van der Leeuw 2014, 223–224), I elaborated that transition as a narrative written from the perspective of the relationship between societal information processing and societal organization. In the next section of this chapter, I will first pick up on that perspective. That discussion will be followed by description of this transition in terms of a dynamic model of the processes involved.

THE "FLOW STRUCTURE" MODEL

The information-processing feedback loop that drives the growth of societies (as outlined in the box from this chapter's preface) interacts with the natural environment of such societies in the form of what I have called a dynamic "flow structure," a feedback loop between the processing of energy and resources on the one hand, and information on the other. Humans need energy and resources to live and flourish individually. To obtain them, people have to organize the identification, acquisition, and transport of such resources from their environment into society. That part of the feedback loop involves collective information processing: Which plants or animals are appropriate resources? For which societal needs? How to ensure their availability? How to transport them? How to prepare them for use? How to consume or use them?

The answers to these questions are, of course, different from one local society to the next. Although some resources or practices may be shared, such as the choice of maize as a staple, because they are suitable for a variety of ecological areas, others will differ across areas, such as the favored way of preparing such a foodstuff, the tools and techniques used for cultivation, harvesting, and so on. Many more (and more profound) differences are likely to occur in societal and cultural domains. In its coevolution, each society shapes its own organization, institutions, techniques, ideas, beliefs, and norms, and it does so path dependently: the outcome is directly related to the starting point and the trajectory of development concerned.

In the process, the members of the societies concerned have aligned themselves on and around their society's "culture," "worldview," and "traditions." That alignment is what distinguishes these societies from each other, and what ensures their members' ability to understand each other and collaborate. It enables the members of the society to refer to themselves as having a collective identity, while allowing them to develop a personal identity—to distinguish themselves from the other members of "their" society. This responds to two fundamental, but in some ways opposite, needs of every person: to belong and to be different—needs that are essential for the healthy functioning of each and every human society but which are expressed in different ways in different societies.

In the Maya case, I would argue that all of the Preclassic sociopolitical units, whether at the organizational level of tribes or chiefdoms, were based on villages of different sizes and would have implemented their own "culture," "worldview," or "traditions." That state of affairs is maintained as long as there is a relatively low level of communication between the individual entities, because of spatial isolation (distance, absence of roads, absence of incentives to communicate), low levels of communication technology (absence of writing or other material means to transmit ideas), or cultural barriers (absence of a shared language, e.g.).

As all these local societies, in the Preclassic stage, were essentially agricultural societies, most of their ideas, institutions, and technologies would have emerged around, and dealt with, their subsistence base. Differences were due to different environmental circumstances (valley, hill, mountain, slope, orientation, need for irrigation or not, etc.) and different ecologies (availability of nondomesticated crops; cultivated crops and technologies used), and so on. In the transition toward the Classic stage, these communities entered into enhanced contact with each other and, under the impact of that contact and a further growing population, developed their organization, institutions, technologies and values, becoming truly (low-density) urban.

Rural and Urban Dynamics

In designing an appropriate framework to understand the dynamics behind this transition, I have refined a model originally developed in the 1990s with James McGlade (van der Leeuw and McGlade 1997) to explain the "urban revolution," which has, in the meantime, been used to understand recent (post–World War II) developments in rural Epirus (van der Leeuw 2000) and elsewhere. The size limitation of this chapter, however, does not permit me to present the full argument in mathematical-modeling terms (van der Leeuw 2019, 263–284). For the purposes of discussion, we assume that the dynamic of urban emergence can be described in information-processing terms as an innovation-communication (reaction-diffusion) dynamic in which a human component and an environmental component become interlocked.

Of these two components, the former consists of relatively few superimposed rhythms and can potentially be accelerated with relative ease (people can learn and do innovate), whereas the latter is a very complex composite of myriad different embedded rhythms in all the food webs and nutrient cycles involved, and thus changes very slowly. One might say that in the rural situation, the (faster) human dynamic has locked onto the (slower) environmental one: people have adapted their way of living to the rhythms and dynamics of nature, and natural diversity is what stabilizes the symbiosis between people and their environment. As in most rural environments, change is relatively slow. In urban contexts, on the other hand, we see that all processes have accelerated. There, the human dynamic increasingly sets the pace for, and thus dominates over, the environmental dynamic.[2]

---

[2] This reversal is a fundamental constituent of our present world. In order to achieve it, humans reduce the environmental dynamic in many places to a much simpler set of rhythms and/or uncouple food webs spatially. As a result, the symbiotic system has become less stable in the classical ecological sense (diversity has been reduced), but it has gained in resilience and now survives through more rapid adaptation.

Rural and urban environments also differ in the relative importance of the two major forms of communications networks that seem relevant to our investigation. The village-level communities are predominantly connected by hierarchical communications networks in which

- family ties are strong, the elders in the family have a dominant role, and much communication remains within the family; and
- the majority of the people do not communicate much outside their community. Only a few do, those who accept/take responsibility as head officials, mayors, representatives of their communities in regional councils, and so on.

Such networks are very efficient in their use of (mostly local) energy and information (news spreads quickly) but relatively slow to adapt because the decision makers are few and of limited diversity and because the well-being of the group is more important than that of the individual.

In towns, on the other hand, contacts (mainly professional) outside the traditional kinship system become more and more important and lead to the development of distributed communication networks that crosscut family and village ties in many different ways. The communications transmitted through these networks are different, tied into the professional activities concerned, and offer alternative means to a rewarding social life. They thus contribute to a differentiation of value systems. Such networks display a relatively high degree of adaptive flexibility, allowing for an acceleration of change (whether due to demographic factors or others).

The Dynamics of Rural-Urban Transition

Now let us look at the transition from a rural system to an urban one. Timewise, this transition seems to extend from the Middle Preclassic (1000–400 BCE) to the Classic (300–800 CE) Maya periods. It is here described in theoretical terms, without my trying to fix the components of the transition in time, as they may have occurred at different moments in different places.

Increasing exposure to communication and the sharing of ideas will accelerate the social dynamic in some places, and, where that happens, it first leads to a cyclical periodicity in which the nonlinear coupling of the relatively structured, slow environmental dynamic and the more rapid and stochastic human one generates an oscillation between phases in which the dynamic is more structured, and phases in which it is more stochastic. In other words, in such communities, one will initially see a debate and an alternation between more conservative and more innovative ways of thinking and doing, but as change becomes the norm conservative foot-dragging will diminish.

Ultimately, such an oscillation is unsustainable, and villages in the rural system will inexorably move toward a bifurcation. A choice is forced on each community: it can remain rural by isolating oneself from what happens around it (by severing some of the communications links), or it can accept the increase in communication and allow itself to change. Although the former choice is, of course, only a temporary solution, it will be implemented in some villages. The result is an increasing differentiation between areas that are still governed by the traditional ways of exploiting the land (socionatural dynamics dominated by the slow rhythms of the environment), and others in which new approaches are introduced, human control over the environment is enhanced, and a quicker pace of change appears.

Such a bifurcation might, for example, be triggered by the (highly probable) situation that in some places, a more rapid adaptation is required of the total human/environment system than in others, which is equivalent to stating that in some places the total dynamic is more dependent on the human component of the symbiosis than in others.[3] That would, for example, be the case in areas that have a less favorable ecology than others, such as areas of poorer soils that might require heavier human investment. But, conversely, in the richest agricultural areas, the social dynamic might be what forces the system toward rapid adaptation because people hold less resistance toward new opportunities. The result is the same, but the dynamic involved is very different. Increased spatial separation between the people partaking in the two "worldviews" would relieve both kinds of communities from the constraints imposed on them by the other one, and would thus allow them to grow in those precise environments for which they are best suited.

Communities organized along predominantly horizontal communication networks would spread (their dynamic being the more adaptable), and would create spatial connectivity over relatively long distances, through specific "communication corridors." Prime candidates for such corridors would be valleys, roads, coastal waters, and so on. By implication, other parts of the society would conform to a slower rate of adaptation, through their more hierarchical communications systems.

But once horizontal communication systems grow in size, they, in turn, become much less adaptable. At that point in their evolution, an oscillation is likely to emerge that drives them to differentiate into individual nodes (towns).

---

[3] Joel Gunn drew my attention to the fact that this might explain why El Mirador / Calakmul accelerated ahead of the Tikal region. Calakmul was more exposed to the fluctuations of the tropical/subtropical ecotone than the Tikal environ deeper in the tropics; it required more rapid adjustments to lesser fluctuations in the global/Bermuda-Azores High that controls the duration and intensity of the rainy season. Tikal, more embedded in the tropical environment, benefited from the greater biomass of the tropics and was less susceptible to shifts in the global environment. Tikal's come-later emergence required the intervention of the greater Mesoamerican interaction sphere to achieve a breakout.

The extent to which this divergence occurs is initially variable in space and time. It manifests itself as the acquisition of stronger urban characteristics by some rural areas, which begin to dominate the dynamics of the surrounding area, and the development of increased social stratification. Both occur, but the degrees to which they do may be crucial in the local dynamics of the individual centers. The overall effect is that the growing long-distance communication networks differentiate to some extent, with denser interaction in the centers, and less-dense interaction between them. Thus, there is room for a degree of local independence and differentiation among the centers. For a while at least, such partial uncoupling might have allowed sufficient localized dynamics within the network to maintain adaptability for the overall system.

WATER MANAGEMENT AS INFORMATION PROCESSING

The emergence of different forms of water management in each of the core areas of the Maya world is one of the most notable phenomena accompanying this process. It reflects an increasing control over the environment and particularly one of its dimensions that is essential for the survival of the emerging urban communities. But the aspect that I want to accentuate here is that the water infrastructure itself is an information-processing tool, as it reduces the information load involved in dealing with natural, unconstrained aspects of climate, agriculture, and land management by regulating, or at least constraining, when and where water goes, and how it is used.

I am making this point because looking at infrastructure and artifacts, including such things as arrowheads, pots, houses, temples, and the like, as information-processing tools is not frequent in archaeological (or other) contexts. Yet, artifacts and infrastructures are societally constructed and accepted "tools for thought and action"; they not only are material manifestations but also represent concepts that are part of the society's mental organization and that contribute to organizing the daily life and thought of a society's members. That is one reason why I find Vern Scarborough's (and, e.g., Lisa Lucero's) work on the "watery world" in which many Maya lived so interesting: it offers an entry point into the structure of their societies' information-processing apparatus.

To return to the rural-urban transition, an assessment of the complexity of the water management structures in the different urban centers could give us a proxy measure relative to the progress of information processing in each center. As it is my contention that a society's information-processing capacity is related to the size of the community involved (see Bettencourt 2013; Bettencourt et al. 2007 on the superlinear relationship between city size and innovation), this might be another proxy to calculate population size of individual agglomerations.

The Expansion of the Rural "Value Space"

Of course, it is impossible to see the deliberations in rural and urban areas through the data recoverable by archaeologists. However, if we define the "value space" of each society as the totality of dimensions along which that society accords value to individuals, artifacts, actions, institutions, infrastructure, and other aspects of societal organization, we may be able to devise a proxy for the transition, as well as identify another aspect of information processing as the fundamental driver of the urbanization process (van der Leeuw 2019).

To understand that, we have to, again, go back to the feedback loop in the box at the beginning of this paper. It essentially argues that when more brainpower is put to work solving challenges encountered by a society, that results in more knowledge, more "tools for thought and action," and the emergence of such new tools enables the cognition of new challenges, and therefore the accumulation of yet more knowledge. Some of these are—and always will be—immaterial, but others will take the (material) form of different, new artifacts, processes, institutions, and elements of infrastructure. The feedback loop thus also implies that a growing number of people engaged in a particular society's ways of solving challenges expands the "value space" of that society by cognizing more dimensions along which "value" can be monitored and assigned. The accumulation of different forms of material culture—including newly introduced artifacts (such as the range of pottery shapes), innovations in the domain of communication (such as writing), infrastructure (such as water management and temple building), and institutions (such as leadership, taxes)—seems therefore an appropriate proxy for the degree of expansion of a society's "value space," and the latter an appropriate proxy for the degree of interactivity in the society, including the number of active participants involved, the frequency of their interaction, and the quantity of information exchanged.[4]

This concept opens an important perspective on the transition between rural and urban societies. Clearly, rural societies interact essentially among themselves about the agricultural value space in which they live, with important dimensions relating to their climate; their physical, biological, and hydrological environment; the infrastructure, techniques and tools used to interact with these; the functions and values of the crops they cultivate, and so forth. But

---

[4] In reviewing this chapter, Joel Gunn commented: "There are two possible avenues to quantifying these dimensional value spaces. One is a binary, presence or absence scheme. The other would be quantification of the continua. There should be interconnectivities between the dimensions of different avenues that aids estimations where the quantities are lacking. The quantities will be irregularly present among sites but estimating formulas can be used to fill in the un-quantified dimensions with possibilities of applying corrective constants to account for local conditions."

these things make up, in effect, a limited number of dimensions of value, and that limitation of the society's value space also limits the number of individuals that can durably and coherently interact about those values.

I would argue that the size of the value space needed to maintain frequent interactions among a much wider community, such as the network of agglomerations that develops in the Classic Maya period, is indeed much larger. Or to put it into everyday language: the number of topics about which that wider community interacts needs to be more diverse for the interaction to be maintained at a sufficient level to involve the individuals participating in the expanding network. Larger populations with too little primary production-related value space must, as an aggregate, develop a bigger value space to enable sufficient interaction among them accommodating the range of things they provide locally, as well as those related to importing, exporting, and transporting other dimensions. Only communicating about the agricultural basics would not be enough to retain the interest of the whole network.

It seems to me that this need is met by the introduction of arts and crafts, novel objects (and their values) introduced by long-distance trade, and so forth. Among these, writing is of paramount importance, as it is the means to transcend time and space in information processing, which is necessary to enable communication over long distances. It would thus be interesting to try and (roughly) quantify and map these new dimensions of information processing to get a sense of the change in the complexity of the value space that accompanies the transition from the Preclassic to the Classic Maya periods.

The Postclassic from an Information-Processing Perspective

This approach, which places the growing information-processing capacity of societies at the center of their evolution, also adds a new dimension to the question of the demise of the Classic Maya toward the end of their period of glory. We could ask the question "Is there an aspect of information processing in the Maya area that prevented Maya society from integrating and expanding even further?" And that is, in my opinion, where we need to pay some attention to the environment's impact on information processing.

As argued by Gunn (chapter 5 in this volume), a particularity of the tropical environment in which the society flourished is its high biodiversity, which has rendered very high population aggregations spatially difficult. This trait differs fundamentally with instances of societies in desert environments, which favored high concentrations of population in areas with sufficient water and hindered a more equal spread of the population in the surrounding dry areas. And this environment is also different from temperate zones, where high population concentrations were feasible if the information-processing capacity of the society engendered them. In tropical forest areas, the nature of the vegetation itself limited the aggregation of population centers at a level below that of either deserts or temperate climes. That, in turn, limited the information-processing capacity of Maya society and thus the growth of the Maya sphere of influence. Pushing into the uplands would have hedged the limitations of the bioactive tropical lowlands by moving into an inherently drier if more rainfall-precarious terrain.

How would the limit of information-processing capacity in the area have made itself felt? I would argue that it would have been through a tipping point at which the society could no longer deal with the unexpected consequences of its earlier (systemic) actions. In an expansive phase, any society deals with challenges by experimentally implementing "solutions" for them. But in that process, due to the enormous difference in dimensionality between the human capacity for information processing and the complexity of the social and environmental dynamics in which it functions, it generates many unobserved and unanticipated consequences of its interventions. Moreover, it "solves" frequent and imminent challenges, but the unintended consequences of the actions undertaken to do so involve a much wider spatiotemporal sphere. Hence, some of these unintended consequences play out much later than the "solutions" implemented. Cumulatively, that implies the emergence of a "risk barrier" often many years, even centuries, after the implementation of the "solutions." I would argue that this phenomenon is sufficiently general to be proposed as a cause for the demise of many societies after a period of intensive growth. The proximate causes may have been very different—including maladaptation to changing climate, famines due to overexploitation of the environment and erosion, incapacity to maintain infrastructures, warfare to deal with societal challenges, economic crises—and many other kinds of dynamics may have manifested themselves. But all of these are, of course, instances of the society's no longer being able to constructively deal with the unintended consequences of earlier (systemic) decisions.

CONCLUSION

In this short chapter, I have tried to highlight some aspects of a perspective on societal dynamics that views societies as collective information-processing organizations. Whereas here I focused on the Maya, I believe that the approach is also interesting for archaeologists and historians studying other complex societies. Due to the inherent limitations of the publication, this has been done in a very condensed form and referring to a relatively high number of my own publications. I hope the reader will understand that and forgive me. The literature on information processing is vast—ranging from computer science to telecommunications to evolutionary biology, mathematics, and other fields—far beyond any single person's capacity to master, unless this is done (such as in my case) over some forty years. And even then, of course, I have only lifted the tip of the veil. As an introduction to the field for archaeologists, I recommend James Gleick's *The Information: A History, a Theory, a Flood* (Vintage, 2012). In my recent book, *Social Sustainability Past and Future: Undoing Unintended Consequences for the Earth's Survival* (van der Leeuw 2019), I have presented many other aspects of this approach.

REFERENCES

Bettencourt, L.M.A. 2013. "The Origins of Scaling in Cities." *Science* 21 (June, 340) (6139): 1438–1441. https://doi.org/10.1126/science.1235823.

Bettencourt, L.M.A., J. Lobo, D. Helbing, C. Kühnert, and G. B. West. 2007. "Growth, Innovation, Scaling, and the Pace of Life in Cities." *Proceedings of the National Academy of Sciences* 104 (17): 7301–7306. https://doi.org/10.1073/pnas.0610172104.

Costanza, R., S. E. van der Leeuw, K. Hibbard, S. Aulenbach, S. Brewer, M. Burek, S. Cornell et al. 2012. "Developing an Integrated History and Future of People on Earth (IHOPE)." *Current Opinion in Environmental Sustainability* 4: 106–114.

Dearing, J., S. E. van der Leeuw, and R. Costanza. 2012. "How to Learn from the Past?" *The Solutions Journal*, March 2012.

Gleick, James. 2012. *The Information: A History, a Theory, a Flood*. New York: Vintage Books.

Rockström, J. W. Steffen, K. Noone, Å. Persson, F. S. Chapin III, E. F. Lambin, T. M. Lenton et al. 2009. "A Safe Operating Space for Humanity." *Nature* 461: 472–475.

Scarborough, V. L., and G. G. Gallopin. 1991. "A Water Storage Adaptation in the Maya Lowlands." *Science* 251 (4994): 658–662.

Steffen, W., W. Broadgate, L. Deutsch, O. Gaffney, and C. Ludwig. 2015. "The Trajectory of the Anthropocene: The Great Acceleration." *Anthropocene Review* 2 (1): 81–98. https://doi.org/10.1177/2053019614564785.

van der Leeuw, S. E. 2007. "Information Processing and Its Role in the Rise of the European World System." In *Sustainability or Collapse?*, edited by R. Costanza, L. J. Graumlich, and W. Steffen, 213–241. Dahlem Workshop Reports. Cambridge, MA: MIT Press.

van der Leeuw, S. E. 2012. "Global Systems Dynamics and Policy: Lessons from the Distant Past." *Complexity Economics* 1: 33–60.

van der Leeuw, S. E. 2014. "Transforming Lessons from the Past into Lessons for the Future." In *The Resilience and Vulnerability of Ancient Landscapes: Transforming Maya Archaeology through IHOPE*, edited by A. F. Chase and V. Scarborough, 215–231. Archaeological Papers of the American Anthropological Association, 24. New York: Wiley.

van der Leeuw, S. E. 2019. *Social Sustainability Past and Future: Undoing Unintended Consequences for the Earth's Survival*. New York: Cambridge University Press, Open access. https://www.cambridge.org/core/services/aop-cambridge-core/content/view

/811395DC3A8D82EAD39C45657B2FD1AD/9781108498692AR.pdf/Social_Sustain
ability__Past_and_Future.pdf?event-type=FTLA.

van der Leeuw, S. E. 2000. "Land Degradation as a Socio-natural Process." In *The Way
the Wind Blows: Climate, History and Human Perception*, edited by R. McIntosh and
J. Tainter, 364–393. New York: Columbia University Press.

van der Leeuw, S. E., and C. Aschan-Leygonie. 2005. "A Long-Term Perspective on Resilience in Socio-Natural Systems." In *Micro Meso Macro: Addressing Complex Systems
Couplings*, edited by H. Lilienström and U. Svedin, 227–264. London: World Scientific.

van der Leeuw, S. E., R. Costanza, S. Aulenbach, S. Brewer, M. Burek, S. Cornell,
C. Crumley et al. 2011. "Toward an Integrated History to Guide the Future." *Ecology
and Society* 16 (4): 2. http://www.ecologyandsociety.org/vol16/iss4/art2.

van der Leeuw, S. E., and J. McGlade. 1997. "Structural Change and Bifurcation in
Urban Evolution: A Non-linear Dynamical Perspective." In *Archaeology: Time, Process
and Structural Transformations*, edited by S. E. van der Leeuw and J. McGlade, 331–372.
London: Routledge.

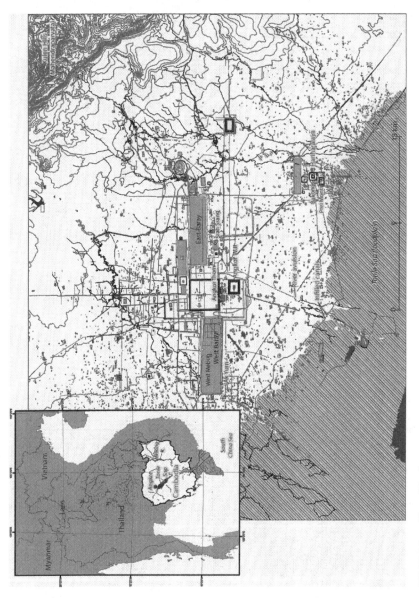

FIGURE 9.1. *Map of Angkor.*

9

Scale and Impact in Southeast Asia

Resilience and Complexity at Angkor

Dan Penny and Roland Fletcher

Human-environmental interactions in premodern civilizations in Southeast (SE) Asia provide insights into sustainability, resilience, and fragility in the use of natural resources in the region. Cultures in the tropical environments of Southeast Asia developed into complex agrarian societies that supported large populations. In the case of Angkor (figure 9.1), the urbanized population may have reached about three-quarters of a million (Fletcher et al. 2003; Lustig 2001). Feeding such a large community and resourcing the ponderous state apparatus without depleting natural resources catastrophically would have been a challenge both politically and economically.

Ongoing research is slowly uncovering not only information on the methods employed by the populace to harness the productivity of the environment without destroying it, but also on the systemic vulnerabilities that they confronted, and that they created for themselves. This chapter considers the environmental consequences of Angkor's growth into the world's most extensive preindustrial settlement and the wider implications for tropical forest environments.

https://doi.org/10.5876/9781646422326.c009

Angkor was the capital of the medieval Khmer kingdom. The first recognizably "Angkorian" settlements, characterized by axial urban design focused on a central ritual space dominated by a temple-mountain, were established at Ak Yum in the seventh century CE (Pottier and Bolle 2009). By the mid-eighth century, an urban settlement was established at Hariharâlaya, and, with very few exceptions, the capital remained on the Angkor plain for more than 600 years, forming the vast, low-density urban complex of Greater Angkor. B.-P. Groslier (1979) linked, influentially, the decline and eventual abandonment of Angkor in the fourteenth and fifteenth centuries to environmental degradation and the silting up of its water system. What has become apparent is that the physical size and organization of the settlement and the redundancy and inertia in its water system were crucial contributing factors in the demise of Angkor (Fletcher et al. 2008; Fletcher et al. 2017; Penny et al. 2018). Recently, climatic variability has also become a likely contributing factor in Angkor's demise (Buckley et al. 2010; Cook et al. 2010; Day et al. 2012; Hua et al. 2017; Penny et al. 2018), a factor Groslier, perforce, set aside for want of empirical evidence (Groslier 1979, 189). The issue is consequential because there is a pattern to the demise of agrarian-based, low-density, dispersed urban settlements (Lucero, Fletcher, and Coningham 2015) with some implications for the future of present-day urbanism (Fletcher 2018).

Unlike the environmentally disparate polities of the Maya world, Angkor rose to become a centralized power in a relatively uniform physical environment, supported by a network of trade routes to strategically located Khmer centers elsewhere in the region (Hendrickson 2010). Central Cambodia is dominated by the Tonle Sap Lake, its expansive floodplain, and the prodigious alluvial plains that surround them. These Quaternary-aged alluvial plains, upon which Angkor was established, are weathered from Mesozoic sandstone and so are sandy, easily leached, nutrient poor, and friable (White, Oberthür, and Sovuthy 1997). Rainfall in Siem Reap is highly seasonal, with nearly 90 percent of the average annual rainfall of approximately 1,200 mm falling while the summer monsoon (May–October) is active and a long period of water deficit during the rest of the year (Kummu 2003). As a consequence, Cambodian rice soils are commonly subject to both drought and submergence during the course of the year, with sensitivity to either varying according to slight differences in rainfall, topography, and sand content of the soil (Seng et al. 2007). Under these circumstances, one might expect Angkor's growth as a settlement to have been constrained to areas with suitable rice soils. We know, however, that Angkor grew to around 1000 km² in area (Evans et al. 2007; Evans et al. 2013; Fletcher et al. 2003) and supported a population of many hundreds of thousands of people (Lustig 2001).

In part, Angkor's success as a massive, low-density settlement is a function of the Tonle Sap Lake. The Tonle Sap is one of the world's most productive fisheries, yielding hundreds of thousands of tons of fish each year (see Lamberts 2006, regarding difficulties in quantifying fish yield from the lake), which represent a large proportion of the Cambodian diet (Bonheur and Lane 2002). Excavation of the prehistoric occupation site Ko Ta Meas, located within the West Baray reservoir at Angkor (Pottier 2006), yielded nearly 3,000 fish bones, representing sixteen families (Voeun and Seng 2006), suggesting that the lake was equally important in antiquity. It is reasonable to assume that the lake was similarly important to the people of Angkor as a source of protein (Roberts 2002, 171–172), in keeping with other civilizations around the world (Gunn, chapter 5 in this volume), though there have been few successful attempts to systematically collect fish bones from Angkorian period sites, in part because of the poor preservation conditions typical of the areas' soils.

The lake is linked to the Mekong River, some 120 km to the southeast, by the Tonle Sap River, which feeds floodwaters from the Mekong to the lake during the wet monsoon. This "backflooding" from the Mekong increases the volume of the lake by, on average, 58 km^3, resulting in the inundation of approximately 13,000–15,000 km^2 of riparian land, depending on the intensity of the monsoon (Kummu et al. 2008). The floodwaters bring a huge volume of suspended sediment from the Mekong River to the Tonle Sap Lake—an average of 5 million metric tons—around 80 percent of which is retained in the basin and almost all of that in the vegetated floodplain (Kummu et al. 2008). The deposition of large volumes of suspended sediment, to which nutrients typically adsorb, drives very high productivity on the floodplain of the Tonle Sap and permits multiple cropping of rice in the receding flood.

The lake, then, receives the bulk of its water and nutrients from the Mekong River, and the size of the flood pulse and its consequent productivity are a function of rainfall and runoff in a catchment nearly 800,000 km^2 in area. The great size and environmental diversity of the Mekong River's catchment mean that the pulse of the Tonle Sap Lake is relatively inured to local (Cambodian) environmental conditions or land use practices, meaning that the resources it provides (fundamentally, water and nutrients) were never threatened by any development in the Cambodian catchments. The cornucopian Tonle Sap, then, was a constant throughout Angkorian history, and undoubtedly supported agricultural communities in central Cambodia since the early Holocene.

Moreover, groundwater levels are relatively high on the floodplain, due in large part to recharge from the Tonle Sap Lake (Kazama et al. 2007). Groundwater levels are particularly high at Angkor, according to R. Acker (2006), ranging uniformly between −5 and 0 m depth (Kummu 2009). High, stable, and readily accessible groundwater resources were extensively exploited by the Khmer of

Angkor, both for state-level constructions such as temple moats, and the small village-scale *trapeang* (water tank) that were the foundation of Groslier's "hydraulic suburbs" (Evans et al. 2007; Groslier 1979; Pottier 1999). This enduring pattern of low-density settlement at Angkor—an excavated and groundwater-fed basin associated with a moated shrine and encircling house-mounds—was deployed with little variation and with apparently great success over a vast area, extending far beyond Angkor (Evans 2007). This is in stark contrast to the approaches adopted to water management in the karstic Maya lowlands, where limited surface water and groundwater greatly sharpened seasonal water scarcity (Dunning et al., chapter 2 in this volume).

Scale and Impact

The spatial scale of Greater Angkor is astonishing. Even after one recognizes that Angkor is a settlement pentimento rather than a single coeval settlement per se, the physical footprint of Angkor remains undeniably massive. Such a large settlement, supporting a population in the many hundreds of thousands, must have required extensive conversion of (presumably) primary forest to agricultural land, and indeed traces of premodern bunded field systems can be discerned in remotely sensed data extending across the flat alluvial plain on which Angkor sits, and north to the Kulen Hills (Evans 2007, 208; Hawken 2013). Unfortunately, the scale and timing of this implied deforestation are unknown, as is the type and status of the forest that was removed. Indeed, the ability to measure the impact of the Khmer on their natural environment is hampered by a lack of environmental archives, such as pollen records, that predate the development of large-scale Angkor-period occupation. Very few natural depositional basins on the Tonle Sap floodplain provide suitable environmental conditions for the long-term storage of sediment, and virtually none of these have been left undisturbed after millennia of agricultural occupation in a seasonally dry environment. The Tonle Sap itself has a long sediment record (Carbonnel and Guiscafré 1965; Darby et al. 2020; Day et al. 2011; Kummu et al. 2008; Penny, Cook, and Im 2005; Tsukawaki et al. 1994), but net sedimentation accumulation in the central lake basin is so low, and wind-driven sediment mixing so pervasive, that no reliable record of the last millennium can be recovered. Most of the environmental reconstruction at Angkor is based, therefore, on pre-Angkor and Angkor period excavations such as temple moats, trapeang and larger *baray* (reservoirs) and reveal nothing about conditions prior to their construction.

Despite the limited empirical evidence, there is no doubt that Angkor's expansion was associated with a profound transformation of the local environment, analogous to the "terraforming" around Caracol in the Maya lowlands (Chase et al., chapter 7 in this volume). Groslier (1979, 192) identified deforestation as the "primary consequence" of Angkor's growth away from the lake, making an explicit link between increasing size and increasing environmental impact. D. Evans et al. (2007, 14281) claim that the scale of Angkor was sufficient to produce "a number of very serious ecological problems, including deforestation, overpopulation, topsoil degradation, and erosion." V. Lieberman (2011, 943) writes, "The search for fuel, building materials, and perhaps fresh arable land pushed peasants to clear forests ever farther north of Angkor in the Kulen Hills, erosion and sedimentation began to clog streams and canals connected to great royal reservoirs . . . these pressures began to constrict settlement and population, to intensify peasant distress and intra-elite factionalism, and thus to leave the realm vulnerable to Tai attacks."

PHYSICAL TRACES OF ENVIRONMENTAL IMPACT

The link between scale, environmental impact, and deleterious social outcomes at Angkor is frequently asserted, particularly with respect to erosion, loss of soil productivity, and "siltation," yet the idea lacks any significant empirical rigor. Soil loss and excess sedimentation can, of course, leave physical traces in the landscape, particularly in depositional basins. Material mobilized in actively eroding catchments is often brought into storage in wetlands, floodplains, and lakes, which collectively constrain the flux of material from the continent to the oceans, in accordance with the sediment-routing system concept (Allen 2008). Accumulations of sediment within lakes, in particular, have been used to provide evidence for periods of soil erosion in the past, commonly associated with land clearing for agriculture (e.g., Gale and Haworth 2005; Wren and Davidson 2011). This evidence is commonly expressed as a change in the type of material being stored in the lake basin (reflected by changes in mineralogy, mineral particle size, geochemistry, magnetism, etc.) and/or the rate at which the sediment accumulates (determined by an absolute chronology based on isotopic decay dating).

It is well known that agriculture can dramatically increase rates of soil erosion well above rates of soil production, resulting in a loss of agricultural potential. The impact of agricultural settlement on soil and soil productivity is perhaps best illustrated in those regions of the earth formerly naive to such land use. In Australia, for example, where European agricultural practices supplanted hunting-and-gathering economies abruptly in the late eighteenth and early nineteenth centuries CE, soil erosion was immediate and so ferocious as to, in some instances at least, strip catchments of already skeletal soils and reduce the supply of new sediment to those minerals being weathered from bedrock (Gale and Haworth 2005; Wasson et al. 1998). In the twelfth and thirteenth centuries CE, the removal of forest on upper slopes as a result of slash/burn agriculture on the island of Rapa Nui (Easter Island) resulted in dramatic slope mobilization and soil loss (Mieth and Bork 2005), just as it did in the uplands of northern Thailand in the second/third century CE (Penny and Kealhofer 2005). In Cambodia, too, historic land use practices have resulted in soil mobilization and excess sedimentation. Sediment cores taken from two pre–Angkor period dams in the Kulen Hills (Thnal Dak and Thnal Mrech), north of Angkor, reveal episodic deposition of sand in these reservoirs, in one instance forming an 18 cm thick lens of medium to coarse sand, deposited most probably in the twelfth century CE (Penny et al. 2014). While the specific triggers for these episodes of erosion and deposition are unknown, and probably unknowable, it is tempting to link them with slash-and-burn and swidden agriculture in catchments with undulating topography, which yield friable soils weathered from the sandstone bedrock. Indeed, accelerating soil loss as a result of human activities, very commonly agriculture, is so ubiquitous it has become one of the defining characteristics of the putative "Anthropocene" concept (Syvitski and Kettner 2011).

However, it does not necessarily follow that large-scale conversion of land from forest to paddy is inevitably associated with greater rates of soil erosion, or with decreased soil capacity. Bunded rice fields, much like the extensive terrace systems created by the Maya (Lentz et al., chapter 3 in this volume), trap and retain water and other materials, and are low-energy, highly productive environments representing important sinks for organic carbon and which expand wetland habitat (Lawler 2001). Paddy soils are highly organic, fine-grained and cohesive, forming a near impermeable clay pan after a number of years' tillage. It is also recognized that rice paddy acts as traps for sediment, effectively reducing the loss of material from actively eroding areas at a range of geographical scales (e.g., Kang et al. 2006). Loss of nutrients from bunded rice systems, then, is not through soil erosion but through direct removal of the growing biomass, drainage losses, and volatilization. In contrast to the friable, permeable, and sandy soils beneath open-canopied deciduous monsoon forest, paddy systems are far more stable and conservative both in terms of soil erosion and water movement and must represent a net improvement in soil organic carbon.

It follows, therefore, that the widespread replacement of deciduous forest with paddy systems as the settlement expanded may be associated with a net *decrease* in sediment mobility across the landscape, rather than a net increase as is so often asserted. Critically, this proposition can be tested empirically, using sediment records from depositional basins at Angkor to assess the flux of mineral sediment as the city grew northward, away from the invariably productive floodplain of the Tonle Sap. We will make the case that "traditional" agricultural practices in the hydraulic suburbs of Angkor were conservative, extensive, monotonous, and stable and did not necessarily result in a loss of soil or soil productivity (and in many cases may even have provided a relative reduction in porosity and a relative increase in nutrients and carbon in the soil). In contrast, attempts to manage channelized water flow resulted in extensive erosion and

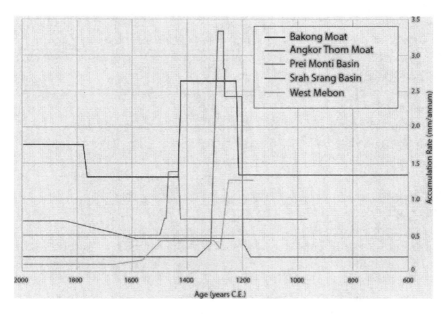

FIGURE 9.2. *Sedimentation rates in five depositional basins across Angkor.*

sedimentation that must have triggered numerous problems through the water management network that, at a large scale, became unresolvable.

SEDIMENTATION AS A PROXY FOR SUSTAINABILITY

As we have discussed, unsustainable land-use practices result in the increased mobilization of soil and higher rates of sediment accumulation elsewhere in the sediment-routing system, and these processes can be readily observed in stratigraphic sections and drill cores. In this context, sediment cores from Angkor period temple moats, baray, and trapeang may be instructive.

B.-P. Groslier (1979, 192) claimed that sedimentation rates in the temple moats were 2–3 mm per annum (mm/a⁻¹) during the Angkor period, and *de l'ordre du mètre* since Angkor's abandonment—equivalent to around 1.82 mm/a⁻¹. This, he argued, was evidence of aggressive siltation as a result of the ponding of sediment-laden water on the extremely flat alluvial plain. It is unclear how Groslier derived these accumulation rates, and he does not specify which moat was sampled. In actuality, sedimentation rates in depositional basins across Angkor are lower than Groslier anticipated. Five sites at Angkor (the central pond of the West Mebon temple, a small trapeang within the enclosure of Prei Monti, Srah Srang reservoir, and the moats of the Bakong and Angkor Thom; a total of twenty-nine radiocarbon dates from Penny et al. 2007, 2006; Penny, Cook, and Im 2005; Penny unpublished data; figure 9.2) reveal an average linear sedimentation rate of around 1.33 mm/a with a minimum linear sedimentation rate of 0.09 mm/a (post–Angkor period, West Mebon), and a maximum linear sedimentation rate of 3.31 mm/a (Angkor period, mid-late thirteenth century CE; Angkor Thom).

These simple linear sedimentation rates conflate several processes, however, and may mask the true magnitude of changing supply of sediment from the catchment. Most of the temple sites indicate a dramatic shift from predominantly mineral sedimentation during the Angkor period to predominantly organic sedimentation in the late and post-Angkor periods (and in some cases much earlier, such as at the Bakong; Penny et al. 2006), said to represent the colonization of the sites by swamp plants in the absence of regular maintenance (Penny, Pottier et al. 2005).

In any event, the temple moats and small, groundwater-fed reservoirs are frequently "closed" features with, in some cases, a hydrological catchment that is restricted to the banks of the excavated basin. This arrangement being the case, these deposition loci may not be representative of broader patterns of soil loss and mobility during the Angkor period. The great baray, however, are fed primarily by a complex network of canals that capture the natural rivers. The West Baray, for example, receives the majority of water from an artificial catchment of canals and embankments exceeding 240 km² in area (Penny, Pottier et al. 2005). The baray, then, represent the final storage for suspended sediment passing through Angkor's water management network and should, therefore, be sensitive to changes in the concentration of suspended sediment related to land use practices within their catchments.

Remarkably, however, very little sedimentation has occurred in the two largest baray: the Yashodharatataka (East Baray) and the West Baray. This absence has been demonstrated by radiometric dating of the East Baray (Tsukawaki et al. 1998), and recent archaeological excavations in the West Baray (see Penny, Cook, and Im 2005; Pottier 2006). The lack of sedimentation is, perhaps, best demonstrated by the litter of pre-Angkor ceramics, masonry, and built features (including the enclosure walls of the first pre-Angkor city of "Banteay Chou," which was partially consumed by the West Baray), which lie exposed on the bed of the West Baray and which are plainly visible from the air or on the surface when water levels are low. Many of these features were mapped by Georges Trouvé in 1935 and were later included in Christophe Pottier's map of southern Angkor (Pottier 1999). Clearly, then, there had been insufficient sedimentation in the great baray to smother the remains of pre-Angkor settlement, and as little as 30 cm since the Neolithic period in the case of the West Baray (Pottier 2006). This observation may be taken as evidence in support of Groslier's (1979, 193) hypothesis that the ponding of surface waters within the extensive and convoluted water management system iteratively reduced suspended sediment concentrations ("la décantation des eaux limoneuses") and thus prevented the delivery of nutrients to field systems "downstream."

However, M. B. Day et al. (2012) have provided a detailed stratigraphic record from the southwest corner of the West Baray that indicates nearly 2 m of vertical sediment accretion. They claim it is a result of the preferential settling of suspended sediment in the lowest part of the reservoir (the southwest corner), consistent with patterns of reservoir sedimentation elsewhere. The highest sedimentation rates in this record—approximately 6.1 mm/a—occurred in the thirteenth century, bracketed by two radiocarbon dates at 1.03 m (SUERC-29787; 700 ± 37 ^{14}C yrs BP) and 1.55 m (SUERC-29790; 804 ± 35 ^{14}C yrs BP) below lake floor. These rates are markedly higher than other depositional loci at Angkor, perhaps reflecting the larger catchment and open hydrology of the great baray. Sediment may also have been yielded to the site by the erosion of the baray's enormous earthen dykes—immediately adjacent to Core WB1–20-XII-03 MWI-1—and this may have been particularly the case during the supposed renovation and reexcavation of the West Baray and the West Mebon associated with Jayavarman VII in the late twelfth century. Lowered sedimentation rates, and changes in sediment strontium isotope values, are taken to reflect a decrease in the rate of erosion and weathering in the catchment following the abandonment of Angkor (Day et al. 2012). Qualitatively, this record is broadly consistent with other dated stratigraphic profiles throughout Angkor, which all tend to indicate a higher rate of sediment mobilization during the peak of the Angkor period (twelfth–thirteenth centuries), consistent with the expectation of more intense land-use during these periods and of lower rates of sediment accumulation during the late and post Angkor period.

Clearly, then, there is no compelling evidence for accelerating sedimentation in the moats, reservoirs, and baray of Angkor coincident with the settlement's decline and abandonment. The implication is that either soil erosion was minimal or that, more probably, eroded sediment was being retained elsewhere in the system as Groslier had suggested. It is possible that the network of agricultural fields themselves acted as a sink for eroded material, particularly in the north of Angkor, effectively filtering the bulk of mobilized sediment that would otherwise have reached the rivers and canal network via overland flow.

Rivers

In contrast to patterns of sediment accumulation in temple moats and reservoirs at Angkor, erosion and sedimentation within the canal system itself were far more dynamic and suggestive of episodes of extensive soil mobilization. Instances of rapid, possibly instantaneous (single event) filling of major canals have been documented recently from the south of Angkor (Fletcher et al. 2008; Kummu 2009; Lustig et al. 2008). Sediment—principally coarse sand, granules and gravel—filled one of the major canals connecting the moat of Angkor Wat to the lake, most probably in the mid-fourteenth century CE (631 ± 69 ^{14}C yrs BP), during the late Angkor period. Well-developed cross-bedding is apparent throughout the profile, suggesting rapid deposition during one or more unusually high-energy events. B. M. Buckley et al. (2010) have suggested that these events relate to unusually strong wet-season monsoons during the middle fourteenth and early fifteenth centuries. The likely consequences of such rapid sedimentation must have been serious—in the case above the displacement of water into the surrounding fields may have damaged the rice harvest, and any transport between the lake and the city along the canal must have been strangulated. Recent numerical modeling of Angkor's water management network indicates that disruption (in the form of erosion or sedimentation) within the canal network can create a cascading failure that causes the entire system to fragment and cease to function (Penny et al. 2018).

It seems probable that the bulk of the material filling these canals came from numerous breaches in earthen embankments higher in the network. These breaches, still clearly apparent, are the result of unregulated, perhaps catastrophic, water flow (Evans 2007). Perhaps more significant as a source of sediment supply to accreting canals in the south of Angkor was the incision of the Siem Reap River some 6–8 m into its bed and banks in its middle reaches (Kummu 2009; Lustig et al. 2008; Player 2018). The incision of the Siem Reap River, and the ongoing erosion associated with knick-point migration up through the catchment, would have yielded massive volumes of sediment that appear to have been deposited in canals cut through the lower floodplain.

The implication of this perspective is that severe erosion and deposition during the late Angkorian period were a product of erosion from *within the channel itself*, related to some of the most intense wet monsoons of the last millennium (Buckley et al. 2010, 6749, and supporting information), and not large-scale topsoil loss and slope mobilization related to unfettered conversion of forest to paddy in the catchment.

CONCLUSION

Angkor was massive, and its scale is often correlated with the likely magnitude of environmental damage caused by its growth. It is frequently asserted that soil erosion and siltation are associated with a loss of productivity and resilience at the landscape scale. However, the large-scale replacement of primary dry deciduous forests with intensive rice agriculture may have acted to stabilize the landscape and reduce soil erosion. The sustainability of Angkor as a massive, dispersed urban settlement was ultimately undermined, not by its scale per se, but by the complexity of the water distribution network that was developed to mitigate a sharply seasonal climate. Angkor's urban form, at least at the scale of the extensive hydraulic suburbs, was very conservative and based on the exploitation of resilient resources—high groundwater, fertile floodplains, and productive fisheries. So resilient was this land use strategy that, once the state had migrated to the margins of the old agrarian kingdom (Lucero, Fletcher, and Coningham 2015; Penny et al. 2019) and climatic variability had shattered the sclerotic water management network, the low-density subsistence economy resumed in the same manner, and in roughly the same areas, as during the pre-Angkor period (Groslier 1985). In the case of Angkor at least, the relationship between scale and environmental impact may be subtler than is generally thought.

REFERENCES

Acker, R. 2006. "Hydrology and the Siting of Yasodharapura." In *Phnom Bakheng Workshop on Public Interpretation*, edited by J. C. Chermayeff, J. Rousakis, and J. Gilmartin, 73–86. Phnom Penh: Centre for Khmer Studies.

Allen, P. A. 2008. "Time Scales of Tectonic Landscapes and Their Sediment Routing Systems." *Geological Society, London, Special Publications* 296 (1): 7–28.

Bonheur, N., and B. D. Lane. 2002. "Natural Resources Management for Human Security in Cambodia's Tonle Sap Biosphere Reserve." *Environmental Science and Policy* 5 (1): 33–41.

Buckley, B. M., K. J. Anchukaitis, D. Penny, R. Fletcher, E. R. Cook, M. Sano, L. C. Nam, A. Wichienkeeo, T. T. Minh, and T. M. Hong. 2010. "Medieval Climate Extremes and the Demise of Angkor." *Proceedings of the National Academy of Sciences of the United States of America* 107 (15): 6748–6752.

Carbonnel, J. P., and J. Guiscafré. 1965. "Grand Lac du Cambodge: Sedimentologie et hydrologie 1962–63." Paris: Ministere des Affaires Etrangeres.

Cook, E. R., K. J. Anchukaitis, B. M. Buckley, R. D. D'Arrigo, G. C. Jacoby, and W. E. Wright. 2010. "Asian Monsoon Failure and Megadrought during the Last Millennium." *Science* 328 (5977): 486–489.

Darby, S. E., P. G. Langdon, J. L. Best, J. Leyland, C. R. Hackney, M. Marti, P. R. Morgan et al. 2020. "Drainage and Erosion of Cambodia's Great Lake in the Middle-Late Holocene: The Combined Role of Climatic Drying, Base-Level Fall and River Capture." *Quaternary Science Reviews* 236: 106265.

Day, M. B., D. A. Hodell, M. Brenner, H. J. Chapman, J. H. Curtis, W. F. Kenney, A. L. Kolata et al. 2012. "Paleoenvironmental History of the West Baray, Angkor (Cambodia)." *Proceedings of the National Academy of Sciences* 109 (4): 1046–1051.

Day, M. B., D. A. Hodell, M. Brenner, J. H. Curtis, G. D. Kamenov, T. P. Guilderson, L. C. Peterson, W. F. Kenney et al.2011. "Middle to Late Holocene Initiation of the Annual Flood Pulse in Tonle Sap Lake, Cambodia." *Journal of Paleolimnology* 45 (1): 85–99.

Evans, D. 2007. "Putting Angkor on the Map: A New Survey of a Khmer 'Hydraulic City' in Historical and Theoretical Context." PhD diss., University of Sydney.

Evans, D., R. Fletcher, C. Pottier, J.-B. Chevance, D. Soutif, B. S. Tan, S. Im et al. 2013. "Uncovering Archaeological Landscapes at Angkor Using LiDAR." *Proceedings of the National Academy of Sciences of the United States of America* 110 (31): 12595–12600.

Evans, D., C. Pottier, R. Fletcher, S. Hensley, I. Tapley, A. Milne, and M. Barbetti. 2007. "A Comprehensive Archaeological Map of the World's Largest Preindustrial Settlement Complex at Angkor, Cambodia." *Proceedings of the National Academy of Sciences* 104 (36): 14277–14282.

Fletcher R. 2018. "Sprawl at Risk." In *Disrupted Balance: Society at Risk*, edited by J. Vasbinder, 48–51. Singapore: World Scientific Press.

Fletcher, R. J., Michael Barbetti, Damian Evans, Heng Than, Im Sokrithy, Khieu Chan, Daniel Penny et al. 2003. "Redefining Angkor: Structure and Environment in the Largest, Low Density Urban Complex of the Pre-industrial World." *UDAYA* 4: 107–121.

Fletcher, R., B. M. Buckley, C. Pottier, and S.-Y. Wang. 2017. "The Case of Angkor and Monsoon Extremes in Mainland Southeast Asia." In *Megadrought and Collapse: From Early Agriculture to Angkor*, edited by H. Weiss, 275–313. New York: Oxford University Press.

Fletcher, R., D. Penny, D. Evans, C. Pottier, M. Barbetti, M. Kummu, T. Lustig, APSARA. 2008. "The Water Management Network of Angkor, Cambodia." *Antiquity* 82 (317): 658–670.

Gale, S. J., and R. J. Haworth. 2005. "Catchment-Wide Soil Loss from Pre-agricultural Times to the Present: Transport- and Supply-Limitation of Erosion." *Geomorphology* 68 (3): 314–333.

Groslier, B.-P. 1979. "La Cité hydraulique angkorienne: Exploitation ou surexploitation du sol?" *Bulletin de l' École française d'Extrême-Orient* 66: 161–202.

Groslier, B. P. 1985. "For a Geographic History of Cambodia." *Seksa Khmer* 8: 31–76.

Hawken, S. 2013. "Designs of Kings and Farmers: Landscape Systems of the Greater Angkor Urban Complex." *Asian Perspectives* 52 (2): 347–367.

Hendrickson, M. 2010. "Historic Routes to Angkor: Development of the Khmer Road System (Ninth to Thirteenth Centuries AD) in Mainland Southeast Asia." *Antiquity* 84 (324): 480–496.

Hua, Q., D. Cook, J. Fohlmeister, D. Penny, P. Bishop, and S. Buckman. 2017. "Radiocarbon Dating of a Speleothem Record of Paleoclimate for Angkor, Cambodia." *Radiocarbon* 59 (6): 1873–1890.

Kang, M. S., S. W. Park, J. J. Lee, and K. H. Yoo. 2006. "Applying SWAT for TMDL Programs to a Small Watershed Containing Rice Paddy Fields." *Agricultural Water Management* 79 (1): 72–92.

Kazama, S., T. Hagiwara, P. Ranjan, and M. Sawamoto. 2007. "Evaluation of Groundwater Resources in Wide Inundation Areas of the Mekong River Basin." *Journal of Hydrology* 340 (3): 233–243.

Kummu, M., 2003. "The Natural Environment and Historical Water Management of Angkor, Cambodia." *Proceedings of the 5th World Archaeological Congress* (Washington, DC): 1–27.

Kummu, M. 2009. "Water Management in Angkor: Human Impacts on Hydrology and Sediment Transportation." *Journal of Environmental Management* 90 (3): 1413–1421.

Kummu, M., D. Penny, J. Sarkkula, and J. Koponen. 2008. "Sediment: Curse or Blessing for Tonle Sap Lake?" *AMBIO: A Journal of the Human Environment* 37 (3): 158–163.

Lamberts, D. 2006. "The Tonle Sap Lake as a Productive Ecosystem." *International Journal of Water Resources Development* 22 (3): 481–495.

Lawler, S. P. 2001. "Rice Fields as Temporary Wetlands: A Review." *Israel Journal of Zoology* 47 (4): 513–528.

Lieberman, V. 2011. "Charter State Collapse in Southeast Asia, ca. 1250–1400, as a Problem in Regional and World History." *American Historical Review* 116 (4): 937–963.

Lucero, L. J., R. Fletcher, and R. Coningham. 2015. "From 'Collapse' to Urban Diaspora: The Transformation of Low-Density, Dispersed Agrarian Urbanism." *Antiquity* 89 (347): 1139–1154.

Lustig, E. 2001. "Water and the Transformation of Power at Angkor, Tenth to Thirteenth Centuries A.D." BA honor's thesis, Department of Archaeology, University of Sydney.

Lustig, T., R. Fletcher, M. Kummu, C. M. Pottier, and D. Penny. 2008. "Did Traditional Cultures Live in Harmony with Nature? Lessons from Angkor, Cambodia." *Modern Myths of the Mekong: Helsinki UT, Helsinki, Finland*, edited by Kummu, Matti, Keskinen, Marko & Varis, Olli, 81–94. Helsinki: Helsinki University of Technology.

Mieth, A., and H. R. Bork. 2005. "History, Origin and Extent of Soil Erosion on Easter Island (Rapa Nui)." *Catena* 63 (2): 244–260. Museum National d'Histoire Naturelle de Paris.

Penny, D., J. B. Chevance, D. Tang, and S. De Greef. 2014. "The Environmental Impact of Cambodia's Ancient City of Mahendraparvata (Phnom Kulen)." *PloS one* 9 (1): e84252.

Penny, D., G. Cook, and S. S. Im. 2005. "Long-Term Rates of Sediment Accumulation in the Tonle Sap, Cambodia: A Threat to Ecosystem Health?" *Journal of Paleolimnology* 33 (1): 95–103.

Penny, D., T. Hall, D. Evans, and M. Polkinghorne. 2019. "Geoarchaeological Evidence from Angkor, Cambodia, Reveals a Gradual Decline rather than a Catastrophic 15th-Century Collapse." *Proceedings of the National Academy of Sciences* 116 (11): 4871–4876.

Penny, D., Q. Hua, C. Pottier, R. Fletcher, and M. Barbetti. 2007. "The Use of AMS 14 C Dating to Explore Issues of Occupation and Demise at the Medieval City of Angkor, Cambodia." *Nuclear Instruments and Methods in Physics Research Section B: Beam Interactions with Materials and Atoms* 259 (1): 388–394.

Penny, D., C. Pottier, R. Fletcher, M. Barbetti, D. Fink, and Q. Hua. 2006. "Vegetation and Land-Use at Angkor, Cambodia: A Dated Pollen Sequence from the Bakong Temple Moat." *Antiquity* 80 (309): 599–614.

Penny, D., and L. Kealhofer. 2005. "Microfossil Evidence of Land-Use Intensification in North Thailand." *Journal of Archaeological Science* 32 (1): 69–82.

Penny, D., C. Pottier, M. Kummu, R. Fletcher, U. Zoppi, M. Barbetti, and T. Somaneath. 2005. "Hydrological History of the West Baray, Angkor, Revealed through Palynological Analysis of Sediments from the West Mebon." *Bulletin de l'École française d'Extrême-Orient* 92 (1): 497–521.

Penny, D., C. Zachreson, R. Fletcher, D. Lau, J. Lizier, N. Fischer, D. Evans, C. Pottier, M. Prokopenko. 2018. "The Demise of Angkor: Systemic Vulnerability of Urban Infrastructure to Climatic Variations." *Science Advances* 4 (10): 1–8.

Player, S. 2018. *The Sands of Angkor: A Sediment Record of the Later Angkorian Channel Network*. PhD thesis, University of Sydney.

Pottier, C. 1999. *Carte archéologique de la région d'Angkor: Zone Sud*. PhD diss., Université Paris III, Sorbonne Nouvelle, Paris.

Pottier, C. 2006. "Under the Western Baray Waters." In *Uncovering Southeast Asia's Past: Selected Papers from the 10th International Conference the European Association of Southeast Asian Archaeologists*, edited by Elisabeth A. Bacus and Ian C. Glover, 298–309. Singapore: NUS Press.

Pottier, C., and A. Bolle. 2009. "Le Prasat Trapeang Phong à Hariharâlaya: Histoire d'un temple et archéologie d'un site." *Aséanie* 24 (December): 1–30.

Roberts, T. R. 2002. "Fish Scenes, Symbolism and Kingship in the Bas-Reliefs of Angkor Wat and the Bayon." *Natural History Bulletin of the Siam Society* 50 (2): 135–193.

Seng, V., R. W. Bell, P. F. White, N. Schoknecht, S. Hin, and W. Vance. 2007. "Sandy Soils of Cambodia." In *Management of Tropical Sandy Soils for Sustainable Agriculture: Symposium on the Management of Tropical Sandy Soils* (November 27–December 2, 2005, Khon Kaen, Thailand), edited by C. Hartmann and N. Chinabut, 42–48.

Syvitski, J. P., and A. Kettner. 2011. "Sediment Flux and the Anthropocene." *Philosophical Transactions of the Royal Society of London A: Mathematical, Physical and Engineering Sciences* 369 (1938): 957–975.

Tsukawaki, S., M. Okawara, K. L. Lao, and M. Tada. 1994. "Preliminary Study of Sedimentation in Lake Tonle Sap, Cambodia." *Journal of Geography (Chigaku Zasshi)* 103 (6): 623–636.

Tsukawaki, S., M. Okuno, M. Okawara, M. Kato, and T. Nakamura. 1998. "Underground Structures of the Site of East Baray Reservoir in the Angkor District, Central Cambodia." *Summaries of Researchers Using AMS at Nagoya University* 9: 272–280.

Voeun, V., and S. Seng. 2006. "Fish Remains from Koh Ta Meas Site." In *Mission archéologique Franco-Khmère sur l'Aménagement du Territoire Angkorien (MAFKATA)*, edited by C. Pottier, 129–151. Rapport sur la campagne 2006. Siem Reap, Cambodia: APSARA-MAE-EFEO.

Wasson, R. J., R. K. Mazari, B. Starr, and G. Clifton. 1998. "The Recent History of Erosion and Sedimentation on the Southern Tablelands of Southeastern Australia: Sediment Flux Dominated by Channel Incision." *Geomorphology* 24 (4): 291–308.

White, P. F., T. Oberthür, and P. Sovuthy, eds. 1997. *The Soils Used for Rice Production in Cambodia: A Manual for Their Identification and Management.* Manila: International Rice Research Institute.

Wren, D. G., and G. R. Davidson. 2011. "Using Lake Sedimentation Rates to Quantify the Effectiveness of Erosion Control in Watersheds." *Journal of Soil and Water Conservation* 66 (5): 313–322.

10

Acequias

Trust and Hydrosocial Territory

Sylvia Rodríguez

ACEQUIAS AND MORAL ECONOMY

New Mexico's acequias belong to a family of hand-dug, gravity-flow, small-scale, farmer-managed irrigation systems found all over the world. Some are historically related, but others are not. Despite their differences in terms of environment, geography, climate, regional and national setting, language, and culture, these systems all seem to operate in strikingly similar ways. This alignment has led one anthropologist to propose that their common operating principles are the result of a rare process of convergent evolution, whereby the same form emerges independently in different places and times, because it is highly adaptive (Trawick, Reig, and Salvador 2014). Such systems—which are found, for example, in the Andes, Mexico, Spain, Switzerland, China, India, Nepal, the Philippines, Africa, and Bali—have proven to be sustainable and resilient within their respective ecological settings, whether arid or humid. Nevertheless, many have disappeared under the onslaught of modernization, while those that still exist struggle to survive in the face of myriad adverse political, economic, social, demographic, environmental, and climatic forces.

https://doi.org/10.5876/9781646422326.c010

This chapter examines the dynamic interface between acequia governance and the broader hydrosocial regime and territory in which it is embedded. My discussion explores the question of acequia sustainability in light of ethnographic-, historical-, comparative-, political-, and ecological systems–modeling perspectives. This analysis moves from microsocial to macrosocial levels and back again, focusing on how the tension between local and regional water politics has evolved through time.

ACEQUIA AGRICULTURE AND GOVERNANCE

The term "acequia" refers to both the irrigation canal and the association of *parciantes* who own and operate it. The association consists of farmer-rancher parciantes, or water right and landowners who share a common *presa* (stream diversion) into a hand-dug *acequia madre* ("mother ditch") from which *linderos*, *venitas*, *sangrías* (laterals) convey water to individual properties. Their basic canal structure and operating principles derive from Islamic-Iberian rules, technology, and practices introduced to the semiarid upper Rio Grande valley by Spanish colonial settlers who occupied *mercedes reales*, or grants of land awarded by the Spanish Crown, starting in the late sixteenth century.

Acequia agriculture extended riparian habitats, transformed regional ecology, and created the northern New Mexican landscape seen today. Acequia irrigation was integral to the agropastoral economy that persisted into the twentieth century and survives today in reduced and modified form among rural and semi-urban Nuevomexicanos. Even though few parciantes today subsist entirely or even primarily on agriculture, acequias remain the organizational backbone of many rural Nuevomexicano communities.

The moral economy model of community irrigation management posits a system of principles and values that supports and guides cooperative, independent economic practice. Drawing on ethnographic research in highland Peru and Valencia, Spain, understood in light of Elinor Ostrom's work (1990), Trawick identifies nine operating principles common to all small-scale, farmer-operated irrigation systems: autonomy, alternation or turn taking, contiguity in distribution, uniformity, proportionality, transparency, boundary maintenance, direct feedback, and graduated sanctions (Trawick 2003; Trawick, Reig, and Salvador 2014, 88). Like their Islamic-Iberian forebears and modern cognates in Valencia, New Mexico's acequia irrigation systems exhibit these attributes.

Parciantes

Parciantes are obligated to pay dues, contribute labor to the cleaning and maintenance of acequia infrastructure, observe the customs of water sharing, and annually elect a *mayordomo* (ditch boss) and three commissioners who oversee ditch management and governance. Labor contribution and water allocation are proportional to the amount of acreage a parciante irrigates. The mayordomo allocates water proportionally to parciantes in good standing on the basis of equity and need, supervises communal labor on the ditch, and resolves disputes over water. Commissioners include a secretary, treasurer, and president. Acequia communities define themselves as place-based, territorial, and linked through time by kinship, spatial contiguity, and a continuous round of sacred and secular calendric and life-cycle rituals.

Today middle- and working-class semiurban parciantes continue to irrigate and stubbornly defend their water rights and agricultural interests. They no longer maintain their acequias as a primary source of livelihood, but also as a source of social, cultural, and emotional connection, identity, and meaning. Given the premier value of land with attached surface water rights on the New Mexico real estate and water markets, there nevertheless can be little doubt that Nuevomexicanos' main wealth resides in their property. Some even operate their *ranchitos* at a loss if personal time and labor investment are taken into account. Pressed to explain why she and other parciantes continue to irrigate and maintain their ditches without monetary gain, a *mayordoma* in San Cristóbal replied, "because it's tradition"; she then paused and added, "If I didn't irrigate I would never have to talk to my neighbors. It's the connection. It's community."

ACEQUIA CONFLICT AND SUCCESS

All acequias operate in roughly the same way, some more cooperatively than others, many slowly unraveling or fractured by bitter conflict. Each has its own unique history, and acequias are not uniform when it comes to particulars. They struggle with decaying infrastructure, knowledge loss, and the dilemma of attrition: *delincuentes* who don't irrigate, or contribute labor, or pay their dues. They doggedly hang on in the twenty-first century under regional and global conditions that threaten to drive farming, neighborhoods, and extended families into extinction.

Every ditch, like every community and neighborhood, has its own character, circumstance, location on a stream, and long-standing families with parciantes who irrigate, come to (or avoid) meetings, vote for officers, negotiate ditch matters, and serve as mayordomos or commissioners. As with all self-managed irrigation systems, the successful operation and persistence of an acequia come down to the commitment and ongoing interaction of a critical number of individuals. At this scale, individual personalities make a difference, something easily observed in day-to-day exchange.

For example, a senior acequia and water district commissioner from Santa Cruz who mediates ditch disputes all over the state commented that every single instance he has seen of paralyzing, irreconcilable conflict on a ditch "comes down to two people who hate each other's guts." Or asked to pinpoint the critical difference between an acequia that operates well and one that is dysfunctional and falling apart, a commissioner and Taos Soil and Water District officer answered: "one or two people who are totally dedicated to the ditch."

The most committed parciantes and proponents of acequias are not necessarily those who benefit most from them economically. Typically, they devote considerable time, energy, and personal resources to other local institutions as well, such as their (Catholic) parish, mutual domestic water association, land grant association, extended family, and *morada* (chapter house for a lay religious confraternity). In the enacted but unspoken moral economy of the ditch, those individuals who demonstrably serve the welfare of the "community," who enact a spirit of mutualism (see Rivera 2011) and show *respeto* (respect) for others—but who do not talk about it—tend to be trusted, watched, and listened to when it comes time to make a collective decision. Such individuals seldom register on the radar screens of outsiders or bureaucrats.

AN ACEQUIA COMMUNITY IN THE UPPER VALLEY OF THE RIO HONDO WATERSHED

Anthropologists who work closely with contemporary autonomous irrigation communities describe remarkably similar internal processes of water governance and management. Ethnography at the community scale foregrounds the local or internal operation and practice of governance, management, and ritual activity, usually analyzed in relation to cultural ecology and/or the intervention of state bureaucracy. My work involves ethnography and ethnohistory in an acequia community in the upper valley of the Rio Hondo watershed, a tributary of the Rio Grande in northern Taos County. I am a parciante and serve as secretary of this acequia, learning in my golden years how to irrigate an acre of alfalfa.

Of seventy-six listed parciantes on this acequia, roughly fifty are active members who pay their dues, contribute labor for the annual ditch cleaning, and irrigate. Almost all grow alfalfa; some have orchards and/or kitchen gardens; some have livestock and/or chickens. None depends exclusively on agriculture for their livelihood, though most who grow alfalfa for their cattle, or to sell, derive some economic benefit from it. San Antoneros assert that everyone in the valley and nearby communities is related through blood, and/or marriage, *crianza* (adoption), and/or *compradrazgo* (fictive kinship). They routinely narrate convoluted genealogies that boggle an outsider's mind.

The quality and dynamism of interpersonal relationships between individuals through time are what most captivate me about how acequia associations operate. At the microsocial scale, what social scientists call mutuality or mutualism and social capital show their human face. Mutualism has a long tradition in northern New Mexico, found at the core of acequia associations, *Penitente cofradiás* (lay religious confraternities of La Hermandad de Nuestro Padre Jesus

Nazareno, also known as the Penitente Brotherhood), mutual domestic water associations, and burial and other mutual aid societies, all known generically as *mutualistas*. According to José Rivera, "Despite their variety in size, composition, and location, these societies were founded on the common principle of *ayuda mutua*, a mutual help response to the harsh realities of survival during periods of social change and economic difficulty" (Rivera 2010, 9).

Participation-observation convinces me that mutualism/reciprocity, kinship, self-interest, *and* personal investment in the common good are what keep the ditches flowing and a multigenerational network of people cooperating to irrigate and defend the integrity of their self-identified, place-based community. My ability to observe how mutualism (e.g., *confianza*, or trust) and social capital (e.g., respeto) function at the local level, and to understand how people perceive, assess, feel, and talk (or not) about these characteristics, depends on the degree to which I myself participate in such exchanges.

Although Pierre Bourdieu is often cited for his use of the term social capital ("a capital of social connections, honourability and respectability" related to but distinguishable from economic and cultural capital; 1984, 122), it is the groundbreaking work of Ostrom that sheds a useful light on how self-organized associations can sustainably govern a common pool resource such as water. "We have selected three types of social capital that are particularly important in the study of collective action: (1) trustworthiness, (2) networks, and (3) formal and informal rules or institutions. We view social capital as an attribute of individuals and of their relationships that enhance their ability to solve collective-action problems" (Ostrom and Ahn 2008, 5).

Two concepts help to illuminate my understanding of how acequias manage to keep operating under today's increasingly difficult economic and climatic conditions: trust and the hydrosocial cycle. At the end of her career, Ostrom was focused on the central role of trust in sustainable and resilient common pool regimes. In her Nobel Prize address, she reported the following: "Building trust in one another and developing institutional rules that are well matched to the ecological systems being used are of central importance for solving social dilemmas. The surprising but repeated finding that users of resources that are in relatively good condition—or even improving—do invest in various ways of monitoring one another relates to the core problem of building trust" (Ostrom 2009, 435).

My focus is on the dynamic relation between trust, or confianza, and mutualism, ritual participation, attachment to place, and social capital in an acequia community that intersects also with a constellation of spheres and scales of power encompassing neighboring communities, local institutions, government agencies, interest groups, tribes, and corporations.

THE HYDROSOCIAL CYCLE

The hydrosocial cycle concept of water as a connective *process* illuminates the social-political agency of water and its ontological inseparability from the human domain (Latour 1993; Linton 2010; Linton and Budds 2014). The conceptual division between the natural and human or social domains is foundational to modern science and underpins its technological mastery over the physical world. In his brilliant critique of what he calls "modern water," Jamie Linton observes that "as the dominant epistemological mode of Western culture, scientific practice has produced a distinctive way of understanding and representing water that makes it appear timeless, natural, and unaffected by the contingencies of human history" (2010, 74). Modern water is an abstraction signified by the chemical formula H_2O and the hydrological cycle diagrammed by Robert Horton in 1931, often reproduced in introductory science textbooks. Science explains water as an objective phenomenon external to human society. Its cyclical transformation into liquid, vapor, or ice is predictable, universal, and everywhere the same (Linton 2010).

Hydrosocial theorists argue instead that water and its social context are co-constituted as historical, local, socionatural process. Conceived in conventional scientific terms, acequia systems mediate, or serve as a hydrological and social buffer between, separate and distinct human and natural domains. Conceived as hydrosocial assemblages, acequia systems are ecologically, historically, and politically situated socionatural hybrids. No one who has irrigated or worked on an acequia for any length of time would deny the palpable agency of an acequia or of water, and especially of water running in a ditch. The acequia is a living process that connects neighbors on a stream who together must manage the flow and equitable distribution of water among deserving parciantes.

ACEQUIAS AND THE STATE

A peculiar twist in acequia history is that Iberian canal irrigation came to northern New Spain as a top-down technology of colonization, but over a period of time under harsh and remote conditions, acequias self-organized into hydrosocially networked autonomous irrigation communities. Colonizers arrived in the New World with a body of Spanish law and seven hundred years of Iberian-Islamic water management history. We can only speculate about how first contact, or the hypothetical hydraulic horizon, unfolded between Iberian and Indigenous Pueblo irrigators, or how they and pre-Columbian Mexican water regimes syncretized over the following centuries, evolving differently in different locations. Historian Michael Meyer offers the following account of how acequia associations or *acequias de común* emerged in New Mexico:

> Through a process of *mancomunicación*, the community of rural irrigators or
> *parciantes* (called *parcioneros* in some parts of New Spain and *aparceros* on others),

voluntarily formed associations (*mancomunidades*) to build, maintain, and administer the ditches as well as to resolve future disputes. The agreements, in part modeled after the municipal water systems, were much more likely to be oral than written and were passed down from generation to generation of irrigators. There is no indication in the surviving documentary record that they required ratification from any nearby municipal or provincial authority. For each ditch they devised water sharing plans on an informal basis. The type of agreements were similar, but not identical, from one *acequia* to another on the same watershed. Most were simple, as each *parciantes'* rights were of equal dignity, but some encompassed a more complicated nexus of priorities, rotations, and water relationships. While the mechanism of self-restraint was enshrined and cooperation anticipated, compliance was not taken for granted. Some form of protection was needed, and the rural irrigators opted for administration without government. ([1984] 1996, 183–184)

They elected a mayordomo to apportion water, oversee fatigue labor, resolve disputes, and work in concert with other mayordomos on a stream, where "most important . . . was the need to protect acequias lower on the stream during periods of droughts" (188). Curiously, Meyer concludes that "the resilience of the system defies ready explanation" (188).

Acequias functioned according to unwritten but well-understood customs and practices under both Spanish (1598–1821) and Mexican (1821–1848) rule. Meyer reports that mayordomos, nevertheless, "fell under the scrutiny of the provincial government," and "in 1826, shortly after Mexican independence, a commission appointed by the *ayuntamiento* of Santa Fe had a statute enacted that provided for the fining of *mayordomos* who were derelict in their duties" (1996, 188). Codification of customary governance and practice under territorial and then state and federal law began in the late nineteenth century after the conclusion of the Mexican-American War and annexation of half of Mexico's territory into what became the US Southwest. US territorial legislation formalized the corporate status of acequias and required them to elect three commissioners annually along with the traditional mayordomo, or ditch boss, an arrangement that continues today.

Acequias became enmeshed in state bureaucracy when American law changed how irrigation water was to be measured, appropriated, owned, and transacted. The modern abstraction of New Mexico's water enabled water rights to be severed and sold separately from the land. Furthermore, instead of according to temporal or proportional practical usage, water was measured by the volumetric acre-foot (325,851 gallons). American law protected individual but not common property rights. This led to massive dispossession of ejido, or common *merced* or grant lands, which ended up in the eager hands of speculators or as state or federally controlled public domain. "Natural waters" were likewise declared

Table 10.1. Acequia Governance vs. State Management

Acequia Water Governance	Management by State Engineer
Water attached to the land	Water transferable, bought and sold like property
Water rights determined locally	Forfeiture of water rights by state
Self-governance by local community-elected leaders	Decisions by centralized bureaucracy
Repartimiento—equity, flexibility, Indigenous knowledge	Strict priority administration—static technocratic knowledge

Source: Courtesy of the New Mexico Acequia Association.

public property and placed under the centralized supervision of a territorial and then a state engineer. A crucial difference inheres between customary acequia water sharing practice based on equity and need and Western water law based on prior appropriation. The new regime usurped the sustainable ethic of sharing the shortages in times of scarcity and instead empowered an owner of the senior or prior water right to take it all.

Acequia associations began keeping ledgers and written records in the twentieth century, and most now have written bylaws that must be filed with the State Engineer's Office in order to qualify for loans and grants-in-aid programs (Rivera 1998, 60–62). Their ever-expanding administrative burdens include filing annual financial reports and showing compliance with Open Meetings and Public Records legislation. Nevertheless, they still routinely conduct their business on a face-to-face or telephone basis at the local internal level. Apart from publicly accessible ledgers, some mayordomos have kept personal *cuadernos* (notebooks) over the years that record temporal *tiempos* (water allocations) and other quotidian and seasonal information. Today, acequias operate as autonomous common property regimes while at the same time as legal subdivisions of the state, subject to state statute. This is a precarious line to walk. Their authority to enforce the rules is backed up by the coercive and judicial power of the state, but in turn they are subject to its scrutiny and control.

Anthropologists commonly report an inherent tension between local irrigation systems and the state. In Paul Gelles's words, "Irrigation politics in widely diverse settings such as Peru and Bali must be understood in terms of conflict between bureaucratic and local forms of understanding" (2000, 159). Table 10.1, provided by the New Mexico Acequia Association (NMAA), illustrates this point.

Irrigation and the State

The relationship between irrigation and the state has been a well-chewed bone of contention ever since Karl Wittfogel proposed his famous hypothesis about despotism and the ancient hydraulic state (1957). Linking political power to water control, few formulations have proved more provocative to scholars across a range of disciplines—even though most subsequent archaeological, historical, and ethnographic research has either refuted or vastly complicated Wittfogel's thesis. Scholars generally agree that the emergence of primary and secondary states in both wet and dry regions of the world required the elaboration of hydrotechnology and water management, but the question of how irrigation relates to power has evolved from the premise of centralized, despotic control to increasingly refined understandings of how local irrigation communities operate internally and become externally articulated with states under different temporal, spatial, environmental, and political-economic conditions. Still, the relationship between irrigation and "the state" remains a compelling question with practical and theoretical implications (see Scarborough 2003).

Inspired by Wittfogel, Donald Worster's prizewinning environmental history *Rivers of Empire* (1985) examines the massive federal reclamation and dam-building projects along the major rivers of the American West that made it possible for cities and industrial agriculture to flourish in the desert. Worster surpasses Wittfogel by making the imaginative leap to water modernity and what he calls the hydraulic capitalist state that emerged in the twentieth century. He distinguishes local subsistence, agrarian, and capitalist state types or developmental stages of hydraulic society and proposes that "capitalism has created a new, distinctive type of hydraulic society, one that demonstrates how domination of nature can lead to the domination of some people over others" (50). In the modern hydraulic society, Worster argues, "there are roughly two centers of power: a private center of agriculturists and a public center of bureaucratic planners and elected representatives. Neither group is autonomous. Both need each other, reinforce each other's values, compete for the upper hand without lasting success, and finally agree to work together to achieve a control over nature that is unprecedentedly thorough" (51).

The modern private agricultural sector Worster refers to is wealthier and better organized than "the archaic peasant class" (1985, 51) that presumably includes acequias, which he mentions in passing but finds of little interest. Still, his characterization of modern water cannily prefigures the hydrosocial critique:

> Water in the capitalist state has no intrinsic value, no integrity that must be respected. Water is no longer valued as a divinely appointed means of survival, for producing and reproducing human life, as it was in local subsistence communities. Nor is water an awe-inspiring ally in quest for political empire, as it was in the agrarian states. It has now become a commodity that is bought and sold and used to make other commodities that can be bought and sold and carried to the marketplace. It is, in other words, purely and abstractly a commercial instrument. All mystery disappears from its depths, all gods depart, all contemplation of its

flow ceases. It becomes so many "acre-feet" banked in an account, so many "kilo watt-hours" of generating capacity to be spent, and so many bales of cotton or cartloads of oranges to be traded around the globe. And in that new language of market calculation lies an assertion of ultimate power over nature—of a domination that is absolute, total, and free from all restraint. (52)

This massive reengineering of the Western waterscape, or hydrosocial territory and hydraulic grid, created the backdrop against which the seemingly insignificant social drama of acequia persistence plays out. As we shall see, acequias are profoundly affected by the 1948 Upper Colorado Basin Compact that divided the waters of the Colorado River among claims made by the western states of Colorado, Arizona, California, and New Mexico, the last of which was allotted 11.25 percent. This project imported "new" water into the fully allocated Rio Grande in order to accommodate future urban growth. The San Juan–Chama Diversion Project channeled water from the Colorado River through mountain tunnels and across the Continental Divide into the Rio Grande, constructing reservoirs and activating a series of state and federal adjudication lawsuits that pitted the indigenous Rio Grande Pueblos, who claim prior rights from "time immemorial" against all junior claimants, starting with acequias and including municipalities, water and sanitation districts, conservancy districts, mutual domestic water associations, and other entities that claim water rights. The ongoing consequences of the New Mexico adjudication suits will be discussed below.

ANTHROPOLOGICAL VIEWS

In the meantime, the question of irrigation and the state leads to other scholars whose work can shed light on how acequias are faring in the twenty-first century. In *Seeing Like a State*, James Scott examines historical case studies of disastrous efforts by "high modernist" authoritarian states to engineer entire regions or landscapes/waterscapes and their resident populations according to rational principles of science and technology. The imperative of statecraft, Scott observes, is to render populations legible for the purposes of "taxation, conscription, and the prevention of rebellion" (1998, 2). They do this through a process of "simplification" that involves mapping, census, and measurement. He contends that "the most tragic episodes of state-initiated social engineering originate in a pernicious combination of four elements. All four are necessary for full-fledged disaster" (4). First is the administrative ordering of nature and society that all statecraft must pursue. Second is a "high-modernist ideology that uncritically believes in the power of scientific technology to execute projects of comprehensive planning and social engineering" (2). Third is "an authoritarian state that is willing and able to use the full weight of its coercive power to bring these high modernist designs into being . . . A fourth element is closely linked to the third: a prostrate civil society that lacks the capacity to resist these plans" (4–5).

Interestingly, Scott's other books focus on how subaltern populations, such as peasants in Southeast Asia, slyly manage to resist the coercive and regulatory powers of the state through indirect, covert, subversive tactics he calls "weapons of the weak" (Scott 1985), often enacting a "hidden transcript" of resistance under the guise of conformity to the "public transcript" (Scott 1990). Scott is an early proponent of the moral economy concept of how peasant society subsists through an ethic of reciprocity and mutualism, and he proposes that it is their overlord's violation of those principles that can lead to peasant revolt (Scott 1976) or induce more mobile populations to retreat to marginal hinterlands lying beyond the zone of direct control (Scott 2010). He sees the fatal flaw of imperial or hegemonic planning as its exclusion of "the necessary role of local knowledge and know-how." He contrasts imperial technocratic knowledge with "the indispensable role of practical knowledge, informal processes, and improvisation in the face of unpredictability" that enables local subsistence populations to survive and adapt in a particular landscape or habitat through time (Scott 1998, 6). He calls this tactical knowledge *metis*, borrowed from the Greek.

Both Worster and Scott are critical of the social and environmental destruction wrought by unchecked instrumental reason wed to centralized state power, irrespective of whether it serves a capitalist or socialist agenda. Scott goes further: "Formal order . . . is always and to some considerable degree parasitic on informal processes, which the formal scheme does not recognize, without which it could not exist, and which it alone cannot maintain" (1998, 310). Dismissing local knowledge as backward, irrational, and inefficient, the modern state excludes metis, or practical local knowledge, at its peril. Metis "represents a wide array of practical skills and acquired intelligence in responding to a constantly changing natural and human environment" (313). Scott echoes Worster and others who see the state and the local rural community as inextricably bound, but his anthropological eye dwells closely on the nature, operation, and indispensability of local knowledge.

The most famous example of how the state can disrupt a highly adaptive system of farmer-managed irrigation comes from Bali, where for decades Steve Lansing has studied the ancient temple-regulated system of *subak* irrigation. Lansing was able to discover, through ethnography and computer simulation, how an elaborate system of water temple rituals regulated the timing of water release from higher to lower canals in a manner that suppressed pest infestations in the rice paddies. Then, in the 1970s, the green revolution introduced—or imposed—industrial agricultural technologies to expand commercial rice production. This gradually threw the ancient system into disarray and to the brink of ecological disaster (Lansing [1991] 2007). Lansing's research played a role in persuading the ruling powers to dial back their potentially catastrophic innovations, and the temple system has been restored in some areas.

Lansing does not attribute the genius of the system to what Scott calls metis however, but to something deeper and more complex (Lansing [1991] 2007, xxviii). He admits that he would probably have been content to understand the water temples as repositories of an extraordinarily rich body of metis had he not crossed paths with a systems ecologist and a complexity theorist. The latter asked if the temples might be a self-organized system. In short, "Were the temple networks a solution, or a device for finding solutions? In other words, had the subaks solved a problem, or built themselves a problem solver?" (Lansing 2006, 14). Lansing concludes that the water temple network is a bottom-up, self-organized system that more resembles an immune system than a technologically engineered network. It evolved through natural selection, "which does not focus on optimizing one solution, but rather on improving the features of the system that enable it to learn and adapt" (15). His conclusion that the network is self-organized, moreover, sheds light on the old debate about irrigation and the ancient state. Having persisted through precolonial kingdom, Dutch colonial, and modern state eras, the Balinese system is widely considered an instructive case. Was the system ever centralized? Lansing's collaboration with other scientists confirms their initial hypothetical scenario: "We imagined a historical scenario for Bali that might have begun with the appearance of a few small systems. As irrigation expanded, these systems would have come into contact with their neighbors and begun to interact. The ability to vary the scale of water control in response to changing conditions would have been the key to success. If water temples began to function like nodes in a network, then an efficient and adaptable system of control would have emerged with no need for centralized planning" (16).

Unlike Java, where a somewhat different political economy took shape, in Bali, "the sheer number of these small-scale irrigation systems and the need for continuous, intensive management would have made it difficult for state functionaries to control them. Instead, the rulers sensibly chose to leave the farmers in control, while taxing the fruits of their labors" (Lansing 2006, 63; for a theoretical approach to the transition from rural to urban settlement and water management, see Van der Leeuw, chapter 8 in this volume; for a comparison of centralized and dispersed water management strategies among the ancient Maya in response to different microenvironments, see Chase et al., chapter 7 in this volume).

Ancient and modern states alike have often found it expedient to leave the day-to-day practical management of irrigation (including canal maintenance and cleaning, distribution of water, internal conflict resolution) in the hands of local farmers while at the same time, such systems become embedded in, and subject to, various levels, branches, or agencies of state oversight and regulation.

The relationship between local irrigation communities and the state is far from monolithic, however. Nor is "the state" a monolithic entity. J. Mark Baker's characterization of state-*kuhl* (local irrigation system) relations in northern India could easily apply to acequia-state (including municipal, county, state, and federal) relations in northern New Mexico: "We must view the state as an internally fractured set of institutions competing with one another, connected to a wider set of policy concerns and directives, and entering into strategic alliances and negotiations with local groups in a manner that both strengthens state authority and benefits segments of the local 'community'" (Baker 2005, 40).

Political Ecology and Scale

The theme of dueling, intertwined, codependent state and local modes of water governance runs also through the geographical literature on water communities, most notably in work by political ecologists. But rather than moral economy or cultural ecology, geographers focus instead on the macropolitics of how marginalized water communities are embedded in larger hydrosocial regimes and territories, locked in unequal yet mutually transformative struggle for whatever shred of local control they can salvage. Hydrosocial cycle theory appears to have emerged among geographers engaged in the study of hydraulic modernization projects in authoritarian nation-states such as Franco's Spain (Swyngedouw 1999) and Pinochet's Chile (Budds 2009, 2013). Writing about the Andes, Rutgerd Boelens calls the forced engagement between official and local, often peasant systems a "shotgun marriage" (Boelens 2009, 315). This coerced wedlock is charged with inequity and conflict: "The State and its legal system face the need to incorporate local fairness constructs [customary law] and solve normative conflicts in order not to lose legitimacy and discursive power in the eyes of its citizens. Local law systems, in turn, are intrinsically hybrids, and cannot operate without relating to formal law systems. But the marriage is unhappy and extremely complicated" (Boelens 2009, 315).

Hydrosocial theorists attribute the Andean version of "marital discord" to the region's successively traumatic history of Inka rule, Spanish colonization, and modern nation building, processes that evolved and continue to unfold differently in Peru, Chile, Bolivia, and Ecuador. Indigenous and peasant communities vary widely in how they articulate with state and corporate interests, but nevertheless it remains "the aim of the State and dominant groups . . . to resolve only ad hoc, secondary conflicts, without changing the primary, fundamental conflicts based on class contradictions and power structures that reproduce gender and ethnic positions" (Boelens 2009, 315–316). Paul H. Gelles sees Andean culture as "created from a hybrid mix of local mores with political forms and ideological forces of hegemonic states, both indigenous and Iberian" (Gelles 2010, 123). He reports that "indigenous Andean culture and cultural identity continue to be key elements in local social relationships in rural peasant communities, and . . . these cultural orientations and ethnic identities are intimately linked to agricultural and pastoral production, in general, and to irrigation water in particular" (119). The struggle for water in rural Andean communities is also a struggle for power, identity, autonomy, and territory. The same is true of traditional water communities on the northern frontier of the Spanish American colonial empire.

Geographers proceed on the premise that "society and nature are intrinsically linked and interdependent" (Boelens et al. 2016, 3). As noted earlier, hydrosocial theorists reject the Western or modern scientific separation of nature and society into ontologically separate domains. Their relational, dialectical approach posits nature and society as a socionatural hybrid: mutually constituted and historically situated. The biophysical and sociocultural are a single (or multiple) hybrid *process*. These scholars focus on the political dimension of the shotgun marriage played out in particular spaces under prevailing contemporary neoliberal economic policies. Rutgerd Boelens and colleagues (2016) deploy the concepts of hydrosocial territory and hydrosocial network to analyze at multiple scales the struggle between local and bureaucratic control over water. They define hydrosocial territory as "the contested imaginary and socio-environmental materialization of a spatially bound multi-scalar network in which humans, water flows, ecological relations, hydraulic infrastructure, financial means, legal-administrative arrangements, and cultural institutions and practices are interactively defined, aligned, and mobilized through epistemological belief systems, political hierarchies and naturalizing discourses" (Boelens et al. 2016, 2).

Regarding networks, they continue, "water, technologies, society and nature are intrinsically interrelated and mutually determining elements that together organize as specific socionatural networks. The networks of relations constituting hydrosocial territories can be termed 'hydrosocial networks.' These networks are intentionally and recursively shaped around water and its use; they are precarious and reversible outcomes of ordering" (Boelens et al. 2016, 3–4). In their view, "most resource and territorial struggles in water-control systems are rooted in how new water governance proposals undermine, transform, incorporate and/or reorder existing local forms of collective self-governance and territorial autonomy" (10). This perspective is useful for looking at the New Mexico water rights adjudication suits. Mandated by the 1907 New Mexico water code, they are among the oldest ongoing cases in the US court system.

HYDROSOCIAL TERRITORIES IN NEW MEXICO

The purpose of each adjudication is to determine the amount, priority in time, and location or point of diversion of every drop of water in the state. These lawsuits oppose inalienable aboriginal surface water right claims dating from "time immemorial" to all junior claims, starting with parciantes, who possess the next-oldest but nonetheless alienable water rights. Mandated more than 100 years ago, several cases drag on well into the twenty-first century with no end in sight. Some have yet to be filed. Each case represents a unique configuration of parties, history, and hydrosocial networks and territory. Each covers a specific watershed.

The most notorious adjudications are probably Aamodt (filed in 1966) and Abeyta (1969), which deal with the Pojoaque and Rio Pueblo de Taos watersheds, respectively. Aamodt involves the "Indian Pueblos" of Nambé, Pojoaque, Tesuque, and San Ildefonso; the state of New Mexico; the United States of America, the city of Santa Fe, Santa Fe County, and representatives of non-Pueblo water users. The Abeyta suit involves Taos Pueblo, the state of New Mexico, the United States of America, the town of Taos, The El Prado Water and Sanitation District (EPWSD), twelve mutual domestic water associations (MDWAs), and the Taos Valley Acequia Association (TVAA). Although a final settlement was reached in Aamodt in 2013 and a final decree was issued for Abeyta in late 2016, neither settlement appears to be making a smooth transition to the implementation phase that will result in major changes to their respective infrastructural or hydraulic grids.[1]

Eric Perramond analyzes the New Mexico water rights adjudications as an example of high modernist statecraft, implemented in this instance by a liberal rather than an authoritarian state, hence exhibiting only the first two of Scott's four conditions for societal disaster (Perramond 2013, 85; also see Perramond 2018). He discusses how the adjudication "is a legal and spatial practice by the state" that seeks to codify or map, quantify, and rank all water rights according to priority dates tied to a binary biopolitical/ethnic distinction between "Indian and non-Indian" users (Perramond 2013). This glacially slow, enormously complex, and costly legal process is now coming to a head in an era of climate change and pervasive neoliberal economic policies. As one *acequiero* put it, the ultimate goal of adjudication is "to measure, meter, and market" all the water. It represents a critical step on the road to total commodification, in a region where every drop of water is already allocated and a ravenous, escalating market valuates water rights according to demand and priority in time.

Perramond describes how "the state's adjudication process has inserted new vertical relationships between local users and state experts and has often

---

[1] Full disclosure: over the years I have been involved with the TVAA in two capacities: first as a research consultant and expert witness for the Abeyta case (1996–2006), and since 2014 as a member of the board of directors, representing the Acequia de San Antonio. My book *Acequia: Water Sharing, Sanctity and Place* is based on the ethnographic research I conducted and gives a detailed account of my relationship to the TVAA. In 2014 I was invited to serve on the board and have done so at the request of the mayordomo and president of my acequia.

disrupted horizontal social relationships on the ground between water users" (2016, 173). While recognizing that adjudication redefines and territorializes water rights, the crux of his argument is "that the process of territorialization is not about water itself, but about the water users. It is an attempt legally and politically to capture and metabolize water users into a single framework that is at cultural odds with how water is perceived, used, valued, and reproduced at the community level" (173–174). Perramond shows how the adjudication disrupts and alters usual parciante practices by, for example, prompting them to irrigate more in order to prove beneficial use, or by pitting neighbors against each other, sowing new seeds of suspicion and mistrust. But like Scott, he also attends to how parciantes resist and attempt in small ways to subvert and shape the process even while they have no choice but to comply with it.

This shotgun marriage, slow dance, or dialectic of resistance-accommodation and mutual entanglement has fostered the emergence of hybrid organizational forms that reticulate between grassroots and bureaucratic sectors. In the late 1970s local acequia associations began to form alliances and coalitions with each other: first in the same watershed, then between neighboring watersheds, and eventually at regional and statewide levels. They organized to defend themselves against specific threats to their water rights such as proposed resort or urban developments on agricultural lands. They proved effective episodic if not permanent associations. One precursor in Taos was the Committee to Save the Rio Hondo, an alliance between Hispano and newcomer (Anglo environmentalist) parciantes who protested pollution of the river by an expanding upstream ski industry.[2] Another was the Tres Ríos Association, organized by parciantes on three adjacent streams in the Taos basin to oppose the creation of a conservation district and reservoir that would have stored purchasable San Juan Chama water rights for which they would have been taxed. Incidentally, this controversy inspired John Nichols's novel *The Milagro Beanfield War*.

The TVAA, a federation of fifty-five (originally; now fifty-four) mainstream acequias in the Taos basin, was founded in 1986 in direct response to the Taos Pueblo water rights adjudication, known as the Abeyta case. As a representative body, its board of directors consists of acequia commissioners from the six streams in the central Taos valley involved in the lawsuit. In 1990, the NMAA organized acequias on a statewide basis. Both nonprofit corporations are missioned with the protection and defense of acequia and related agricultural interests.[3] The NMAA, based in Santa Fe, provides a variety of educational and practical programs and self-consciously seeks to "build an *acequia* movement."

---

[2] Anyone who buys irrigated property automatically becomes a parciante on the associated acequia.

[3] The TVAA achieved 501c3 nonprofit status in 1989 and the NMAA in 1995.

The TVAA has a pursued an almost exclusive focus on coordinating acequia response to the rigorous procedural requirements of the Abeyta adjudication. Hence, it became one of five local parties to the suit.

The course of the Abeyta case has been arduous and long for those individuals directly involved for nearly three decades in active, ongoing legal consultation and negotiation. In 1990, the TVAA proposed the parties enter a formal process of negotiation in order to avoid costly, bitter, and protracted litigation. Throughout the ensuing decades of negotiation, the parties were simultaneously preparing for litigation (Rodríguez 1990b, 2012). In 2006, after hundreds of tense and emotionally grueling meetings conducted regularly over a period of seventeen years, the parties managed to reach a negotiated settlement. Only a handful of individuals were involved from start to finish, including two men from Taos Pueblo and two from the TVAA, one being their lawyer who has since died. Other representatives of the parties came and went as they changed jobs, left office, retired, or passed away. The TVAA and Taos Pueblo agreed at the outset to maintain complete confidentiality and keep the story out of the newspapers because they believed publicity would endanger the process. Strict confidentiality surrounded the negotiation process as well as concurrent preparations for litigation. Reputedly fraught negotiation sessions revisited every dispute and resolution ever documented between Taos Pueblo and "non-Indian" or mestizo settlers along the Rio Pueblo and adjacent streams for the past 400 years.

Each party to the suit had its own set of concerns. The Town, Taos Pueblo, and the EPWSD all aimed to secure their existing claims but also to acquire more water for growth. The MDWAs, represented by a single attorney, sought additional water to meet their existing needs and to remedy inequities in their current supplies. The presumption and expectation of continuous growth are together a universal given, not merely of the adjudications or of all long-range planning in the Southwest; they are foundational to capitalist civilization. Only the acequias sought simply to keep what they had. The TVAA's objective in the negotiation process was therefore not to lose parciantes' water rights and to "keep the *acequias* whole."

The crux of the Taos case comes down to Taos Pueblo's prior claim to all the waters in the basin from time immemorial. Hence, it claims historical rights to several thousand more acre-feet of water than it presently uses. The oldest documented acequia water right in the valley is from 1715.[4] If the pueblo were to make a priority call on all of its surface water rights, it could dry up many, if

---

[4] This is the oldest documented date for an acequia in the Taos valley. The digging of an acequia was necessarily the first act of colonial settlement in New Mexico (starting with the founding of San Gabriel by Juan de Oñate in 1598). There can be little doubt the first Taos-area acequias were established in the early 1600s, but no archival documentation for them exists.

not most, neighboring acequias. Parciantes would then be unable to irrigate, and no one else would have much either. In the past, as well as today, everyone enjoys more or less sufficient water for their needs because it has always been shared, and except at moments of crisis, there has been more than enough to go around. Under Spanish and Mexican law, the perennial vicissitudes of competition, encroachment, and crisis were alleviated through compromise and cooperation that crystalized into customary water-sharing agreements between and within acequia communities and the pueblo known as *repartimientos* or *repartos*. Each was forged according to local conditions and an underlying ethic or moral economy primarily based on principles of equity, need, and nonimpairment (see Meyer [1984] 1996, 145–164). Today, comparatively little agriculture is practiced at Taos Pueblo, and the water it claims far exceeds its past, present, or foreseeable demographic needs.

According to the terms of the Abeyta Settlement, the pueblo agreed never to make a priority call and thereby to forbear on the exercise of its unused rights until a corresponding amount of water could be acquired by them through purchase. Doing so allows the rights to be retired in order to offset the deficit caused by the present and future pumping of groundwater. The depletion of groundwater depletes surface water and vice versa, while at the same time, an interstate compact compels New Mexico to deliver so much water to its downstream neighbor, Texas. Hence, the Rio Grande and its tributaries, like the Colorado and other major rivers in the West, amounts to a large hydraulic zero-sum shell game. Because New Mexico's water is already overallocated, all growth requires the transfer of water rights away from other sources or uses—that is, until the Colorado compact delivered thousands of acre-feet of "new" water into the system. Rights to San Juan–Chama water can be acquired through government contracts. This brings us to the mind-boggling irony that sits at the heart of the adjudication: San Juan–Chama water is being used to solve the very dilemma triggered by its introduction into the Rio Grande system.

Key to the Abeyta Settlement is the importation of San Juan–Chama water. The following summary can be found on the webpage of the Office of the State Engineer:

> In exchange for adjudication of the Pueblo's water rights with senior priorities, the Settlement Agreement provides funding for Mutual Benefit Projects and mitigation mechanisms for offsetting surface water depletion effects of groundwater pumping, preserves existing *acequia* water uses and historic water sharing arrangements between the Pueblo and non-Pueblo *acequias* on the Rio Lucero and Rio Pueblo, and authorizes the United States to allocate 2,621 AFY of water supply contracts from the San Juan-Chama Project for the Pueblo, the Town of Taos, and EPWSD. (Office of the New Mexico State Engineer n.d.)

Because Taos sits north of the point where actual imported wet water enters the Rio Grande, this new water has to come out of the ground. Integral to the settlement are the "Mutual Benefits Projects," which will require the construction of either an aquifer or a surface storage project involving two deep wells near the village of Arroyo Seco, plus a nearby stream gauge; five new deep groundwater wells for the Town of Taos; two new deep groundwater wells for the EPWSD; and five mitigation wells to offset Taos valley tributary depletion effects. These mitigation wells are intended to inject groundwater into the streams from which the acequias divert their irrigation water to offset the depletion of stream water caused by groundwater pumping.

As soon as the complicated, densely legalistic 100-page settlement document had been signed and made public, the TVAA and other parties began holding public meetings to explain the details to Taoseños. A number of protests were filed against the settlement but dismissed in district court. The final decree was issued just three months short of its March 31, 2017, deadline. The practical ramifications of the mitigation wells slowly dawned on parciantes and rural MDWA members when the project began to enter the preimplementation and administration phase that is to be overseen and executed by the Bureau of Reclamation. Curiously, it is the mitigation wells, intended to supplement irrigation and MDWA water, that seem to disturb parciantes and environmentalists more than the deep groundwater wells planned by the town and the EPWSD, which would cause stream and shallow aquifer depletion in the first place. The TVAA became the popular scapegoat—not the town, not the Mutual Domestics nor the EPWSD, and certainly not the pueblo.

Rumors began to circulate about the secret, self-serving deals the TVAA negotiators had cut with developers that would result in Taos water being exported downstream to Santa Fe and Albuquerque while Taos's acequias and residential wells would become contaminated with chlorine and other chemicals. Environmentalists voiced concerns about the possibility of "cones of depression" and geochemical contamination of the shallow aquifer caused by deep aquifer drilling. They denounced interbasin water transfers and the absence of conservation measures in the settlement. They predicted that once the "sinking funds" provided by the settlement for the maintenance and administration of the Mutual Benefits Projects were exhausted, acequias and MDWAs would go broke from the sheer magnitude of future electrical bills and other maintenance costs. They warned this outcome would ultimately drive parciantes and MDWA members to sell their farmlands and water rights to developers.

A local environmental group took out full-page ads in the *Taos News* denouncing the settlement and even tried to capture journalist Amy Goodman's attention when she came to town. As of May 2017, three acequias had voted against their mitigation wells and one MDWA was debating whether to reject theirs. One critic predicted that all the proposed acequia beneficiaries would end up doing this. But after so many decades of negotiation and expense, not to mention federal and state approval and allocation of many millions of dollars for the construction of what amounts to a new hydraulic grid, none of the parties believe the settlement can be nullified. Nullification would return the parties to the point where they began, facing litigation—an unthinkable prospect for the exhausted participants who struggled to reach the settlement.

Nevertheless, the settlement contains a provision that allows for modification of the Mutual Benefits Projects (by all five parties) should they prove infeasible, presumably for hydrological and/or economic reasons. If the projects do proceed, a workable administrative process and structure must be created to coordinate cooperation between potential beneficiaries and government agencies. A local acequia commissioner and retired government worker stood up at the 2017 annual TVAA membership meeting and asked exactly how this was supposed to happen. He was urged to pursue this, and subsequently he devised and proposed a working framework to the TVAA board. After hours of intense debate, they approved it.

One must ask why the most vulnerable, grassroots party to the Abeyta suit is the one under attack from the very sector it serves. The TVAA seems more accessible and accountable to its constituents than the other parties. One local observer suggests that perhaps parciantes and environmentalists feel betrayed by the TVAA because while they already expected the town and the EPWSD to "sell out" (in terms of hydrological greed and overextension), acequias and the TVAA are "supposed to be sustainable." Taos Pueblo, regardless of what its future plans may be for the allocation and use of all the water it will control, remains implicitly beyond reproach in the popular imagination, an important aspect of modern interethnic relations in Taos.[5] Perramond notes that despite their role to push back against the adjudications, by their very nature defensive organizations such as the NMAA and TVAA simultaneously reinforce bureaucratization and enhance acequia legibility in the eyes of the state. Yet, they also empower parciantes, promote advocacy and activism, and inspire popular, as well as scholarly, interest in acequias. They represent a New Mexican version of the hydropolitical shotgun marriage—with its alternately condemned and celebrated hybrid progeny.

CAN ACEQUIAS SURVIVE?

Hydrological research on acequias confirms their performance of an array of ecosystem services, including sustenance of riparian habitat, vegetation, and biodiversity; aquifer recharge and return stream flow; and seepage dilution

---

[5] See Rodriguez (1987, 1989, 1990a) for discussions of this phenomenon.

of agrochemicals and septic leachate (Boykin, Samson, and Alvarez 2017; Raheem et al. 2015). Of particular concern to scientists are questions of acequia sustainability, resilience, and tipping points in response to socioeconomic, demographic, environmental, and climate change. A five-year multidisciplinary study employing an National Science Foundation (NSF)–funded Coupled Natural and Human Systems (CNH) approach uses systems dynamic modeling to calibrate potential tipping points and test the hypothesis that "traditional *acequias* create and sustain intrinsic linkages between human and natural systems that increase community and ecosystem resilience to climatic and socioeconomic stresses" (Fernald 2009, 3).[6] Mutualism figures as a key variable in the causal loop diagrams generated by this systems dynamic modeling approach (Fernald et al. 2012; Fernald et al. 2015; Turner et al. 2016). These researchers identify the long experience, small size, cohesiveness, self-governance, and water-sharing customs of acequias as potential assets in the face of drought and climate change. They further note modern acequias' potentially resilient "desire to adopt new forms of hydrologic data and modeling techniques and incorporate them into [their] approaches" (Rango et al. 2013, 84). In sum, their findings "identified agricultural profitability (crop and livestock), community demographics (percentage of population having local historical roots), and land use (irrigated or residential/built-up) as key determinants of socio-economic and biophysical system response. Results also point to the important role of community mutualism in sustaining linkages between natural and human systems that increase resilience to stressors" (Turner et al. 2016, 1019).

Another line of inquiry, by Ostrom's student Michael Cox, focuses on the Taos valley acequias. Cox deploys a social-ecological system (SES) framework to explore "the combination of social and biophysical features that have enabled the *acequias* to persist as subsistence-based irrigation systems in a high desert environment since their initial period of settlement" (Cox 2011, 1; see also Cox 2014a; Cox and Ross 2011).[7] But he also sees a sampling bias in SES studies, which tend to "focus disproportionally on successful systems." He therefore seeks to redress this imbalance by also analyzing the conditions under which "long-lasting community-based resource management systems deteriorate" (Cox 2014b, 213). In this vein he reports:

By examining longitudinal data we find that the *acequias* are producing less than they have in the past and have mostly lost their common-property-based livestock pasturing system. While some of these changes can be attributed to similar declines in water availability, much of the change results from social drivers including demographic changes, regional-to-global market forces, and public policies. Overall the shift of the *acequias* to their current state is a result of their integration into a much larger-scale set of social and economic forces than they have experienced in the past. This shift will be very difficult to reverse, meaning the *acequia* farmers must adapt to the current condition. (213)

Given the irreversibility of many of the changes acequias are facing, Cox believes their survival will depend on an ability to adapt to new conditions. He offers a fresh interpretation of the universally lamented problem of knowledge loss: "The loss of traditional knowledge in a community may be an adaptation to a disturbance rather than a failure, if it is replaced by knowledge that is better suited to the post-disturbance environment" (221). He considers the future of acequias uncertain: "Whether or not they can transform themselves into a new type of system that succeeds based on novel performance criteria is an open question" (222).

The emergence of acequia activism and heightened self-awareness arguably are signs of resilience. The popular and scholarly interest they inspire has reinforced the value of acequias for more than just parciantes. A few newcomers who purchase irrigated properties become active parciantes and even effective advocates. Not unlike alienated parciantes, others ignore and neglect the acequia or damage it by selling or losing (through abandonment or forfeiture) their precious water rights. Female leadership has become significant. There are now more female commissioners, mayordomos, and TVAA board members than a decade ago, and women have led the NMAA since the 1990s. A few activists have contact with counterparts in other countries and identify as part of a global Indigenous/rural water movement. Virtually all parciantes share a deep concern about the over-fifty age range of most practicing farmer-ranchers. Despite a surge of regional and national interest in organic farming and local food production, and the revitalization of small-scale agriculture, acequia-based farming-ranching is not seen as a viable subsistence option for most young people.

All acequias exist in a state of precarity, and they will survive or disappear on a regional basis. Yet there is enough variation within and between stream systems and watersheds to indicate that some are at more immediate risk than others. Notwithstanding the considerable amount of research and bureaucratic data collected on them, little is known about the day-to-day management and interpersonal relations on any given acequia, except by its officers, active parciantes, and attentive long-term residents. Each is a world unto itself and despite their commonalities, acequias are microsocially heterogeneous and often respond differently to the same problems.[8]

---

[8] Social science and ecological approaches to questions of water management follow divergent pathways reflected in their respective, apparently mutually nonconversant literatures. Although not entirely ignoring political and historical context, as do strictly ecological approaches, the SES framework does not take on the macrosocial issues of power at the center of political ecology. Scarborough alludes to this limitation:

> The integration of water management into a meaningful social science framework has been inhibited, in part, by its overwhelming focus on ecological relationships. Clearly, the social relations underpinnings of the economy direct the course of decision making. At this level of analysis, the cooperative and conflictual dynamics of water management affect culture change and stability. The ecological laws of water systems do not cause centralization or decentralization. Rather, the organizational planes within a culture regulate the rates of cultural change and influence the processes or overall organizational outlooks of a group. (Scarborough 2003, 38)

Two approaches to the survival of modern small-scale irrigation systems exemplify this divergence.

Drawing on ethnographic fieldwork, Baker seeks to explain why the *kuhls* of northern India have survived through precolonial, colonial, and modern eras under conditions "of persistent long-term stress and short-term shocks that common property resource theory (SES) suggests should lead to their demise" (2005, 197). He deploys an "explanatory tapestry" consisting of four analytical "strands," each involving a different "scale and set of relations." The first "is composed of local-level social and ecological processes that facilitate or hinder collective action—a domain of inquiry commonly addressed in theories of common property regimes." The second involves potentially cooperative relations, including latent networks, with neighboring resource management regimes, "that link irrigation systems within a hydraulically defined landscape unit" (such as a watershed). Next comes "relations between kuhl regimes and state entities." He presents a nuanced, longitudinal view of state and irrigation community interaction or "statemaking" that encompasses precolonial, colonial, and postindependence modern periods. Baker defines statemaking as a mutually constitutive process that under specific conditions can enhance or undermine kuhl durability. His fourth level of analysis "concerns the importance of place and region in accounting for the forms and persistence of common property regimes" (12–15). He explores how modern responses to nonfarm employment are mediated by high local (economic) reliance on kuhl water and the degree of socioeconomic differentiation within a community. He predicts (and his research confirms) that "when reliance is high and differentiation low, increasing nonfarm employment will minimally affect the kuhl regime," and formalization of management or state intervention is unlikely. "When reliance and differentiation are both high, increasing nonfarm employment will lead to conflicts" and is likely to result in formalization of management and state involvement. Low reliance and high differentiation are likely to lead to a high degree of internal conflict and eventual collapse, or to state intervention and control (167–173).

Based on case examples from Nepal, Thapa et al. propose a multidimensional framework for characterizing the adaptive capacity of farmer-managed irrigation systems (FMIS). They identify Generic Adaptive Capacity (GAC) and Specific Adaptive Capac-

An uneasy balance of ecological, socioeconomic, demographic, and political factors shapes the larger context within which each acequia operates. But the day-to-day work of canal maintenance, the delivery and sharing of water, and the act of irrigation itself all come down to the decisions and cooperative inter-action of individuals. The extent to which they trust, and feel they can rely on, each another is crucial to the quality and durability of their acequia and sense of community. This is equally true of Balinese subaks. In Lansing's appraisal, subaks "are surprisingly fragile institutions . . . vulnerable to disturbances created by self-ish and ambitious men" (Lansing 2006: 193). In order for these irrigation systems to function, he continues, "individuals must be persuaded to bear in mind their dependence on the goodwill and willingness to cooperate of other . . . members. They must actively participate in the process of self-governance, and choose to bear the high costs of contributions to public goods. They require, in short, a state of mind that is in many respects strikingly different from that of *homo eco-nomicus*" (193–195).

The acequia to which I belong seems to operate more amicably than many others I hear about in the neighboring vicinity. This remains a matter of opin-ion, since I have no firsthand, practical knowledge of how any other acequia manages itself—only hearsay. An unusual degree of cooperation in the com-munity of San Antonio derives, I believe, from several factors: small size, clear geographical circumscription in a deep narrow valley, social and kinship density, collective ownership of an intact land grant, upstream position in the valley, an unobtrusive enclosed *placita* (a small plaza or village) with a chapel, and a critical mass of trusted and well-respected individuals who, as the soil and water district supervisor put it, "are totally dedicated to the ditch" and to other core commu-nity institutions, including the parish and mutual domestic water system that supplies the placita area. San Antonio's hydrosocial territory lies just outside the scope of the proposed Abeyta Settlement Mutual Benefits Projects. But for rea-sons that remain unclear, as a result of the adjudication it lost a substantial part of its traditional one-third proportional allocation of the river to a junior upland community. Lifelong residents maintain a defensive vigilance against perceived threats from an expanding upstream ski resort, encroaching real estate devel-opment, the gentrifying upland neighbor that now diverts a disproportionate

---

ity (SAC) and study "the interconnections between seven key dimensions of adaptive capacity: the five capitals (human, financial, natural, social, and physical), governance, and learning," concluding that "long-term adaptation requires harnessing the syner-gies and tradeoffs between generic adaptive capacity that fosters broader development goals and specific adaptive capacity that strengthens climate-risk management. Measuring and addressing the interrelations among the seven adaptive capacity dimensions aids in strengthening the long term sustainability of farmer-managed irrigation systems" (Thapa et al. 2016, 37).

amount of water from the river, and an old downstream neighbor that covets San Antonio's portion of a once-shared land grant (having sold its own portion) and that complains of no longer getting its fair share of irrigation water.[9]

The case of New Mexico's acequias speaks to many of the issues and questions that preoccupy irrigation and water management scholars and policy makers. Acequias exemplify the moral economy of water management and the complex relationship through time between local and state levels of control in an arid environment under changing and now increasingly stressful environmental, political, and economic conditions. The ability of acequias to adapt and survive in the coming decades will likely serve as a portent of how humanly habitable the desert borderlands of North America will remain in the twenty-first century.

REFERENCES

Baker, J. Mark. 2005. *The Kuhls of Kangara*. Seattle: University of Washington Press.

Boelens, Rutgerd. 2009. "The Politics of Disciplining Water Rights." *Development and Change* 40 (2): 307–331.

Boelens, Rutgerd, Jaime Hoogesteger, Erik Swyngedouw, Jeroen Vos, and Philippus Wester. 2016. "Hydrosocial Territories: A Political Ecology Perspective." *Water International* 41 (1): 1–14.

Bourdieu, Pierre. 1984. *Distinction*. Cambridge, MA: Harvard University Press.

Boykin, Kenneth G., Elizabeth A. Samson, and Guillermo Alvarez. 2017. "Acequia Ecosystems." In *Acequias of the Southwestern United States: Elements of Resilience in a Coupled Natural and Human System*, edited by Adrienne Rosenberg et al., 21–32. Research Report 796. Las Cruces: New Mexico State University Agricultural Experiment Station.

Budds, Jessica. 2009. "Contested H2O: Science, Policy and Politics in Water Resources Management in Chile." *Geoforum* 40 (3): 418–430.

---

[9] I believe that acequias, or at least some of them including the present-day Acequia de San Antonio, represent an example of the Kantian equilibrium proposed by economist and game theorist John Roemer. According to Roemer, the Kantian equilibrium obtains in collective situations where participants are motivated by self-interest that leads them to behave as they would like others to behave. In short, they operate by a kind of golden rule. This contrasts with the widely cited Nash equilibrium, in which participants are constrained to act in the collective interest by threat of negative sanction. Roemer considers the Nash equilibrium to be implicit in Ostrom's model of how common pool resources are sustainably governed. My ethnographic observation over many years suggests that while negative sanctions are built into acequia governance (those who don't abide by the rules don't get the water), the moral economy of water is at least equally sustained through personal example. In other words, leadership among equals on a ditch is modeled, taught, or inspired by individuals who consistently act in behalf of the common good. One is moved to serve the common good by the behavior of those who do. Elsewhere I have argued this ideal is embodied by the saints (Rodríguez 2006). Roemer argues that the Kantian equilibrium is nevertheless maintained out of self-interest rather than altruism (Roemer 2015, 2019).

Budds, Jessica. 2013. "Water, Power, and the Production of Neoliberalism in Chile, 1973–2005." *Environment and Planning D: Society and Space* 31 (2): 301–318.

Cox, Michael. 2011. "Applying a Social-Ecological System Framework to the Study of the Taos Valley Irrigation System." Workshop in Political Theory and Policy Analysis, Indiana University, Bloomington. https://seslibrary.asu.edu/sites/default/files/seslibrary/cases/165/Cox%202011.pdf.

Cox, Michael. 2014a. "Applying a Social-Ecological System Framework to the Study of the Taos Valley Irrigation System." *Human Ecology* 42: 311–324.

Cox, Michael. 2014b. "Modern Disturbances to a Long-Lasting Community-Based Resource-Management System: The Taos Valley Acequias." *Global Environmental Change* 24 (1): 213–222.

Cox, Michael, and Justin M. Ross. 2011. "Robustness and Vulnerability of Community Irrigation Systems: The Case of the Taos Valley Acequias." *Journal of Environmental Economics and Management* 61 (3): 254–266.

Fernald, Alexander (Principal Investigator). 2009. "Acequia Water Systems Linking Culture and Nature: Integrated Analysis of Community Resilience to Climate and Land Use Changes." Research Proposal to National Science Foundation (Number 1010516).

Fernald, Alexander, S. Guldan, K. Boykin, A. Cibils, M. Gonzales, B. Hurd, S. Lopez et al. 2015. "Linked Hydrologic and Social Systems That Support Resilience of Traditional Irrigation Communities." *Hydrology and Earth System Sciences* 19 (1): 293–307.

Fernald, Alexander, V. Tidwell, J. Rivera, S. Rodríguez, S. Guldan, C. Steele, C. Ochoa et al. 2012. "Modeling Sustainability of Water, Environment, Livelihood, and Culture in Traditional Irrigation Communities and Their Linked Watersheds" *Sustainability* 4 (11): 2998–3022. https://doi.org/10.3390/su4112998.

Gelles, Paul H. 2000. *Water and Power in Highland Peru.* New Brunswick, NJ: Rutgers University Press.

Gelles, Paul H. 2010. "Cultural Identity and Indigenous Water Rights in the Andean Highlands." In *Out of the Mainstream*, edited by Rutgerd Boelens, David Getches, and Armando Guevara-Gil, 119–144. New York: Earthscan.

Lansing, J. Stephen. (1991) 2007. *Priests and Programmers.* 2nd ed. Princeton, NJ.: Princeton University Press.

Lansing, J. Stephen. 2006. *Perfect Order.* Princeton, NJ.: Princeton University Press.

Latour, Bruno. 1993. *We Have Never Been Modern.* Cambridge, MA: Harvard University Press.

Linton, Jamie. 2010. *What Is Water?* Vancouver: University of British Columbia Press.

Linton, Jamie, and Jessica Budds. 2014. "The Hydrosocial Cycle: Defining and Mobilizing a Relational-Dialectical Approach to Water." *Geoforum* 57: 170–180.

Meyer, Michael C. (1984) 1996. *Water in the Hispanic Southwest.* 2nd ed. Tucson: University of Arizona Press.

Nichols, John. 1974. *The Milagro Beanfield War.* New York: Holt, Rinehart and Winston.

Office of the New Mexico State Engineer. n.d. "Taos Pueblo Water Rights Settlement Agreement." Accessed November 4, 2021. https://www.ose.state.nm.us/Legal/settlements/Taos/Taos_IWRS.php.

Ostrom, Elinor. 1990. *Governing the Commons*. Cambridge: Cambridge University Press.

Ostrom, Elinor. 2009. "Beyond Markets and States: Polycentric Governance of Complex Economic Systems." [Nobel] Prize Lecture, December 8: 408–444, accessed February 5, 2015. https://www.nobelprize.org/prizes/economic-sciences/2009/ostrom/lecture/.

Ostrom, Elinor, and T. K. Ahn. 2008. "The Meaning of Social Capital and Its Link to Collective Action." In *Handbook on Social Capital*, edited by Gert T. Svendsen and Gunnar L. Svendsen, 1–34. Northhampton, MA: Edward Elgar.

Perramond, Eric. 2013. "Water Governance in New Mexico: Adjudication, Law, and Geography." *Geoforum* 45: 83–93.

Perramond, Eric. 2016. "Adjudicating Hydrosocial Territory in New Mexico." *Water International* 41 (1): 173–188.

Perramond, Eric. 2018. *Unsettled Waters, Rights, Law, and Identity in the American West*. Oakland: University of California Press.

Raheem, Nejem, S. Archambault, E. Arellano, M. Gonzales, D. Kopp, J. Rivera, S. Guldan et al. 2015. "A Framework for Assessing Ecosystem Services in Acequia Irrigation Communities of the Upper Río Grande Watershed." WIREs Water. https://doi.org/10.1002/wat2.1091.

Rango, Albert, A. Fernald, C. Steele, B. Hurd, and C. Ochoa. 2013. "Acequias and the Effects of Climate Change." *Journal of Contemporary Water Research & Education* 151 (1): 84–94.

Rivera, José A. 1998. *Acequia Culture*. Albuquerque: University of New Mexico Press.

Rivera, José A. 2010. *La sociedad*. Albuquerque: University of New Mexico Press.

Rodríguez, Sylvia. 1987. "Land, Water, and Ethnic Identity in Taos." In *Land, Water and Culture*, edited by Charles Briggs and John Van Ness, 313–403. Albuquerque: University of New Mexico Press.

Rodríguez, Sylvia. 1989. "Art, Tourism, and Race Relations in Taos: Toward A Sociology of the Art Colony." *Journal of Anthropological Research* 45 (1): 77–99.

Rodríguez, Sylvia. 1990a. "Applied Research on Land and Water in New Mexico: A Critique." *Journal of the Southwest* 32 (3): 298–315.

Rodríguez, Sylvia. 1990b. "Ethnic Reconstruction in Contemporary Taos." *Journal of the Southwest* 32 (4): 541–555.

Rodríguez, Sylvia. 2006. *Acequia: Water Sharing, Sanctity, and Place*. Santa Fe, NM: School for Advanced Research Press.

Rodríguez, Sylvia. 2012. "For the Sake of Peace in the Valley: The Negotiated Settlement in the Taos Water Rights Adjudication." In *One Hundred Years of Water Wars* in *New Mexico 1912–2012*, edited by Catherine Ortega Klett, 198–205. NM Water Resources Research Institute. Santa Fe, NM: Sunstone Press.

Rodríguez, Sylvia. 2017. "Key Concepts for a Multidisciplinary Approach to Acequias." In *Acequias of the Southwestern United States: Elements of Resilience in a Coupled Natural and Human System*, edited by Adrienne Rosenberg et al., 4–11. Research Report 796. Las Cruces: New Mexico State University Agricultural Experiment Station.

Roemer, John. 2015. "Kantian Optimization: A Microfoundation for Cooperation." *Journal of Public Economics* 127: 45–57.

Roemer, John. 2019. *How We Cooperate: A Kantian Explanation*. New Haven, CT: Yale University Press.

Scarborough, Vernon L. 2003 *The Flow of Power*. Santa Fe, NM: School of American Research.

Scott, James C. 1976. *The Moral Economy of the Peasant*. New Haven, CT: Yale University Press.

Scott, James C. 1985. *Weapons of the Weak*. New Haven, CT: Yale University Press.

Scott, James C. 1990. *Domination and the Arts of Resistance*. New Haven, CT: Yale University Press.

Scott, James C. 1998. *Seeing Like a State*. New Haven, CT: Yale University Press.

Scott, James C. 2010. *The Art of Not Being Governed*. New Haven, CT: Yale University Press.

Swyngedouw, Erik. 1999. "Modernity and Hybridity: Nature, *Regeneracionismo*, and the Production of the Spanish Waterscape, 1890–1930." *Annals of the Association of American Geographers* 89 (3): 443–465.

Thapa, Bhuwan, Christopher Scott, Philippus Wester, and Robert Varady. 2016. "Towards Characterizing the Adaptive Capacity of Farmer-Managed Irrigation Systems: Learnings from Nepal." *Current Opinion in Environmental Sustainability* 21: 37–44.

Trawick, Paul. 2003. *The Struggle for Water in Peru*. Stanford, CA: Stanford University Press.

Trawick, Paul, Mar Ortega Reig, and Guillermo Palau Salvador. 2014. "Encounters with the Moral Economy of Water: Convergent Evolution in Valencia." *WIREs Water* 1 (1): 87–110. https://wires.onlinelibrary.wiley.com/doi/abs/10.1002/wat2.1008.

Turner, Benjamin, Vincent Tidwell, Alexander Fernald, José Rivera, Sylvia Rodríguez, Steven Guldan, Carlos Ochoa, Brian Hurd, Kenneth Boykin, and Andres Cibils. 2016. "Modeling Acequia Irrigation Systems Using System Dynamics: Model Development, Evaluation, and Sensitivity Analyses to Investigate Effects of Socio-economic and Biophysical Feedbacks." *Sustainability* 8 (10): 1019. https://www.mdpi.com/search?q=Modeling+Acequia+Irrigation&journal=sustainability&volume=8.

Wittfogel, Karl. 1957. *Oriental Despotism: A Comparative Study of Total Power*. New Haven, CT: Yale University Press.

Worster, Donald. 1985. *Rivers of Empire: Water, Aridity, and the Growth of the American West*. Cambridge: Cambridge University Press.

11

How Do We Get Out of This Mess?

Landscape Legacies, Unintended Consequences, and Tradeoffs of Human Behavior

Christian Isendahl

> *Throughput is the metabolic flow by which we live and produce. The economy in its physical dimensions is made up of things—populations of human bodies, livestock, machines, buildings, and artifacts. All these things are what physicists call "dissipative structures" that are maintained against the forces of entropy by a throughput from the environment. An animal can only maintain its life and organizational structure by means of a metabolic flow through a digestive tract that connects to the environment at both ends. So too with all dissipative structures and their aggregate, the human economy.—Daly (2006, 40)*

Most archaeologists with an interest in detailing the significance of water in past societies will have come across the work of Vernon Scarborough. Scarborough's examination of the technological, economic, social, and political dimensions of water management in the distant past, particularly in the Maya lowlands, forms world-leading scholarship on the archaeology of water, influential well beyond the field of Maya archaeology. Furthermore, exploring the points of interaction between archaeology and sustainability scholarship (e.g., Chase and

https://doi.org/10.5876/9781646422326.c011

Scarborough 2014; Scarborough 2009, 2018; Scarborough and Burnside 2010), Scarborough pushes the boundaries of an archaeological discipline that not only is concerned with understanding the past but that details the past with the ultimate purpose of tackling global sustainability challenges, those associated with global warming in particular. Whether examining Maya urban form and blue-green infrastructure, detailing issues of long-term sustainability and resilience from an archaeologist's vantage point, or exploring the discipline's potential to provide practical insights that address contemporary challenges, Scarborough's scholarship is characterized by a combination of deep knowledge accumulated over a long academic career; an unrelenting curiosity to discover, understand, and explain; and innovative and independent thinking that moves beyond orthodox models of interpretation and points to previously unconsidered linkages.

To a large extent inspired by Scarborough's work, in the following I loosely shape a deliberation from the preceding ten chapters that make up the substance of this volume by highlighting three concepts that I find particularly useful to contour archaeology as sustainability scholarship: the landscape legacies (Arroyo-Kalin 2019), unintended consequences (Scarborough 2018), and trade-offs (Hegmon 2017b) of human behavior. With some points of overlap, these concepts direct attention to different dimensions of what people have done in the past, why they did so, and the outcomes of their actions. Collectively, they form tools to explore the significance of intentional vis-à-vis unintentional outcomes of human behavior from archaeology's long temporal vantage point, thereby shedding some reflective light on the challenges of sustainability.

LANDSCAPE LEGACIES, UNINTENDED CONSEQUENCES, AND TRADEOFFS

Landscape legacies are part of the core source material of archaeological examination and explanation. Essentially, landscape legacies refer to all impacts of past human behavior on the environment perceptible, however subtly, in contemporary landscapes. Defined thus, landscape legacies overlap with a generic understanding of the archaeological record but focus on detailing components of the geo-, bio-, and atmospheres that past human behavior has altered at the scale of the landscape, how and why, and the significance of these vestiges in the contemporary world. It is a central idea of historical ecology that past generations' continuous acting on, in, and with the landscape (i.e., their cumulative landscaping [Arroyo-Kalin 2019]) influences the trajectory and durability of successive socio-ecological systems (e.g., Balée 1998, 2006; Balée and Erickson 2006; Crumley, Lennartsson, and Westin 2018; Isendahl and Stump 2019b). Archaeologists, trained to understand in detail the formation processes of the archaeological record, are specialists in disentangling human–landscape history from the soil by deciphering the many kinds of sequential human behaviors and their causes, effects, and longevity of influence that collectively have generated the landscape palimpsests we observe today (see Balée and Erickson 2006).

Typically, the legacies of past human behavior in the landscape reference how past land-use plays out to influence land-use in the present (Arroyo-Kalin 2019). In many world regions—for instance, the Maya lowlands and the Amazon Basin—the locations where long-term and large-scale human settlements of villages, towns, and cities in the past concentrated human organic waste are often those that contemporary smallholders favor when selecting field plots for cultivation. In Amazonia, the pyrogenic carbon deposited in pre-Columbian settlements contributed to the generation of anthropic soils (i.e., soils with properties that record the effects of past land-use [Eidt 1985]) commonly referred to as Amazonian Dark Earths (ADE). Compared to the strongly weathered Ferralsols of the landscape surrounding these archaeological sites, the anthropic soils have an elevated long-term soil-nutrient-holding capacity, including higher soil pH, soil organic carbon, phosphorus, calcium, and magnesium content (Araújo et al. 2015; Arroyo-Kalin 2019; Woods et al. 2009). To generate higher yields, contemporary Amazonian smallholders' field plot selection draws on the landscape legacies of soil nutrient enhancement that pre-Columbian populations' clustering released over time, thus providing substantial benefits for local livelihoods in the present. Landscape legacies may also record negative impacts on environments, limit livelihood options from local landscapes, and involve high investment costs for restoration. The salinization of agricultural soils that late third to early second-millennium BCE field irrigation in southern Mesopotamia generated is the most widely cited example (e.g., Jacobsen and Adams 1958; Redman 1999).

Manuel Arroyo-Kalin (2019) draws on Robert Eidt's (1985) distinction between anthropogenic (soils deliberately modified by humans) and anthropic soils to emphasize that landscape legacies make no difference between deliberate and unintended anthropic transformations of landscape. For instance, the formation of ADE is a long-term consequence of human behavior to cluster in settlements and/or repeatedly inhabit some locations, thereby concentrating organic matter at certain points in the landscape—which might not have been either a particularly intentional or unintentional practice but a cumulative consequence of daily routines. Mesopotamian salinization was clearly an unintended consequence of land use but also a long-term tradeoff of landesque capital investments—that is, agricultural installations or modifications of the land or soil made to endure beyond the cropping cycle (e.g., field demarcations, windbreaks, hillslope terracing, and soil humidity management), typically with the intent to increase productivity (Brookfield 1984; see also Arroyo-Kalin 2019; Håkansson and Widgren 2014). Irrigating field systems to increase production and feed growing urban populations, to meet elites' demands to accumulate and control energy and matter, or both, over time denuded these landscapes of their production potential.

Scarborough (2018) suggests that since the archaeological record is the outcome of humans' causal agency, archaeologists' forte to trace past human behaviors (whether deliberate or unintended) from their material consequences forms theoretical, methodological, and interpretive skills fundamentally useful in planning for sustainable futures. Specifically, he argues that archaeologists' knowledge of causal behavior from examining outcomes observed in the landscape can be helpful to inform the kinds of decisions, actions, and behaviors that are called for to address our global challenges (e.g., United Nations 2015). Equipped with tools to describe and explain complex cause-effect relationships of human behavior from observable outcomes, Scarborough (2018) argues that archaeologists can reverse that logic to contribute their insights to outline the human behavior needed to arrive at projected desired outcomes. Essentially, we should not only be asking, "How did we get into this mess?" (see Monbiot 2016), which is perhaps what we expect archaeologists or historians to inquire but also "How do we get out of it?"

A myriad of individual actions and kinds of cultural behavior leave material consequences, some of which have considerable longevity. Human action resulting not only in the intended but also in undesired outcomes relates to the idea of tradeoffs. Since it is a colloquial term, there are many different understandings of what a tradeoff is, with the dictionary definition, the "giving up of one thing in return for another" (*Merriam-Webster Dictionary* 1984, 1250, cited in Hegmon 2017a, 3), among the most generically common. A relatively oft-applied concept in sustainability scholarship and resilience thinking to examine, describe, and evaluate cost–benefit leveling in human decision-making (Carpenter et al. 2001), Michelle Hegmon's (2017b) recent edited volume is the first to critically test its analytical strengths in archaeological contexts, tracking past socio-environmental processes as well as exploring what "tradeoffs" entail when viewed from the long-term and kaleidoscopic perspective that is an archaeological comparative lens. Hegmon (2017a) stresses that there are multiple perspectives on tradeoffs among archaeologists, and the following expands on ideas previously explored in Isendahl and Heckbert (2017b).

In its strictest sense, a tradeoff forms part of a behavioral and deeply ethical process: intention and purpose, calculation and leveling of costs against benefits from different potential courses of action, and purposeful action. Arguably, this process requires access to information and an understanding of causal relationships, which may be generative or constraining, the one tending to trigger further action and the other restrict it. "Generative tradeoffs" are those that produce negative effects (e.g., doing A to achieve desired outcome B will also result in undesired outcome C), while "constraining tradeoffs" limit future options (e.g., doing A to achieve desired outcome B forecloses desired outcome C). The tradeoffs of group behavior are similar, but the evaluative phase of intention, foresight, and calculation of cost-benefit analysis is more indistinct, negotiated, and integrated.

To examine behavioral processes archaeologically, past practices need to result in lasting, tangible material consequences in the physical world—in other words, landscape legacies. Isendahl and Heckbert (2017b) argue that archaeology's most pervasive contributions to the study of tradeoffs are (1) to track how they play out over long time periods (at temporal scales of several centuries or millennia), and (2) to examine tradeoff mechanisms in socio-cultural contexts of the past that are beyond the scope of other disciplines. The first point makes implicit that the "giving up" aspect of a tradeoff may well be suffered by those that do not benefit from behavior, a distributed effect that may not only play out over time but across space and among social domains (Hegmon 2017b). With significant challenges to detail from the archaeological record how gauged and informed decision-making in the distant past actually considered a range of anticipated but undesired outcomes (and assuming they chose the least damaging in relation to the benefit gained), these kinds of distributed tradeoffs are analytically indistinguishable from the unintended consequences of human behavior. When applied in archaeological analysis, however, both concepts direct attention to the integrated physical manifestation of the past in the present. The tradeoffs of people's actions and the unintended consequences of human behavior generate landscape legacies that constrain, present challenges, or enable opportunities beyond the predicted and imagined, and are timescale dependent. To examine these issues from the vantage point of archaeology involves, in some sense, a position that relates the observable in our contemporary world to outcomes of past reason. Studying those chains of causal relationships over different timescales not only adds new insight into the profound consequences of human behavior, but also highlights that there will be outcomes that contest intention and that we will not be able to predict.

The urgency and severity of our contemporary global challenges call on the scientific community to generate as broad and deep a knowledge base as possible to draw from in the pursuit of solutions (Isendahl and Smith 2013, 132). A most fundamental contribution from archaeology is to add the field's long-term perspective on human behavior to assess predicted outcomes of contemporary and future behavior (including behaviors motivated by sustainability concerns [Hegmon 2017b]), as well as maintain an ambitious and yet unassuming attitude to predict *and* explore the full range of material outcomes of human intention. Hence, by focusing on the landscape legacies, unintended consequences, and tradeoffs of human behavior, one rich field of exploration among many lies ahead for archaeologists to contribute constructively to sustainability scholarship (e.g., Isendahl and Stump 2019b). As with any field of scientific knowledge production, our archaeological understanding of these processes is cumulative and we have now a better grasp of the range of outcomes associated with past human behavior than we had a decade ago, as well as being consequently better equipped than ever to predict with increasing degrees of certainty the magnitude of the challenges that lie ahead.

ARCHAEOLOGY ON THE PATH TO SUSTAINABILITY?

The chapters in this volume offer an eclectic sample of archaeological and anthropological approaches to explore water management and sustainability in our era of burgeoning climate change. The title of the volume suggests that its contents detail how the past generates insights that inform sustainable future water management. Overall, the volume complements a growing body of scholarship on the archaeology of water, many following Scarborough's lead (most recently Holt 2018; Sulas and Pikirayi 2018), as well as contributes to the vital development of applied archaeology, "a branch of the discipline that is explicitly concerned with the application of knowledge about the past generated from archaeological research to address practical problems perceived in the present" (Isendahl and Stump 2019a, 585). Given global concerns for social, economic, and environmental sustainability, climate change, and freshwater security, the volume's main theme is patently urgent.

Since notions of sustainability are not only at the center of an inter- and transdisciplinary global academic discourse, but colloquially reach far into every domain of social life, it is critical to be transparent on what the term implies in archaeological analysis (is it normative or an ethic, is it quantifiable, will idiosyncratic colloquial jargon suffice?). To the backdrop of the preceding discussion of landscape legacies, unintended consequences, and tradeoffs of human behavior, this concluding discussion focuses on how "sustainability" and derivable terms are used in the volume. The motivation for this selective choice is that clear definition and shared understanding of core concepts across disciplinary boundaries are a matter of some importance in integrative past–future research. The immediate tradeoff of this focus is, however, that most of the brilliant points the authors are making throughout the volume are left without comment. Hence, to no extent are these concluding remarks doing full justice to the research and insights presented. Nevertheless, in a volume that places heavy emphasis on sustainability as a lead concept, with all chapters—except Freidel et al. (chapter 6)—applying sustainability thinking to archaeological analysis, "a multitude of perspectives on sustainability" (Larmon et al., chapter 1) are represented within its pages. In their introductory chapter, the editors establish the Brundtland Report of the World Commission on Environment and Development's (Brundtland et al. 1992) definition of sustainable development as a baseline for the volume: "development that meets the needs of the present without compromising the ability of future generations to meet their own needs." However, to characterize how the chapters in the present volume conceptualize sustainability, the Brundtland Report's definition is a too general frame of reference.

One alternative is Hernan Daly's (2006, 39) suggestion that there are two broad responses in sustainability scholarship to the query of what it is that is projected to be sustained: (1) nondeclining *utility*, that is, "the utility of future generations is to be non-declining," with utility referring to "average per capita utility of members of a generation" and the aim that the "future should be at least as well off as the present in terms of its utility or happiness as experienced by itself"; and (2) nondeclining *throughput*, that is, "the entropic physical flow from nature's sources through the economy and back to nature's sinks is to be nondeclining." Daly endorses the latter, arguing that while the utility definition is the most common, and very useful in economic theory, utility is an experience and therefore nonmeasurable, and, even if it were quantifiable, the immateriality of utility cannot be passed on to future generations: "to define sustainability as a non-declining intergenerational bequest of something that can neither be measured nor bequeathed strikes me as a nonstarter" (2006, 40). To Daly, nondeclining throughput makes more sense, "the capacity to generate an entropic throughput from and back to nature" (2006, 40) being both quantifiable and transferable across generations. Below I suggest that most chapters in this volume—and, I would claim, most archaeological approaches to examine sustainability in the pre-Columbian Maya past, my own attempts included (e.g., Isendahl and Heckbert 2017a, 2017b; Isendahl, Lucero, and Heckbert 2018)— tend to adhere more closely, albeit loosely, to the non-declining utility than the throughput conceptualization of sustainability.

First, however, we need to ask what archaeology's unique contribution to sustainability scholarship is. Drawing on arguments recently pursued elsewhere (cf. Isendahl and Heckbert 2017a, 2017b; Isendahl, Lucero, and Heckbert 2018; Isendahl and Stump 2019a), I suggest that archaeology's scope as the science of long-term social change, primarily through studying material remains, is uniquely situated to (1) detail the long-term character of sustainability, particularly examining factors that condition sustainability's implied qualities of durability and longevity; and (2) generate case studies that identify factors and processes that build resilience and introduce vulnerabilities for the sustainability of socio-ecological systems. Both approaches have potential to add depth of reflection on the nature and potential of sustainability. For instance, Isendahl, Lucero, and Heckbert (2018, 33; emphasis in original) argue that the "archaeological perspective is particularly important in focusing on the very long-time perspective when thinking about the sustainability of socio-ecological systems or institutions, such as approaches towards managing freshwater security," cautioning that "sustainability is hardly ever defined and commonly vaguely associated with *indefinitely*." Sustainability is unimaginable without the temporal dimension; it is supposed to be durable, to have considerable longevity, to persist over the long term. All of these qualities, however, are vague and relative, their connotation context-dependent, while we might think sustainability should not be. Paul Lane (2019) demonstrates how dependent the temporal scale of "the long-term" is on the kind of processes each discipline analyzes, arguing the importance to specify concepts of time. The same applies to "longevity" (another timescale) or "durability" (a vaguely time-dependent concept, much as sustainability). Joseph Tainter and colleagues' (Allen, Tainter, and Hoekstra 2003) insightful four-point query of sustainability—of what, for whom, at what cost, and for how long—forms a critical analytical framework to define dimensions of time, scale, function, and outcome that arguably can be put to greater widespread use in the archaeological examination of sustainability than presently is the case. Hence, in archaeology (and anything else), conceptualizing sustainability as nondeclining utility will need to involve definition of what is the object of non-declining utility, for whom it will be sustained (e.g., what social domain), what is the spatiotemporal scale of analysis, and which outcomes are there of maintaining sustainability, for instance in terms of tradeoffs?

In the introductory chapter, Larmon et al. direct thinking toward generating case studies that detail water management strategies "employed by the ancient Maya to sustainably live and flourish within their environments" (chapter 1) and "explore the ways in which political control of water sources, the maintenance or degradation of sustainable systems, ideological relationships with water, and fluctuations between the extremes of water availability have impacted or been impacted by social change" (chapter 1). Emphasis is on examining hydro- and agrotechnological and institutional solutions that support nondeclining utility of (urban) social systems in the context of climate change. It is a general path of investigation that several chapters largely follow. For instance, in their most comprehensive and useful overview of water harvesting, collection, and storage practices in the Elevated Interior Region (EIR) of the pre-Columbian Maya lowlands, Dunning et al. (chapter 2) suggest that "the evolution and sustainability" of Maya urban settlements and society depended on the development of hydrologic engineering that addressed the opportunities and challenges to freshwater security that karst landscapes presented. The different techniques discussed add to a pool of knowledge on rainwater harvesting, their resilience and vulnerabilities, to draw from for the future, indicating a form of applied archaeology by which past technologies or institutions inform practices in the present that are projected to be sustainable (e.g., Caponetti 2019; Cooper and Duncan 2019; Herrera 2019; Kendall and Drew 2019; Spriggs 2019; see also Ashmore, chapter 4 in this volume). The argument is persuasive: the IPCC recommends "expanding rainwater harvesting, improving water storage, conservation, and re-use among other strategies to offset negative impacts of climate change in Latin America (Intergovernmental Panel on Climate Change 2007). These are precisely many of the techniques that the ancient Maya honed while seeking sustainable occupation of the EIR and that could inform present-day population expansion in the region" (Dunning et al. chapter 2).

Similarly, Lentz et al. (chapter 3) outline "the sophisticated land management practices that allowed the ancient Maya to develop large cities and sustain them for several centuries." Hence, focus is on detailing how the agricultural economy was able to build food security for large urban populations, "thus creating a sustainable system of food production that could maintain the growth of urban centers" (chapter 3)—a statement largely coherent with the nondeclining utility version of sustainability. However, in arguing that "for many decades it had been presumed that the ancient lowland Maya practiced an extensive type of long fallow (fifteen to twenty years) swidden (slash-and-burn) or milpa agriculture that relied upon the regrowth of forests to replenish lost soil nutrients, thus creating a sustainable system of food production that could maintain the growth of urban centers," Lentz et al. (chapter 3) seem to shift to a nondeclining-throughput emphasis. This change in perspective is only temporary, for they later note that "the 'short fallow' part of this assessment comes from the observation that there was not enough land to feed 40,000–50,000 inhabitants and have twelve to fifteen years of land set aside in fallow [at Tikal]. Evidently, the Maya could not rely solely on short fallow swidden agriculture, however, and developed several other kinds of intensive agriculture that were more productive and more sustainable" (chapter 3).

Chase et al. (chapter 7), comparing Tikal to Caracol, argue that "initially prompted by the need to manage soil loss and water flow in hilly terrain to be agriculturally sustainable, the ancient Maya at Caracol used their technological prowess to completely modify the landscape." At Caracol, a highly complex agro-urban landscape interfingering civic-ceremonial and residential buildings, infrastructure, water reservoirs, and cultivation spaces "likely permitted more than one crop per season (with crops being cycled or mixed for nitrogen fixation), indicating that the site was agriculturally self-sustaining" (chapter 7). They suggest that Caracol landscape modification "demonstrate[s] a focus on long-term sustainability that represents a different strategy from the one used at Tikal" (chapter 7), where sustainability "may have been dependent in the Late Classic period on the importation of food across flooded *bajos* [low-lying wetlands] during the rainy season, presumably under centralized control" (chapter 7). These arguments of Caracol's sustainability loosely fit in with a nondeclining utility understanding but also show how seemingly effortlessly this conceptualization merges with standard archaeological analyses of carrying capacity. Essentially, Chase et al. base their interpretation of the sustainability of these urban systems on the assessment that they are food secure, with the main point being that Caracol—on the basis of the agro-urban landscape's capacity for self-sufficiency—was sustainable. Although the ability to maintain food security is an essential dimension of a social system's sustainability, food self-sufficiency is not synonymous with sustainability, nor is food self-sufficiency per se a measure of the system's nondeclining utility, and even less its nondeclining through-put. Furthermore, a most intriguing question is which food system—Caracol's locally focused or Tikal's (more) regionally based—was the least vulnerable to perturbations (see Isendahl and Barthel 2018)? That both cities suffered political collapse and experienced a process toward large-scale abandonment at roughly the same time in the ninth century CE indicates that the scalar properties of these food systems, either entirely self-sufficient or supplemented by imports, were not the only decisive factor for maintaining the sustainability of the larger social or economic system.

Dunning et al. (chapter 2), Lentz et al. (chapter 3), and Chase et al. (chapter 7) focus on anthropogenic landscape modifications to generate a blue-green infrastructure of pre-Columbian Maya cities characterized by significant urban farming (e.g., Isendahl 2012a). The general arguments pursued seem to suggest that human behavior to increase production automatically increased sustainability, since growth signals the system's success to maintain functions intergeneration-ally. From a nondeclining throughput perspective, however, these are separate dimensions of metabolic flows (volume versus longevity), with the potential for an inverse relationship between, on one hand, anthropogenic manipulation of an ecosystem to increase flow and, on the other, durability. In sustainability scholarship, keeping natural resource flows and ecosystem services constant is sometimes referred to as "strong sustainability," whereas keeping constant those in which humans form part constitutes "weak sustainability" (Daly 2006, 40). Readings of "natural" versus "anthropogenic" capital, however, typically draw on contemporary and recent human–environmental interactions, uninformed by archaeologists' deep time analyses of landscape legacies. The formation and legacies of ADE in the Amazon Basin is a case in point of how an unintended con-sequence of past human behavior (waste management or the lack thereof, not least) has integrated with natural capital long-term to increase the landscape's metabolic flow of nondeclining throughput. Similar processes are increasingly being documented in the Maya lowlands, where the unintended consequences of humans' changing the biotic and abiotic environment through land use practices over millennia sometimes lead to increased ecosystem flows and services in the landscape (e.g., Chase and Scarborough 2014; Graham 2006). Hence, histories of place-based socio-cultural behavior, including both large-scale landscape modifi-cation programs and small decisions and daily actions and tasks, have shaped the landscape legacies that archaeologists and other land-users confront.

Among the case-study-focused chapters, Penny and Fletcher's (chapter 9) is different not only by examining sustainability aspects of Angkor in Southeast Asia (rather than the pre-Columbian Maya), but most significantly by more clearly taking the route of nondeclining throughput to examine sustainability. They argue that although large-scale landesque capital investments in blue-green infrastructure for production growth over time increased sedimentation rates that had a negative impact on the political economy of the Angkor state, small-scale land-use strategies that dominate resumed nondeclining throughput to the pre-Angkor-state period level. It brings to mind Isendahl and colleagues' (Isendahl, Dunning, and Sabloff 2014; Isendahl and Heckbert 2017a, 2017b; Isendahl, Lucero, and Heckbert 2018) application of Tainter's (e.g., Tainter and Allen 2019) approach to the concept of energy returned on energy invested (EROI). These studies suggest that investment in landesque capital that increased output and stimulated both population and economic growth entails committing to continuous input (e.g., for maintenance) that, though increasing carrying capacity, locks the social system into path dependence—quite the opposite of maintaining flexibility—and introduces vulnerabilities to future changes in EROI ratios. A socio-ecological system that has sustainable qualities (e.g., technologies that generate freshwater security) does not necessarily mean that these are durable: at some point their utility (simply defined as the ratio between output and input) will begin to decline. Hence, it is hard to see how using "long-term sustainability," in the sense of "the capacity to increase production for a while," will generate significant insights about sustainability per se, other than the methodological reflection that these are not the same thing. Penny and Fletcher's study similarly suggests that investing in large-scale infrastructure is perilous to nondeclining throughput.

In chapter 5, Gunn notably turns the attention to the sustainability of pre-Columbian Maya governance. However, suggesting that "the ability to supply labor, would have been strongly dependent on a sustainable bureaucracy with good potential to provide administrative guidance year after year" (chapter 5) indicates an application of the term very different from Daly's. Indeed, this usage of sustainability appears largely synonymous with "stable," assuming some kind of longevity. Relating Gunn's argument to the Brundtland Report definition, it can be questioned from the vantage point of political economy (see, e.g., Scott 1998), how did the Maya bureaucracy's proficiency to provide a steady supply of labor to the state per se support "the ability of future generations to meet their own needs" (Brundtland et al. 1992)? Put differently, what is the cost of sustainability if it is maintained by coercive labor? In contrast, Rodríguez (chapter 10) shows how small-scale, farmer-managed irrigation systems have high capacity for sustainability—in the sense that these water-harvesting strategies maintain functions and nondeclining throughput in a wide range of geographical settings.

Drawing on Elinor Ostrom's (1990) concept of common pool resource management, Rodríguez's focus on past and contemporary self-organized resource management strategies—while under threat from a series of forces (political, economic, social, demographic, environmental, and climate change)—points to a more convincing path toward sustainable management than centralized bureaucracies.

In chapter 8, van der Leeuw—an archaeologist turned leading sustainability scholar—takes a novel approach to outline a theory of how long-term social change is ultimately driven by problem solving, a process in which information processing is key. While some assumptions made to contrast urban from rural social dynamics are debatable (Isendahl 2012b; Scarborough and Isendahl 2020), van der Leeuw demonstrates how the archaeologist's understanding of long-term patterns and socio-ecological dynamics is vital for understanding how the socio-ecological conditioning of sustainability is in constant flux. As the editors note: "What is sustainable at present may not be possible as climate change continues, requiring diverse and flexible adaptation strategies" (Larmon et al., chapter 1).

Arguably, the most important contribution of archaeology to understanding the complexities of sustainability is its focus on understanding social-environmental interactions by analyzing the landscape legacies, unintended consequences, and tradeoffs of human behavior. What have people done, what were their goals and motivations, what were the consequences of this behavior over different spatial and temporal scales, and what can we learn from these examples?

FINAL NOTE

Asking questions is the fundamental driver of the research process, with archaeological problem-formulation significantly benefiting from engaging with related discourses to compare notes of what we do know, what we need to know, what we can find out, and the significance of that knowledge. Integrating sustainability thinking in archaeological research, thus extending the frame of reference for asking questions and responding to them, benefits both archaeology's relevance to society and generates vital knowledge for understanding sustainability. Pushing the boundaries of the discipline closer to the domain of sustainability scholarship is doubtlessly a great epistemological challenge, but it will prove worthwhile if we, even if ever so slightly, can contribute a response to the daunting question: "How do we get out of this mess?"

ACKNOWLEDGMENTS

I thank Lisa Lucero and Jean T. Larmon for inviting me to contribute to this volume, Vern Scarborough for stimulating my thinking on water and sustainability, and Scott Heckbert for a decisive suggestion. Any errors and shortcomings of this text remain of my own doing.

REFERENCES

Allen, T.F.H., Joseph A. Tainter, and Thomas W. Hoekstra. 2003. *Supply-Side Sustainability*. New York: Columbia University Press.

Araújo, Suzana Romeiro, Mats Söderström, Jan Eriksson, Christian Isendahl, Per Stenborg, and José A. M. Demattê. 2015. "Determining Soil Properties in Amazonian Dark Earths by Reflectance Spectroscopy." *Geoderma* 237–238: 308–317.

Arroyo-Kalin, Manuel. 2019. "Landscaping, Landscape Legacies, and Landesque Capital in Pre-Columbian Amazonia." In *The Oxford Handbook of Historical Ecology and Applied Archaeology*, edited by Christian Isendahl and Daryl Stump, 91–109. Oxford: Oxford University Press.

Balée, William, ed. 1998. *Advances in Historical Ecology*. New York: Columbia University Press.

Balée, William. 2006. "The Research Program of Historical Ecology." *Annual Review of Anthropology* 35: 75–98.

Balée, William, and Clark L. Erickson, eds. 2006. *Time and Complexity in Historical Ecology: Studies in the Neotropical Lowlands*. New York: Columbia University Press.

Brookfield, Harold. 1984. "Intensification Revisited." *Pacific Viewpoint* 25 (1): 15–44.

Brundtland, Gro Harlem, Mansour Khalid, Susanna Agnelli, Saleh Abdulrahman Al-Athel, Pablo Gonzalez Casanova, Bernard T. G. Chidzero, Lamine Mohamed Padika et al. 1992. *Report of the World Commission on Environment and Development: Our Common Future*. http://www.un-documents.net/our-common-future.pdf.

Caponetti, Lorenzo. 2019. "The Invisible Landscape: The Etruscan Cuniculi of Tuscania as a Determinant of Present-Day Landscape and a Valuable Tool for Sustainable Water Management." In *The Oxford Handbook of Historical Ecology and Applied Archaeology*, edited by Christian Isendahl and Daryl Stump, 412–421. Oxford: Oxford University Press.

Carpenter, Steve, Brian Walker, J. Marty Anderies, and Nick Abel. 2001. "From Metaphor to Measurement: Resilience of What to What?" *Ecosystems* 4 (8): 765–781.

Chase, Arlen F., and Vernon L. Scarborough, eds. 2014. *The Resilience and Vulnerability of Ancient Landscapes: Transforming Maya Archaeology through IHOPE*, 43–55. Hoboken, NJ: Wiley-Blackwell.

Cooper, Jago, and Lindsay Duncan. 2019. "Applied Archaeology in the Americas: Evaluating Archaeological Solutions to the Impacts of Global Environmental Change." In *The Oxford Handbook of Historical Ecology and Applied Archaeology*, edited by Christian Isendahl and Daryl Stump, 441–458. Oxford: Oxford University Press.

Crumley, Carole L., Tommy Lennartsson, and Anna Westin, eds. 2018. *Issues and Concepts in Historical Ecology: The Past and Future of Landscapes and Regions*. Cambridge: Cambridge University Press.

Daly, Herman E. 2006. "Sustainable Development—Definitions, Principles, Policies." In *The Future of Sustainability*, edited by Marco Keiner, 39–53. Dordrecht, Netherlands: Springer.

Eidt, Robert C. 1985. "Theoretical and Practical Considerations in the Analysis of Anthrosols." In *Archaeological Geology*, edited by George J. Rapp, 155–190. New Haven, CT: Yale University Press.

Graham, Elizabeth. 2006. "A Neotropical Framework for *Terra Preta*." In *Time and Complexity in Historical Ecology: Studies in the Neotropical Lowlands*, edited by William Balée and Clark L. Erickson, 57–86. New York: Columbia University Press.

Håkansson, N. Thomas, and Mats Widgren, eds. 2014. *Landesque Capital: The Historical Ecology of Enduring Landscape Modifications*. Walnut Creek, CA: Left Coast Press.

Hegmon, Michelle. 2017a. "Introduction: Multiple Perspectives on Tradeoffs." In *The Give and Take of Sustainability: Archaeological and Anthropological Perspectives on Tradeoffs*, edited by Hegmon, Michelle, 1–25. New York: Cambridge University Press.

Hegmon, Michelle, ed. 2017b. *The Give and Take of Sustainability: Archaeological and Anthropological Perspectives on Tradeoffs*. New York: Cambridge University Press.

Herrera, Alexander. 2019. "Indigenous Technologies, Archaeology, and Rural Development in the Andes: Three Decades of Trials in Bolivia, Ecuador, and Peru." In *The Oxford Handbook of Historical Ecology and Applied Archaeology*, edited by Christian Isendahl and Daryl Stump, 459–479. Oxford: Oxford University Press.

Holt, Emily, ed. 2018. *Water and Power in Past Societies*. Albany: State University of New York Press.

Intergovernmental Panel on Climate Change 2007. *Summary for Policymakers of the Synthesis Report of the IPCC Fourth Assessment Report*. IPCC, Geneva. Accessed March 16, 2017. https://www.ipcc.ch/report/ar4/syr/.

Isendahl, Christian. 2012a. "Agro-Urban Landscapes: The Example of Maya Lowland Cities." *Antiquity* 86 (334): 1112–1125.

Isendahl, Christian. 2012b. "Investigating Urban Experiences, Deconstructing Urban Essentialism." *UGEC (Urbanization & Global Environmental Change) Viewpoints* 8: 25–28.

Isendahl, Christian, and Stephan Barthel. 2018. "Archaeology, History, and Urban Food Security: Integrating Cross-Cultural and Long-Term Perspectives." In *Routledge Handbook of Landscape and Food*, edited by Joshua Zeunert and Tim Waterman, 61–72. London: Routledge.

Isendahl, Christian, Nicholas P. Dunning, and Jeremy A. Sabloff. 2014. "Growth and Decline in Classic Maya Puuc Political Economies." In *The Resilience and Vulnerability of Ancient Landscapes: Transforming Maya Archaeology through IHOPE*, edited by Arlen F. Chase, and Vernon L. Scarborough, 43–55. Hoboken, NJ: Wiley-Blackwell.

Isendahl, Christian, and Scott Heckbert. 2017a. "Pathways to Sustainable Development or Poverty: Water Security and Wealth in the Pre-Columbian Puuc-Nohkakab Maya Lowlands." In *Crisis to Collapse: The Archaeology of Social Breakdown*, edited by Tim Cunningham and Jan Driessen, 251–262. Louvain-la-Neuve, Belgium: Presses Universitaires de Louvain.

Isendahl, Christian, and Scott Heckbert. 2017b. "Tradeoffs in Pre-Columbian Maya Water Management Systems: Complexity, Sustainability, and Cost." In *The Give and Take of Sustainability: Archaeological and Anthropological Perspectives on Tradeoffs*, edited by Michelle Hegmon, 125–147. New York: Cambridge University Press.

Isendahl, Christian, Lisa J. Lucero, and Scott Heckbert. 2018. "Sustaining Freshwater Security and Community Wealth: Diversity and Change in the Pre-Columbian Maya Lowlands." In *Water and Society from Ancient Times to the Present: Resilience, Decline, and Revival*, edited by Federica Sulas and Innocent Pikirayi, 17–39. London: Routledge.

Isendahl, Christian, and Michael E. Smith. 2013. "Sustainable Agrarian Urbanism: The Low-Density Cities of the Mayas and Aztecs." *Cities* 31: 132–143.

Isendahl, Christian, and Daryl Stump. 2019a. "Conclusion: Anthropocentric Historical Ecology, Applied Archaeology, and the Future of a Useable Past." In *The Oxford Handbook of Historical Ecology and Applied Archaeology*, edited by Christian Isendahl and Daryl Stump, 581–597. Oxford: Oxford University Press.

Isendahl, Christian, and Daryl Stump, eds. 2019b. *The Oxford Handbook of Historical Ecology and Applied Archaeology*. Oxford: Oxford University Press.

Jacobsen, Thorkild, and Robert M. Adams. 1958. "Salt and Silt in Ancient Mesopotamian Agriculture." *Science* 128 (3334): 1251–1258.

Kendall, Ann, and David Drew. 2019. "The Rehabilitation of Pre-Hispanic Agricultural Infrastructure to Support Rural Development in the Peruvian Andes: The Work of the Cusichaca Trust." In *The Oxford Handbook of Historical Ecology and Applied Archaeology*, edited by Christian Isendahl and Daryl Stump, 422–440. Oxford: Oxford University Press.

Lane, Paul J. 2019. "Just How Long Does 'Long-Term' Have to Be? Matters of Temporal Scale as Impediments to Interdisciplinary Understanding in Historical Ecology." In *The Oxford Handbook of Historical Ecology and Applied Archaeology*, edited by Christian Isendahl and Daryl Stump, 49–71. Oxford: Oxford University Press.

Monbiot, George. 2016. *How Did We Get into This Mess? Politics, Equality, Nature*. London: Verso.

Ostrom, Elinor. 1990. *Governing the Commons: The Evolution of Institutions for Collective Action*. Cambridge: Cambridge University Press.

Redman, Charles L. 1999. *Human Impacts on Ancient Environments*. Tucson: University of Arizona Press.

Scarborough, Vernon L. 2009. "Beyond Sustainability: Managed Wetlands and Water Harvesting in Ancient Mesoamerica." In *The Archaeology of Environmental Change:*

Socionatural Legacies of Degradation and Resilience, edited by Christopher T. Fisher, J. Brett Hill, and Gary M. Feinman, 62–82. Tucson: University of Arizona Press.

Scarborough, Vernon L. 2018. *A Framework for Facing the Past*. In *Water and Power in Past Societies*, edited by Emily Holt, 297–315. Albany: State University of New York Press.

Scarborough, Vernon L., and William Burnside. 2010. "Complexity and Sustainability: Perspectives from the Ancient Maya and the Modern Balinese." *American Antiquity* 75 (2): 327–363.

Scarborough, Vernon L., and Christian Isendahl. 2020. "Distributed Urban Network Systems in the Tropical Archaeological Record: Towards a Model for Urban Sustainability in the Era of Climate Change." *The Anthropocene Review* 7 (3): 208–230.

Scott, James C. 1998. *Seeing Like a State: How Certain Schemes to Improve the Human Condition Have Failed*. New Haven, CT: Yale University Press.

Spriggs, Matthew. 2019. "A 1980 Attempt at Reviving Ancient Irrigation Practices in the Pacific: Rationale, Failure, and Success." In *The Oxford Handbook of Historical Ecology and Applied Archaeology*, edited by Christian Isendahl and Daryl Stump, 395–411. Oxford: Oxford University Press.

Sulas, Federica, and Innocent Pikirayi, eds. 2018. *Water and Society from Ancient Times to the Present: Resilience, Decline, and Revival*. Abingdon, UK: Routledge.

Tainter, Joseph A., and T.F.H. Allen. 2019. "Energy Gain and the Evolution of Organization." In *The Oxford Handbook of Historical Ecology and Applied Archaeology*, edited by Christian Isendahl and Daryl Stump, 558–577. Oxford: Oxford University Press.

United Nations. 2015. *Resolution A/RES/70/1 Adopted by the General Assembly on 25 September 2015*. New York: United Nations.

Woods, William I., Wenceslau G. Teixeira, Johannes Lehmann, Christoph Steiner, Antionette M.G.A. WinklerPrins, and Lilian Rebellato, eds. 2009. *Amazonian Dark Earths: Wim Sombroek's Vision*. Berlin: Springer.

Chill Hill (Aguateca), 85
China, Great Central Plain, 104
Chocop River, 121
Cholan-speaking Maya, 100
Chontal Maya, 99, 102
chronology, at Caracol and Tikal, 147–48
chultuns, 16, 18, 20, 37; Puuc region, 33, 34, 34–35; Xcoch, 39–40
cisterns, 16. *See also* chultuns; tanks
Cival, 109
civic planning, 145; cosmology, 80
CKU. *See* Central Karstic Uplands
Classic period, 7, 68; water mountains, 119–20
clay, as reservoir seal, 24
climate, climate change, 6, 16, 98, 99, 104, 145, 181; adaptation to, 4–5; and sustainability, 3–4; and water management, 10, 233
CNH. *See* Coupled Human and Natural Systems
Cob Swamp, 54, 63
Cobweb Swamp, 54
cohune (*Attalea cohune*), 59, 68
colonization, water values and, 81
Committee to Save the Rio Hondo, 215
communications networks, 104, 105, 180; and community organization, 176–78
communities: bifurcation of rural, 176–77; value space of, 180
concave systems, 19, 20
convex system, 19–20
Copan, 131, 134
Corriental Reservoir (Tikal), 26, 30, 31, 55
Cortés, Hernán, 124; Yucatán expedition, 100–102
cosmology, 80; Maya, 14, 31; water and water imagery in, 7–8, 81, 82–84
cotton (*Gossypium hirsutum*), 54, 58, 59, 63, 64, 68
Coupled Human and Natural Systems (CNH) approach, 220
Cox, Michael, social-ecological system, 220–21
coyol (*Acrocomia aculeata*), 59, 68
Cozumel, 64, 83
crocodiles, in cosmology, 81
Crossroads of the Earth and the Sky, At the (Urton), 82
Cuello site, 54
cultural evolution, Maya, 93–94

Dakota Access Pipeline (DAPL), 81
dams, 25; in Cambodia, 190
deforestation: Angkor, 188–89; impacts of, 189–90

demographics, of Tikal and Caracol, 147–48
divination, water and, 84
Dos Pilas, 80
dredging, reservoir, 26–27, 28
droughts, 39, 68, 98, 109
Dzibanche, 32

earthworks, at Tikal, 55
East Baray, sedimentation in, 192
ecosystem services, acequia systems, 219–20
Ecuador, 212
Edzna, 32, 55, 94
E Groups, 109, 110, 155–56
EIR. *See* Elevated Interior Region
El Achiotal, 8, 120, 121, 122, 123, 135, 136; description of, 124–25; iconography at, 126, 127; on Sihyaj K'ahk, 133–34
Elevated Interior Region (EIR), 68; agriculture in, 52, 54, 63; Classic period reservoirs, 24–32; reservoirs, 18–24, 38–39; sustainability in, 235, 236; water management, 7, 16–17, 41; water sources, 14–16. *See also* sites by name
elites, water management and ritual, 152–53
El Laberinto Bajo, 107
El Mirador, 23, 62, 99, 102, 105, 107, 122, 126, 135, 177(n)
El Peruito, 135
El Perú Laguna, 135
El Perú-Waka, 8, 124, 127; description of, 121–23; royal palace acropolis, 125–26; water mountain at, 120, 129–31, 134; Wite' Naah shrine at, 131–33
El Prado Waste and Sanitation District (EPWSD), 214, 216, 218
El Salvador, volcanic ash in, 56–58
El Tajin, 105
El Tintal (Tintal), 8, 102, 120, 121, 122, 129, 135–36
El Zotz, reservoir at, 25, 27–28
energy returned on energy invested (EROI), 238
environment, 174; Tikal and Caracol, 143–44, 145, 158–59; tropical, 180–81, 185, 186–87
epigraphic records, at Caracol and Tikal, 148–49
EPWSD. *See* El Prado Waste and Sanitation District
Eridu, 97
EROI. *See* energy returned on energy invested
erosion, 55; in Angkor systems, 9, 194
Erythrina sp., 64
Euphrates River valley, 97
Eznab ceramics, 148

Vietnam, French colonialism in, 81
Vilcanota River, and Milky Way, 82
villages, 61, 176; sociopolitical structure, 174–75

WAC. *See* World Archaeological Congress
Wak Chan K'awiil, 134
Wak dynasty, 131–32, 134
walkways, at reservoirs, 28–29
warfare, Maya, 109, 149
Wari Camp, 37
water, 10, 13–14, 38, 80, 119, 205; acequia alloca-
    tion, 201–2; at Caracol and Tikal, 150–53; in
    caves, 85; collection and storage of, 16–17,
    20–21, 38, 238; control of, 86, 105–6, 211; in
    Maya cosmology, 7–8, 94–96, 178; potable,
    29–30; rituals, 82–84; sources, 4, 17–18, 153;
    and sustainability, 5–6
water law, Mexican and US, 206–7
water lilies (*Nymphaea* spp.), 30, 81
water management, 3, 6, 10, 36, 86, 110, 208, 228,
    235–36; at Angkor, 9, 192–93; at Calakmul,
    107, 108–9; at Caracol and Tikal, 150–53, 159,
    160–62; as information processing, 178–81;
    Maya, 4, 7, 8, 37–41; monumental architec-
    ture and, 31–32; and sustainability, 233–34
water markets, in New Mexico, 202
water mountains, 8, 83, 119, 129–31, 135; at El
    Perú-Waka, 120, 134; monumental architec-
    ture as, 31–32
water rights: in New Mexico, 202, 205–7, 214–19;
    political power and, 207–9
water security, 234–35
watersheds, 106, 214; manipulation of, 19–20;
    San Juan River, 127–29
water trails/routes, 100, 120, 135–36; in Central
    Karstic Uplands, 122–23; in Petén, 123–27
wells: filtration, 28; groundwater, 218
West Baray reservoir, 187, 192, 193
West Mebon temple, 191, 193

wetlands, 63. *See also* bajos
Wite' Naah Fire Shrine, 15, 131; at El Perú-
    Waka, 131–34
Wittfogel, Karl, on hydraulic state, 207–8
World Archaeological Congress (WAC), 86
worldview, Maya, 94–96
Worster, Donald, *Rivers of Empire*, 208–9

Xcoch, 18; cave and monumental architecture
    at, 31–32; chultuns at, 35, 39–40; reservoirs
    at, 23, 24, 26, 28–29, 33
Xculoc, 35
Xoxocotlán, 66
Xpotoit Aguada, 23
Xpujil Aquifer, 127
Xuch, 26, 35
Xucub River, 121
Xultun, 23, 39
Xunantunich, 60, 61

Yalahau region, 85
YAP. *See* Yaxnohcah Archaeological Project
Yashodharatataka, 192
Yaxha, 155
Yaxhilan, 119–20
Yaxhom, 23
Yaxnohcah, 18, 31, 37, 55, 62, 102, 152; household
    tanks at, 35–36, 36; reservoirs at, 22–23, 27,
    30, 38–39
Yaxnohcah Archaeological Project (YAP), 35–36
Yucatán Peninsula, 8, 82, 93, 97, 99, 172; Cortés
    expedition to, 100–102; paleoenvironment
    of, 14–16; water supply in, 13–14. *See also*
    Elevated Interior Region; *various sites*
Yuknoom Ch'een the Great, 134

Zoque speakers, 97, 99

Mary Jane Acuña received a *licenciatura* degree in archaeology from Universidad de San Carlos de Guatemala in 2005, a MA degree in Latin American studies from the University of Texas at Austin in 2007, and a PhD in anthropology from Washington University in St. Louis in 2013. Since 2003 her research has focused in the area of northwestern and northern Petén, Guatemala, where she has worked at the sites of El Péru-Waka', La Corona, El Achiotal, and El Tintal. In 2014, Mary Jane began the El Tintal Archaeological Project, which continues under her direction.

Armando Anaya Hernández is a full professor and researcher at the Universidad Autónoma de Campeche, Mexico. He has been conducting research in the Maya area since 1983 and since 2011 has been undertaking research at the site of Yaxnohcah, Campeche, Mexico.

The late Wendy Ashmore was Distinguished Professor Emerita of Anthropology at the University of California, Riverside. She was a leading figure in Maya archaeology who conducted pathbreaking work in settlement patterns, household archaeology, landscape archaeology, the archaeology of place, and gender.

Timothy Beach holds a Centennial Chair and is professor and director of the Soils and Geoarchaeology Labs in Geography and Environment at the University of Texas at Austin. His research ranges from soil profiles to watersheds from the Pleistocene to the present, especially in the Maya and Mediterranean worlds.

Jeffrey Brewer has conducted research in the Maya lowlands since 2006 and has published in archaeology and water management, particularly among the ancient Maya. He is currently an adjunct assistant professor of geography at the University of Cincinnati.

Christopher Carr is research assistant professor of geography at University of Cincinnati. He completed his PhD at University of Cincinnati after retiring from a nearly thirty-year career in engineering at Procter and Gamble. He applies engineering and spatial analysis skills to human-environmental interactions both ancient and modern. He is particularly interested in using LiDAR to better understand ancient Maya infrastructure—for example, water reservoirs.

Arlen F. Chase (PhD in Anthropology, University of Pennsylvania, 1983) is a visiting professor in the Department of Anthropology at Pomona College in Claremont, California. He was previously at the University of Central Florida (1984–2016) and the University of Nevada, Las Vegas (2016–2019). He has been actively engaged in Maya archaeology since 1971. His publications are available at http://www.caracol.org.

Diane Z. Chase (PhD in Anthropology, University of Pennsylvania, 1982) is vice president for Academic Innovation, Student Success, and Strategic Initiatives at Claremont Graduate University. She was previously at Princeton University (1983–1984), the University of Central Florida (1984–2016), and the University of Nevada, Las Vegas (2016–2019). She has been carrying out archaeological research since 1974. Her publications are available at https://www.caracol.org.

Adrian S.Z. Chase (PhD in Anthropology, Arizona State University, 2021) was recently a research fellow at Claremont Graduate University from 2021–2022 and is currently a postdoctoral fellow at the Mansueto Institute for Urban Innovation at the University of Chicago. His research investigates the intersection of urbanism, computational archaeology, and ancient Mesoamerica. He has worked on field projects at Teotihuacan and Chichén Itza in Mexico, Caracol in Belize, and Hibemerdon Tepe in Turkey. He also undertook three internships at Oak Ridge National Laboratory, Tennessee. His publications may be found online at https://www.caracol.org.

Carlos R. Chiriboga is a PhD candidate in the Department of Anthropology at Yale University. He obtained a BA in Archaeology in 2006 from the Universidad del Valle de Guatemala and a M.Phil. in Anthropology in 2012 from Yale University. His work focuses on archaeological mapping and settlement pattern surveys, as well as human-environment interactions and landscape change in the southern Maya lowlands of Mesoamerica.

Jennifer Chmilar has spent copious time dirty and wet, contemplating the ingenuity of ancient engineering feats. She has studied ancient Maya water management and wetland agriculture throughout the southern and northern Maya lowlands, where her research has elaborated on ways that the ancient Maya conspicuously constructed their landscape to adapt to both wet and dry conditions.

Nicholas Dunning is professor and head of the Department of Geography and GIS at the University of Cincinnati. He has undertaken field work on ancient settlement, agriculture, and paleoecology in the Maya lowlands, West Indies, Chaco Canyon, and elsewhere since the mid-1980s.

Roland Fletcher studies settlement dynamics and has, in particular, studied the trajectories of low-density settlements over the past twenty years. His main focus has been working in an interdisciplinary research team on the form, operation, and demise of Greater Angkor in Cambodia.

David Freidel is professor of anthropology at Washington University in St. Louis. He directed three major archaeology programs in the Maya area, at Cerros (Cerro Maya) in Belize, at Yaxuna in Yucatán, and at El Péru-Waka' in northwestern Petén, Guatemala. He has written on Maya settlement, monumental architecture, iconography, and ancient history. He worked with Vernon Scarborough at Cerros.

Liwy Grazioso Sierra is professor of archaeology at Universidad de San Carlos de Guatemala and director and curator of Museo Miraflores in Guatemala City. Her areas of interest include Mesoamerican archaeology, Maya culture, development of complex societies, and iconography and symbolism.

Robert Griffin is an environmental anthropologist whose research focuses on the study of urban and agricultural landscapes using remote sensing and geographic information analysis. He is an associate professor in the Atmospheric and Earth Science Department at the University of Alabama in Huntsville and currently serves as the associate dean for the College of Science.

Joel D. Gunn is a lecturer in the Anthropology Department, University of North Carolina at Greensboro. His publications include books, articles, reports, and online course documents on regional culture change, global climate change, and complex systems, especially focused on regional cultures around the North Atlantic Bermuda-Azores Subtropical High: Maya lowlands, southeastern United States, Western Europe, and West Africa. He has also published on the future sustainability of the post-Columbian world economic system.

Christian Isendahl is professor of archaeology at the Department of Historical Studies, University of Gothenburg, Sweden. His research concerns issues of long-term sustainability and resilience, applying a historical ecological lens to examine urbanism, farming systems, water management, and sociopolitical organization in the Maya lowlands, the Andes, the Amazon, and Cuba. Coeditor (with Daryl Stump) of *The Oxford Handbook of Historical Ecology and Applied Archaeology* (2019), he explores archaeology's potential to provide practical insights into contemporary challenges.

Jean T. Larmon (PhD, UIUC, 2019) is an archaeologist at Historical Research Associates in Missoula, Montana, and teaches at the University of Montana. Her research interests include the intersection of environmental justice and archaeology, climate change, relational ontologies, and public outreach. She applies her research throughout North America, and primarily in Belize, where she works at Ancient Maya sites with contemporary Maya peoples.

David Lentz is professor of biological sciences at the University of Cincinnati. His research activities focus on paleoecology, archaeobotany and anthropogenic landscape changes of the past. He has conducted his studies in Mesoamerica, North America, Central Asia, and Western Europe.

Lisa J. Lucero (PhD, UCLA, 1994) is a fellow of the American Association for the Advancement of Science (AAAS) and a professor of anthropology at the University of Illinois at Urbana-Champaign. Her interests focus on the emergence and demise of political power, ritual, water management, the impact of climate change on society, sustainability of tropical regions, and the Classic Maya. She has been conducting archaeology projects in Belize for thirty years.

Sheryl Luzzadder-Beach is the Raymond Dickson Centennial Professor of Geography and the director of the Environmental Hydrology and Water Quality Lab in Geography and the Environment at the University of Texas at Austin. She is a past president of the American Association of Geographers. Her research interests include hydrology, geoarchaeology, geostatistics, and science and human rights, pursued in landscapes from Mesoamerica to the Mediterranean.

Dan Penny is a geographer and geoarchaeologist who specializes in the application of palaeobotany and sedimentology to explore interaction between human communities and the rest of the earth system. He has worked extensively through the global tropics, particularly Southeast Asia and Mesoamerica.

Kathryn Reese-Taylor received her PhD in 1996 from the University of Texas at Austin and has taught archaeology in the Department of Anthropology and Archaeology at the University of Calgary since 2000. Her principal research focuses on landscape archaeology, urbanism, and the development of complexity in the Maya lowlands. Reese-Taylor has directed archaeological projects in Belize, Guatemala, and Mexico. Her current project is a multidisciplinary program of research located in southern Campeche centered in the region surrounding an extensive wetland, the Bajo Laberinto.

Michelle Rich is the Ellen and Harry S. Parker III Assistant Curator of the Arts of the Americas at the Dallas Museum of Art (DMA). Since 2003, she has been a member of the US-Guatemalan-led Proyecto Arqueológico El Perú-Waka´ (PAW). Her aim is to contextualize and analyze works of art and cultural heritage through curatorial practice and archaeological understanding, and her research interests include Maya and Mesoamerican art and figurines, ritual objects, and ritual architecture.

Cynthia Robin is professor of anthropology at Northwestern University. She has conducted fieldwork at Maya archaeological sites in Belize. Her research focuses on the everyday lives of ordinary people in the past and the development of sustainable lifeways.

Sylvia Rodríguez is Professor Emerita of Anthropology at the University of New Mexico.

William Saturno is the former director of the San Bartolo–Xultun Regional Archaeology Project. He is now an independent scholar living in Connecticut.

Vernon Scarborough is Distinguished University Research Professor and Charles Phelps Taft Professor in the Department of Anthropology at the University of Cincinnati—and now emeritus. His work emphasizes sustainability and global water systems. By examining past engineered landscapes, he addresses both ancient and contemporary societal issues from a comparative ecological and transdisciplinary perspective. Geographically, his published work includes studies about the US Southwest, Guatemala, Belize, Indonesia, Greece, Pakistan, and the Sudan.

Payson Sheets is professor in the department of anthropology at the University of Colorado in Boulder. He earned his PhD at the University of Pennsylvania. His career has focused on the relationships of ancient Mesoamerican and Intermediate Area societies with volcanic activity. He continues to investigate the ancient Maya village of Cerén, El Salvador, buried by a volcanic eruption in the seventh century AD.

Michael Smyth is president of the Foundation for Americas Research, Inc. (www.FARINCO.org) and received his PhD in anthropology from the University of New Mexico. Working and researching for over thirty-five years in the Yucatán's Puuc region at Sayil, Chac II, and Xcoch, as well as in the Colombian Andes, he has published numerous articles on Maya storage and subsistence systems, ethnic interactions, hydraulic chiefdoms, and human ecodynamics and is currently researching the Preclassic settlement hierarchy and early farmers of the Xcoch hinterland.

Fred Valdez Jr. (PhD in Anthropology, Harvard University, 1987) is a professor in the Department of Anthropology at the University of Texas at Austin. He has directed and codirected archaeological research in the Maya area for more than three decades and currently serves as director of Center for Archaeological and Tropical Studies (CATS) at UT-Austin.

Sander van der Leeuw was trained in prehistory and medieval history in the Netherlands. Having taught at Amsterdam, Leiden, Cambridge, and Paris (Sorbonne), he is currently emeritus dean of the School of Sustainability of Arizona State University. Widely published, his latest book is *Social Sustainability—Past and Future: Undoing Unintended Consequences for the Earth's Survival* (Cambridge UP, 2020 (open access)). In 2012 he received United Nations Environment Programme's (UNEP's) highest award, "Champion of the Earth for Science and Innovation."

Andrew Wyatt is associate professor in the Department of Sociology and Anthropology at Middle Tennessee State University. He received his BA in literature at Antioch College and his PhD in anthropology from the University of Illinois at Chicago in 2008. He has conducted archaeological research in Mexico, Guatemala, Belize, Belgium, and the midwestern United States. He has published numerous articles, book chapters, and reports.